FRANKLIN CLARK FRY

Franklin Clark Fry *Sketch by Donald W. Kern, 1968*

FRANKLIN CLARK FRY

A Palette for a Portrait

EDITED BY ROBERT H. FISCHER
PROFESSOR OF CHURCH HISTORY
LUTHERAN SCHOOL OF THEOLOGY AT CHICAGO

Supplementary Number of
THE LUTHERAN QUARTERLY, Volume XXIV, 1972

Library of Congress Catalog Card Number: 72-78582

THE LUTHERAN QUARTERLY

DANIEL F. MARTENSEN, EDITOR

A Theological Journal sponsored by

Printed in the United States of America
by the Times and News Publishing Company, Gettysburg, Pennsylvania

Distribution Office for this volume:
THE LUTHERAN QUARTERLY
Wittenberg University
Springfield, Ohio 45501

The LUTHERAN QUARTERLY gratefully acknowledges the generous grant from the members of Aid Association for Lutherans, Appleton, Wisconsin, which has made possible the publication of this volume and its distribution to LUTHERAN QUARTERLY subscribers, to ministers of the Lutheran Church in America, and to certain libraries interested in contemporary church history.

CONTENTS

The International Range of Dr. Fry's Churchmanship

PART TWO *Memos from the American Lutheran Church and the Lutheran Church–Missouri Synod*

PART THREE *Memos from Lutherans outside America*

PART FOUR *Memos from American Christians of Sister Churches*

PART FIVE *Memos from Overseas Christians of Sister Churches*

PREFACE

By any standard of judgment, Franklin Clark Fry was one of the most eminent and influential Christian churchmen of the mid-twentieth century. For a decade and a half, no Protestant name was more widely known around the world, with the exception of W. A. Visser 't Hooft. No man was more influential in drawing world Lutheranism into the mainstream of the ecumenical movement, and in leading Lutheranism out into a prominent and cooperative position in American Christianity. Dr. Fry's interests decisively touched many different areas of the life of Christendom. His career, therefore, becomes one important window through which to view the course of Christianity in the mid-twentieth century, both in America and on the world scene. Indeed, this period cannot be understood without reference to him.

But now that Dr. Fry is gone, how shall we interpret him and his times? What is our access to what really happened in Christendom as his life participated in it? He published comparatively little. His official reports were impressive. But what were the dynamics of problems, personalities, and thought behind these reports? Still alive in thousands of memories is a colorful Fry legend, with a large stock of anecdotes. But in the long run, do the anecdotes illumine, or perhaps obscure the person? Does the legend make him more real and near, or more remote? We have a little volume of tributes by ten colleagues, entitled *Mr. Protestant,* presented to Dr. Fry on his sixtieth birthday anniversary in 1960. But valuable though it is and sincere though its intentions, to what extent must it be discounted as a church-sponsored "court chronicle"?

Out of such questions came the seed from which this volume germinated, namely, the idea of producing not a portrait of Franklin Clark Fry the churchman, but a *palette for a portrait.* Let me explain.

If we want to learn the *dynamics* of crucial events and trends in the church and Dr. Fry's role in them, if we try to go backstage behind the visible historical drama, we should turn to the persons intimately involved in it. Since Dr. Fry came to prominence in the church at a fairly young age, many of these persons were older than he—twenty-five of our authors, for instance. If we are to secure candid testimony about these historical developments, especially that of his older colleagues, we must get it while their memories are still vigorous.

Early in 1969, therefore, I requested a number of prominent churchmen in America and abroad, clergymen and laymen, Lutherans and non-Lutherans, to write memos about their experiences with Franklin Clark

Fry. I asked them to avoid eulogy, rather to point out key events and issues, tensions and clashes, insights and evaluations, which will need to be assessed in any effort fairly to appraise the man. In short, how do things get done—or not get done—in the church? The writers were not to try to write polished and well-balanced biographical sketches, but simply to comment on those areas in which they were personally associated with Dr. Fry. The volume would deal with Dr. Fry, the churchman, not pry into his private life.

The memos are fragmentary, of course. But they have the compensating quality of concreteness, color, and intimacy. Surely there is no contributor who will not learn something about Dr. Fry which he had not known before. There is inevitably an uneven and overlapping character to the collection. But each writer had to form his own concept of what he should write; few have seen the memos of any of their colleagues. The overlapping, indeed, I considered more valuable than an edited homogenization. Varying angles of vision and diverse viewpoints are a contribution to realism. As the memos began to come in—the majority of them date from 1969—I found it advisable to seek out divergent judgments on the same subjects. I looked for persons to deal with some areas of Dr. Fry's churchmanship which were not treated by the original group invited. And I invited persons who sharply opposed Dr. Fry as well as those who admired him. Thus the modest project was unabashedly expanded to immodest proportions. Freshness and diversity, rather than edited neatness, became one justification for the present size of the volume.

There was a second justification. This volume is not about Dr. Fry alone. Most of the writers are themselves history-makers. This book, therefore, becomes a document illuminating an entire period, and particularly a collection of case-studies on the diversity of approaches to leadership in the church.

The response of those invited to contribute was overwhelmingly positive. Though some needed persuasion, not many declined to write. This fact itself is a remarkable tribute to Dr. Fry. One churchman was not convinced that the project should be encouraged: "Not all writings printed in this kind of publication are worth it, and I have no desire to add to their number." But almost all others applauded the idea, and most caught the spirit of trying to make the volume analytical rather than eulogistic. Their task of writing was not always easy, however. Some persons admired Dr. Fry, others disliked him, still others feared him. But I have yet to hear of a churchman who did not genuinely respect him. Some authors, accordingly, wrote with alacrity. Said one: "I have enjoyed doing this; it has done me good." Another, who often disagreed with Dr. Fry: "Quite frankly, I had considerable satisfaction in setting down on paper my reflections." Others wrote very reluctantly. One or two submitted their memos but added a note such as this: "I hope you will decide not to publish this. All in all I have no pride in it." One reluctant author wrote, however: "Thanks for holding me accountable."

Because of the fragmentary and somewhat informal character of the memos, the reader must refrain from drawing undue conclusions from what the authors do *not* say. No writer has said all that he *could have said.* The reader also is not entitled to draw conclusions from the absence of certain names from the list of authors. There is a whole gamut of reasons why several persons did not choose to contribute. A few men actually sat down to write their promised memos, but finally declined when they could not be satisfied with what they were able to produce. For all that, we can be grateful for the rich variety of what the authors *did say.* Not only do they shed light on one man and on a period of Christian experience; I think it would also be fair to say that our writers have revealed a good deal about themselves.

The resulting collection, consequently, is not really a portrait of Franklin Clark Fry—not even a mosaic portrait. More accurately, the volume is a *palette for a portrait*—daubs of paint with which the reader may compose and sketch his own picture of Dr. Fry.

To the best of my knowledge, this "palette" is a new type of historiographical tool. Differing in principle from the familiar memorial volume, which generally is ruled by the axiom, *De mortuis nihil nisi bonum,* it aims not to draw conclusions but to open up inquiry. It is more than an archive between two covers, but less than a biography. Certainly, however, no future biographer of Franklin Clark Fry and no historian of mid-twentieth century Christianity will be able to overlook the rich hints of data and opinion which Dr. Fry's colleagues have brought together here.

This volume, then, may be read in at least four ways. (1) For sheer human interest. People who did not know Dr. Fry at first hand will find a fascinating, colorful personality to explore. (2) For insights into a period only recently past, with its achievements and problems, its dynamics and its trends. (3) This volume can actually serve as a sourcebook for a study of various styles of Christian leadership. (4) As a collection of data for future historians and future students of this era. For their benefit as well as that of contemporary readers, the *Source Register* of materials by and about Dr. Fry was compiled, and a collection of these materials made at the Library of the Lutheran School of Theology at Chicago.

It is a great pleasure to express my thanks to the many persons who have aided and encouraged me in this project. I am grateful above all to five special advisers: Paul C. Empie, Helen M. Knubel, Erik W. Modean, George F. Harkins, and Samuel M. Cavert—all of whom have also contributed memos. Though I must have fatigued them all with my questions, they cheerfully and unselfishly devoted a great deal of time to providing helpful answers—suggesting names of persons to be invited to write memos, areas of Dr. Fry's career to be covered, and leads for securing information about his activities and his addresses. I deeply appreciate it also that Margaret Duhme, Dr. Fry's devoted secretary, aided the project in a number of thoughtful ways, though she deemed it wisest not to write a memo for the volume. If I were to mention all those who helped me track down the information for the Source Register, the list would exceed a hundred names, including contributors of specific items to the collection of Franklin Clark Fry materials in the Library of the Lutheran School of Theology at Chicago, who are acknowledged in the register. I must name a few persons, however, who went far out of their way to aid me in the search: the late Elson Ruff, editor of the LUTHERAN; R. Marshall Stross, Dorothy J. Marple, and William P. Cedfeldt, executives of the Lutheran Church in America; Rollin G. Shaffer, director of Lutheran World Action Promotion, and Alice M. Kendrick of the Office of Research, Statistics and Archives of the Lutheran Council in the USA. Special thanks also are due to Erik Modean of the LCUSA News Bureau and Albert P. Stauderman, now editor of the LUTHERAN, who at the beginning of the project kindly published notices requesting persons to inform me of the whereabouts of Fry materials—notices which produced useful results.

I express herewith my deep gratitude to Mrs. Franklin Clark Fry and her son, the Reverend Dr. Franklin Drewes Fry, for their courtesies to me during the preparation of this work. Since they had no part in launching the project, it is understandable if initially they had many misgivings over it. Only after the project was well under way and was taking tentative shape did I get into direct touch with them, for I wished to allay all suspicions that this was in any way a family-inspired or family-sponsored enterprise. The Fry family, I think I may say, came to trust in the soundness of our procedures. Mrs. Fry and her son, accordingly, have been most kind in aiding me when I approached them with questions; but I wish also to testify here that they have made absolutely no attempt to steer or shape the project.

The Reverend Donald W. Kern graciously permitted us to use as a frontispiece his sketch of Dr. Fry, drawn from memory for a memorial service bulletin in June 1968. Mr. Kern, at that time minister in St. Boniface, Manitoba, is now minister in Reserve, Montana. My warm appreciation to Pastor Kern is here recorded.

I want to express my personal thanks to Aid Association for Lutherans of Appleton, Wisconsin, for its subsidy of the volume. The members of Aid Association for Lutherans have supported this project as a contribution to the wider and deeper understanding of the Lutheran heritage.

Others who have aided in the production of the volume have also earned my sincere thanks. Robert E. Karsten, managing editor of the LUTHERAN QUARTERLY, not only has handled the business affairs of this project with his customary competence and good humor, but also has been a helpful consultant in determining its character. It has been a pleasure to work with my friends, Mahlon P. Hartzell, Jr., Paul B. Ramer, and William H. Small of the Times and News Publishing Company, Gettysburg, who saw the work through the press. John Kendrick of the University of Chicago Press gave me friendly advice on editorial technicalities. I record my thanks also to Lowell C. Albee, Jr., assistant librarian at LSTC, for aiding me with research and translating a couple of memos submitted in Swedish (I myself translated the memos which were written in German), and to B. Penrose Hoover and Alice Hilgendorf, my research assistants.

Some of the footnotes to the memos have been prepared by the authors; in the majority of cases they have been supplied by the editor.

Lutheran School of Theology
Chicago, Illinois
February 28, 1972

ROBERT H. FISCHER

Two *comprehensive sketches* of Dr. Fry introduce the collection. The first is the *obituary article* prepared by Erik W. Modean, head of the Lutheran Council News Bureau, for distribution to the news media and the churches on June 7, 1968. The second presents the wide-ranging *reminiscences and reflections* of nonagenarian Luther D. Reed, Franklin Fry's seminary teacher and later colleague in the church.

1

Dr. Franklin Clark Fry One of Towering Figures of the Christian World

June 7, 1968

By Lutheran Council News Bureau

A buoyant intellectual and physical giant, the late Rev. Dr. Franklin Clark Fry was acknowledged in religious circles as one of the towering figures of Christianity in the twentieth century.

A striking personality, coupled with great mental capacity and creative ability that bore the authentic stamp of genius, earned Dr. Fry worldwide eminence as a church statesman.

His innate talent, as a master of dynamic prose, a consummate administrator, an impeccable parliamentarian, and an astute politician, was fused with a deep spiritual zeal and an unlimited zest for hard work—all leavened by an incisive wit and a strong sense of humor.

Out of this awesome combination of attributes, he forged an unrivalled record of leadership in church activity at home and abroad for a quarter century. The major posts of responsibility he occupied over the years impinged on nearly all areas of non-Roman Christendom. For just cause he was known as "Mr. Protestant."

Shortly before he died on June 6 at the age of sixty-seven, knowing the end was imminent, he resigned midway through his second and final four-year term as first president of the 3,288,000-member Lutheran Church in America, the nation's largest Lutheran body. Brought into being by a four-church merger in 1962, the LCA included the United Lutheran Church in America, which he had guided for eighteen years.

Dr. Fry was forty-four and had been pastor of Holy Trinity Lutheran church in Akron, Ohio, for fifteen years when the ULCA's fourteenth biennial convention at Minneapolis, Minnesota, in 1944 chose him as the second president of the denomination, then numbering about two million members.

Elected on the fourth ballot, with 358 of 517 votes, he succeeded the late Rev. Dr. Frederick H. Knubel, who at seventy-four had completed twenty-six years of distinguished service to the church.

From that day, Dr. Fry steadily gained prominence in the national and international activities of organized Protestantism. As a staunch advocate of confessional, ecumenical and interdenominational unity, he was a prime mover in the formation of the Lutheran World Federation in 1947, the World Council of Churches in 1948, and the National Council of Churches in 1950.

The constitutions and bylaws of these cooperative agencies were largely the product of his hand, his mind, and his heart.

Dr. Fry served as treasurer of the LWF from 1948 to 1952 when the Rev. Dr. Ralph H. Long, then executive director of the National Lutheran Council, died a year after he had been named to the post. Dr. Fry then served as first vice-president to 1957 and then as president to 1963. He was elected to the latter office at Minneapolis where, thirteen years earlier, he began his rise to world renown. He was a member of the Federation's Executive Committee until his death.

For the first six years of the World Council's existence, Dr. Fry served as vice-chairman of its policy-making Central Committee. He was elected chairman of both its Central Committee and its Executive Committee in 1954, was re-elected in 1961 and was to retire from these vital posts at the WCC's Fourth Assembly at Uppsala, Sweden, this summer.

Frequently he said of himself that he was more readily recognized in some foreign cities than he was in his own New York City, a reference to his global travel in behalf of the LWF and the World Council.

In 1967, for example, he visited eight foreign countries and in the first few months of 1968 had been in six countries before he was stricken with his fatal illness. Much of this time was devoted to the myriad details of planning for the WCC assembly. He had almost completed his report for Uppsala when he was hospitalized.

Although a leading member of the General Board of the National Council of Churches, and a former chairman of its Policy and Strategy Committee, Dr. Fry never held office in the NCC. But only because he declined nomination repeatedly as its president.

Had he accepted, he could have accomplished an unprecedented religious "grand slam"—leader at one and the same time of a major denomination, a confessional body, an interdenominational agency, and an ecumenical organization.

Dr. Fry was in the chair at the opening session of the National Council's constituting convention at Cleveland in 1950. So meticulous was he in hewing to the line on prescribed principles of organization that he insisted upon forty-four amendments to the governing documents. This was said to have caused one prominent churchwoman to sink into her seat one day after an absence from the sessions and whisper to her neighbor: "What do the Lutherans want now?"

When this remark reached Dr. Fry by the grapevine, he slapped his thigh and roared with laughter, a habitual reaction to anything that struck him as particularly funny. People not quick enough, or subtle enough, to follow his unspoken mental processes, were often startled and wondered what on earth he was laughing at.

Without doubt, Dr. Fry was at his superlative best as a presiding officer. That view was shared by many, including reporters who cover religion for the nation's press. Usually sparing in their accolades, they ranked Dr. Fry as the foremost of church parliamentarians. When he was in the chair, the press tables were sure to be crowded.

It was a fascinating sight to watch Dr. Fry, pectoral cross dangling on his clerical vest, an unruly lock of dark hair falling across his high forehead, preside over a large assembly.

The tall, broad-shouldered churchman—he was 6 feet, 1½ inches and topped 200 pounds—came into a meeting saturated with knowledge of every matter due for consideration, its past, present and possible future. These details seemed to be filed in his capacious mind in perfect order, waiting to be pulled forth for application at just the proper moment.

Always in command of any situation, he never lost control of the proceedings as he slashed through parliamentary tangles with penetrating speed and dexterity, letting the quips fall where they may.

In one plenary session, a delegate questioning an intricate legislative maneuver said he wanted to consult an expert on Robert's Rules of Order as to its propriety. To which Dr. Fry suggested, "Why don't you ask me."

On another occasion, an enraptured delegate jumped to his feet and cried, "I move what the president thinks."

When he himself once made a slip in reading a proposal to provide closer coordination between church boards, he quipped: "There's no more coordination between my brain and tongue than between the boards of the church."

On a television show, when the master of ceremonies expressed ignorance of the vestments worn by the clergy and asked for a description of clerical garb, Dr. Fry retorted tartly, "Why not go to church and find out for yourself."

One measure of Dr. Fry's greatness was the wealth of stories told about him. His quickness of wit often made him the target of similar sallies. At a dinner in his honor, the toastmaster praised his infinite patience, pointing out that Dr. Fry always gave the church's Executive Council "all the time it needed to come around to his way of thinking."

Most of the stories were apocryphal, many adapted from other sources and other subjects. Such as the one attributed to an underling, who said, "When he tells me to sit down, I don't even look for a chair." But he enjoyed them all, at least the first time he heard them. He had a standing offer of twenty dollars, it was said, for anyone who came up with a new anecdote. Few, if any, collected.

An associate recently ran across a matchbook cover promoting tomato sauce for hot dogs under the intriguing slogan, "Fancy Frank Fry." Needing a double sawbuck, he showed it to Dr. Fry (with palm outstretched), only to be told that he had already received scores of the matchbooks from all over the country.

Dr. Fry's four major interests, in the order of importance in which he listed them, were: (1) The Lord; (2) The Lutheran church; (3) The family; (4) The New York Yankees.

The Yankees were a passion with Dr. Fry. When the Lutheran World Federation was formed at Lund, Sweden, in 1947, as he waited to appear on an international radio hookup, Dr. Fry said to the engineer across the Atlantic: "How did the New York Yankees do today? I won't go on the air until you tell me."

In one of his last public appearances, he represented the LCA at the seventh convention of its Texas-Louisiana Synod in late April. At an "Evening With the President," it was reported, he was "at his incisive, hard-hitting, witty, serious best" in an informal question and answer session before a packed church which proved to be "the exciting highlight" of the meeting.

"For nearly an hour and a half," said the synod's periodical, "Dr. Fry shot back pungent and sometimes sharp answers from the hip to pre-submitted, but not pre-digested, questions ranging from the concern of delegates and visitors for racial and urban tensions to his continued loyalty to the Yankee baseball team and the Democratic party."

When the Yankees were involved, as they usually were in their heyday, in a World Series during a biennial convention of the ULCA, inning-by-inning scores were relayed to Dr. Fry at the podium on placards held up to his view from the press table. He was even known to halt proceedings to announce the final score. But only, of course, when the Yankees won.

Despite his worldwide interests, he maintained an unswerving dedication to his own communion and exercised a phenomenal influence in the ULCA and later the LCA and in American Lutheranism. For more than two decades, he was closely identified with the National Lutheran Council as a member of its Executive Committee and chairman of its Division of LWF Affairs. For many years he headed the NLC's program of aid to orphaned missions.

When Lutheran World Relief was organized after World War II in 1946 as the material aid agency of the NLC, Dr. Fry was elected president and remained in that office until his death. Many of his numerous trips abroad were made to war-devastated countries in the interest of church relief and reconstruction.

In January of 1951, he made a round-the-world flight in behalf of the "One Great Hour of Sharing" appeal of the National Council of Churches' Church World Service, inspecting conditions and needs of displaced persons and war refugees. On his return he reported in person to the president of the United States and to the nation via radio and television.

Also in 1951, he was appointed vice-chairman of American Relief for Korea, a service for which the government of Korea conferred upon him honorary citizenship.

His efforts in relief work earned the Grand Order of Merit in 1952 and the Grand Cross First Class of the Order of Merit in 1960 from West Germany and the Austrian Great Silver Cross with Star in 1955. All of which he accepted in the name of American Christians and as a tribute to their generous outpouring of help to helpless brethren overseas.

West Germany also gave him the Knight's Commander Cross with Star in 1960 for leadership in the ecumenical movement. In addition, he received thirty-four honorary degrees from universities, colleges and seminaries both in this country and abroad.

One of his last two doctorates was conferred in absentia by Augustana College at Rock Island, Illinois, on June 2 while Dr. Fry was hospitalized. The other was to be awarded posthumously two days after his death by LeMoyne College at Syracuse, New York, on June 8.

Largely through Dr. Fry's labors, the four-church merger that established the Lutheran Church in America in 1962 was accomplished after only six years of negotiation between the ULCA, Augustana Lutheran Church, American Evangelical Lutheran Church, and Finnish Evangelical Lutheran church, known as the Suomi Synod.

He had hoped for an all-inclusive union of the eight bodies comprising the National Lutheran Council but the other four denominations merged into the American Lutheran Church. The latter was organized in 1960 by the old ALC, Evangelical Lutheran Church, and United Evangelical Lutheran Church, and was joined in 1962 by the Lutheran Free Church.

With the NLC reduced to two church bodies, its executive director, the Rev. Dr. Paul C. Empie, proposed efforts to achieve a broader cooperative relationship among Lutherans in America, particularly with the Lutheran Church-Missouri Synod, which had remained aloof from the Council.

On Dr. Fry's motion, the NLC initiated action in 1958 that was to end its forty-eight-year existence at the close of 1966. Taking its place was the Lutheran Council in the USA, in which the LCA and ALC were joined by the Missouri Synod and the Synod of Evangelical Lutheran Churches. Together the four bodies represent more than ninety-five percent of the nation's nearly nine million Lutherans in a cooperative program of theological study and Christian service.

In what was destined to be his final report to the LCA, to its fourth biennial convention at Atlanta, Georgia, June 19-27, Dr. Fry hailed the "new feeling of family solidarity."

"Rarely in anyone's lifetime do hopes come true as richly as mine have in the first year and a half of the Lutheran Council in the USA," he said.

It was while Dr. Fry was pastor of Holy Trinity, where he brought the membership from a depression-time low of 1,200 in 1929 to more than 2,700 in 1944, that he began to demonstrate his administrative gifts. A year after his arrival in Akron, when he was thirty, he became secretary of the ULCA's Committee on Evangelism and served eight years.

A few years later, following the death of his father, who was the first executive secretary of the Board of American Missions of the ULCA, Dr. Fry was elected to membership on that board and plunged into its program of organizing new congregations.

When the Rev. Thomas B. Kline went to Holy Trinity to serve as Dr. Fry's assistant, he arrived by car at 8:30 in the morning. Dr. Fry immediately began initiating him into his duties. Within the hour, the two men were visiting the sick at St. Thomas hospital.

"About three weeks later," Kline recalled, "I finally got all my bags out of the car."

In 1938, Dr. Fry was asked to make the commemorative address on the twentieth anniversary of the founding of the United Lutheran Church. In 1942 he was named to a four-year term on its Executive Board, interrupted two years later when he was elected to the denomination's presidency.

Said one colleague admiringly: "He works like a horse from morning to night, and he expects everyone around him to work like a horse from morning to night."

"Father believes," said his son Franklin, "that the children of light must work as hard or harder than the children of darkness. And he believes the children of light must be just as smart, too, in using their brains."

An only child, Franklin Clark Fry was born in Bethlehem, Pennsylvania, August 30, 1900, but was taken to Rochester, New York, before he was a year old. His childhood and youthful memories centered around the Church of the Reformation, where his father, the Rev. Dr. Franklin Foster Fry, was pastor of a large congregation for many years.

"You keep off," he was heard to say to another little boy of four, "this is my father's church."

From the time he could toddle, young Franklin went to church and enjoyed his father's sermons. He eagerly absorbed what he later described as the "colorful words" and the "interesting imagery."

When he visited his grandfather, he listened to more sermons. The grandfather, the Rev. Dr. Jacob Fry, climaxed a long career in the ministry as the pastor of the Church of the Ascension on the campus of [the Philadelphia] Lutheran Theological Seminary, where he was professor of homiletics and pastoral theology for nearly thirty years.

Born in Trappe, Pennsylvania, in 1834, Grandfather Fry, while pastor of Trinity Lutheran church in Reading, founded five other congregations and a Sunday school, meanwhile publishing three books and various sermons and tracts.

He frequently remarked, in words that could have been echoed by his grandson, "if we rest, we rust," and he was still in harness when he died with his shoes on one day at the age of eighty-six.

"My grandfather was probably the best preacher of us all," observed Dr. Fry some years ago, "for in a formal age when most men had a stiff and formal style, as indeed my own father did, my grandfather spoke off the cuff, and spoke vividly and well."

Perhaps this childhood enjoyment of sermons developed Dr. Fry's emphasis on the precise use of words. And he used them, to the despair of reporters, without an advance text. When he did provide notes, the tiny script in a neat, fine scholar's hand required 20-20 vision to decipher until one became familiar with it.

The rapier-like quality of his mind was often attributed, at least in part, to his keen-minded mother, to whom he was adoringly devoted. After a very active life, she had been bedridden with a lingering illness before her death at ninety-three in February of 1961.

Franklin Foster Fry, father of Dr. Fry, was a great organizer, too. He held the delicate post of chairman of legal matters when the General Council, United Synod of the South, and General Synod merged in 1918 to form the United Lutheran Church in America. The elder Dr. Fry spent twenty-six years as pastor of Reformation Lutheran church in Rochester. During part of this period he was president of the ULCA's New York and New England Synod. For six years before his death in 1933 at sixty-nine he was executive secretary of the Board of American Missions.

Young Franklin never had any other idea but that he would be a preacher. In preparation, he studied Greek three years in high school. Then, with his special long bed, the gangling youth went off to Hamilton College at Clinton, New York, for a thorough grounding in the classics, enjoyed debating and chess, and topped off his studies with a year in the American School for Classical Studies in Athens, Greece.

"He was first in his class," said one of his professors, "and there was no second."

By the time he was ready for his theological studies at Philadelphia, his grandfather had died. The grandson headed the student body and led a student movement to advise the faculty on curriculum revision.

Dr. Luther D. Reed, president emeritus of the seminary, testified that Dr. Fry was a constructive critic. "The seminary," Dr. Reed said some years ago, "has caught up with him now; he was simply ahead of the faculty."

During his first pastorate at Yonkers, New York, from 1925 to 1929, young Fry married a "very superior wife," Hilda Drewes, who sang in the choir of the Church of the Redeemer. Early in 1967, when Dr. Fry cancelled a sermon, explaining "it's the second time in my life I've ever done that," it was to rush to the bedside of his wife, who had suffered a sudden attack of pneumonia in Cedar Rapids, Iowa.

Two sons and a daughter were born to Dr. and Mrs. Fry. One son, the Rev. Franklin Drewes Fry, is pastor of Christ Lutheran church in York, Pennsylvania;[1] the other, Robert Charles Fry of Pleasantville, New York, is a business developer. Their daughter, Constance, is the wife of the Rev. Richard I. Preis, pastor of Trinity Lutheran church in Ann Arbor, Michigan.

Although ineligible to succeed himself in 1970—bylaws of the LCA rule out re-election of an officer after he has passed his sixty-seventh birthday—Dr. Fry was not content to rest on his laurels during his final years in office. To the contrary, he seemed more active than ever.

A statement on the racial emergency in the United States in January of 1968 earned widespread distribution through the communications media when he told his "dear partners," the thirty-two synod presidents of the LCA, that "for all who are not yet awake, a shrill alarm is sounding."[2]

"Unstop your ears and be startled," he said. "What is commonly called the 'racial crisis'—until to some, I fear, it sounds hackneyed—is real. The grievances fomenting it are just. Time for its amelioration is fast running out.

"Unpleasant as it is for me to say and for you to hear, the United States confronts a time of spiralling and spreading violence to make one's blood run cold unless a massive improvement of the lot of Negro ghettos comes quickly."

Dr. Fry read one of the scripture passages at the Morehouse College funeral service for Dr. Martin Luther King, Jr., the civil rights leader and winner of the Nobel Peace Prize, who was slain last April 4.

In recent years, Dr. Fry had turned considerable attention to Protestant-Roman Catholic relations. Speaking to the North American Area Council of the World Alliance of Reformed Churches last January, he noted the "natural affinity" which exists between Lutherans and Roman Catholics because of grounding in doctrinal roots. "Unity in the church corresponds to unity in God," he said.

His consuming interest in the World Council of Churches was motivated by his belief that "the spirit of the ecumenical movement is the spirit of Luther to the extent that it is a movement back toward the center of the Christian faith."

To Dr. Fry, real faith could not, must not be merely a thing of vague emotion, but a product, too, of the intellect, founded on a sturdy theology, one "to teach, to saturate, the inquiring and absorptive mind of man."

Nothing was more important, he believed, than to preach the gospel and administer the sacraments and, over the quarter century that he gave himself unstintingly to other areas of Christian service, he looked forward to returning some day to the parish ministry. But that was not to be.

Many things contributed to Dr. Franklin Clark Fry's stature as a giant of modern Christianity, but above all was the clear, strong evangelical witness that marked him as a dedicated man of God.

---

[1] Since 1971 pastor of St. John's Lutheran Church, Summit, New Jersey.

[2] "Dear partners" included all LCA pastors, who received Dr. Fry's monthly *Ministers Information Service* releases entitled "The State of the Church."

2

Luther D. Reed

Franklin Clark Fry, The Churchman

One of the happy occasions I shared with Dr. Fry was a dinner in 1955 given in his honor and celebrating his tenth anniversary as president of the United Lutheran Church. Members of the executive board and of other boards, and secretaries and staff members from the Church House gathered in New York City. Speeches were made by men who had known Dr. Fry and his work at various stages in his career. I had been asked to speak of his years as a student in the Philadelphia Seminary (1922-1925).

The Early Years

On this occasion, I recalled that as a seminarian Franklin Clark Fry had been a brilliant student, faithful and conscientious in his work, and even in class attendance, but highly critical of the curriculum and of many members of the faculty. It had been fully expected that his father, Dr. Franklin Foster Fry, would be elected to succeed his grandfather, Dr. Jacob Fry, as professor of practical theology in the Philadelphia Seminary. When the board of directors met, however, for some reason unknown to me, they elected Dr. John Conrad Seegers to this position. Franklin Clark Fry took this as an insult to his family, and he came to the seminary with chips on both shoulders. He himself had had the advantage of excellent education with a year as graduate research student in Athens after graduation from Hamilton College, in New York State. He soon detected weaknesses in the curriculum and in the faculty and openly showed his scorn of both, while meticulously meeting all requirements of the institution.

As one of his professors in the seminary, I somehow escaped his sharp barbed criticism. We then and there cemented a close friendship which endured unbroken until the day of his death.

I also said that during his pastorate of Holy Trinity church in Akron,

---

(1873-1972) Dr. Reed, eminent liturgiologist, was librarian (1906) then professor (1911-45) and president (1938-45) of the Lutheran Seminary at Philadelphia. He was the first president of the Lutheran Liturgical Association (1898-1906), secretary of the joint committee which produced the *Common Service Book* (1917), and chairman of the joint commission which prepared the *Service Book and Hymnal* (1958). He served on several committees of the United Lutheran Church in America and of the former Federal Council of Churches.

Ohio, and at meetings of the Ohio Synod he had crossed swords with many persons and had inflicted wounds that were difficult to heal. I thought that many eyebrows had been lifted on the Mount Airy campus and in the Ohio Synod when on Columbus Day, 1944, in Minneapolis, Dr. Fry had been elected president of the United Lutheran Church.

This all reminded me of a dog story, I told them. A man entered a movie theatre and found a seat in the dark. He then recognized a big dog sitting next to him with paws outstretched on the back of the seat in front of him, looking intently at the screen. The man spoke to the owner of the dog: "Your dog seems to like the picture." "Yes," said the owner, "it's strange, isn't it? He didn't care for the book." If in those early years some did not like the "book," all present at the dinner, and thousands of others, would agree that the "picture" was superb, and that Dr. Fry's leadership of the church during the previous decade had been a magnificent achievement, and all accomplished in a truly Christian spirit.

When I congratulated Dr. Fry on the day of his election as the president of the United Lutheran Church, he said to me, "I know that I will have to discipline myself and curb my tongue." And this he did to a great degree, even as he accomplished other things by hard and constant self-discipline. He did not mellow with the years, but he came to respect the rights and the feelings of others and to be patient and civil with opponents and with other points of view. In the last few years of his life there were occasional flashes of the old acerbity. Several years ago I was in the Church House in New York when one of the secretaries in the building came downstairs from Dr. Fry's office. He said, "Don't cross swords with him today; he'll cut your head off right above the shoulders."

Dr. Fry was a highly gifted, highly developed and truly great leader of men. Others will speak more fully of his work as pastor, preacher, negotiator, administrator, and world figure. His thought had the depth of sound scholarship, the breadth of the continents and the height of a truly spiritual character—all controlled and directed by massive powers, not only of analysis but of construction as well.

Dr. Fry's flair for the flamboyant often led him into extravagant expression in the manner of the actor or the artist who gains immediate attention by gilding solid thought with extravagant phrase, or emphasizing beautiful lines by the use of brilliant color. In spite of this dramatic quality, he was not an individualist, seeking self-expression for its own sake, or for applause or personal advancement. He was first and last a churchman who measured all things by the church's rule of thought and life. This quality of churchmanship gave wings to his thought and strength to his work. It is of this special quality in his work and leadership that I would speak, first of all.

Churchmanship

Dr. Fry's awareness of churchly values was shown at the first convention of the United Lutheran Church after he was elected president. Up to this time the ministers who conducted the opening services of holy communion at the church's national conventions had officiated in vestments of many sorts. Some wore black gowns, others gowns with stoles, and one or two wore surplices and stoles. Dr. Fry before the convention contacted Dr. H. Torrey Walker of the Publication House and asked him to send ten cassocks, surplices and stoles to the convention hall so that all the officiating clergy would be vested alike. This masterful handling of a ticklish question was an example of his churchmanship, for the dramatic effect of this new procedure was quickly felt in synodical and congregational services throughout the church.

When Dr. Fry became involved in policy making in interdenominational groups such as the Federal Council of Churches, he strenuously objected to the prevailing practice of "co-opting" men of special qualifications and appointing them as members of important commissions or committees without their having been elected to these positions by the churches themselves. This relatively minor but yet important instance of good churchmanship later became accepted in practically all the non-Lutheran groups with which he was associated. It established the full authority and responsibility of the church in these matters and gave greater strength and tone to all cooperative endeavor.

In its early years the United Lutheran Church had a standing committee on Church Architecture of which I was chairman. Much of its work had been to examine, correct and approve of plans for mission congregations which received loans or other support from the general church. Dr. Fry thought this work should be strengthened and he personally came before the committee with a plan proposing the creation of a strengthened committee, with a salaried director, functioning as a department of the Board of American Missions. I strongly objected to placing this work entirely in the hands of any board, as it was a matter of great importance for the entire church and not exclusively related to missions. Dr. Fry heard me patiently and left the meeting. He came to the next meeting with a fully developed plan for a department of Church Architecture responsible to the Executive Board of the church itself. I heartily approved this proposal, the committee was pleased, and the Department of Church Architecture was established. Other departments of Worship, Stewardship, and Press, Radio and Television followed in the next year or two. Dr. Fry had welcomed the suggestion of larger church responsibility and service and had translated this enlarged thought into action.

At the convention of the United Lutheran Church in Minneapolis in the fall of 1944 the Common Service Book Committee presented a final report of its five years' study of the hymnal of the church. This concluded with a request for authority from the church to complete the nearly finished work and proceed with publication of a new and thoroughly revised hymnal. A motion of approval was before the house when Dr. Oscar Blackwelder of Washington, D. C. proposed an additional sentence which instructed the committee in completing its work to invite the cooperation of all other Lutheran church bodies in the country in an endeavor to produce, "as nearly as may be possible, a single and common hymnal for all Lutheran congregations in America." This was a bold stroke, and the amended motion was promptly and enthusiastically adopted by the convention.

Some weeks later, as chairman of the Common Service Book Committee, I asked Dr. Fry if he could give me an hour or so for discussion of this matter. We met for a luncheon conference at the University Club in Philadelphia. I asked if he, as president of the church, would take the initiative and extend the church's invitation to the presidents of all the other Lutheran bodies in the country. His prompt reply was to the effect that the church had officially instructed the Common Service Book Committee to carry out this action, which he would heartily support, but that the initiative should come from the committee and not from him. Our discussion resulted in my writing the invitation as chairman of the committee, with Dr. Harvey Hoover, secretary of the committee, signing it jointly with me and sending it personally to the presidents of all Lutheran churches in America. This was the beginning of the joint endeavor which eventually, in 1958, produced the *Service Book and Hymnal* by joint action of eight Lutheran church bodies in America.

During the twelve years of common effort by thirty representatives of these eight churches, Dr. Fry gave this important work his fullest support. I did not wish him to depend upon garbled reports or backstairs gossip as the work proceeded. I kept him fully informed about all important decisions of the joint commission and of sub-committees. My files contain copies of ninety letters which I wrote Dr. Fry during these years, and seventy replies which I received from him. These occasionally were inquiring, rarely questioning, generally applauding.

Many of his letters came from unexpected places, for whenever he went abroad he carried his "homework" with him, or his jewel of a secretary, Margaret Duhme, would see that he received all important documents at various points on his itinerary. I recall receiving one quite lengthy letter from him from Stahlheim in Norway, where he was attending a conference. I well remember the magnificent view from the porches of the hotel perched on top of an 800-foot cliff and affording a magnificent view of a deep descending valley, enclosed by lofty mountains, perhaps the most impressive bit of scenery in all Norway. Dr. Fry began his letter by saying: "In the midst of this magnificent scenery I have been thinking of you and your work on the Liturgy and Hymnal of the Church."

As a churchman, Dr. Fry was not interested merely in the liturgy or the hymnal themselves. He was greatly interested in a common book of corporate devotion which would be a powerful instrument of the whole church. Here, again, was the churchman, heartily supporting an important work of the whole church.

Centralization

An outstanding example of Dr. Fry's workmanship as a churchman came with the organization of the Lutheran Church in America, which church in many respects was practically his creation. He spent days and nights in correspondence and in preparation of the constitution and by-laws of the new continental church body which emerged under his leadership and of which he became the first president. At the beginning of these studies I seriously questioned the wisdom of the policy of centralization which Dr. Fry was proposing. I did not publicly oppose this policy, as did Dr. Bagger, Dr. Stoughton and others. I, however, pointed out that in nearly all Protestant churches throughout America the form of church organization had always been diocesan, presbyterial or synodical. Large powers of control and administration had been left in the hands of these regional bodies and not in a central governing body. As one of the founding fathers of the United Lutheran Church I recalled that in 1918 we never would have succeeded in uniting the separated synods in one general body if we had not specifically agreed to leave the direction and control of all the seminaries in the country in the hands of the synods that had established and supported them, instead of placing them under the Board of Education of the whole church. I also noted that liberal trends in the Roman Catholic church were all in the direction of placing more responsibility and more authority in the hands of local bishops. Were we not missing the bus?

Dr. Fry, however, believed that we must adopt this policy not only to get the Augustana Church into the new body, but also to promote the best development in a reasonably uniform way of all our colleges and seminaries, as well as in our work of parish education and administration throughout the country. Dr. Fry's proposals appealed to the laymen, particularly to executives and men of affairs, and they were adopted.

Some dozen years later I wrote Franklin that the extremely successful operation of the Lutheran Church in America up to that time had delighted me and that I now believed that the verdict of history would be approval of the course he had taken as the best possible action at that particular time. He replied that my letter had given him greater comfort and strength than any other of the many letters he had received on this subject, which seemed to indicate that possibly he had had a few carefully concealed scruples himself.

Americanism

A determining factor in Dr. Fry's leadership in this and other matters was the fact that he was an American through and through. His family history in this country began more than a hundred years before the American Revolution. Heinrich Frey and his family settled in Trappe, Pennsylvania, in 1670. Franklin's education was soundly American with graduate study and travel abroad. This gave it breadth and depth. He lived in a full understanding of his country's expanding greatness, and so far as his church was concerned he deplored the divisions into separate bodies which kept it in weakness and unable to achieve its potential. He was the first of our leaders to see that the things which divided us were fundamentally nationalistic and linguistic rather than doctrinal, as was so generally supposed. His faith in the country's future and his certainty that these divisions could be overcome by an advancing tide of Americanization and Anglicization led him to project his planning into future decades, and not to be satisfied with things as they were. He was convinced that if the church was to serve the nation and to endure in it, it must speak the language of the land and share in the culture of the land, and not perpetuate European or other languages or cultures. Behind his policy of centralization was his conception of future American growth and unification. He wanted all Lutheran groups in the country to come together in a few larger units and have a truly American development. The Civil War had weakened the powers of individual states and had strengthened the power of the central government. A stronger and more united nation had developed under the general policy of central authority and responsibility. What had proved good for the nation should be good for the church.

Under his dynamic leadership and deep personal involvement in the program of Lutheran World Action and Lutheran World Relief the church lifted its eyes to the need and the distress of peoples of many faiths and languages in other lands in a united effort of all Lutheran groups in America to give food, clothing, comfort, help, and the assurance of Christian brotherhood and concern to millions in other lands.

A minor example of Dr. Fry's deep Americanism came to expression in the way he conducted his business as president of the church. Every now and then some foreign queen or other head of state would come to New York to seek his aid or counsel. If the noble lady, according to European custom, sent an aide asking him if he would not request an appointment with her majesty and come to see her, Dr. Fry would say, "My office is open every day except Sunday and I shall be glad to see Her Majesty there at any time that is convenient for her." "This," Dr. Fry said, "is the American way."

Pan-Lutheranism

Dr. Fry's deep concern for the good estate of the whole church went far beyond the continental range of Lutheranism in his own church body. A man of power himself, he deplored the divisions which kept Lutherans in separate national bodies and often in bitter rivalry, debating, maintaining institutions and agencies which duplicated each other and which failed to achieve the power and influence which could result in united effort. "Freedom and unity" became a slogan with him. No other person surpassed him in striving to achieve a form of Lutheran unity which would permit united action even before absolutely common agreement in minor doctrinal matters had been attained. Cooperating with many others in all groups in the country, he was a commanding figure in the efforts which produced the Lutheran World Federation and the Lutheran Council in the USA. In fact, if Dr. Fry became a member of any important organization, it was never long before he became its head, or a member of its governing body. At the third assembly of the Lutheran World Federation in Minneapolis he was elected president, a position he held for six years. In preparation for this meeting he had drafted a document of 3,500 words which, in well-rounded terms, defined the role of the Lutheran church in the world.[1]

Mr. Protestant

Leaping beyond the limits of Pan-Lutheranism, Dr. Fry's thought and effort embraced total Christianity in America, and he became a powerful figure in the National Council of Churches. He presided over the constituting convention of that body in Cleveland in December 1950. His prominence there gave him national recognition. TIME magazine called him "Mr. Protestant" and published a feature story, a carefully documented study of his life and work.[2]

The Ecumenical Movement

All this would seem enough to exhaust the energy of a very able leader. But Dr. Fry soon entered upon worldwide endeavors in the ecumenical movement. His three-dimensional spirit of world Christianity responded to the guiding principles of this world endeavor which he was convinced was "a turning back toward the center of the Christian faith." He soon became a highly respected figure in the innermost councils of the World Council of Churches. For fourteen years he was chairman of the powerful central committee and the executive committee of this body. In its interest he not only helped mold world policies but himself circled the globe, meeting with leaders of Christian churches in many lands. Within a period of two years he had criss-crossed the map of Europe, including Russia and Hungary, and had visited India, Japan, Australia, and many other lands.

I shall not go into details concerning Dr. Fry's very important part in the ecumenical movement. Others who were actively engaged in the inner councils of this movement will speak of his activities there. I had no part personally in them except to serve as a member of the Faith and Order Commission of the World Council of Churches in Lund, Sweden, and as an official visitor at the Lutheran World Federation meeting in Hannover, Germany. I will simply ask you to stand with me in awe and admiration before the memory of the man who could grasp the details and supervise the activities of these world endeavors and not neglect the responsibilities and activities of a great church at home in America of which he was the head. He had made the Lutheran church in America known and respected in Europe by the quality of his leadership, but he was able to do this because of his magnificent and successful management of his own church in America.

Before we leave this particular topic I may quote Bishop Johannes Lilje, Bishop of Hannover, Germany, and also a former president of the Lutheran World Federation. Bishop Lilje, who has a gift for saying the right thing at the right time and place, has well written: "There are very few who equal Dr. Fry in this gift for combining sound theological evaluation with a precise judgment of the actual situation and the objective appraisal of attainable ends. If one adds to this his tremendous gift of formulation which serves him in the critical moments of a debate and helps to overcome an impasse by expressing the mind of a majority of the meeting, then you have all the details of the masterly way in which Dr. Fry fulfills his high ecumenical position."[3]

Recognition

We have briefly sketched the work of this wonderful servant of God. That all this was recognized and appreciated by others is evident in the recognition of Dr. Fry received not only in academic circles within the church but within educational circles throughout the world. He was the recipient of about thirty honorary degrees from many of the ranking institutions throughout the world—from Harvard, Yale, Princeton, etc., in America and from many universities and governments abroad. This volume of tributes is further testimony that his work in and for the Lutheran church and as a world figure and eminent Christian statesman who dealt with great issues in a masterful way, was recognized and applauded everywhere.

A Great Human

So much for the man and his work. What of the man himself? Dr. Fry was a big man, physically nearly 6 ft. 2 in. tall and solidly built. Intellectually and spiritually he was a giant. A strong man can swim with the storm; it takes a great man to exercise leadership and chart the course.

I have referred to great conceptions which directed and controlled Dr. Fry's life and work: Americanism and churchmanship and ecumenism. In day by day work in his office, and in all official transactions, he always wore clerical attire and a pectoral cross. There was nothing slovenly about him. Every morning when he was in his office in New York City, he left his desk at the sound of the chapel bell, inviting any visitors or whoever might be with him to go with him to the twenty-minute service in the chapel of the Church House.

Dr. Fry's decisions and his actions were not motivated by desire for personal recognition or gain, but for the church's sake. He believed that the church was the divinely appointed custodian of spiritual gifts, graces and powers, and he wanted to work in and through it. As a leader and administrator in the church he was superb. The NEW YORK TIMES religious editor who regularly attended all manner of church assemblies throughout the country has said that Dr. Fry was the ablest parliamentarian in all the churches. Knowing his own church from coast to coast and from the Gulf to Nova Scotia he was able to make wise appointments and build up a strong staff.

Dr. Fry's preaching had a searching quality which probed the depths of one's spiritual consciousness. It had a quickening power which lifted one's thought and aspiration to the heights. His thought might range to the circumference but it never lost contact with the center. His mind constantly sought the highest potential, but his planning rarely went beyond the possible. The past, present and future seemed one to him. He studied the past, not for its own sake, but to make it serve the future.

Dr. Fry sought out and dealt with the deep things of the spirit, with the serious problems of life and death, but humor was always just around the corner. When in a jovial mood, which was quite often, he would listen to a good story or crack a joke himself, and slap his thigh in a characteristic and resounding gesture.

I did not know his inner family life intimately. I did know how jealously he guarded his vacation month of August which he always spent somewhere with Hilda, their three children, and half a dozen grandchildren.

No engagements or business matters were permitted to interrupt these precious weeks of rest and refreshment.

I recall his affection and tenderness when his talented and lovely wife Hilda became seriously ill. He said to me, "I am terribly afraid that I may lose her. But if this has to be, we have had those wonderful years together." Standing together beside his still open grave on the day of his burial at Trappe, Dr. Edward T. Horn, III, said to me, "He had 'class.'" I said, "Yes—style." Other great leaders will come and go, but we shall not see his like again.

---

[1] LCA President's Report, Minutes, 1956, pp. 29-38.

[2] Number of April 7, 1958. Reprinted by permission in *Mr. Protestant, An Informal Biography of Franklin Clark Fry*. Philadelphia: The Board of Publication of the United Lutheran Church in America, 1960.

[3] *Mr. Protestant,* p. 39.

Part One

Memos from the United Lutheran Church in America *and (since* 1962) the Lutheran Church in America

Memos 3 to 7 focus on Dr. Fry's *early life* and his nineteen-year *parish ministry.*

3

William H. Stackel

From half a century of service through the church, Mr. Stackel reflects on the maturing and the career of Franklin Fry, whom he knew intimately from boyhood.

A Boy Becomes Father to the Man

His Genealogy

This account of Franklin Clark Fry begins with his ancestors, for that is the stock from which he grew. His was the third generation in a direct line of Lutheran ministers. His son, Pastor Franklin Drewes Fry, makes the fourth Lutheran minister in that line, each with a distinguished career.

I have seen all four of these Frys in action, and I worked closely with Franklin Foster Fry, who was my pastor, and a generation later with Franklin Clark Fry as president of the United Lutheran Church in America. The boy, Franklin, grew up in the congregation of which I was a member.

(b. 1885) A Rochester banker and long-time councilman at Reformation church, Mr. Stackel was a delegate at the formation of the United Lutheran Church in 1918. He served on its Board of Education (1918-26), its Executive Board for sixteen years, and on the Executive Committee of the Lutheran Laymen's Movement for Stewardship. Chairman of the ULCA Commission on Investments 1934-54, he helped design the church's Common Investment Fund which was launched in 1954.

When in 1900 Franklin Clark Fry was born in Bethlehem, Pennsylvania, his grandfather, the Rev. Jacob Fry, D. D., was professor of homiletics and pastoral theology in Philadelphia Lutheran Seminary. He was a distinguished scholar, seasoned pastor, and elder church statesman. His impressive sermons at the seminary church gave his students a fine example of his teachings. As pastor he had been popular with young people and his keen observations often sparkled with humor. His devoted wife was greatly beloved. The religious influence of these parents led two of their sons, Charles L. Fry and Franklin Foster Fry, into the Christian ministry.

In 1901 the Rev. Franklin Foster Fry was called as pastor to Lutheran Church of the Reformation, Rochester, New York. He brought from Bethlehem, where he had been pastor of Grace Lutheran church, his charming bride of a few years, Minnie Clark Fry, and their infant son, Franklin.

Home Influences

Franklin was blessed with a stimulating home life. Sharply differing characteristics of his parents were clearly woven into his character and carried to his maturity.

His mother of Scotch-Irish descent was a born leader with a keen mind and decisive opinions openly expressed and ably defended. She was a tower of strength both in home and in congregation, loved people, and was gifted in conversation. She was devoted to every good cause and formed many enduring friendships.

Franklin's father had a deep passion for souls and gave himself utterly for the congregation's development. His sermons were delivered with moving passion and revealed deep spiritual conviction. His open-minded dealings developed the best in his lay leaders. He strove for Lutheran unity and encouraged wider Christian fellowships. He was a stalwart leader in synod and in the church at large.

But this father found time daily out of his busy life to pal with his lively son and to match wits with him. He was exceedingly resourceful with a keen sense of humor and a stubborn driver for higher and yet higher goals.

Franklin's parents encouraged their only child in his eager search for knowledge. At an early age he was widely read and was remarkably versed in the Bible and in a wide variety of subjects. He heard church policies and problems discussed from all angles in his home.

But home topics were of broad dimensions. To illustrate, when the Progressive party was formed in 1912, there were three political leanings in the family of three. This proved that nothing was accepted or approved without thorough discussion and testing.

Course in Churchmanship

A great factor in Franklin's development was his opportunity for close observation of the remarkable growth of Reformation congregation in an unusual period of its history. Suburbia was unborn. Autos were scarce. Distractions were fewer. But uppermost with many churches was the language problem. Members flocked to this English-speaking church. Its pastor, Dr. Fry, eagerly seized this opportunity and majored in sermonizing and calling. Both members and prospects were within near radius of the church and other residential areas. Many calls could be made in a single afternoon. Thus favored and under the dynamic leadership of the pastor, the congregation expanded immensely, both intensively and numerically.

Boyhood and Youth

In such an aura of religious dedication and with such a ringside seat at the arena of congregational performance, the boy Franklin grew to manhood. Yes, it was difficult at times to determine whether his wisdom or stature had the greater girth. His physical frame bore the semblance of dignity and endurance. It housed a massive mind and a God-fearing soul.

But as a boy he was a genuine boy. He entered eagerly into sports and the fun side of life. Boys who sang with him in the church choir thought him a prankster. His restive mind boomed in all directions. From boyhood he was a regular fellow but with keen insights and mature judgments.

He was an avid baseball fan and when later in life he presided at church conventions, his multifarious mind enabled him to follow both the Yankees' game and any tangled convention proceedings concurrently without muffing the ball. His hearty laughter joined with leg slapping often aroused by his own quips shook his massive frame and perchance the rafters. This levity in his maturity became an escape from excessive strain or from an impasse in any *Hier steh' ich* conference.

One of Franklin's classmates who later became a lawyer and judge expressed deep disappointment that Franklin had decided to be a minister, for he said that his classmates were aware of Franklin's keen executive ability and that his country needed him. What a creditable appraisal of his many-sided abilities from his own peers! Although clearly a leader from youth, he was not a showoff but was humble and deferential, respecting his elders and teachers.

Strength Through Union

When in 1918 the gavel passed from that towering churchman, Dr. Theodore E. Schmauk, last president of the General Council and temporary convention chairman, to a new resourceful leader, Dr. Frederick H.

Knubel, as president of the United Lutheran Church in America, it signaled a new surge in that branch of the Lutheran church and new dimensions in cooperation. Joining of forces multiplied effective leadership and removed the divisive feeling of varying shades of Lutheranism in the merging bodies. Bold expectations for significant progress were released, implemented by better organization and wider use of the laity. Here was a new era in the church's history marked by a strong spirit of union which erased all distinguishing loyalties to the merging synods, the General Council, General Synod, and United Synod in the South.

It had taken years of prayer and patience to effect this God-leading consummation. When the going was tough to the point of impasse, the voice of determined laymen on the merger commission aided greatly in achieving the merger goal.

Each of the merging synods heard the commission's report and voted for the merger. How well I recall as a delegate to the General Council witnessing the march of the commission onto the platform singing with the delegates that most appropriate hymn, "Lord Jesus Christ, Be Present Now."

Other Steps in Lutheran Unity

Is it not the truth that as separated Christians draw nearer to our Lord and Savior they instinctively draw nearer to one another? Jesus Christ is the rallying point for the union of all faithful Christians because all who walk with him in faith and humility are already in spirit and truth companying together.

When Jesus fervently prayed (John 17) "that they may all be one," he did not leave it there, but through the Holy Spirit he bestirs our consciences and our hearts to face squarely that oneness in Christ which must finally be achieved to obey his holy will.

Therefore, in less than a half-century after the 1918 merger another Lutheran union was consummated in 1962 by four churches into the Lutheran Church in America. It is significant that this brought into this second merged body the Augustana Synod (Swedish), because there had been strong hope for the inclusion of the Augustana Synod in the 1918 merger. In fact, a representative of that body spoke at the merging convention in 1918, indicating how the General Council and the Augustana Synod had over many years cooperated in common projects and how close were their ties.

This second merger added much strength to the new body and brought into the larger fellowship many strong leaders and influential congregations. It also effected wider congregational coverage in areas such as New England, the Midwest, the Far West, and certain metropolitan centers where one or another of the merged bodies had been sparsely represented.

The constitution and policies of the merged church also effected a stronger union in the main church body in place of the somewhat diffused powers of individual synods.

Broader Ecumenicity

In three great areas of broader church cooperation the United Lutheran Church in America made notable advances during the early years of Dr. Franklin Clark Fry's presidency. In 1947 the church took an active part in the founding of the Lutheran World Federation, in 1948 the World Council of Churches, and in 1950 the National Council of Churches of Christ in the USA.

In all of these ecumenical advances Dr. Fry was a leading participant and eventually a top leader. His ecumenical assignments had started in 1936, when he was a member of the preaching mission of the Department of Evangelism of the Federal Council of Churches. From 1954 until his death he served as chairman of the Central and Executive Committees of the World Council of Churches. From 1957 to 1963 he was the president of the Lutheran World Federation.

Who Is My Neighbor?

That question and Jesus' incisive answer spoken nearly two thousand years ago (Luke 10) resounds with great emphasis in our day. Human want and suffering—physical and spiritual—in this land of affluence with tens of millions of Christians are truly appalling. Racial bias and injustices are also most disturbing. Great resourcefulness on the part of the church and its members is needed to do our part in averting confusion and catastrophe.

Greatly to the credit of our Lutheran church be it said that it has become increasingly aware and concerned over social problems and at each church convention its Board of Social Ministry has come with recommendations calculated to give our faith stronger expression in our attitudes and our works. In this significant application of the gospel to everyday living, Dr. Franklin Clark Fry has been an effective leader. It will take a lot of prayer and good judgment to guide this important phase of our church's commitment into wise channels which will be supported by the great majority of its membership and avoid extremes to right or left.

Church Business Administration

As a member of the Executive Board of the ULCA and chairman of its finance committee for some years during Dr. Fry's presidency, I worked closely with him and so observed his outstanding business acumen. He was a whiz on budgeting, knowing instinctively where appropriations would be most effective. His memory and familiarity with procedures and previous actions were remarkable. He exhibited rare judgment with all business affairs of the church. He would have been a marked success as head of some large commercial enterprise. Devoting his business ability to the church over his whole active life has been a contribution of truly incalculable value.

He was a stickler for correct procedure and could quickly adjust his own thinking where required. To illustrate: I pointed out to him after studying the church constitution that formal hearings with the boards were required when preparing the biennial budget. At once he arranged for such hearings at the next budget period, and the thorough procedure involving budgets and forecasts was installed and continues to this time. During the two days required for board hearings, Dr. Fry presided and revealed his vast knowledge of every part of each board's financial operations.

Finally, let me witness to Dr. Fry's patient and considerate attention in every conference I had with him. He always would leave his seat at the desk, and coming near me would make me feel that my matter in hand was of supreme importance to him. He made one feel like an important cog in his intricate machinery.

In Summary

Here was a leader whom God in his wisdom called to administer the affairs of a great church. His great strength lay in his towering faith in God's leading and in his utter dedication to his church's welfare and progress.

4

Charles M. Cooper

From his experience as assistant pastor in Akron, Dr. Cooper comments on Dr. Fry's parish ministry. Then as his later colleague in executive affairs, he adds some reflections on President Fry's churchmanship.

The memoranda I can supply on FCF are, first, of my three years with him at Trinity, Akron, 1933-36[1]; second, of the years I was on the United Lutheran Church in America Executive Board and on the Joint Commission on Lutheran Unity, through the merger into the first biennium of the Lutheran Church in America, 1954-64. They certainly picture his interests in those years, more fully in the thirties than later, since we were more intimate then; they go deeply into his personality to illustrate the problems a good biographer will have to face; and they do include anecdotes illustrative of his character.

In the parish FCF's sole interest was his ministry. When I arrived on the scene, he was going full tilt, seven (not six) days a week. Gradually he eased off a bit on Sunday afternoons, taking his family for an occasional drive, and including me, since I was single the first year. But if we went down through Wooster he would be tempted to stop and call on the local pastor; if we went up to Cleveland, we might see Joe Sittler, Jr., on the east end or somebody else on the west side. But there were no avocational interests: no general reading, no sports, no solitary listening to the radio unless it was a spot of news. It hardly seemed necessary to read books—a glance would tell him all he needed to know. His one relaxation came after lunch: twenty minutes to smoke a cigar (often the only one of the day). His real interest outside of work was talk, preferably about church matters; but if the conversationalist with whom he engaged preferred, it could range to sports, travel, himself and his family, school days, politics, the world at large—only to circle around again to the church. He loved the church.

Holidays were also days for work. Thanksgiving Day was required to

---

(b. 1909) President of the Pacific Lutheran Seminary since 1961, Dr. Cooper was formerly Old Testament professor at the Philadelphia Seminary (1945, joined the faculty in 1936) and president of the Pennsylvania Ministerium (1953-61). He was a member of the Joint Commission on Lutheran Unity (1956-62), and a delegate to the assemblies of the World Council of Churches (1961) and the Lutheran World Federation (1963).

tot up the pledges received at church the previous Sunday, estimate how far short they fell of the coming year's budget, list some more men who should be commissioned the following Sunday for the canvass of all who had failed to show up with a pledge card. New Year's Day was dedicated to making out the annual parochial report. One month at Lake Skaneateles each summer was vacation. I cannot believe he thought, spoke or did anything even there that was not related to the coming year in the church.

The weekly pattern was almost invariable. Monday morning he visited the offices of Hurl Albrecht of Acme Stores, a layman dedicated to the advancement of Trinity church. By Tuesday he was thinking about the sermon blurb he must put into Sunday's bulletin with the full page of announcements—the blurb referring to the sermon of the subsequent week. Correspondence took less time than planning that bulletin, thinking about parishioners, setting up calling lists, getting out on the depression-days' constant job of finding work for unemployed men, making contacts with prospective members, being a pastor. Every afternoon, from 1:30 (after the cigar and a minute's grooming) he started out on calls. He stopped only when he found people at early suppers. He came home to eat his with the family and departed to do more calls. The total was usually from six to ten a day. They might start with three or four the first hour at a hospital. They could range over a whole quarter of the city, systematically scoured for shut-ins (giving an hour to enjoying a baseball radio broadcast with a man, or two minutes to congratulations and a sincere prayer of thanksgiving after childbirth to a woman); for prospects (no stranger turned up in church on Sunday but his home was visited that week); and for nudging, challenging, seeking, demanding parish work of his members (no one was called by phone to teach a class—they might say No—they were personally seen and convinced they could do it and should at least give it a try).

This calling schedule kept up until Friday evening. Then he started writing the sermon for Sunday. He kept at it all day Saturday. Saturday night or at dawn Sunday he was committing the six-page, thirty-five-minute discourse to memory, practicing its phrases, rephrasing a bit of it, inserting changes in the typed copy in that ineffably neat, tiny script. But because the subject and the predication of that sermon had been decided upon ten days before he wrote it, so as to be announced in the prior Sunday's bulletin, it was taking form in his mind all week. His somewhat erratic and too heavy-footed automobile driving was partly due to his complete lack of manual dexterity (he was not naturally an athlete in spite of his build). But even more it was due to his preoccupation in the car with thinking about the sermon. He knew every street in Akron, never needed to refer to the map for a member's locale; could make a list of house numbers opposite the names on that day's calling schedule almost without referring to the card file of membership, and so eased up to house after house, thinking *both* of the person to be seen, or the situation in which that call would probably involve him, *and* of some topic or aspect or emphasis or illustration that would go into the coming sermon or perhaps some future one.

His mind was not only quick but fertile. A page of reading gave him six or seven ideas, although the author had only projected two or three. In writing, the job was to simplify, prune adjectives away, find synonyms of simpler cast than the rich, Asiatic and even Pindaric style he naturally affected. The bulletins of the years 1929-33 will give proof of this, as well as any sermon manuscripts that his family may still have. Flowers for the altar were announced as follows on December 31, 1933:

> The gracious charm of ———— has inspired her sister and brother ———— [the full names supplied] to consecrate the chancel flowers for her today, as it will many another to cherish her memory in unfading affection.

Here is the blurb that appeared on June 21, 1936:

> "The Days of Our Years"—and the tides of worthy achievement with which an open-handed God justly intends to fill them full —will be Pastor Fry's challenging, insistently practical theme at 10:30 o'clock one week from today in his final appearance in Trinity Church's pulpit until August. A sober reflection finds in them —those days—the only complete democracy which exists. They present the solitary equality which applies to all men, as wealth, opportunity and even native talents cannot. How about today? Or next Sunday? What, do you estimate, is its capacity—for love, for joy, for peace, for wholesome activity, for reverence? The culture of your soul in worship before God will enable you beyond all else to expand your days to the utmost.

By this date I was planning to leave for a teaching post at Mount Airy. But I had been imbued with his style. I wrote the bulletins and he edited them and got them to the printer. But his own blurbs were of course his own compositions. This is mine on that same "penultimate" Sunday in June, 1936 (as he would have identified it):

> A contemporary by-product of Christianity in strife-torn Oriental lands finds expression in policies of pacifism and non-resistance. Just how truly these exhibit the spirit of Christ is perhaps questionable to many minds. A Church Militant at all events cannot be composed of flabby spirits [a Fryism!] nor of complacent souls

which cry, "Peace, Peace!" when there is no peace. So the Scripture for the Third Sunday after Trinity will call through Pastor Cooper's sermon at the 8:00 o'clock service to "Resistance of Evil."[2]

Church meetings, parochial or general, denominational or ecumenical, did not appeal to him as a pastor. Of course, he attended and *reported in writing* at every monthly meeting of the council and went to conference and synod. He took Hilda Fry to the rather elegant luncheon meetings of the select ladies who composed the altar guild. He tried to do his duty to the Luther Leagues until I could relieve him of that. But other organizations had to be content with his turning up in the course of their meeting, greeting them cordially and leaving promptly thereafter with the explanation that he had calls to make. At the monthly interdenominational ministers' meeting, he attended the Monday morning devotions and heard the speaker, took part in discussion of the address, and stayed for lunch (and, conditions permitting, his cigar). Then he lit out on calls, when New Business might engage the brethren in some task-force effort in the community, some special committee project, some social or community issue. I was stuck with these things for several years as the treasurer of the group—since my predecessor in office, an Evangelical and Reformed man, was also named Cooper and the Akron clergy thought it a good trick to keep the same name for the office (and perhaps get some revenge on Fry for his complete indifference to their organization, apart from its devotional and educational uses, which he did not despise but to which he limited his participation). Social action in those days was tame and often blundering. He knew its limited value and weighed his parish responsibilities (and opportunities) as of more worth than protests to city council on immorality in the streets or calls on industrial management to alleviate unemployment, and the like. He particularly abhorred ecumenical pronouncements that did not come out of a properly organized council of churches, giving scope to what he regarded as a properly evangelical point of view. He also knew the brethren envied him as pastor of the biggest and livest downtown church, and one that throughout the worst years of the depression seldom failed to net a hundred new adult members a year, won by direct evangelization and thorough adult catechization and held by vigorous, if somewhat flamboyant, preaching and a dedicated pastoral concern.

These were features that matured and developed in his later career as churchman. Forcing the evangelical and representative principles upon all councils of churches in which ULCA people affiliated; giving every other denomination a run for its money; competitively engaging in the Lord's work, glorying in every advance—but still confessing, as admonished by Jesus, that he was an unprofitable servant.

There were ups and downs in his temperament. He would chuckle and glow about a sermon idea. When he had spent himself all week by unremitting parish labors, hammered out the sermon manuscript and preened and pruned it to what in his judgment was perfection, committed it to memory, preached it with a clarion voice, clear as crystal, devastating in its denunciation of evil and shimmering with the beauty and sincerity of his faith—he would hand out the offering plates and sink, exhausted and dismayed, into his clergy seat in the chancel, out of everyone's sight except mine in the corresponding seat on the other side. He felt he was a failure. That sermon had not come off as it should have. He knew its more purple patches contained some bombast. His honest mind saw through his own choicest bits of oratory. Sometimes he smiled bravely—as if to say, "I tried." Often he mopped his brow and looked the picture of dejection. But the ushers returned with full plates. His free pastoral prayer (never written down, to my knowledge) was so much more eloquent in directness and condensation than the sermon, and he turned to pronounce the benediction in a glow of spiritual refreshment. At the door he was himself again, gladdened by his people's appreciation, uplifted by their enthusiasm, delighted by their frank criticism, and thrilled, not with himself and his effort, but his sense of being the Lord's servant among the Lord's people in the Lord's work.

I think a biographer's biggest problem will be to penetrate and justly judge his temperament and character. He had plenty of ego—why not? He was the only son of somewhat older than average parents who doted on him—of course. He did not make friends easily. Men came easily to hate and fear him. But he yearned for companionship and hungered for men's friendship. He was afraid of women. I don't think he understood them. He had little gallantry. But he was a Christian gentleman, clean-minded. The healthy cleanliness of mind, though, was inseparable from sharpness of intellect, keenness of perception, devotion to the truth as he saw the truth. He was aglow with the Spirit but he had too capacious a mind to permit that glow to run into emotionalism. His great temptation was that of despising others. He steadfastly resisted it. It always seemed to me it was as if his wise and witty parents, whom I found it much easier to be with than with him, had impressed upon him through all his years at home that he had incomparable gifts and tremendous abilities and needed not to fear any man; but that with these gifts went a corresponding responsibility to employ them for Christ and his church. To that he was wholly committed.

Then in the later years, he ran the ULCA Executive Board as he would have liked to run Trinity's council—but couldn't, with a lay president at Trinity. He wrote out every committee report and attached all the pertinent documents and added all the resolutions he considered appropriate. The committees looked all this over and duly moved the resolutions. Exceptions were keen lawyers like Judge Henninger or later Ober Hess, who insisted on doing their own homework, or some good friend, like Frederick R. Knubel or myself, whose "improvements" of his wording or even dissent from his judgments he would welcome. He loved his friends and was delighted to accept their counsel. Others who differed with him would get keen debate from him. But he did not fight to win. He fought to get results. He was glad for correction, eager for reproof (from those who could dare to give it), prompt to recognize worth in any quarter or from any source. But one could seldom improve on his work and never outsmart or outflank his agile mind. He was several steps ahead of every parliamentary maneuver.

The problem is, how to balance all this off? To those closest to him, admirers and friends, this was leadership of high order. To those at a distance and in opposition, or slow to understand, this was autocracy and egotism on a gigantic scale. Where does the truth lie? Given his home circumstances, his superb education at Hamilton and Athens (after which seminary was a terrible letdown), his native gifts and his dedication to his calling, an achievement of high order seems inevitable. But it cost him dearly. With no one his equal, except momentarily in some single aspect of the field of his work, he was a lonely soul.

I speak of his parents in this connection because he was fiercely proud of and attached to his father and his mother. Harry J. Kreider[3] either did not know or omits to tell in his chapter on seminary years that the antagonism FCF felt for the Mount Airy faculty was not merely the result of his intellectual superiority to many of them. I know it was resentment regarding what he understood to have been his father's expectation of succeeding old Dr. Jacob Fry as professor of homiletics and pastoral care. Apparently some seminary authorities had led Dr. F. F. Fry to expect this call and had induced him to begin buying books and giving time to preparation for its duties. But the call went to another. FCF took it as an insult to his father (I do not know that his father was as much put out by it as the son was). Similarly, when he became president of the ULCA he rode the Board of American Missions hard on plans and procedures his father had worked out for its operations and which he felt were being violated or put aside. This began, in fact, before he was elected president but was a member of that board. He could laugh with others at his uncle's eccentricities. But he loved his father. We looked forward in high anticipation to Christmas, 1933, when his parents and my fiancée were to be visiting Akron. But his father suddenly died and I went with Frank and Hilda to the train in Cleveland, returning their big Buick to Akron for them. Then my fiancée came down with bronchitis and after the midnight Christmas service and the early Christmas dawn service, I spent the rest of Christmas Day on a day coach bound for Boston. Our mutual disappointments were very real. But his loss was the permanent one.

Because after 1954 I also presided annually at a big convention, in the Ministerium of Pennsylvania (actually a more intense one than the leisurely paced ULCA convention and sometimes exceeding it in numbers of delegates), I felt I had a special right to gauge and appreciate his powers as a parliamentarian. His quick mind and ready tongue made him a superb presiding officer. I think he was less objective than he might have been. He cared more what actions were taken. For one thing, they couldn't be changed the next year: ULCA conventions were biennial. For another, his relations to boards and synods were more remote than a synod president's relations to pastors, committees and boards of synod. So more was perhaps at stake. But he gave his best on these occasions. He encouraged timid laymen and younger pastors. He fenced with those he thought could take it but spoke softly to the less able or less assertive. He lived the convention days intensely and spent hours at night devising strategy. He excelled in the ability to untangle procedures and to state the gist of motions and to clarify for the house what was at stake and what one course of action would result in as compared with another. But he tended also to be a strict constructionist: a motion meant what it said and a series of resolutions was to be read through word by word (preferably by himself) after all amendments had been adopted and it was finally up for action. He really wrote the LCA constitution. The rest of the commission or even of the merging convention simply touched it up here and there—except some item like the preamble which he graciously permitted Dr. Bergendoff to write. I can still identify a word or phrase there that I contributed; for example, in section 3 of Article II, "for which the Old Testament prepared the way and . . ." is my addition. But nothing that substantive can I recall adding to the pages and pages which FCF poured out, clear and definitive and complete in his drafting.

There was a suprising strictness in his Lutheran identification and practice, considering his wide and deep ecumenical attachments. One might feel at Helsinki (1963) that he was carrying a vendetta with President Schiotz a bit far when he did not commune at a service conducted by the American Lutheran Church. But I do not believe he ever communed at other than an altar in his own parish or his own synod or church body. Not that he disapproved my having communed elsewhere—in Presbyterian, Episcopalian, and even Congregational churches, when invited to do so. But he loved his own with a fervid attachment. His confirmation promises were sacred vows. His doctrine of the Lord's Supper was genuinely deep as well as strict. At his first administration of the sacrament in Trinity, Akron, he told me, he wept at the indifference and what he regarded as irreverence of the communicants. That was all changed by the time I came. It was still only a quarterly communion in their old General Synod style, except that he had introduced one more on Ash Wednesday. They still used grape juice, except that when he and I and President Joseph Sittler, Sr. of the Ohio Synod communed at my ordination it was with wine in the chalice of the Augustana congregation (Trinity had stacks of trays but no chalice). But the tone of devotion and, for him, of rapt adoration of the very present Lord, was certainly evident and real.

He rests now with nearly fourscore Frys in Old Trappe churchyard. When he learned that Claude Schick, then secretary of the Ministerium, had bought an adjacent lot, he joked that if disturbed there he would rise up and "bop him one" from where they lay, almost side by side. Like all men whose religion comes naturally and flows deeply, too deep for outward show of shallow piety, he could make a joke of sacred or solemn matters. But only if the subjects or objects were of merely mortal stuff. There was no blasphemy on his tongue.

So I think he knew his own worst faults and shortcomings. I think he hated the egocentricity that seemed to envelop him as a leader, a winner, an exceptional churchman. I think he confessed privately before God that he loved the applause of men, that he liked to have his own way, that he found himself thinking he could do things better than others could. And if such honesty and humility prevailed in his heart when he opened it to the Lord, how shall we judge those lapses in which a besetting sin caught up with him? I hope a biographer can be realistic, can find evidence (I am sure it is there) of growth in grace (or what men call "mellowing"), and in the final analysis can deal gently with a great heart, a gallant soul, a devoted servant of Jesus Christ.

---

[1] For another glimpse of Dr. Fry in the parish, see the chapter in *Mr. Protestant*, pp. 14-20, by Thomas B. Kline, Dr. Cooper's successor as assistant pastor and now pastor in Georgetown, Connecticut.

[2] In 1942 Dr. Fry described his homiletical technique, including the "blurb," in a "sermon biography" accompanying his contribution to S. J. Sebelius, ed., *A Faith for These Times*, Rock Island, pp. 125-133.

[3] "At the Philadelphia Seminary," in *Mr. Protestant*, pp. 7-13.

5

Walter E. DeBruin

From intimate experience Mr. deBruin writes of the pastorate of Dr. Fry.

The Akron Pastorate of Dr. Franklin Clark Fry (1929-1944)

To try and record accurate recollections and observations upon the personal development of Franklin Clark Fry during the fifteen years of his chief pastorate in Holy Trinity church, Akron, Ohio, is a herculean task for one who was privileged to know this great Christian leader as both pastor and intimate friend over at least fourteen of those memorable years and to the date of his death. I have tried to draw upon the recollections of others in the congregation and thus temper my own admiration and affection with different points of view. The very subject "personal development" suggests to the reader an improper premise—a progress from immaturity toward maturity. Even though he was only twenty-eight years of age and out of the seminary with four years of parish experience when he arrived in Akron, he certainly was not immature. Some of his closest friends relate that in the intellectual environment in which he grew to manhood, they can't imagine him ever being a child. Others have accurately said that intellectually he was superior to the seminary faculty under which he studied. So I write rather of what changes in perspective and in sense of mission he may have disclosed to those who knew him well in that period of his life.

He came to a sixty-one-year-old congregation the year after they had celebrated the twenty-fifth anniversary of Dr. E. W. Simon's ministry among them. Dr. Simon was sixty-nine years of age and remained as minister emeritus for life. The young pastor was handicapped by the doubts, suspicions, and personal loyalty of parishioners to whom he was an unknown. The congregation was soon to realize the prodigious vitality and dedication of the new shepherd. From early in the morning until late at night he made calls on members and prospective members of the congregation. The writer and his wife attended Holy Trinity on their first Sunday in Akron, and within the week they were visited by Franklin Fry

---

(b. 1905) A former attorney of the Goodyear Tire and Rubber Company in Akron, Mr. deBruin has been for several decades a prominent member of Holy Trinity Lutheran church. He served as secretary of the church council for many years during Dr. Fry's ministry in Akron.

who received their letter of transfer from their home Lutheran church and engaged them to assist in the Sunday school.

In the pulpit the young evangelist preached the most profound sermons which he had memorized from his script and in a magnificent voice which filled every corner of the sanctuary. The rhetoric was beautiful, but on many occasions the intellect which had created it was far above the understanding of some of his flock. None, however, could miss the reverence and the spiritual comfort of the entire service of worship.

In the sick room or beside the hospital bed, the intellectual giant became a warm-hearted, wise comforter who was ever present when most needed. He bore with his parishioners the great number of tragic episodes which are so large a part of normal living in a community. When the Great Depression struck, he voluntarily insisted upon taking a twenty percent cut in salary. In religious instruction, Franklin Fry was meticulous and insistent. His catechumens were thoroughly drilled in the faith in which they were confessing. And as a teacher of the Bible, he was without a peer. He made the biblical characters come alive, and his great knowledge of the subject and his informal manner of presentation were so captivating that many of his congregation would return again and again to listen and learn. Franklin Fry's chief interest was the parish ministry, and he gave himself completely to it. He sacrificed his vacations, and he was critical of other ministers who seemed to spend large amounts of time away from their church work. He had no time for service clubs and felt that loose associations of churchmen of various faiths accomplished little good. Strong Lutheran theologian that he was, he could not understand so-called Christian churches which had no specific creeds or articles of faith. At this stage in his life he was far from ecumenical in his thinking, but so were most churchmen.

For fifteen years, as his children grew toward maturity, he and they lived, camped, worshiped and experienced good times and bad with families in the congregation. When slanderous, false rumors threatened the professional career of one of the congregation, Dr. Fry's quick action both at the church and through the public press averted a crisis. On a number of occasions, people who found their minds at the breaking point because of the stress of living owed their recovery to the wisdom and the dedication with which he ministered to their needs. His family went camping with other families in the parish where they swam, played volleyball and had stunt nights together. When, on one occasion, he came from the parish to spend a night at camp, the man who became president of the United Lutheran Church in America was greeted at the camp entrance with signs typical of the roadside Burma Shave ads of that era, two of which read, "Come in Brother" and "Yea Fatso." The next day before the outdoor altar in camp attire, Franklin Fry preached to the same families about the Good Samaritan in a manner neither adults nor children ever forgot. When his wife underwent repeated serious surgery, his parishioners prayed with him and later thanked God for her miraculous recovery. At the last service in Trinity before he left, he stepped to the altar rail and took communion with members of his congregation. Small wonder it is that in his resignation letter to the parish he said in part, "Today, with a heavy heart, I am faced by one of the most difficult and painful duties of my life. By action of the United Lutheran Church in America which has elected me its president, I must resign as the pastor of Trinity Lutheran church. My ministry, my labors, and my very being have become so intertwined with this congregation after more than fifteen years of intimate, blessed fellowship that it means a deep wrench for us all." As one member of the congregation, I can agree with his statement that his leaving did mean a deep wrench for all of us.

Dr. Fry was later to say of his elevation to the presidency that "The Lord called me into the ministry and the church called me away from it. I would much rather have a pastorate than have to squirt grease into ecclesiastical machinery."[1] But, regardless of personal wishes, he did accept the call of the church, with what degree of success others far more eloquent and knowledgeable than this writer have already recorded. There is one facet of his remarkable success in this position that I should like to dwell upon because it casts some light upon his personal development. That is the growth of the ecumenical movement among the Christian churches and the important part Dr. Fry played in it.

The formation of the Lutheran Church in America by the merging of four of those branches was a tremendously complicated labor into which he poured his intellect and his organizational skill. In the same period of time, however, he became one of the planners who organized and directed the National Council of Churches of Christ in the United States. W. A. Visser 't Hooft, general secretary of the World Council of Churches, has accurately recorded Franklin Fry's long and valued service to that organization. Bishop Lilje of the Lutheran Church of Hannover, Germany, in speaking of his leadership in the Lutheran World Federation, said that there were few people in the ecumenical movement who equaled Dr. Fry's gift for combining sound theological evaluation with a precise judgment of the actual situation and the objective appraisal of attainable ends. TIME magazine called him a new kind of Protestant leader—"the Ecumenical Man."[2]

The limits of this essay do not permit the elaboration of his labors in the field which won him the accolade of "Mr. Protestant." I only mention them to demonstrate two points: First, the development of a dedicated Lutheran parish pastor who felt his first duty was to the people in his parish, and who had little time for anything that would interfere, into a worldwide Christian who demonstrated his compassion for all people and exhausted his physical powers as a modern St. Paul. How noticeable it was in his later sermons. No one who heard him from the pulpit or from the podium or from TV broadcasts could miss the terrific impact. His message still had the beautiful, flowing rhetoric but along with it the warmth and earnestness and the empathy of a man who labored and lived as his Master would have him live among people across the world. I have had the opportunity of looking into the eyes of grateful Arab refugees as well as Jordanian officials and hearing from them the fulsome praise that the very name Fry brought forth. And I am sure that the same appreciation and adulation would have been evident in Addis Ababa, Iceland, India and even in the imperial garden in Tokyo where Dr. Fry had an audience with the emperor of Japan. Government officials and laymen alike marveled at the magic accomplished by Lutheran World Relief under his inspired leadership. This was the parish pastor whose parish became the world.

The second thing about Franklin Clark Fry's genius to which I would direct attention was even more remarkable. Here was a dynamic leader who not only dedicated himself to the "greasing of ecclesiastical machinery" but to its rebuilding, all the while assuming responsibilities for the worldwide organization of all Lutheran groups and also a similar organization of all Protestant denominations. Spanning continents by air became almost a weekly occurrence, and his work exceeded the capacity of two secretaries. In spite of the demands on his time and the drain of his energies, he never was too busy to remember his many friends.

There was the time when delegates from the four Lutheran bodies and several corps of lawyers were attempting to wade through mountains of constitutions, resolutions, and paper work necessary to the formation of the new Lutheran Church in America, and Dr. Fry was the key negotiator working about twenty hours of each day. He heard of the tragic death of the wife of a former member of his Akron congregation, and he immediately wrote a longhand, personal note of comfort to the bereaved husband. At conventions of the church when he was not presiding, he would leave the platform and seek the society of old friends among the visiting laymen.

Although New York was his home, when he or his wife Hilda had some time for relaxation, they invariably spent some time with their Akron friends. Within a year of his death, Dr. Fry was in Akron for a brief visit. Although he turned down all invitations for speaking engagements and the visits of his host of acquaintances, he found time to call at the home of one old friend who was suffering a terminal illness and spent a full hour in family conversation with her—and then he moved to the home of another critically ill friend whom he surprised and comforted with his thoughtfulness. "Mr. Protestant" was never too big or too busy to help a friend.

---

[1] Quoted in the TIME magazine cover story of April 7, 1958, reprinted in *Mr. Protestant,* p. 59.

[2] References to Visser 't Hooft and Lilje are from *Mr. Protestant.* The expression from TIME is found in the story quoted above.

6

Robert W. Stackel

Dr. Stackel analyzes Dr. Fry's Akron ministry.

Dr. Fry's ministry in the Evangelical Lutheran Church of the Holy Trinity, Akron, Ohio, in relation to the later concerns of his life

1. *Fierce struggle over priority of loyalties.* In his early years in Akron young Pastor Fry found such strong loyalties in the congregation toward the Sunday school that many members were giving only secondary loyalty to the life and worship of the church itself. Considered in some quarters to be brash and immature, this young pastor butted heads solidly with status persons in the congregation about this. It was the greatest struggle of his early ministry in Akron, as the archives of the congregation will reveal. With courage and determination he never gave up. Undoubtedly this struggle, demanding broad-gauge strategy, was a proving ground for many bigger struggles he encountered in later life which required much sharper strategies and even firmer determination. Indeed, out of such beginnings evolved the superb strategist.

2. *Revision of constitution.* Not long after he took up his ministry in Akron, he was engaged in a revision of the congregation's constitution, along with a committee of laymen. Adopted in 1933, this was such a remarkable document that it stood for over three decades. Some of his thinking can clearly be seen in this constitution. Here we find an early exhibition of his lifelong interest in drafting constitutions, as well as his deep regard for basic documents in the life of any organization.

3. *His interest in persons.* In the rapidly growing congregation he related warmly to persons, always remembering names. One member of the congregation still recounts with glee how he stood in line to greet Dr. Fry fifteen years after the pastor left the congregation, the two of them not having met in between. "You won't remember my name," this layman said. "Fouts," Dr. Fry shot back, "*Omer R.* Fouts." The warmth of

---

(b. 1913) Dr. Stackel, a son of William Stackel, has been pastor of Holy Trinity church, Akron, since 1958. He directed the ULCA Evangelism Mission of 1956-57. He has been a member of the ULCA Executive Board (1958-62) and the LCA Executive Board (1958-62) and the LCA Executive Council (1962-66), and a participant in the work of the National Council of Churches and the World Council. He was the preacher at the funeral of Dr. Fry in 1968.

his personal relationships is indicated by the first-name basis on which he dealt with people. Many years later I saw him telephone the chairman of the board of a very large government operation and secure over the phone on the spot consent of this chairman to take a heavy church assignment. The personal relationship between the two men was so strong that just a phone call could accomplish this. The whole career of this man was based upon a pastoral approach.

4. Influence of the great depression. Severe hardships were suffered by many members of the congregation and also the pastors' families during the great depression of the thirties. Widespread unemployment in the rubber factories plunged many families into deep need and despair. This weighed heavily on the young pastor's heart. He worked desperately with families to help them. Out of this anguishing experience grew a profound compassion for the poor and downtrodden easily manifest throughout the later life of Dr. Fry. He was a champion of those at the bottom of the ladder of life.

5. Importance of evangelism. In the twenties and thirties Akron grew by leaps and bounds as the rubber companies required more and more workers. Holy Trinity church grew by leaps and bounds also. It burgeoned to a very large congregation. Evangelism was a "front-burner" concern. During some of those years Dr. Fry was secretary of the Evangelism Committee of the United Lutheran Church in America. During the Lutheran Evangelism Mission (1955-1957) he gave a week from his president's office to be a missioner himself in a Maryland congregation.[1] His lifelong interest in evangelism never burned out.

Ohio Lutheranism and Dr. Fry

As a prophet in his own country, Dr. Fry had some strained relationships with the Synod of Ohio of the United Lutheran Church in America, to which the congregation he served belonged. During his years as a pastor of the synod, he made some frontal attacks on things he thought were not right with the Establishment, whether it were Wittenberg College or the synod or Hamma Divinity School, as the minutes of synod conventions will show. These earned him some antagonism. Perhaps part of the opposition was based on jealousy toward a pastor with such a constellation of abilities. Then, too, he had an impatience toward those who could not see obvious need for change and who stubbornly resisted it. This is not to say that he did not have excellent personal relations with persons, clergy and lay, across the synod. Yet the fact remains that a somewhat disturbed relationship with this synod existed during his whole life.

His concern for a stronger ministry

Throughout his life Dr. Fry lamented that the ministry of the Lutheran church was not of a higher quality. For this reason a major interest of his life was theological education for pastors. He was always trying to buttress the seminaries. As president of the church, he had a vital interest in the master plan for theological education of the newly merged Lutheran Church in America. He saw seminary deployment from the eagle's point of view, churchwide and ecumenical, as opposed to some who saw it from the robin's point of view, whose whole territory is just a neighborhood.

A parallel interest of Dr. Fry was the continuing education of pastors during their ministry. He would plead with groups of pastors to spend less money on food and more for books. He kept challenging them to prepare for a much different future that was already knocking on the door. Continually he kept his eye peeled for sharp, young pastors and tried to guide them into opportunities for their further development. As much as one person could, he was committed to seeing that the level of the ministry of the church was lifted high.

---

[1] In the March 1957 *Pastor's Desk Book* Dr. Fry reported on his evangelism mission in Hampstead, Maryland.

7

B. Evangeline (Mrs. Louis A.) Witzeman

An Akron parishioner views Dr. Fry as an impressive pastor and an interesting friend.

My husband and family were friends and admirers of the Frys. I became a Lutheran during Dr. Fry's period at Trinity. It was a strong introduction to the Lutheran faith and a lasting friendship developed. My husband was a Lutheran and Dr. Fry left no stone unturned when he found I was among the sinners who somewhat resisted church organizations. I felt Dr. Fry represented the church and all its bigotry and I did not hesitate to say it, and as per usual he was not helpless in the rebuttal. We finally both got disgusted and he said, "If that woman wants to join my church, she will come to me." I did. The climax came one day when he came to our home. Our deaf Irish Catholic maid answered the doorbell with her favorite salesman repellent, which was, "We don't want any." I was coming down the stairs and heard him boom out, "That's not the way I heard it. She called me." Just as I came to the rescue, the maid noticed his clericals under his overcoat and reeled around saying, "My God, it's the father and I almost shut the door in his face!"

Dr. Fry was a pastor of the first order. After he left Akron, I had occasion to meet many who wondered how that erudite parliamentarian could have been a good pastor. There are many here who can testify this is just one of the "many" unusuals of this person. One outstanding characteristic of Dr. Fry was his ability to sense our troubles. It seemed he was there almost before the blow came. He had a strong sense of how a pastor could literally help people. He was a "doing" helper, not only a giver of advice. He literally knew every one of his flock by name.

My husband and I traveled a great deal. We liked the places, sights, and peoples of the world. Dr. Fry traveled much but he could do only limited sightseeing per se. When he returned from his trips our friend-to-friend communication about what he did, saw, and experienced afforded us some of the very richest experiences of our lives. His interpretations of the peoples and events added a plus to our own traveling which could

---

(b. 1897) Mrs. Witzeman is a former psychologist to the Akron Juvenile Court Center and faculty member of the University of Akron. She and her late husband were the closest of friends with the Fry family across the years. She was a ULCA delegate to the World Council of Churches assembly at Evanston in 1954.

have come no other way. Long after the Frys left Akron this kind of communication continued and I have frequently wished the whole world could have listened in on these sessions. He said so much in those hours when he capsuled total conferences and world sessions as well as interviews with world persons. Dr. Fry provided us with another less direct but most potent form of communication when we traveled. He made it possible for us to contact church people and others in all parts of the world. This gave us firsthand appreciation of the world church which we could not have gotten otherwise. Since my husband's death he continued to make world contacts possible. I feel a great loss when I cannot call Dr. Fry and say, "We are going to Tombouctou; will I find any Lutherans there?"

Memos 8 to 13 place the *accent on the personal,* in a variety of settings.

8

Charles B. Foelsch

From intimate experience with Dr. Fry's family and with his later career in the ULCA and the LCA, Dr. Foelsch draws on a wealth of incidents to analyze the personal qualities of Dr. Fry.

There's a growing legend that Franklin Clark Fry was superhuman, infallible, never at a loss for an answer to a problem, never wrong about anything at any time, sprung perfect from the head of Jove. As with every legend, when all's sifted and precipitated, there is a residuum of fact to give it substance.

There were certainly times when Franklin Clark Fry's matter and manner and mien hinted that he had no doubt that he was to the manner born, equipped to speak ex cathedra on anything, anytime, with every utterance flawless in toto and in detail.

This on occasion almost intolerable superiority of the man bred the unkind "stories" that were sometimes told about him in convention corridors and cloakrooms. The very splendor of his endowments and deeds inevitably produced backlash tales that were seldom genuinely "funny"; indeed, the tales often told more about the teller than about the subject of his tale.

For example, that one, surely in bad taste if not brazenly sacrilegious, that was bruited abroad during the 1960 United Lutheran Church convention in Atlantic City (at which Fry presided with his usual aplomb) that when Franklin at last got to heaven, it immediately became imperative to prepare a new constitution for the heavenly realm and, naturally, Franklin was appointed to write it. When at last the finished version appeared, it was discovered that under the new constitution God was vice-president.

(b. 1891) Still active as interim pastor of Christ Lutheran church in Manhattan since 1965, Dr. Foelsch began his ministry in 1915. He served as president of Chicago Lutheran Seminary 1942-47 and of the new Pacific Lutheran Seminary 1952-61. He has been a member of the ULCA Executive Board (1940-48, 1956-62), president of the ULCA Board of American Missions for several years, and secretary of the LCA Court of Adjudication since 1962. He is currently chairman of the board of the Hymn Society of America.

Now, no one who knew him dared doubt that the man had a magnificent astuteness, a unique perspicacity, a towering imagination, a prodigious memory at instant command with facts and figures to stagger belief—and with all that, a deep distaste for anything sloppy or shoddy or incompetent.

Whence this awesome mental equipment? In no small measure it was inherited. His father and mother were both keen intellects. Both were deeply involved in human, especially church, affairs and both were outgoing, outspoken, outstanding people of faith and works, of culture and movement and enthusiasm.

Franklin Foster Fry (1864-1933, ordained 1888) was an indefatigable toiler, ever eagerly on the go, with an unflagging and admiring interest in all that pertained to the church and the kingdom, plus a penetrating understanding of human nature and alert administrative gifts. These were the factors of weight that collaborated to make him the first executive (1927) of the Board of American Missions, the new agency that was bringing together the United Lutheran Church's fragmented home missions operations, and these were the qualities which in earlier years had made their indelible impression on his lad, Franklin.

Minnie Clark Fry, Franklin's mother, was a woman of similar faith, competence, acumen, industry, and breadth of spirit. The child of such parents could hardly be less than a prodigy.

Beyond this, Franklin was a lone child in the home; there was no baby patter dialog with brothers and sisters. So he listened steadily to the adult conversation of his parents, often about the church, often about the community's affairs and the world's. Again, it is to the point to note that the parents were not happy-go-lucky teenagers in 1900, the year their son was born, but grownups of mature years, the father thirty-six, the mother thirty-two. So Franklin was an adult mind—and a churchman—from a boy.

When I would visit his mother at her 10 Rich Street apartment in New York's suburban Mount Vernon (during the years I was her pastor at Holy Trinity, New York), she'd love to talk, usually with amused motherly pride, about Franklin's precocity, and particularly his boyhood interest in "synod matters."

Especially pleased she seemed one time, telling me about her husband's coming home from a trip toward noon one Saturday, greeting her and in the same breath asking, "Where's Buster?" She explained to him that the minutes of synod had come and that the lad—was he seven?—was up in his room, deep in the minutes, dead to the world!

This was in Rochester, New York, where the Frys were the parsonage family of our Reformation church for a quarter of a century, plus. Reformation congregation was and continues to be a citadel of Lutheran strength and an influential community institution; to live in its parsonage would give the most modest child a sense of assurance, and prestige, to boot, among the children of the parish and community.

In due course at Hamilton College, to this day one of America's top-notch humanities schools, Franklin took his bachelor's degree, achieving an academic record—with great ease—that made him the not unenvied cynosure of all campus eyes.

Franklin knew that all this did not make him everybody's favorite character at Hamilton. With his penchant for hyperbole routing any native reluctance he may have felt, he confided to some of us one day that he was certainly the most cordially detested member of his class! When I asked one of his Hamilton classmates about this, a decade or so ago, he thought that that estimate of Fry's place in the affections of his fellows was not completely wrong!

However that may be, it is not to be doubted that Hamilton put more than a little iron into Franklin's blood and, yoked up with the other gifts and influences we've catalogued above, made him a person of adequacy in everybody's eyes, his own not least.

Anywhere and everywhere this self-assurance showed itself justified. He was never the president of the National Lutheran Council, but always (we who sat with him on the council admitted this freely) its most brilliant member. Not that he was always on his feet, debating issues. Far from it. He had the astonishing ability to be—it seemed—totally engrossed in his favorite Sunday TIMES or SATURDAY REVIEW OF LITERATURE double-crostics, yet (how could we know that this was so?) *sub rosa* acutely alert to every syllable crossing the lips of every participant in the discussions.

Sometimes we lesser mortals would find ourselves in a conferential cul-de-sac. Silence would fill the room. Then, with a patient sigh and a studied show of understanding sympathy for the group's helplessness, he would rise, his puzzle page and pencil in hand, at the ready to resume crosswording the instant he had helped the assembly out of its pickle.

With leisurely insouciance, he'd glance all around the room; then, with a very few impeccably fit words he'd quickly unravel the conferential tangle which the meeting had counted a Gordian knot, and with a look that some thought was commingled pity and triumph, he'd resume his seat and his puzzle.

His confidence in his all-round competence revealed itself eloquently in almost everything, even in so small a matter as that crossword business. In mid-October of 1952, when the strenuous Seattle convention of the ULC was at last over, Franklin and his wife Hilda were our houseguests at Berkeley for several days. He was on our campus to induct the new Pacific Seminary's first faculty and then, that done, to relax a bit. I came upon him, comfortable in a big armchair in our living room, doing a New York Times crossword puzzle, and asked, "Is it coming out all right?" "It always does!" was his reply.

Having struggled week by week with the for me always difficult puzzles of the Times, I said, *sotto voce,* "I wish I could say that!"

The towering self-assured superiority of the man understandably made him impatient with mediocrity and intolerant of shoddy thinking. One day, years ago, veteran pastor Paul H. Krauss was telling me about a commission's meeting. With Fry in the chair, the session was nearing its end. Some member came up with an idea that everybody saw was silly. The chairman, choosing words that were not semantically harsh, but spoken in tones close to asperity and with a grimace that might easily have degenerated into a sneer, put the man in his place. The man colored an unpretty rosé, but said not a word.

The meeting soon ended. Rees Edgar Tulloss, then Wittenberg College president, walked down the hall with Paul and remarked sadly, "If only Frank Fry could be more gentle when he's vexed. This man is going to resent that for a long time."

Patience with people who failed to see "eye to eye with Fry" was not one of Frank's strong traits, especially not in the early years of his career. At Philadelphia in the mid-thirties, for example, at a meeting of the commission charged to work out a plan for the consolidation into a single new agency of the ULC's Inner Mission Board, Evangelism Committee, and Moral and Social Welfare Committee, there were some very human verbal exchanges between Fry, secretary of the Evangelism Committee, and Dr. Gustavus H. Bechtold, the Inner Mission Board's spokesman.

Each man let it be known that he was seeking only the best for the cause and of course each passionately believed that what he espoused was the best! So, while each sought to preserve the amenities (Fry was by far the cleverer at that), the air was often tense with smothered waspishness to negate the gentlemanly rhetoric that marked the discussions. In the end the contest was a draw!

During the early fifties, while I was president of the Board of American Missions, arose a desire and need to build a, for those times, costly "annex" to the Lutheran Church House in New York. The president of the church thought it a tremendous idea to launch a churchwide appeal—in the millions—for capital funds to finance the expanding church extension program of the board, and adroitly proposed to attach a rider to the appeal to seek extra money to pay the cost of the new church house construction.

The board, sold on the idea of raising increased funds through building up the general stewardship willingness of the people, and remembering the disastrous American Missions Appeal of 1938, was less than happy in the contemplation of a possible second debacle and dragged its heels (that's putting it mildly).

Frank wrote me sharply, on the eve of the ULC's Toronto convention:

> New York, September 9, 1954
>
> Dear Charles:
>
> This is the eve of the crucial Executive Board meeting for the Board of American Missions' Oliver Twist act. And I don't think that good old BAM is going to fare any better than poor little Oliver. . . .
>
> At least this episode will add spice at Toronto. It will be a big bang when the Executive Board and the Board of American Missions collide head-on and that is exactly what they are going to do. . . .
>
> What I regret most is the fatal blow which the Board of American Missions has struck against a special financial appeal in 1955 and 1956, which, I believe, could have been a rich harvest for the United Lutheran Church. We shall be weaker and sadder as a result of this development and I am half grieved at the thought of it. . . .
>
> Cordially yours,
> Frank

The two plans did collide at Toronto, but not disastrously. For though the convention agreed with the BAM that there should be no special appeal at that time, we did not seem to grow "weaker and sadder as a result." Instead, the smile of heaven beamed upon the church as it financed the church house annex another way and also upped its regular benevolence giving. And more, the president soon showed himself in his normal mood of genial cordiality.

The word normal is good here, for it was his basic bent, deep down, to be kind and understanding and—yes—compassionate. To illuminate the point, let me spin memory's wheel and permit its indicator to stop at whatever of a thousand recollections it will.

There was that unforgettable evening—at the end of an arduous executive board day in New York—when in the Fry home in suburban New Rochelle, after Hilda's simple but delicious dinner, our host gave a half hour, replete with willing patience and sage counsel, to the guest couple who had a difficult decision to make.

Another evening, after another exhaustingly long meeting in the church house, when on the way to the installation of Dr. F. Eppling Reinartz as secretary of the United Lutheran Church, at Manhattan's Holy Trinity church, the taxi driver pulled a bizarre traffic boo-boo. Expecting a rebuke, he received instead from Frank an understanding word of encouragement and a tip a little more generous than customary ("the man has his problems, too").

Yet again, that 1952 Sunday, when in the narthex of our First church in Oakland, California, at the end of a service which he had attended unannounced, he gave a warm, brotherly, well-merited word of gratitude to the young pastor whose heart (he told me later) had been quaking in the presence of the mighty man before him in the pew.

Once more, that to me precious Tuesday morning that saw the arrival at my house of Frank's far-beyond-the-call-of-courtesy response to my sympathy note after his dear mother, over ninety, had passed on; his words were choice, tender, kind, meticulously hand-done in his own neat small script:

13 February, 1961

Dear Charles:

My gallant old mother loved you and never thought of you without putting you very close to the Throne . . . . What higher praise could there be—or tighter bond to draw us together?

Thanks for all you have been to her and to me.

Sincerely,
Frank

These are but four little diamond chips lifted at random from a great tray of blue white sparklers in my memory chest, samples of the man's myriad kindly words and deeds when the demons of weariness and overwork and nettling problems and antagonists' machinations were not harassing his spirit and the real Franklin could come through with characteristic good will.

I've been asked: Did Franklin Clark Fry "grow"? That he grew in many directions none may doubt. I knew him at first hand—in his thirties and in his forties and in his fifties and in his sixties—and he loomed bigger and bigger to me as his years marched into the record books.

In some directions, to be sure, he grew more than in others. His knowledge grew, for he was a compulsive reader and observer and listener, too. His astuteness was native, it seemed to me, and there was not much room for its growth; or for growth in his quickness to grasp a point, or discern a weakness, or discover a solution to a problem. These cerebral assets of his bore the sterling hallmark from his young manhood and kept it to the end.

Did he outgrow any weaknesses? Some he did, but not all. As with the "young Luther," there were imps in Franklin Clark Fry's spirit that more than a few times tormented him and needled him into retorts and gestures and voice tones which, alas, got under the hide of some of his contemporaries and made them squirm, sometimes grow angry, God be thanked seldom bitter. Yet, though never completely exorcised, these imps not for one day had free rein in his spirit and more and more, as the years went by, the basic kindliness of his soul showed itself in his relationships with others.

Yes, his understanding of people grew with the years and especially his concern for the weak and the poor and the ill and the sorrowing. His little personal notes of appreciation or suggestion became kinder and richer and dearer over the years and often brought along a bit of the truest balm of Gilead to soothe the soul and perchance to comfort the recipient's physical body, too.

As his presence recedes from among us, his stature grows, and this is as it should be.

Franklin Clark Fry was a great man. None greater among churchmen is our generation likely to produce. But he was no demigod. That fact must keep the image in focus, lest a plaster saint emerge, towering high but lacking humanness and honest reality.

While there is yet time, before the image jells and hardens, it is surely needful to note for the record some things, for example certain incidents included above, that do not add luster to the image. They are terribly important for an understanding of the real Franklin Clark Fry, and they may help to keep tomorrow from putting his towering figure high against the sky to vie with God. Frank was never guilty of such *hubris*. He always humbled himself under the mighty hand of God and he always loved God's people.

We who knew him miss him still and shall miss him, poignantly, until the last man of us who knew him intimately and long as a friend—a legion of thinning ranks they are—has gone on, to renew friendship with him yonder.

9

Helen M. Knubel

A close friend of Dr. Fry and his family, Miss Knubel writes of Franklin Fry as student, pastor, friend, and intimate of her brother and father.

Franklin Clark Fry was a close personal friend to the members of my family ever since his seminary days, and it is of this relationship that I am glad to write. In fact, the relationship goes back even before that time, for he and my future sister-in-law both grew up in his father's church, and his father and my father were co-workers in the formation and early days of the United Lutheran Church in America.

I first met Franklin in 1922 at his home in Rochester, New York, where his father, Dr. Franklin Foster Fry, was pastor of Reformation church and my brother was his assistant. Franklin had just returned from Greece after his year of graduate study at the American School for Classical Studies in Athens. As we sat on the porch after dinner, Franklin, ebullient and enthusiastic, told of his days in Greece. He was never an antiquarian and I believe his great attachment to Greece was his joy in the intellectualism, the classic beauty.

I like to remember the Franklin Fry of his seminary days. He was a good-looking young man with something of a football player's build, warm and friendly with a ready smile, deeply sincere and fun to be with. His critical nature was active, to be sure, and his great wit was always present. Even as a young man he could be ruthless under certain circumstances, but his sense of humor along with wit, and his sense of joy in life at that time were counterbalances.

My brother, Frederick R. Knubel, had just come to Rochester and he and Franklin became admiring and devoted friends. Dr. and Mrs. Fry welcomed Fred into their home as another son, urging frequent visits, for Fred was as yet unmarried. Upon my visits to Rochester, I would be included in the invitations.

(b. 1901) Miss Knubel served from 1954 to 1970 as director of Research, Statistics, and Archives of the National Lutheran Council and as associate director in its successor, the Lutheran Council in the USA. Prior to this she was engaged in parish education and in public relations work. She was a delegate to the WCC assembly in 1954. Since 1968 she has been secretary of the Lutheran Historical Conference. At present she is a consultant in library services and archival management. She is a daughter of Frederick H. Knubel, Dr. Fry's predecessor as president of the ULCA, and a sister of Frederick R. Knubel, former president of the ULCA New York Synod.

Mrs. Fry liked to watch Dr. Fry's pride in the two boys, particularly on the occasions when Franklin would be home at seminary vacation times and would take part in the church service. "Dr. Fry struts like a rooster behind the two tall boys in the procession," she would say.

In pastoral ways Franklin was like his father, able to develop strong congregations and to appeal to intellectual minds. Both had the same manner of preaching, with the excellent upswing at the end of each sentence so that nothing was ever lost on the listener. But Dr. Franklin Foster Fry was a quiet man, somewhat short in stature, strongly benign and gentle.

In temperament Franklin was like his mother. She was the firebrand, outspoken, with strong likes and dislikes, and unfortunately some personal prejudices. But all this was within a basically motherly nature, encompassing the congregation and a host of friends who loved her. Her pride in her only child was immense. As she would recount the escapades of outwitting his teachers, choirmaster, and his peers, a slight sense of shame would soon be blotted out by her expressions of delight and glee. Franklin also inherited from her, I believe, his energy; and from both his parents a great decisiveness.

To those who were his friends he was loyal and appreciative. His friendship with my brother, I am convinced, was one of the most meaningful things in Franklin's life. They were members of each other's wedding parties and after that there was a kidding rivalry as each child arrived in the two families. Eventually, each family was complete with three children. A letter from Fred to Franklin in May, 1935, ends with this paragraph:

> I didn't care much for the insulting close of your letter: all about greetings from 5 to 4. Such insufferable pride receives just rebuke in the fact that we hope it will be 5 to 5 around the first of December. Yea!

In the private correspondence recently sorted by Hilda Fry, there are some letters she has shown me from my brother and my father. Some excerpts from Fred's indicate the warm and mutually admiring friendship which continued through the years as each pursued his pastoral work.

> July 30, 1942—So the threatened storm has broken! Never fear—it will clear the air, make *something* grow, and you'll soon dry off in the sunshine, no matter which way the Lord leads you to decide.

> July 29, 1943—Helen was with us for the month of July and taught in the vacation Bible school. I tried to teach her to yell the length of the building the way you used to, but she was a poor pupil.

November 9, 1943—This is just a ray from the bright afterglow of the anniversary celebration. Your message couldn't have been more fitting. It gave us the open path of the future. It was something I can bank on, and remind the congregation of. It gives me a tremendous boost and leverage for my heart's desire for the church. It was so much better than a mere congratulation. And it got behind and above buildings and mortgages to the real thing.

When my brother was elected president of the United Lutheran Synod of New York, he wrote to Franklin as follows:

June 26, 1944—It was my good fortune to get many letters of good wishes, but none more welcome than yours; and it is now the first one to be answered, for I have finally found a moment to start the pile.

I shall never forget your comfort and friendship in those miserable moments of soul-searching, and you are doubly my friend forever.

Now I'm eager to roll up my sleeves and get into a fight bigger than I; and to put on seven league boots and rush in where angels fear to tread.

Pray for me.

When my brother died in 1957, Franklin rushed to the hospital immediately and was there with Alice, my sister-in-law, and me. His thoughts and concern were for us then. But the next morning, in the privacy of his office, he thought of his own loss. His secretary told me that she found him there, his head in his hands, and heaving with sobs—no dramatics, just utterly giving way to his sorrow. She immediately shut the door and left him, as she knew he wished her to. She added, "That is the only time I ever saw him weep. There was no one closer as a friend to him than your brother."

Among the letters shown me by Hilda are some from my father. Doubtless in the ULCA archives there are many others. Some excerpts from these follow.

November 12, 1938—It does not surprise me to learn of your decision to remain on the Board of American Missions. Personally I do not believe that you are making a mistake although I continue to be much concerned over the future of the Board of Social Missions. You could help there greatly, but I continue to be confident that constructive plans for the work of that board will develop before long. An organization meeting is to be held soon at my call as convener. My hope is to be able in opening the meeting to suggest the wide opportunity now possessed by the board. Our Lord is concerned as to that meeting also and will, I trust, accomplish His own purposes. Where you find opportunity to drop a helpful word to some individual on the Board, please do so.

February 20, 1939—Your good letter of the 15th arrived promptly but I have been unable to reply to it until now because I could not read the enclosure until Sunday evening. It was the finest of Sunday reading for me especially because I so often hear from pastors of their troubles. Your support was quite to the contrary, and I believe it must have heartened your people as fully as it heartened me. First of all, however, it must have heartened you that you could write a report of that character. You have, I am sure, often had occasion to thank our Lord for his grace to you and your people. All the more do you merit this manifestation of His favor because of the difficulties that you have of necessity faced and that you have overcome by the same grace. I am grateful for the opportunity to read this record of the past.

I was all the more surprised because on Sunday also I read a book review concerning Akron telling the story of its times of trouble as a city during recent years. Reflections of that trouble were to be discovered in your report.

June 8, 1940—I am at home restfully recuperating from weeks of journeys and talks. The rest began definitely with the evening hour with Hilda and you. I was much refreshed when I reached my train. It was good also to talk over a number of items with you. You were all thoughtfulness for me all that day, and my heart is grateful.

During severe illness in Franklin's family, father wrote:

January 30, 1941—It was wonderful to read your letter of the 22nd with its news of the help of our God's providence once more in your home distresses. Meanwhile, Mrs. Knubel or Helen had had a little letter from your mother. We rejoice with you and keep on trusting.

I have written of Franklin's faithfulness at the time of my brother's death. Twelve years earlier also he was with us immediately when father died, and again when my stepmother died. His participation in the funerals was difficult for him and blessings to us.

He was a gallant friend to me, including me in his seminary commencement celebrations, laughing and playing with me, grieving with me, and caring for my personal comfort at many meetings. I cannot remember him ever calling me "Helen"—it was always "girl." This remained, although much of the joy and playfulness was gone with the weight of the years, and much of the humor was missing from the wit. Others will write of his churchmanship and of his genius, but I like to remember the younger student, pastor, and friend.

10

W. Carl Satre

A brother-in-law and ministerial colleague assesses Dr. Fry's personal characteristics.

It is always difficult to write an evaluation of a man who has become to many people a legend in his own time. It is most difficult when you have known such a man intimately and have had and still have a great affection for him. My real acquaintance with him began in 1942 when I returned to the Ohio Synod; before that I knew him through occasional committee work and hearsay. It was not until 1949 that I became a part of the family through marriage to Miss Dorothy Drewes, a sister of Mrs. F. C. Fry.

One thing which comes to my mind as I write is the saying, "Being dead he yet liveth," for to me it still comes as strange that I do not see him about in the familiar places, the executive council, synod, at the Lutheran Church in America conventions, at his home.

I had the opportunity to observe Frank at all the conventions of the United Lutheran Church in America and the LCA over which he presided. I was a delegate at the election convention in Minneapolis and a delegate at every convention thereafter and never missed a session. I saw not only his masterly control of the conventions but also his kindness to the new delegates (his sharpness was reserved for the old pros who tried to manipulate through parliamentary maneuvering or misleading arguments) as they tried to express themselves on some subject of interest to them.

A characteristic of Dr. Fry was his absolute dedication to his church and the task it had given to him to do. Whatever the job at hand he did it to the best of his ability. He always prepared himself for whatever task might develop. He gave the same dedication to small tasks that he did to the great tasks he was asked to do. In fact, I have thought he prepared himself for the great tasks by taking such excellent care of the small tasks.

His thoughtfulness for others came through in many ways, in condo-

---

(b. 1902) Since 1942 Dr. Satre has been pastor of Augsburg Lutheran church, Toledo, Ohio. He was chairman of the ULCA's Committee on Organizational Structure which reported to the 1954 convention. He has served on several boards of the church and on the Evangelism Commission of the National Lutheran Council, and has been a member of the LCA Executive Council since 1964.

lences, congratulations, and remembrances of events in other people's lives. Many people treasure the handwritten notes they received from him at the loss of a loved one or in congratulation of some recognition that came to them. This, I am sure, was possible for him to do, busy as he was, because he constantly used fragments of time. I have traveled with him by train and plane and always the brief case was there and he would write notes, read minutes, go over constitutions or read or discuss church matters. I have been with him as he watched Yankee games on TV and he would be using intervals to go over materials or plans. To him every moment was precious.

His intensity toward life perhaps helped in his devotion to the church and his willingness to sacrifice himself for it. He never accepted an office for honor; to him it meant work and if he could not do the work he would not accept but if he did accept he felt compelled to attend the meetings the office called for. Duty loomed large in his vocabulary and this applied to others as well as himself. He gave short shrift to men who accepted office and then refused to accept the responsibility and work and expenditure of time that went with it. He thought honor, duty, and responsibility walked hand in hand.

Dr. Fry had great respect for his co-workers in the official life of the church but his special concern always was the pastor in the parish and in the congregation. He often pointed out how everything planned and projected by conventions and by boards and agencies of the church depended on the response of the pastors and the congregations of the church if they were to be successfully completed. He never lost his pastor's heart in the maze of committee meetings, conventions, national, and international responsibilities. He never became a professional who felt the churches were responsible to him but rather he always felt keenly his responsibility to the church, the congregations, and the pastors whom he served as president.

He always was a Christian first and a churchman who served God in faith. God to him was a living reality in Jesus Christ his Lord. God and his church were too sacred to Frank to ever be used as a means of cheap notoriety. To him God was ever alive and the church the body of Christ. He believed that a man of the church whether a pastor or layman should always represent the church in everyday living as well as in periods of worship. He endeavored to live his faith as best he could and expected the same of other men.

I could not close without a tribute to one who was dedicated to her task as the wife of Dr. Fry and mother of their children and thus freed him to more thoroughly pursue his work; he often spoke of her devotion and helpfulness, Hilda Drewes Fry.

11

Joseph A. Sittler

Sketching some piquant observations about his friend, Professor Sittler explores the problem of really understanding the man.

Any effort to get at the personal reality of Franklin Clark Fry is an enterprise in historical futility. For whereas the objective words, deeds, positions taken, causes espoused, changes championed are there (fully documented) for all to see, the central motivating and driving substance escapes capture. In one sense that is not true; for gospel, church, and mission, all affirmed in clear and passionate fidelity, shine through and illuminate everything as the ordering center. But the soul of the man was shrouded in the heart's secret encounter with her Lord; and speech about that is an effort as futile as it is unbecoming. That there was such an encounter and that in its grip and struggle and joy a rich life was engendered and great accomplishments driven to fulfillment there can be no doubt. The rest is silence.

His great body, a kind of sign of the spirit and purpose of the man, stays large and alive in the memory of all of us who knew and loved him. The huge head, always leaning a bit forward from the shoulders, his hands with fingers curled half-hidden by the always too long sleeves of his coat—or, at a meeting, tapping out arpeggios upon his knee! And, after some apprenticeship in Fry-mood-exegesis one could know from the beat of those fingers if their rhythm was born of excitement, or anger, or impatience, or frustration, or affirmative exultation! Only his ingenuous joy in his own powers of mind and quickness of comprehension made one forgive him his gusto in the exhibition of these.

And there, too, that unpredictable war whoop of booming laughter accompanied by a thigh-slap that cracked like a rifle shot. But one never knew for certain what that meant! It could be humor; it could be derision. It could also be a disorganizing break-up of tangled negotiations preparatory to a fresh start—and usually along lines closer to something *he* wanted done or said.

(b. 1904) A pastoral neighbor of Dr. Fry in the 1930's, Dr. Sittler attained the name of one of America's outstanding theologians and preachers, as professor at Chicago Lutheran Seminary 1943-57 and at the University of Chicago Divinity School since 1957. He has been long prominent in ecumenical affairs, nationally and internationally.

It has been said that it is the incongruities that disclose and charm in the humanity of even the most dominant and forbidding of persons: the dimple in the cheek of the masterful face, the stray, girlish curl at the nape of the neck of the severe woman with the tightly bound hair. The delightful give-away in the instance of F. C. Fry—all dignity and force from the knees up—was the way he stood on those out of scale, too small, slightly pigeon-toed feet, always close together, like a lad being reprimanded by his mother, but impish and unrepentant like a little boy who had just made off with the cookies. As, in most cases, he had!

I smile as I remember these things—and as I here record them the purpose of this volume is, I hope, advanced. For the portrait of the churchman, the statesman, the precise formulator of constitutions and position papers is enriched and made more consoling to us all as we recognize that, in Joseph Conrad's phrase, "he was one of us." He was a man on a large scale; but a man.

Franklin Fry drinking tea during recess of sessions at World Council meetings is a hilarious memory. The European setting of most of these meetings, and the Anglican tea habit, meant that Fry could on such occasions be found standing in courtyard, foyer, or garden, towering above a chatting group and holding a fragile teacup. Fry and teacups were not meant for each other. He held the silly thing as if it were a time-bomb, a forlorn, beseeching look upon his face as if appealing to some higher power to get him out of so compromising a circumstance. Thomas Aquinas surprised at dalliance could not have looked more pathetic.

It was an unseasonably warm September in New York. Our committee had begun its work on Friday afternoon, worked after the dinner break, and was about to adjourn at the end of Saturday morning. Fry slipped me a one-line note. "The game begins at 2 p.m.; come to my office at one o'clock."

I did; and there he was in his black suit—but with a difference. The vest and clerical collar had been discarded for a sport shirt open at the neck. En route to Yankee Stadium I was assured that New York's manifested superiority to the Chicago White Sox was going to make this a pleasant afternoon—an insouciant slaughter of the hapless.

But this was not Frank's, or the Yankees,' day. Chicago did everything right, nothing went well for New York. Billy Pierce was pitching superbly and New York was baffled. Yogi Berra got spiked and was out of business for the day. A ninth inning threat ended when a sharp sure single—was scooped up by Luis Aparicio in an incredible play.

Frank's world of Yankee-pride was demolished; he was a large lump of utter dejection. Sensing that he needed pastoral care in his misery, I muttered as gently as I could, "Allah is merciful." "Merciful, rot!" he thundered. "That little guy had no *right* to that ball!"

It is recorded of Gilbert K. Chesterton that when he first saw a hippopotamus he asserted, "It isn't possible!" There is a sense in which Franklin Clark Fry was an impossible man. All that Luther meant by *simul justus, simul peccator* was held in taut suspension within the gifted richness of this remarkable man: he came fully equipped with faults and graces—both out-size. He believed in omelettes, and felt called to lead the church to make the best ones possible; and along with that calling he accepted the realistic necessity that in this life one cannot make omelettes without breaking eggs. Decisiveness, courage, the willingness to bear the burden of doing hurting and popularly inexplicable things—these are not endearing qualities. To be tough for the sake of the right result is an invitation to loneliness, a kind of official necessity to advance what the gentle want done, but by necessary means that the gentle then deplore. That vocation, at sea or in church and state, is what has been called "the loneliness of command." It has its rewards; it also exacts its price.

That price forms a man to its exactions—and known only to himself and to God are its torments. What we saw, through the carefully guarded outside, were only external hints—and these were the marks of them: brusqueness and charm, warmth and icy decisiveness, gentleness to anguish and harshness to the obtuse, an enveloping love of men-in-Christ and occasional curtness toward individual men, grace and guts. Apparent contradictions coexisted, and could coexist in him because, for all of his ego-certainty, his intentions and powers were not finally at the service of himself. He really did his fierce best to be obedient to the Pauline injunction, "I implore you by God's mercy to offer yourselves to him: a living sacrifice, dedicated and fit for his acceptance, the worship offered by mind and heart" (Romans 12:1, New English Bible).

12

Krister Stendahl

Dr. Stendahl comments briefly on Dr. Fry's manner.

My first meeting with Franklin Fry had a lasting influence on me. I have met few people who gave as total an impression of what he was and what he stood for in a short time. I may have had twenty minutes at most in his office. But I felt I knew him. That was in 1952. We came to meet many times since, in the United States and abroad. And the more I think about it, the more it strikes me that I had met the whole man already the first time.

That could have been boring or disappointing, but we all know that it was not. It was rather due to his directness, and that element of mental and spiritual health. His ways and style did not suggest humility. He enjoyed life and work, faith and order (also with the capital letters that make those words into the ecumenical movement) too much to be concerned about the humble style. His genuine humility came rather from a realistic awareness of human foibles and limitations, his own included. That made it possible for him to encourage and to trust.

Intelligent he was indeed, but hardly an intellectual. Consequently he did not make his decisions by subtle analyses and glittering dialectic. He often seemed to act and take his stand on the gut level, by instinct informed by the basic Lutheran tradition, by a disdain for irrelevancies, and by a good dose of common humanity.

In many way he was the man of and for the era that he helped to shape. Ecclesiastical ecumenism, and neo-orthodox excitement for both scriptures and tradition was the setting that supported and harmonized well with his instincts. One may wonder whether he could have been as strong a leader now when the issues and the demands force the church into a more radical quest for its identity and its place within God's plan.

I would rather guess that he was the man for his time to such a degree that his work, his style, his contribution will be easily dated by the historians. To some that does not sound good enough. For him who wants to serve, it surely is, for it means that the *charisma* and the *kairos* fitted just right.

(b. 1921) A pastor in Sweden before coming to the United States, Dr. Stendahl has been professor of New Testament at Harvard Divinity School since 1954, and dean since 1968. For many years he has been a leader in the Lutheran World Federation and the ecumenical movement; he was one of the chief drafters of the LWF's "Minneapolis Theses" in 1957. Since 1970 he has been a member of the LCA Executive Council.

13

Robert E. Van Deusen

Dr. Van Deusen offers three vignettes, and brief observations on Dr. Fry's personality.

Fry Vignettes

Franklin Clark Fry was a complex and many-faceted person. The following are a few brief glimpses into what made him tick:

He was on the way from the airport by car to a meeting of Protestant ministers from the Washington area. I asked him how he managed to prepare for his many speaking appointments.

He said, "I don't put everything I have into everything I do. I size up the group and the situation, and give them only as much time and energy as their importance deserves. This one was easy . . . ."

* * *

The only time that Dr. Fry testified before a Congressional committee was in regard to a relatively obscure issue, but one which affected the clergy. He reported the action of the LCA Board of Pensions favoring the mandatory inclusion of ministers in Social Security, except for those who elected not to be included for reasons of conscience.

It was the behind-the-scenes relationships that were significant. Robert J. Meyers, the chief actuary of the Social Security Administration, was a member of the Board of Pensions. Dr. Fry's testimony placed before a congressional committee a change favored by the executive branch of the government. Quietly, the committee recommended and both houses of Congress passed an amendment plugging a loophole in the Social Security law, which had favored clergy by making their participation optional.

* * *

A Washington area pastor was ill with rapidly progressing cancer. Dr. Fry accepted an invitation of the local church council to meet with

---

(b. 1909) A veteran interpreter of national affairs, Dr. Van Deusen has been Washington (D. C.) secretary of the National Lutheran Council 1949-66, and subsequently director of the Office of Public Relations of the LCUSA, with headquarters in Washington.

them and the pastor for a service of prayer with the laying on of hands. In a brief devotional service in a small chapel, he spoke simply and profoundly of the meaning of life and the power of faith.

Dr. Fry joined in the laying on of hands and the prayer of commitment and faith. On leaving the chapel he remarked, "It has been a long time since I have been in this close a circle of love."

* * *

As a non-parish pastor serving a national church agency, it was my privilege to have an annual conference with Dr. Fry. In his role as "pastor of pastors," he encouraged me to share my personal and professional concerns. These contacts on a one-to-one basis opened windows of insight into Dr. Fry as a person which I valued highly.

He was essentially a lonesome man, separated from most of his fellow pastors by official relationships and by the often unwelcome decisions required by his job as top administrator. He thought with lightning speed and felt intensely, suffering inwardly over the slowness of others to recognize trends that seemed obvious to him. He disliked displays of emotion, but his own emotions, often well hidden, played a key role in his complex character.

Memos 14 to 30 range far and wide, but share a common focus on *life in the United Lutheran Church in America* (to 1962).

14

G. Elson Ruff

The late Dr. Ruff, veteran journalist and long-time friend, has probed Franklin Fry's maturing and his character in his presidency of the ULCA.

Robert Fischer has urged us to be candid in writing about Franklin Clark Fry in this series. He says he doesn't want eulogies. I hope not to overstep the bounds of propriety in my candor, but I knew Frank for so long and so well that I wish to write about him as I knew him. In whatever I write there can't help being reflected the inordinate respect and affection for this man which I felt increasingly through the years.

There were probably not many fellow-students on the Philadelphia Seminary campus in the early twenties who really liked Franklin Fry. He had been at a much better college than most of us and had an additional year of travel and graduate study in Greece. Also he gave full evidence in his youth of phenomenal mental capacity. So he knew more than most of the rest of us. He used his knowledge in a pedantic manner to put us in our places and demonstrate his keen sense of superiority.

Frank was abrasive in belittling those who ventured to disagree with him. Also at that time he was an orthodoxist, almost a fundamentalist, not only in church doctrine but especially on political and social questions. I recall his alarm during the presidential campaign of 1924 with the possibility that the third party candidate, Robert La Follette, might be elected. He said that under normal circumstances he would support the Democratic candidate but, in view of the La Follette threat, he would have to vote for Calvin Coolidge. He was jubilant the morning after the election in deriding the small handful of La Follette supporters at the seminary since our man had carried only one state.

It was more than a dozen years after seminary days that I had occasion to begin to see Frank again at various church meetings. I found that time had brought a great change in him. He had gone through the

---

(1904-1972) A Philadelphia Seminary schoolmate of Dr. Fry, Dr. Ruff was editor of THE LUTHERAN, official organ of the ULCA and then of the LCA, 1945-72, and editor-in-chief of the United Lutheran Publication House 1946-62. He was president of the Associated Church Press 1953-55.

depression years as a parish pastor with his people and had learned compassion and social concern. A serious health crisis in his family had deepened him in spirit. There was still very much of the old asperity on occasion, but he was making efforts to keep it under control.

And somewhere along the line he had made a fresh and thorough study of biblical criticism and had caught up with the twentieth century. He was among the handful of floor leaders at the United Lutheran Church convention in 1940 in opposing "the Pittsburgh Agreement,"[1] a biblicistic statement which he would have endorsed a decade earlier.

When Dr. Fry was elected president of the ULCA at the 1944 convention, I was also elected editor of the church paper to take office a year later. From then on he and I sat together in literally hundreds of meetings, traveled many thousands of miles together, and talked about almost every imaginable subject. There was still this problem of his impatience with the slow-moving minds of most people around him and his eagerness to demonstrate his superiority. But he fully understood this problem and was trying to get it under control.

At one time I told him I had decided I was temperamentally unsuited to go on with the work of a church paper editor. He wrote this to me on September 26, 1946:

> Man to man and friend to friend, Elson, do you think that I am better adapted instinctively to the share of the church's work that I have been elected to than you are to yours? You have known me intimately since we were both even younger and fresher sprouts than we are now. You know how explosive and caustic I like to be when I can be only myself. It has been a hard schooling and often an irksome trial to me to have to submerge my own natural characteristics and to discipline myself so that I may serve the church better. . . .

But a small sample of the shock treatment he still gave out when off guard is this: A well-known church leader was making a long and dull speech at a ULCA convention. When he concluded, Dr. Fry told the convention, "You may wake up now. Dr. ——— has finished speaking."

Over the years I came to understand that Franklin's self-confidence and self-dramatization were the necessary price to be paid for the enormous leadership ability he had. He had to believe in himself implicitly to feel justified in shaping the world around him as he did.

Dr. Fry could easily dominate practically any group he entered, and did it by having done his homework better than anyone else. He was better prepared on the agenda of a meeting which he was attending than others were and kept more acutely alive to every nuance of the developing discussion of very subject. Often I dozed at some dull meeting, hardly aware of what was being said, and was startled to hear Dr. Fry snap up some obscure point a man made in a lusterless speech and compare it with a contrary decision the group had made in a resolution two days before.

Considering this constant aliveness, and the pitiless schedule of travel, speaking, and presiding at meetings which he set for himself, there was always a question of whether he could survive physically. I saw him often when he was so weary he could hardly hold up his head. He had these resources, though: the huge gusto of his humor, his roaring laughter, his constantly quick wit. He refreshed himself in these and in quick change of pace. And I was impressed by his ability to turn off completely in an instant, to fall into deep sleep in a chair in an airport, and awake without any evidence of having missed a night's rest. Also he lived deeply in his family and took great joy in what little time he had with his wife, children, and grandchildren.

Dr. Fry had very little small talk and shunned the innumerable polite conversations which his work made constantly necessary. Once he told me that he felt less alone among complete strangers than in a roomful of casual acquaintances. There seemed to be a growing edge of melancholy in him in his late years, partly because he was aware of how rapidly times are changing in the world and in the church. He said he felt an increasing gulf between himself in the presiding officer's chair at a church convention and the folks sitting out in front of him. He admitted that he could not understand today's youth and was glad that at his age he didn't really have to try.

If necessary he would have sized up the changing times and developed useful answers to present-day problems. He didn't really resent attacks on the church as an institution because he wasn't an organization man, although he spent much of his time writing church constitutions and putting ecclesiastical machinery together. He never fulfilled his role of chief executive by patrolling his colleagues to see that they did things as he wanted them done but took for granted their freedom to do as they thought best. At nuts-and-bolts executive functioning he wasn't very good. But he had limitless loyalty to colleagues in encouraging and supporting them, especially when they felt obliged to appeal to him for help.

For twenty-five years I was editor of the magazine of the church of which he was president, and there was never a time when he tried by even the faintest shadow of a frown to influence me in what I wrote or caused to be published (except one scowl about something Reinhold Niebuhr wrote in our magazine during the Wisconsin heresy trials period).[2] Dr. Fry upheld my freedom of expression even when I took stands on a few important questions which I knew to be opposite to his own positions. But on occasion when I needed help in getting some policy decision determined, and appealed to Dr. Fry with my problem, he gave me his complete attention and cooperation.

Each year Dr. Fry gave me stronger assurance that he was my close personal friend, and especially in my own intense personal bereavement in recent years. I have no doubt the world is full of people who remember him as I do, and who love him because he gave us so much evidence of loving us.

---

[1] An agreement of the ULCA and the American Lutheran Church on the inspiration of the scriptures. Text in *Doctrinal Declarations,* St. Louis, 1957, pp. 69-70; abridged in R. C. Wolf, *Documents of Lutheran Unity in America,* Philadelphia, 1966, Document 157. See also memos by Henninger (No. 15), Krauss (16), and Fendt (49).

[2] Niebuhr's article in The Lutheran, December 21, 1955. Fry commented on the trials in the *Pastor's Desk Book,* January 1956.

15

James F. Henninger

Drawing on experiences covering three decades, a late jurist and leading layman of the ULCA has analyzed Dr. Fry's ideas and style as a church executive, contrasting him with President Knubel. Examples include relations between the ULCA and the former American Lutheran Church, and the church polity change in the new LCA.

In writing a "Now It May Be Told" about Dr. Fry, I ought in all honesty to state that while I worked in close cooperation with him for a quarter century, I could not qualify as a confidant.[1] By the same token, I was not his henchman and this is greatly to his credit. Close as we were, he never asked me to throw any stones for him, to advocate any policies he sponsored, or to make any political maneuvers. It is true that I, as well as others, paid close attention to the business of the ULCA and of its Executive Board and, if we believed we knew Dr. Fry's mind and if we were in agreement with him, we would make what we considered the proper parliamentary maneuver to further the business of the board or convention. Often we guessed wrong and were soundly beaten by the convention, but the man-hours saved by a right guess compensated for the disgrace of a wrong guess. We must emphasize, however, that all such efforts were voluntary, unsought and, what's more important, unmentioned.

My first clash with Dr. Fry occurred before we ever met. He had questioned the right of the board of Wittenberg College—as it was then known—to issue a call to a seminary graduate, which call was the basis for his ordination. I was then a member of the ULCA Commission of Adjudication, and the Synod of Ohio, having ordained the man, made an appeal to the commission. I well remember that some of the older members—in my late forties I was a youngster—felt that Dr. Fry was merely harassing the Wittenberg board. We decided that since the man had been ordained and there was no immediate threat of another such situation, the question was "moot." This was a permissible disposition of such questions, but one to which the commission had not consistently held.

(1891-1970) For thirty years judge of the Lehigh County Court of Common Pleas, Allentown, Pennsylvania, this distinguished layman served as member of the ULCA Commission of Adjudication (1933-42), then of the executive board for sixteen years, the Joint Commission on Lutheran Unity, and the LWF Executive Committee (1952-57). He was also a ULCA representative to both the National Lutheran Council and the National Council of Churches.

In 1942 Dr. Fry and I were elected to the Executive Board of the United Lutheran Church in America, worked together there for eight years and then for another eight years from 1954 to 1962, the date of founding of Lutheran Church in America. Meanwhile, I served with him for five years on the National Lutheran Council and the Executive Committee of Lutheran World Federation and for more years than I can count on the Commission on Relations to American Lutheran Church Bodies, which later resulted in the Joint Commission on Lutheran Unity, from which developed the Lutheran Church in America.

As a fellow member of the executive board, I did not find Dr. Fry the disturber of the peace that many people believed him to be. Forthright and fearless, yes; intransigent and trouble-making, no. Our first cooperation was as a committee to induce the U. S. chief of chaplains to make some changes in the V-12 program[2] and then to induce the Philadelphia Seminary to accept the program. Dr. Fry's persuasive powers succeeded in both objectives.

For two years Dr. Fry sat at Dr. Knubel's feet in the executive board. He and his older friends and associates, Dr. Paul H. Krauss and Dr. Henry H. Bagger, were the "young Turks" on the board. They did not hesitate to speak up or to show their displeasure with reactionary actions. One of these was the "Pittsburgh Agreement," which was intended to bring about pulpit and altar fellowship with the American Lutheran Church. It was dissented to by the entire delegation of the Central Pennsylvania Synod and by Drs. Bagger and Krauss, who felt that this compromised the church's position on the Word of God. The name of Dr. Fry does not appear among the dissenters although he, with the others, resented the idea that, while it was a permissible parliamentary procedure, Dr. Knubel left the chair to press passage of the resolution.[3] Later the same indignation was felt when Dr. Knubel and Dr. E. Clarence Miller wanted the executive board to direct the Board of Publication to demand changes in the Alleman New and Old Testament Commentaries, still in the vain hope of conciliating the American Lutheran Church.[4] Interestingly enough, almost twenty-five years later in his 1966 President's Report, Dr. Fry, in a dozen words and without advancing any argument, opposed consideration of ordination of women, undoubtedly to avoid offending other Lutheran bodies with whom we hoped to achieve pulpit and altar fellowship.[5] Whether or not this earlier Commission on the Doctrine of the Ministry was indignant I cannot say, but they were surely chagrined by this premature attack, which certainly encouraged others to attack other propositions in their report.

One is tempted to compare the presidencies of Dr. Fry and Dr. Knubel. Both were parliamentarians par excellence. Perhaps the easiest—and therefore the most dangerous—way to differentiate is to say that Dr.

Knubel was "smooth," while Dr. Fry was "sharp," using both terms in their best meanings. Dr. Knubel tried to avoid dissent, Dr. Fry to resolve differences. At Dr. Fry's first convention in 1946, he felt that his task as a presiding officer was simply to rule according to strict parliamentary procedure. He soon discovered that he was dealing with a group indifferent to and generally ignorant of the finer points of parliamentary law and that, if the will of the body was to be expressed, the chairman would be required to guide as well as to rule. This finally led to the occasional motion, "I move what the president has just suggested."

It seems to me that there is a greater percentage of skilled parliamentarians in the other churches merging into Lutheran Church in America than among the constituency of the United Lutheran Church in America. coupled with a greater readiness to invoke unusual parliamentary procedures. I well remember the glee of some leaders of the other churches when they found that Dr. Fry had confused the terms "meeting" and "session" in an early draft of the LCA constitution.

In 1944 at the Minneapolis convention Dr. Fry was elected president of the United Lutheran Church in America. In 1957, also at Minneapolis, he was elected president of Lutheran World Federation. At that time he confided to me that this was his third election to a presidency in Minneapolis, because in his college days he was elected president of his national college fraternity,[6] at a convention in Minneapolis, an interesting coincidental irrelevancy.

What did presidency of ULCA do to him? For one thing, it put him into clerical garb. At the time of his election one of his friends remarked that he would have to dispose of many colorful neckties. His associate pastors at Akron, Ohio, attest to his energy and to his orderly administration of a large parish, while carrying a tremendous load of outside activities.

This energy, zeal, and demand for orderly procedure was carried into the presidency. There is no doubt that there was a continually increasing concentration of power in the headquarters bureaucracy. It was not so much due to a thirst for power as it was to recognition of Dr. Fry's grasp of the problems of the church and a reliance upon his good judgment. Yet he recognized the constitutional rights of boards and synods and yielded to them—after expressing his opinion—in matters subject to their own judgment.

In the executive board he came to the aid of many committee chairmen and frequently his inimitable style shone through the purported words of a committee. Again this did not prevent committees from disregarding his suggestions and bringing their own ideas to the board. Dr. Fry was not by nature a tolerant individual and it is to his credit that he accepted defeat of his plans, as he was compelled to do when the convention of the church occasionally kicked over the traces.

I found him always fair to his opponents, so fair in some cases that he provided an opportunity for them to oppose his own views. This occurred in JCLU, when he used the president of the New York Synod as an alternate in the absence of a regular commissioner, so that he could present that synod's opposition to the proposal to limit the size of synods by splitting some of the larger ones. Incidentally, while the ULCA delegation refused to sponsor the proposition of permitting larger synods, it prevailed in JCLU with the support of some of ULCA's own group. I am not informed as to the forces that eventually led to the splitting of the New York Synod—or of the Synod of Eastern Pennsylvania—but it vindicated Dr. Fry's position.

Although Augustana had grown to be a widely ramified church, it retained a synodical polity, with a concentration of power in the church at large. I believe Dr. Fry welcomed this precedent in JCLU and used it to mold LCA into a church in which the national body exercised authority in matters theretofore considered the sole prerogative of the synod. While the form of many institutional relationships remained the same, the substance was quite different. In ULCA the church was in effect the creation of the synods; in LCA the synods became the localized agencies of the church. While the synods retained the responsibility for support of theological seminaries and for the ordination and discipline of ministers, the church retained a large, although minority, part in all three areas.

Dr. Fry, supported by an analysis by the management consultant firm of Booz, Allen and Hamilton, succeeded in convincing his midwestern colleagues in JCLU that the headquarters of the church should be in New York City; he lost his battle to have the Board of American Missions headquarters there, only to have the board itself after several years ask to be removed from Chicago to New York.

Many persons credit or charge me with "standing up" to Dr. Fry. This surprises me. While we had occasional differences and I did not hesitate to express my opinion on occasion, my own impression is that we were generally in agreement or that our differences were on matters not worth a contest. I thought he drew too fine a line in the elaborate system of sources of call—the same point raised in his early controversy with Wittenberg College—and in naming a Washington, D. C., church to record ministerial acts of Army and Navy chaplains, but I respected his theological position and did not feel obliged to oppose the proposals.

Dr. Fry's molding of the polity of LCA and his administration of it in the five and a half years of his presidency will be of inestimable value to his successors and to the church. Centralization of power cannot be denied, but Dr. Fry himself was the first to recognize the constitutional rights of synods, boards, and congregations and, although he might advise, he was always willing, albeit occasionally reluctantly, to let the synods, boards and congregations act as they had the constitutional right to act.

My assignment is not to evaluate Dr. Fry's personality and character and that is fortunate, for surely it would seem fulsome, with the tremendous admiration I had for the man and for his Christian spirit.

---

[1] Judge Henninger also wrote "An Appreciation" of Dr. Fry in *Mr. Protestant*, pp. 51-57.

[2] For the accelerated training of Navy chaplains.

[3] Reference is to the 1940 ULCA Convention and the "Pittsburgh Agreement" (1940). See *Doctrinal Declarations*, St. Louis, 1957, pp. 69-70, and Krauss's memo (No. 16) in this volume.

[4] The *New Testament Commentary* edited by H. C. Alleman, was first published in 1936. Publication of the *Old Testament Commentary* was delayed until 1948.

[5] In 1966 the LCA considered but did not adopt a statement on the doctrine of the ministry, 1966 Minutes, pp. 434-447. See p. 43 for Dr. Fry's comment on the ordination of women. The LCA ordained its first woman minister in 1970.

[6] Dr. Fry was national treasurer, not president, of the Theta Delta Chi fraternity for a period in the 1920s.

16

Paul H. Krauss

Dr. Krauss focuses upon experiences in the Executive Board of the ULCA, calling attention among other things to President Fry's humor.

My father, Professor Elmer F. Krauss, told me that when he was a senior at Muhlenberg College, at the beginning of the college year in October, 1883, Pastor Jacob Fry, later the distinguished professor of homiletics at Mount Airy, appeared at his dormitory with a young man, introduced him as his son Franklin, and asked if, as a senior student, my father would kindly help his son in getting oriented and established in the school. That "son Franklin" was FCF's father, Franklin Foster Fry, subsequently pastor at Rochester, New York, and later secretary of the Board of American Missions. That goes a long way back! A whole generation later the Muhlenberg Glee Club, of which I happened to be president at the time, sang the anthem at a special service at St. John's Lutheran church, Allentown, Pennsylvania, at which Dr. Jacob Fry was the special preacher. I have never forgotten the kindness of his appreciation of our effort. This at least throws some light on the generous-hearted spirit and quality of the Fry family.

My first contact with Franklin Clark Fry was in a Pennsylvania Railroad pullman car. He and Dr. Henry Bagger, then pastor at Lancaster, Pennsylvania, and I were on the Committee on Constituent Synods of the Executive Board of the United Lutheran Church in America. Frank was then pastor at Akron, Ohio, and I at Fort Wayne. At the time of our impending executive board meeting in New York City, I suggested to him that he come down to Canton, Ohio, and meet me on the night Pennsylvania Railroad train to New York, and Dr. Henry Bagger could get on at Lancaster, Pennsylvania, when we went through there about seven the next morning. This we did, and together at breakfast organized the schedule for our committee activities. It was Dr. Frank C. Fry's first meeting as an executive board member, and on that occasion two of his most striking qualities revealed themselves: (1) a sharp, swift comprehension of issues, and (2) his magnificent sense of humor. When we got

---

(b. 1890) Pastor of Trinity Lutheran church, Fort Wayne, Indiana, from 1920 to 1967, Dr. Krauss has served on the ULCA Executive Board (1938-46), the Joint Commission on Lutheran Unity, the Board of Higher Education (ULCA), and the LCA Board of Theological Education.

to the hotel and continued our meeting as a committee, we had to study and certify to the executive board the constitutionality of the proposed new constitution of the Andhra Lutheran Church of India. Its language contained some syntactical structures that were quite natural, in the circumstances, but we literally rocked with laughter, perhaps out of all proportion to the real humor, but largely at the pungent criticism of the freshman member of our board, Franklin Clark Fry.

Dr. Henry Bagger had the same love of pure fun, and altogether, I think, we obtained "strength through joy." This was the beginning of a working fellowship in the activities of the church that we prized greatly. We met frequently at synod conventions and at the meeting of boards and committees. I remember the time that we met brethren of the American Lutheran Church in Columbus, Ohio, and certainly made progress in mutual respect and understanding with Dr. Fendt and the brethren of the American Lutheran Church. I don't know what the exact issues were in discussion at that time. One of the official statements being hammered out was on the nature and inspiration of the scriptures, later adopted after warm debate at the Omaha convention of the church.[1] Others were on Lutheran union, a perennial ideal. Then and always Dr. Fry, together with Dr. Bagger and myself, to a much less important degree, were committed to the vision of a Lutheranism United in this country. We had, perhaps, too short a patience with the insularities or confessional rigidities of ethnic groups, and, certainly none for the occasional manifestations of personal ambition and sometimes phariseeism that arise in human leadership. With personal pretentiousness Dr. Fry was completely impatient; but with human frailty he was completely considerate and kind.

Concerning the quality of his humor among friends, this story may serve to illustrate. The Four Horsemen, as we sometimes called ourselves, Fry, Bagger, Foelsch and Krauss, happened to be standing together at the back of the auditorium at the Baltimore convention (1938), listening to an eloquent presentation by someone. "That man," Bagger commented, kindly but possibly correctly, "has come further with fewer gifts than any man I know in the church." Swiftly Fry commented, looking at Bagger with a grin, "Well, Henry, you ought to know, you ought to know!" The universal church was greatly blessed with the heart, the mind, the vision, the humor of Franklin Clark Fry. His friends were blessed, infinitely!

---

[1] The so-called "Pittsburgh Agreement," 1940. See *Doctrinal Declarations,* St. Louis, 1957, pp. 69-70; see also the memos of Ruff (No. 14), Henninger (15), and Fendt (49) in this volume.

Five of President Fry's colleagues in the Lutheran Church House at New York offer insights into his manner of work and his personality.

17

Clarence C. Stoughton

Drawing especially from his years in the New York Church House, a former stewardship executive analyzes Dr. Fry's type of leadership, contrasting it with that of President Knubel.

In his sermon at the funeral of Franklin Clark Fry,[1] Pastor Robert Stackel asked the hard question, "Who can take the measure of such a man?" and a bit later made the judgment that "as Muhlenberg was the outstanding Lutheran leader of the eighteenth century, so Franklin Clark Fry looms as the outstanding Lutheran leader of the twentieth century."

This is a judgment that will be accepted by virtually all who knew Frank Fry well. It is one with which I agree, especially after nearly five years as one of his co-workers at 231 Madison Avenue.

Now comes the request to amplify the judgment so that we see some of the facets that make him, not less a leader, but one whose very humanity becomes manifest as a part of that leadership.

There are different kinds of leadership. Some men lead by the gentleness of their spirit—as did Dr. F. H. Knubel—and some by their great concern for other human beings—as do some great pastors—and some by the power of their position—as military leaders must do.

Frank Fry led because he saw himself as the supreme commander of the church. He did not brook opposition. He knew where he wanted to go and the opinion of others was not often asked for or listened to if offered. Typical, for example, were the meetings of the executive board of the church. The reports were, in general, written by Dr. Fry and even when there were some opposing points of view, they seldom prevailed. Dr. Fry did not encourage even verbal changes when the reports were read and acted on.

(b. 1895) Clarence Stoughton has been president of Wagner College, Staten Island, New York (1935-45) and of Wittenberg University, Springfield, Ohio (1949-63). Between these terms he was the executive director of the ULCA Lutheran Laymen's Movement for Stewardship, and the church's stewardship secretary. He was a member of the ULCA Executive Board (1954-62) and the LCA Board of Social Ministry, and has been active in the LWF, the National Council of Churches, and the World Council of Churches.

This commander in chief stance perhaps explains the extremely small number of real friendships in his life. This did not mean that he did not treat men with kindness, but when he charted a course, that was it. He would sometimes use ridicule as he talked of this or that staff officer, but none of us in the Church House laughed very loudly because we were sure none of us escaped the same treatment when we were discussed. And when the commander in chief no longer desired this or that person on his staff, he could eventually make life so miserable for that person that he "resigned."

Franklin Fry was noted for his stories, but again many of them involved ridicule. It is my judgment that many of the stories he told of other Lutheran church leaders were often repeated to them and that their anger and resentment delayed the merger of some of these bodies even to the present day.

Like the superior commander in chief, he never neglected his homework. Conventions were given extraordinary preparation; his copy of the *Convention Bulletin* contained copious notes. He was ready for any questions, any kind of action, and he was the leader every minute of the floor debate. He has rightly been called one of the great presiding officers of our day.

Frank Fry, if he so desired, could have been one of our great politicians. He could have been one of the outstanding lawyers of our day. He could have been a top executive in any great corporation. Thanks be to God that he chose to be a great churchman.

---

[1] The sermon was printed in the LCA *Ministers Information Service,* September 1968.

18

Henry Endress

Another outstanding lay church administrator comments on two sides of President Fry—the efficient executive and the sensitive pastor.

To serve on the staff of Franklin Clark Fry was like working for your father.[1] You loved him deeply. He was the greatest man alive.

Like a little boy clutching to the pants leg of your dad, you looked up and saw a giant who had such a wide range of abilities, agile mind, and inexhaustible energy, that he seemed to be able to do—and almost did—everything he conceived to be necessary to his ministry. This dimension of Franklin Clark Fry often created an obstacle to close personal relationships. His associates were reminded of this man's unusual capabilities through day by day observation and, sometimes overtly, by Dr. Fry himself. When he entered a room conversation often stopped or speakers became self-conscious of what they were saying no matter what the subject; they suspected he might have thought it and said it better. This would amuse Dr. Fry (and, perhaps, twitch his ego) but he regretted it, too, because he was eager to benefit from a free and candid discussion. He became involved easily as he joined the group because he had been thinking about the matter, too. His interjection of opinion began to finalize matters as others respected his lightning grasp of the subject and his perceptive conclusions.

Dr. Fry would try to stimulate discussion so that all would participate. Yet, more than he realized, his total involvement in the discussion would become apparent, climaxed by his own conclusions and position. Sometimes others felt he was guiding discussions toward the end he desired, but there were enough examples of other points of view predominating to counterbalance the suspicion.

Dr. Fry seemed easily irritated by others. He confessed this was true, but insisted that he tried to be generous with patience. The problem was that he couldn't endure stupidity.

(b. 1914) Executive director of the Lutheran Laymen's Movement and of the ULCA Stewardship Department 1949-62, Henry Endress was (along with Oswald Hoffmann) an associate producer of the highly successful motion picture "Martin Luther" and a leader in the production of other films. He served as vice-president and for one year as acting president of Waterloo Lutheran University (1963-69) and is now executive director of the cooperative Lutheran Resources Commission in Washington, D. C. During 1968-69 he was a member of the LCA Executive Council.

Such impatience was evident at times when he would prod and slash while directing and commenting from the podium at conventions. At one session he irked a good friend and lost the sympathy of the delegates at that moment when he criticized the synodical official for doing "the bishop's walk" as the man moved too slowly to a floor microphone. Many times it was with strained patience that he listened to statements and recommendations. In an effort to support a stewardship recommendation I found myself hammered down. And yet, upon reflection later, I realized my point had already been made by someone else and the presiding officer had been right. But that's what got under a man's skin, too!

Believe it, there was the other side to Franklin Clark Fry. His shortcomings bothered him and he regretted, though not always expressed, the hurts he caused. His greatest fear was that he was hurting the cause of the church. During a recess at the Toronto convention of the United Lutheran Church (1954), Dr. Fry called together his immediate staff members in a committee room to find out what he was doing wrong. He was dealing with proposals on the reorganization of the church and recommendation after recommendation was being beaten to the ground or tabled.

Without complaint or bitterness he asked us why the debate was going badly. What was he doing wrong? In what way had he antagonized the delegates?

We loved him for his humility and frankness and his appeal to those around him for advice and guidance. The circumstances were, as I recall them, that the delegates, and Dr. Fry himself, were tiring of the long hours of discussion of constitutional detail. Yet every recommendation seemed so important to him for the more efficient functioning of the church. Many delegates lost patience and consequently wanted both a rest break and something refreshingly different to discuss for a change.

Dr. Fry's interest in what was going on and his concern for better procedure were remarkable. Before a conference or convention, he did his homework in depth. He perched on a stool at the lunch counter and, while munching a sandwich, read reports. When he went to the men's room he carried along synodical bulletins to speed read. When he traveled by train or plane he avoided becoming too involved with anyone, so that he could cover the material in his brief case and then complete the NEW YORK TIMES crossword puzzle. Even his system of going through the mail on his desk was impressive. Upon entering his office one often found him in his desk chair surrounded by piles of correspondence and reports, each heap sorted out for specific purposes. He had a mastery of organization, but also of concentration and memorization. After he worked his way through a pre-convention bulletin (700-800 pages in length) he could cite paragraph, page, and paragraph position on the page of any subject. He delighted in doing this, I suspected, because it spurred everyone else along to do his homework more carefully. And he loved to stop a convention delegate short by declaring from the platform, "My friend, the material to which you refer appears with great clarity in italics at the bottom of page 347 in the pre-convention bulletin!"

The speeches and reports Dr. Fry delivered seemed to flow out of him easily. He once said he prepared his presentations and delivered them as one would prepare to perform on a huge church organ. He sat at the console and played with delight, using the wide variety of stops and volumes, always watching his audience to note its response and to vary his performance to heighten the impact. (Someone *must* gather, select, and publish the best of Franklin Clark Fry's sermons, statements, speeches, and "Dear Partner"[2] letters.)

In 1947 when the stewardship office launched the series of stewardship motion pictures, Dr. Fry agreed to come to Hollywood to give the "trailer speech" at the end of the film, "And Now I See." At lunch he reviewed his notes written on the transcontinental flight. He finalized it, timed it, and memorized it as we walked back and forth on the patio of a Los Angeles outdoor restaurant. Shortly after, in the film studio, he received instructions from Jack Coyle, film director, about body movements at and around a desk in a mock-up of "Dr. Fry's study." He agreed to a rehearsal "with film."

"Good," Dr. Fry said. "I may not be able to do it a second time."

Director Coyle called for silence, action, camera, and sound, and Dr. Fry began to speak. All around him behind the lights and camera stood the cast and crew to witness the film debut of a church president. It was perfect until halfway through the sequence the camera rolled in for a close-up. It was the day before zoomer lenses and so the large Mitchell camera with soundproofed hood was dollied along toward him.

"For heaven's sake!" he declared with eyes popping.

That broke it up and the director called for a second "take." Had it unnerved him? "I'll try again," he said.

Dr. Fry repeated the entire speech from memory without changing one word. When the sequence ended and Jack Coyle cried, "Cut!" the entire studio audience broke out in vigorous applause. "You're the best study (memorizer) in the house," they told him. The number of retakes required for a few of the professionals bore out that statement.

Although he helped to promote most of them, Dr. Fry insisted he never liked films. Some years later we convinced him to see "A Man Called Peter."[3] On one of his rare evenings at home he took Mrs. Fry to a movie theatre in New Rochelle. As she stood waiting, Dr. Fry went to the box office with cash in hand. "Oh, no, Father," declared the cashier, "you are our guest!" He grinned, thumbed in the direction of Mrs. Fry, and asked, "Can I take her with me?"

But films seemed to be among his pet peeves—although he became extremely fond of the LCA's "Davey and Goliath" series for television, begun in 1959. Deaconesses seemed to upset him when it took so long to merge the Philadelphia and Baltimore motherhouses. And outdoor camping. He once asked as he slapped his thigh, "Is it true that one must spend two weeks in a church camp to enter the kingdom of God?"

One evening during a social hour with his staff, the subject of retirement came under discussion. Various ideas were tossed about in good humor, when we finally came up with the "perfect" job for him when he retired from the church presidency: "We shall arrange for you to be appointed the audio-visual aids director of a deaconess summer camp." He enjoyed the suggestion and, I understand, used it as an anecdote at the synod presidents' conference in early 1968 when discussing his retirement "after Minneapolis."[4]

Dr. Fry, at times, seemed too calculating in his work, but it should not be forgotten that there was the soft emotional and even sentimental side, too. His concern for his beloved wife, Hilda, his children, and grandchildren brought tears to his eyes. His greater family—the staff, the church, and the worldwide opportunities to minister were involved too. He talked of the causes of the church as if they were his children. He told of meet-own Christian testimony at a staff conference years ago brought a look from across the room that spoke affection and encouragement. He rarely gave commendation in public, always fearing he'd leave out the name or ing fellow Christians in far-off places with great affection and love. My act of some deserving person. Like the true pastor he was, he spoke these things quietly, person to person. And to have them come from him orally or in a private, handwritten note, gave a troubled man a new lease on life.

Our sharpest difference developed over one of the premieres of the Lutheran motion picture "Question Seven."[5] A crisis developed concerning the position of a theatre chain operator regarding racially integrated performances. While we in the church agreed on principle, there was difference of opinion over procedure and Dr. Fry took a position without conferring with his representatives. The issue was not resolved to the pleasure of any of us but, fortunately, the difference never became a personal matter.

Ordinarily his communication with the rest of us was par excellence. Most refreshing were Dr. Fry's reports to the Church House staff, executive council, and boards upon his return from special missions overseas or in other parts of the hemisphere. Each presentation was memorable because these reports went to the core of matters, were full of interest and had a lot of Franklin Clark Fry in them.

Who can forget the narrative regarding the Budapest sessions of the Central Committee of the World Council of Churches in 1956! Dr. Fry had been designated to give the toast for the World Council in response to the one spoken by the Hungarian government official hosts. He quickly became aware that they had made the most of their toast for propaganda purposes, and so he decided not to fall short of the opportunity to give a Christian witness. In the course of his expanded toast (a speech!) he used the name of Jesus Christ . . . but noted that the Hungarian government interpreter failed to mention Christ by name in his translation into Hungarian. Dr. Fry felt challenged. He continued his toast, again using the name of Christ, and again he found the interpreter avoided use of it. Dr. Fry then continued, in the natural course of speaking, to use the words "Jesus Christ" again and again until the interpreter was embarrassed into using it, too. Dr. Fry loved to share this experience with others. It was a battle of wits but, above all, a testimony for the gospel that was appreciated by his associates who were present.

Another of the Franklin Clark Fry stories was one about his overseas flights with another World Council leader. Shortly after takeoff a stewardess appeared with trays of cocktails and snacks. Dr. Fry, at the window seat, received his Manhattan cocktail with appreciation. When the girl offered his companion a similar tray, Dr. Fry heard him respond: "I don't touch it; take it away!"

"For heaven's sake," intervened Dr. Fry, "Don't do that!" And he lifted the Manhattan off the other tray and placed it on his own.

Dr. Fry loved his roles as church president and traveler. He had a zest for adventure and was eager to meet other persons, in high and low station, to learn what made them "tick." With him he carried his famous autograph book in which he had kings, presidents, artists, and churchmen inscribe their names. It was a book of memories beginning with 1944 throughout his international ministry.

Yet, despite the excitement and enthusiasm he displayed in his role as president, there was evident always the affection for the parish ministry and a nostalgic yearning to be back with former congregations, especially Holy Trinity, Akron, Ohio. He reflected what so many pastors feel after being in general work for a time—almost a guilt complex about spending time in administration away from the person-to-person relationships that parish life offers. University and college faculty members and even specialists in medicine show the same symptoms. St. Stephen himself, after being appointed by the apostles to handle administrative matters, had to satisfy that hunger for personal relationship and testimony by preaching and teaching, too. (I personally have been able to enjoy and find fulfillment in both as a churchman.) To be a synod president or a church president, bishop, and archbishop, is to be pastor of pastors and of laymen as well.

Dr. Fry touched many lives, again and again, including my own. His was a parish ministry in a wider area of operation.

For instance, shortly after the war, we both read Bishop Hanns Lilje's book of wartime experiences in Nazi Germany, "In the Valley of the Shadow" (Philadelphia, 1950). We discussed the suffering of long imprisonment and interrogation and the horror of the sentence of execution and the horror of not knowing on which day this would take place. Each day could have been the day of death for Bishop Lilje. Dr. Fry gave a testimony of respect to the faith and endurance of Dr. Lilje and others under such circumstances.

He said quietly: "I am not afraid to die. My concern about myself is that I would be strong enough to endure long pain and suffering."

God gave Franklin Clark Fry that strength because he certainly knew he was ill and was in pain for many months before his death. Yet he tried to brush it aside and to go on giving a vibrant and significant witness for his Lord in all parts of the world.

Several months before his death as I sat in his office seeking his guidance I remarked that he did not look well. He responded, "Perhaps so. I am not well and don't quite know what to do." He turned the conversation back to my own concerns.

He helped me in this meeting with him, but one of the greatest helps, I believe, came to me in an informal address.

When Dr. Fry returned from his first trip to Russia he included in his report to the Church House staff his experience of worshiping in the Russian Orthodox Church. There was the human setting. So many old people. Women in babushkas. And then the altar with its lights. The impact of lights, music, voice and incense on all his senses. And then the greatest moment of all when the priests prostrated themselves before the altar giving themselves totally—body, soul, mind, and strength—to the Lord of Lords. As he told it, as I write these words, I see Franklin Clark Fry, that big hulk of a Christian pastor, a great and complicated human being, prostrating himself before his Savior in complete submission, obedience, service, and adoration. It might have been difficult at times. But he did it.

---

[1] Dr. Endress also wrote the chapter "In the ULCA" in *Mr. Protestant*, pp. 21-30.

[2] Reference is to the monthly "State of the Church" communications in the ULCA *Pastor's Desk Book* (1947-62) and subsequently in the LCA *Ministers Information Service* (1963-1968).

[3] On the life of the Presbyterian minister and chaplain of the U. S. Senate, Peter Marshall (d. 1949). The movie was adapted from the biography of the same name by his wife, Catherine Marshall.

[4] I.e., the anticipated 1970 LCA convention.

[5] A highly acclaimed film on Christian decision in East Germany, made in 1957 by Lutheran Film Associates, Inc. Dr. Endress had also helped to produce the award-winning and commercially successful movie "Martin Luther" in 1953.

19

F. Eppling Reinartz

A former secretary of the ULCA shares a pair of episodes from life at the Lutheran Church House.

Here are two little mementos of life in the headquarters of the United Lutheran Church in America.

In the years at the Lutheran Church House my service as manager gave me now and then the opportunity to write memoranda of a somewhat personal sort. Some of these, like the following, dealt with the little recognitions that came to our "Morgan Mansion" companions.[1] It was fun giving honor to whom honor was due.

> Greeting to President Franklin Clark Fry of The United Lutheran Church in America on the occasion of his being awarded "Das grosse Verdienst Kreuz"[2] by the West German Republic, in February, 1953:
>
> > Our warmest congratulations on your having been awarded Das grosse Verdienst Kreuz, an honor which has come to you in the compassionate and selfless service of Das grösste Verdienst Kreuz.[3] Your beneficent "posting over land and ocean without rest" has made royal deposits against the day of the final assize when the King of Heaven will take full note of love to the untold, unknown thousands of "the least of these," His brethren. May your present joy be an earnest of that higher, holier and more enduring joy in the Saviour's "well done."
> >
> > The Lutheran Church House Family
> > New York, New York, February 1953

* * *

Attorney Robbin B. Wolf of Pittsburgh, long a member of the ULCA Executive Board, once wrote a letter about Dr. Fry's missing an oppor-

---

(b. 1901) Dr. Reinartz served as executive secretary of Promotion for the ULCA (1938-45), secretary of the ULCA (1947-60), then president of the Lutheran Southern Seminary, Columbia, South Carolina (1961-70). He was a member of the LCA Executive Council (1962-70), and in 1970 was named to the LCA Court of Adjudication. He has been active in inter-Lutheran and ecumenical affairs, as chairman of the ULCA Commission to the Federal Council of Churches (1944-50), for fifteen years councillor of the NLC, and its president (1956-58), and representative to the National Council of Churches (1950-62) and the LCUSA (1966-68).

tunity to become a volunteer fireman. As I recall its premiere, Dr. Fry read it to us in a lighter moment in a meeting of the ULCA Executive Board. It was mimeographed and distributed to us all with Dr. Fry's permission after requests for it came from all sides.

711 Plaza Bldg.
Pittsburgh, Pa.
June 17, 1958

Rev. Dr. Franklin Clark Fry
231 Madison Avenue
New York 16, New York

Dear Dr. Fry:

You are never far out of my mind—could not be in the face of recent press releases, in which your friends have taken solemn pride, and the crossing of our paths at Pittsburgh and Gettysburg.

A hazy recollection of a rhetoric primer suggests that antithesis is the best emphasis.

Recently in the LUTHERAN, I found the obituary of a ne'er-do-well ex-classmate who in some way managed to reach the ministry and I was intrigued to notice that the chief item in his obituary was "He was chaplain of the volunteer firemen." To the biographer that seemed all sufficient.

No one would think of associating the word obituary with the name of Dr. Fry, but one should be forchanded.

When I read in the LUTHERAN about the late Reverend Doctor (probably Oscaloosa) and the volunteer firemen, it occurred to me that this was a field that Dr. Fry had not plowed, an area into which he had not ventured, an opportunity which he had overlooked. I hasten to call the item to your attention and recommend you give it immediate thought, and thereto assign the following reasons:

1. Having at times been somewhat of an incendiary and as well having a record in putting out certain fires, there could be no doubt of your qualification.
2. With a large rural representation at church conventions, membership in the volunteer firemen—with perhaps some help from the asterisk[4]—would assure your winning any and every election.
3. Other Lutheran bodies contemplating merger, while frowning on lodges, would not resent membership in the volunteer firemen.
4. Public applause—the girls never scream so delightedly as when the volunteers parade down Main Street with the chief on the big red wagon.
5. After a brief interval as a private you would undoubtedly be elected "chief." This would serve a double

purpose, (a) you would be in full charge and could delegate the hard work to others, (b) the name Chief would be a splendid solution of the problem among those nearest to you who would like to address you more familiarly but presently feel constrained to address you as Dr. Fry. (Don't be discouraged by the experience of the Lutheran pastor at Tarentum who joined the firemen and at the first meeting was elected janitor.)

6. After the strawberry festival with the treasury bulging, it is customary to supply the members with a sporty leather jacket with large lettering on the back or front. This would seem a relief from the severity of the constant clerical.
7. Descending to the gruesome and giving thought to obituary and tombstone, think of the saving in printer's ink with the obituary confined to "He was a member of the volunteer firemen" and on the monument a replica of the firemen's helmet and crossed nozzles.

If you have read thus far, please forgive the nonsense of an old horse turned out to pasture who indeed would be a dirty ingrate if he did not recall the privileges that were his over a long period of years and find himself casting a longing, lingering look behind. Foolishly trying to come back? No. Unmindful of the ravages of eighty years? No. Just a host of happy recollections centering about you and the many other valued associates on the Executive Board.

You remain always in my affection and in my prayers.

Cordially,
Robbin B. Wolf

RBW:m

Addendum:

8. Beyond the grave, Paradise. Surely any fire extinguishing spirit wandering near Satan's dominion would promptly be told to go to Heaven.

---

[1] The Lutheran Church House is the former J. Pierpont Morgan mansion at 231 Madison Avenue in New York.

[2] The High Merit Cross.

[3] The Cross of *Highest* Merit.

[4] Asterisk on a ballot indicates nominee of the agency itself.

20

Charles C. Hushaw

Observations on Dr. Fry from the viewpoint of a journalist and public relations executive.

Franklin Clark Fry was a personality who would have been the delight of any press agent. He was mine.

I told him often he would have been a great newspaper editor. He knew what news was and he was in a position to create it. And he liked newspapermen and they liked him because he never let them down. Radio and television directors regarded him as a "pro."

Church news, like all other types of news, Dr. Fry once told a meeting of synodical press chairmen, tends to sort itself out on three levels: "news about individuals, news about the church as an organization, and news that catches and shows to the public some of the inner spirit and purpose of what religion really is, what the Christian religion is all about and what makes Christianity tick."

The job of church public relations, Dr. Fry once said, is to create a climate, "to catch the attention of the listless bystander, to put religion into an affirmative setting and whet the appetite for more."

When he came to Southern California Reformation Day of 1953 and urged me to come to New York City to set up the church's first Department of Press, Radio and Television, Dr. Fry told me: "Charley, I'm eager to have you as my trusted and invaluable partner in one of the most wide-awake churches in America. Nowhere else could you serve your Lord or your generation better, I am devoutly convinced."

As his press relations director for more than ten years, I found Dr. Fry a trusted and invaluable partner. And I am convinced that through the final years of the United Lutheran Church in America, the negotiations of the Joint Commission on Lutheran Unity leading to the birth of the Lutheran Church in America—busy years in which Dr. Fry was so involved with the leadership of the World Council of Churches and the Lutheran World Federation—nowhere else could I have served my Lord, my generation, or a great churchman better.

(b. 1911) Charles Hushaw had been a newspaperman for twenty-five years when he became the first director of the ULCA/LCA Department of Press, Radio, and Television (1954-64). He served on committees of the National Lutheran Council, and was vice-chairman of the Broadcasting and Film Commission of the National Council of Churches. Since 1964 he has been assistant director of the Department of Education of Copley Newspapers, Los Angeles.

21

Raymond H. Tiemeyer

A former assistant to the president probes for the principles guiding Dr. Fry's churchmanship, and shares a few insights into the president's personal orientations.

From 1956 to 1962 it was my privilege to serve as administrative assistant to the president of the United Lutheran Church in America. It is from this vantage point that I would like to share a few observations about Dr. Fry, the man and his manner.

Henry Ford is misunderstood when his life is visualized in the image of the Model T. That reduces him to dated structure. He is better seen in the principles which guided his work such as his dedication to the methods of mass production.

Dr. Fry is misunderstood when his life is equated with the Lutheran Church in America constitution or the structures of the ULCA, the Lutheran World Federation, or the World Council of Churches. He too is better seen in the principles which guided his career. Of these there are many—enough to discourage simplistic legend-making—but I would like to emphasize three of the most important.

Vocational obedience. In Dr. Fry's view, offices existed only by right of the church's need for their function. No person, agency, or institution filling those offices was to gain the status of an absolute. Dr. Fry was quick to detect and oppose the effort of any person to institutionalize himself or of any institution to perpetuate itself. People and structures had to remain subject to the changing needs of the church if they were to be vocationally obedient. He once said, "A constitution must be a living organism, adaptable to functional needs."

This principle became quite apparent, for example, when he had to respond to some new development. New problems were not to be satisfied with old solutions. For that reason his response was often unpredictable. He would search for the obedience demanded by the new situation. Any predictions of his course of action could only be extrapolated from previous responses. He would not institutionalize past successes to avoid future failures. This is not to say he wasn't subject to temptations, but he would

---

(b. 1926) Pastor Tiemeyer served as administrative assistant to President Fry from 1956 to 1962. He was ULCA director of Lutheran World Action 1958-62, and councillor to the NLC (1963-64). In 1970 he joined the editorial staff of the LCA Board of Parish Education.

prefer that one take satisfaction from being a martyr than for being self-protective, if personal motives had to be indulged.

Subscription to the principle of vocational obedience is one reason why the Fry image should not be confined to the structures left in his legacy. Those structures were only the functional expression of their moment, not of an indefinite time span, not even of the span of his years. Two reorganizations took place during his presidential tenures, and a third was on the horizon. He recognized that the 1954 restructure of the ULCA was in need of revision already by the time of the merger in 1962, and several parts of the merger structure were beginning to become outdated already by 1968. Were he alive now and at the age of 44 or 55 or 66 his response to the day would be less defensive of the past and more unpredictable than one might think. Institutional servanthood required situational obedience.

Conservative theology–liberal ethics. Elsewhere in this book Dr. Lazareth has identified what is probably the most basic interpretive principle of Dr. Fry's life, that he was theologically conservative and ethically liberal. He came to those stances by deliberate choice. Ethically, by background he would have been conservative, but he underwent a rather radical change of philosophy. He compared his change to that of a few other persons of his day such as the statesman Averell Harriman. Theologically, he had been liberal by inclination of intellect. His shift to the conservative view was crystallized as a result of the suicide of industrialist George Eastman in 1932. He realized that an idealistic humanism provided inadequate interpretations to sustain the satisfactions of philanthropy, the fulfillments of creativity and success, and the well-being of wealth. This liberal-conservative paradox is another reason why his responses were complex and not easily predicted.

Rational integrity–emotional honesty. Dr. Fry was intensely rational but he was repelled by rationalizations. He had little patience when people resorted to "feelings" because they were too lazy to think a problem through. He was impatient when anyone was impetuous because of failure to discipline mental facilities. Yet he did not operate in a sterile logic. He was not a pure theoretician. He distrusted reason when it was either too impersonally detached or too personally involved. Emotions were needed to keep reason real and reason was needed to keep motives honest.

He was repelled by sentimentalism, but he had intense sentiments. Any exploitation of the emotions to charm people and manipulate their spirit was dishonest, he believed. Emotion was permissible only as a genuine and spontaneous expression of worthy feelings, never as contrived display. He had no time for a worship service designed to elicit emotions, yet he always sang hymns with great heart and he could not keep his voice from breaking on the liturgy. His Mother Church stirred deep currents of appreciation in him. He gave it his finest reason.

* * *

My life in the president's office afforded me ample opportunity to learn about Dr. Fry's outlook on a variety of subjects. A few revealing personal opinions are the following:

1. *Evaluation of his Documents*

Of the many reports and documents produced by Dr. Fry, he seemed to take the greatest personal satisfaction in the study on church unity written as the report to the 1956 ULCA Convention.[1] He was particularly pleased with the reception it gained abroad.

Of the documents he produced in team with others, he seemed to take the most satisfaction in the Minneapolis theses on Freedom and Unity written by the 1957 LWF assembly.[2]

2. *Potential Authorship*

When asked once what subject he would choose if he were to write a book, he thought it would be sites of Christian history. His favorite site was Hagia Sophia in Istanbul. It was impressive to him as a phenomenally early architectural achievement for the church, but also as the place where Russian emissaries were first converted to the Christian faith.

3. *Communications Media*

Dr. Fry was very sensitive about allowing a speech to be reduced to writing, or a writing to be delivered as a speech. He considered them two distinct media. Material prepared for one medium lost its quality if conveyed in the other. For this reason he was also uneasy about the presence of tape recorders. He believed a recording distorted material originally delivered in person. He resisted appearances on motion picture film, but he was completely at home on television.

---

[1] Printed in the ULCA 1956 Minutes, pp. 29-38, and in LUTHERAN WORLD, March 1957, pp. 322-334; abridged in Richard C. Wolf, *Documents,* Document 225.

[2] *Proceedings of the Third Assembly of the LWF,* Minneapolis, 1958, pp. 84-91: Theses on the Theme, "Christ Frees and Unites" (popularly known as the "Minneapolis Theses"). Abridged in Wolf, *Documents,* Document 242.

The contributions of two veteran ULCA synodical presidents follow.

22

Dwight F. Putman

Dr. Putman comments on President Fry's manner of leadership in the executive bodies of the church, and his relations with the Central Pennsylvania Synod.

Many have spoken and written eloquently of Franklin Clark Fry's greatness in so many respects. Few subjects that could have been chosen would have given justification for greater eloquence. It is not my purpose to reiterate much that has already been and will be expressed in tribute to this exceptional personality, who, had he chosen a political career, would undoubtedly have stood near the top among modern statesmen.

Having served in rather close relationship with Dr. Fry as a member for sixteen years of the Executive Board of the United Lutheran Church in America and the Executive Council of the Lutheran Church in America, also as a member of the Joint Commission on Lutheran Unity, and as a participant with him in numerous other areas of church work, I have been requested to tell it as it was.

When Dr. Fry sat with a board or committee or other deliberating group, time and again he would contribute greatly to the end of advancing substantially or resolving the matter under consideration. At the same time, unfortunately for the freest exercise of the democratic process, the great weight of his presence and his skillful use of that weight were often a deterrent to full participation by others in the group.

As chairman of the executive board and executive council of the church he presided with his well-known customary skill. In these bodies he truly endeavored to make the members feel free to share fully in the deliberations. While of course there was no direct effort on the part of the chairman to coerce or curb anyone in respect to his stand or vote on an issue, yet he did not always avoid making felt his strong displeasure with positions expressed that were contrary to those of his own about which he felt most keenly.

(b. 1898) President of the Central Pennsylvania Synod 1948-66, Dr. Putman served on the ULCA Executive Board (1950-58) and the LCA Executive Council (1962-68), and on the Joint Commission on Lutheran Unity. He was president of the Pennsylvania Council of Churches 1952-54, and has been a representative to the NLC and the National Council of Churches.

While Dr. Fry's competent and effective leadership was generally recognized and highly regarded, it is true that there were those who felt a certain resentment when the dominant role which he normally assumed in any group of which he was a part tended to thwart the free play of the democratic process, or when he would be sharply severe in his criticism of others as indeed he could be. At the same time any hostility thus generated would be greatly tempered by the fact that at heart he had a deep pastoral concern and expressed the same for the welfare of the individual person.

On one occasion I recall I had reason personally to be especially aware of this concern. An illness had overtaken me during a meeting of the executive board and landed me in a New York City hospital at considerable distance from the place of the meeting. Promptly upon the adjournment of a strenuous board session of several days Dr. Fry was in my hospital room calling upon me.

During my years on the executive bodies of the church I served in the office of the president of the Central Pennsylvania Synod. In this position I was privileged to enjoy numerous official relationships with President Fry. In all my experience in that office his role in relation to the synod president was always performed with meticulous correctness, wholly in keeping with the structure of the church. At no time did he presume to encroach upon the prerogatives of the synod official. For instance, if at any time a member of the synod would take a complaint to the head of the church that would normally come under the responsibility of the synod, Dr. Fry would respond very discreetly—sometimes, depending on the nature of the complaint, making a poignant reply and plainly advising the complainant that the problem did not come under his jurisdiction but that of the synod. And, of course, he would always send a copy of his answer to the president of synod.

Both personally and officially our relationship left little to be desired. However, the synod of which I was president and what it represented did not always seem to be held by Dr. Fry as a shining segment of the Lutheran church.

In the first place, it was and continues to be a very large synod of the church. Being of such size, and for many years having raised its benevolence one hundred percent, it was able to stand first among the synods in the total volume of financial support of the church. However, the president of the church had a different concept of the synod as to size, and to that end sought a different synodical arrangement. He conceived of the matter of shepherding pastors and congregations as resting not with the office of the president or with the synod generally but with the person of the president of synod himself. Consequently, he was certain that the shepherding function could not be carried out effectively in such a large synod.

Furthermore a large synod was more likely to act independently of the church at large and to exercise more power in its life than was conducive to that centralization and unity which Dr. Fry considered essential for a strong church.

Something of this tendency was evidenced in the life of the Central Pennsylvania Synod. For instance, it had operated a kind of pension plan before the church at large was ready to enter into anything like an adequate pension system for its ministers. Then, too, it had traditionally a more open relationship with other denominations, with which policy the church in general was not in sympathy. In the area of social concerns it had played a more active role than the church was willing to assume in the earlier years, and was looked upon as being too legalistic in its approach to social issues and its attitude toward personal behavior. Liturgically the synod was considered "low church" in character, at least not typically Lutheran. Furthermore, it supported a seminary on its territory that represented and promoted many of these characteristics, and which was also held to be left wing if not indeed theologically heretical, at least as far as some of its faculty were concerned. Divergencies such as these in a segment of the church caused the greater concern because they were by no means conducive to the realization of the desired and hoped-for unity of American Lutheranism.

It is hardly necessary to point out that in recent years, in some of these areas such as social action and ecumenical relations, the church has gone even beyond what had been the earlier position of the synod, and generally on a sounder basis. At the same time, in other respects such as liturgical practice, the synod has moved into closer accord with the rest of the church.

Due to the synod's stance on many of these matters, which was at times in contrast with that of the prevailing trend of the church, and because its size was considered by Dr. Fry not to be in the best interest of either the synod or the church, it was evident on occasion that the Central Pennsylvania Synod and its institutions were not among his first loves.

Volumes might be written to tell of the many qualities of greatness represented in Franklin Clark Fry and of his far-reaching accomplishments within and beyond the Lutheran church. My particular contribution in this article is in response to being urged to give it a personal slant and to comment candidly on some of the areas of tension that were sensed during the years of our personal and official relationship.

23

J. Luther Mauney

A southern synodical executive reflects on Dr. Fry's leadership.

The vantage point of a synod presidency affords an insight into the effect of Dr. Fry's leadership. One observation in this regard relates to the cohesion of the church itself. The nature of the United Lutheran Church in America as basically a syncretizing of synods inevitably resulted in strong synods and a somewhat restricted position for the national body. Not having had earlier responsibility for synodical leadership Dr. Fry came to his position as president of the church without that previous influence or that bent of mind that might have been disposed to extend into the future this fragmentation of the church's potential for a full realization or expression of its true unity. He could and did give emphasis to the oneness, the totality of the church, in a way that brought about a willingness to alter its structure and thus enhance its position and ability to carry out its mission. This was at times somewhat frustrating to those responsible for synodical programs and concerns, but it helped to pave the way for the new focus on the unity within our church that became a part of the concept embraced in the Lutheran Church in America, and this he helped to introduce into the governing documents of that body.

As the administrative head of the church Dr. Fry exhibited an unusual diligence in assimilating information relative to developments in all parts of its life. With respect to synodical affairs one was frequently surprised to note the extensiveness of his information and concern. This was matched only by his willingness to consult on these matters when desirable, and his openness of access and readiness to lend assistance whenever it could be fitted into his heavy schedule.

An additional observation relates to the benefit that was observable from having as our president one who was widely known and respected, and its particular effect in a section of the country where our church is in a definite minority position. One could discern a real benefit from having a person of Dr. Fry's stature and ability in that position. It gave added prestige, and encouraged a wider recognition of our church and its life and work.

(b. 1907) Dr. Mauney has been president of the Virginia Synod since 1948. He has served on the Parish Education Board of the LCA. He was president of the Virginia Council of Churches 1962-65, and a representative to the National Council of Churches (1964-70).

The next seven memos shed light on particular facets of life and thought in the ULCA.

24

Earl S. Erb

Dr. Erb discusses problems of Lutheran church polity and administration as these affect the mission enterprise; the merging of world service and overseas missions agencies in the reorganization of the NCCC; and an American problem with the move for Lutheran unity in Japan.

Dr. Fry's intimate and profound knowledge of world affairs, of the church in every corner of the globe and of the personnel involved in that work, continued to amaze me through the fifteen years in which I had the privilege to be associated with him as executive secretary of the Board of Foreign Missions of the United Lutheran Church in America and later of the Board of World Missions of the Lutheran Church in America.

One could go to him for consultation concerning relationships with the sister churches overseas and know that he was already aware of the situation because he had read both the minutes of the board and copies of correspondence which came to him. Nor did he forget what he read. His proposals concerning procedure in a particular situation showed his wide experience, his knowledge of human nature, and his awareness of the implications of what was to be written or done.

Dr. Fry participated fully in the week-long "policy conference" held by the Board of Foreign Missions of the ULCA at Thiel College in 1957. The broad policies of the board were formulated as a result of that conference. Dr. Fry not only participated in the conference but was most helpful in formulating the actual statements of policy which grew out of the Thiel College conference.

Principles of Organization

It was in the area of principles of organization within the church that I did not always agree with Dr. Fry. For him the ideal was that every-

---

(b. 1899) Dr. Erb was executive secretary of the ULCA Board of Foreign Missions and then of the LCA Board of World Missions from 1953 to 1967. He was staff assistant in the Southeastern and Northeastern Pennsylvania Synods 1967-69. He was long prominent in the Division of Foreign Missions of the National Council of Churches, and took part in the New Delhi assembly of the World Council of Churches (1961).

thing should be centered in and pretty much controlled by the executive board of the church. He felt that each board tended to want to be autonomous, a "nest of boards," and actually tried to be just that. My own opinion was and is that the broad policies should be determined by the central church organization but that once the broad policies have been determined, boards should be given full freedom to develop the program within the framework set up by the church. It is my opinion that this will result in a more creative program, using all the gifts of board members and staff. I said to Dr. Fry a good many times that I was quite agreed that the executive council should discipline any board or staff member that overstepped the bounds set by the church, but that the threat of interference should not be expressed. Dr. Fry did not feel that this procedure was sound or effective.

When you look at some of the constitutional provisions of the ULCA documents, Dr. Fry's concepts are illustrated.

The following is a quotation from the ULCA constitution, Article XI, Section 3, dealing with the powers of the executive board:

"9. Review the actions of each board, agency (excepting common agencies), and auxiliary at the first or second meeting of the Executive Board next following receipt of the minutes of the meeting of the board, agency, or auxiliary at which the actions are taken. This power of review and responsibility shall be interpreted as power of veto of any program or enterprise which shall in the judgment of the Executive Board conflict with or be hurtful to the total program of the church."

Dr. Fry's interpretation of Article XI, quoted above, was severe and rigid, in my opinion. I said to Dr. Fry a number of times that if the Board of Foreign Missions would want to make the executive board look foolish we could write to the related churches overseas that the board had agreed to provide certain funds or personnel requested but that we could not actually respond to the request until the Executive Board of the ULCA had passed on our actions. This would often have meant a delay of many months. Of course, we did not act in that negative way.

The LCA constitutional provisions are modified and, in my opinion, are better than the former ULCA provisions.

The following are the provisions in the LCA constitution and LCA bylaws dealing with the powers of the executive council.

LCA Constitution

Article XII. Section 3. The duties and functions of the Executive Council shall be to:

"h. Promote and coordinate the activities of the synods and of the several boards, commissions and auxiliaries of this church, and have the power of review of the actions of said boards and auxiliaries to assure that such actions are in conformity with the policies laid down by the convention."

LCA Bylaws

Section VIII. Executive Council:

"Item 5. The power of the Executive Council to review the actions of the boards and auxiliaries shall be exercised at the first or second meeting of the council next following receipt of the minutes in which such actions are recorded. If a specific action is, in the judgment of the Executive Council, not within the powers of the board concerned or not in conformity with a policy laid down by the convention, formal declaration of that fact shall postpone or suspend the effectiveness of said action. Unless the action in question is meanwhile rescinded, the issue shall be reported to the next convention for adjudication. In the case of auxiliaries this provision shall apply to actions both of their conventions and of their executive bodies."

The LCA provisions give the boards a bit more freedom of movement but wisely make provision for adjudication by a convention if there should be a serious conflict with the executive council. In my opinion this provides for creative programming within the policies set by the church. The term "veto" has disappeared. However, the executive council still has the right to "postpone or suspend the effectiveness of said action."

It seems to me that the spirit of "team work" is expressed somewhat more adequately in the LCA constitutional provisions as over against central control and almost slavish obedience. However, the spirit of teamwork could be fostered even more fully if the threat of the postponement or suspension of an action were removed. The very presence of those words in the bylaws makes for an uneasiness among staff people and board members.

NCCCUSA Reorganization

Dr. Fry was intimately involved in the decisions concerning the reorganization of the National Council of Churches in the USA during the mid-fifties.[1] As a member of the General Board of NCCCUSA and as chairman of the Division of Foreign Missions of the council, I was involved in the plans for reorganization.

The recommendations which were being considered included a merger of Church World Service and the Divison of Foreign Missions into the Division of Overseas Ministries. Dr. Fry felt that this was wrong. In his estimation Church World Service was an agency that should minister to the physical needs regardless of creed or nationality and that to merge with the Division of Foreign Missions would hinder this type of service, since the aim of the latter was to bring people into the fold of the churches.

The vast majority felt that it was the love of Christ that constrained Christians to serve in both areas and that the merger would not hinder the valid aims of Church World Service.

Dr. Fry made a speech at a meeting at which final recommendations were drawn up. His ideas did not get the support of the group. This was a great disappointment to Dr. Fry and I always felt that Dr. Fry's later inactivity in the NCCCUSA basically came because of the pattern followed in the reorganization.

It will be interesting to see what changes in organization will take place in the Lutheran World Federation and in the World Council of Churches in the next few years. Dr. Fry's views were a powerful influence in both of those bodies.

Lutheran Unity in Japan

An event early in my experience on the staff of the Board of Foreign Missions of the ULCA will always be vivid in my mind. I visited Japan to participate in discussions looking to the formation of a single Lutheran Church. European boards of missions, the former Evangelical Lutheran Church, the Missouri Synod, the Augustana Church, the American Lutheran Church, and the ULCA were the major groups involved in the discussions.

I was very much aware of Dr. Fry's feeling about the merger of Lutheran groups. As is well known, it was his conviction that there must be no test of Lutheranism other than the acceptance of the canonical scriptures and the Lutheran confessions.[2] I agreed with Dr. Fry entirely in this concept. However, the Missouri Synod participants pleaded with us for a position which would enable them to get the approval of the Missouri Synod. After prolonged discussion we agreed that a statement of "Doctrinal Witness" to the people of Japan should be formulated by the church. The statement was to be in terms of the issues and religions in the East. I thought that this was valid and that it was not a denial of the position which had been taken by the ULCA.

When I reported to the Board of Foreign Missions of the ULCA, with Dr. Fry present, there was quite an explosion. Dr. Fry was opposed to the position which I had taken but my position had the support of most if not of all the members of the board. Finally the following resolution was adopted:

> *Voted* that we record that we have heard with gratitude and hopefulness the report of negotiations now being carried on by the Japan Evangelical Lutheran Church and other Lutheran groups in Japan and wish them Godspeed in these negotiations, and that we inform our missionaries and the Japan Lutheran Mis-

sionaries' Association that their several activities in these negotiations shall be in connection with and with the sanction of the Japan Evangelical Lutheran Church.

The real point of the resolution was that missionaries of the ULCA could serve as individuals with the church in Japan but not as representatives of the ULCA in developing the plan of organization and the "Doctrinal Witness" statement.

Minutes of the Board of Foreign Missions of the ULCA (June 1956) contain the following restatement of the interpretation Dr. Fry gave the constitution:

> In the United Lutheran Church, the Board of Foreign Missions is not in a position to take official action to delegate authority to the missionaries to serve as the Board's representatives. In their Lutheran Unity negotiations the missionaries proceed only in connection with the JELC and with its sanction.
>
> Matters of inter-Lutheran relationships are the responsibility of the Executive Board of the ULCA. When the amended constitution is submitted to the Board of Foreign Missions by the JELC, the procedure for the approval will depend on the nature of the amendments. Amendments affecting "the doctrinal basis of an affiliated church or its general agreement with the Constitution of the United Lutheran Church in America" (1952 ULCA Minutes, page 204) are to be submitted to the Executive Board for approval.

After that board meeting Dr. M. P. Moller, Jr., president of the board, and I went to see Dr. Fry. I felt I could not serve the BFM if there was no room for negotiation with overseas groups. We did come to an understanding and I want to give testimony here that Dr. Fry was such a "big" man that none of the differences were held against me in later and continuing relationships. I admired Dr. Fry for this and always felt that I could go to him and get a fair hearing.[3]

Autograph Book

An episode in President William A. Tubman's office in Liberia, Africa, will always remain in my mind. Dr. Fry had an autograph book. It contained the autographs of many famous people. Dr. Fry used the book in a most effective way. President Tubman was smoking his usual cigar, as was Dr. Fry. Dr. Fry then asked President Tubman for his autograph and asked him in which part of the book he would like to place his autograph. President Tubman was obviously flattered.

Faithfulness to Christ

Dr. Fry's faithfulness to Christ and to the total gospel was outstanding and was a source of strength to me again and again. For him this was central not only intellectually but also emotionally. In many discussions in church meetings when Christ and the centrality of the gospel would have been glossed over or even forgotten by prominent leaders of the church, it was Dr. Fry who got the discussion back to where it should have been.

I have such a high regard for Dr. Fry that nothing that I have written is to cast reflection on his actions but rather is an attempt to give background for a small part of the vast activities of this man of God.

---

[1] See S. M. Cavert, *American Churches in the Ecumenical Movement,* New York, 1968, pp. 248-250.

[2] This position had been set forth in the Savannah Resolution of the ULCA, 1934. See *Doctrinal Declarations,* St. Louis, 1957, pp. 58-60; abridged in R. C. Wolf, *Documents,* Document 149.

[3] See also the memo of Kishi (No. 64).

25

Abdel Ross Wentz

In a second memo treating church polity, Dr. Wentz concentrates on two subjects: the principles of ecumenical organization, in which he and Dr. Fry agreed, and Dr. Fry's desire for centralization of executive power in the Lutheran church, which Dr. Wentz opposed.

Lights, Not Shadows

Half a century ago when psychoanalysis was in blossom, experts in the science went back through the centuries and tried to lay bare the psyches of great men long since dead. Martin Luther was an easy target; he had left so much evidence of his heart and soul. If the writers of this symposium follow the instructions to abstain from "the ordinary bouquet of eulogies," this collection of essays may provide good material for a future psychoanalysis of Franklin Clark Fry. There will be plenty of evidence to use and plenty of personality to analyze.

Then it will be clear that, as with every great but human personality, his faults and weaknesses were only the shadows of his virtues and strong points. Thus, for example, the abrasive elements in his character were balanced by his uncanny ability to charm opponents into submission, and his pride of power was only the underside of his sincere and humble Christion devotion. A high pole casts a long shadow. The expert biographer will need to explore the shadows as well as the brilliance. But the church historian should be content to point out the tangible contributions, whether good or not so good.

In the course of the Cleveland convention of the United Lutheran Church in America in 1946, the first that was chaired by Dr. Fry, I said to his mother, whom I knew very well: "Aren't you proud of Frank's amaz-

---

(b. 1883) Prominent educator, author, and church statesman, Dr. Wentz has been professor of church history (1916-51) and president (1940-51) of Gettysburg Seminary in Pennsylvania. He was a delegate to the organizing assembly of the Lutheran World Convention (1923), and served on the LWC Executive Committee 1935-47. He wrote the constitution of the Lutheran World Federation (founded 1947), was a vice-president 1947-52, and has been an honorary member of its Executive Committee since 1952. He was active in the Federal Council of Churches, and influential in the provisional committee which created the World Council of Churches in 1948. He was president of the ULCA Board of Foreign Missions (1944-52), and a member of the committee which prepared the Revised Standard Version of the New Testament (published 1946).

ing skill and brilliance in the president's chair?" She replied: "I am only glad that Frank has not yet broken out!" I repeated this to Frank, and he said: "If the people of this convention could realize how hard it is for Frank to keep from breaking out, they would give him more credit than they do!" This was no chance remark. It was true, and it points the index to much of his life and character, as I afterwards learned from close association with him over the years.

Frank was constantly struggling against a measure of asperity in his character, his belittling of those who ventured to disagree with him or were slower in their thought processes, his tendency to prove his superiority and assert his power, his recourse to artifice, and his disposition sometimes to dictate in areas in which he had no expertise, such as theology and theological education. In this magnificent and continuous inner struggle to keep from "breaking out" he achieved a large measure of victory. And through it all he kept a lowly and contrite *heart* and did "walk humbly with his *God.*"

From the many and various areas of Dr. Fry's positive activities and identifiable contributions, I select only two for brief comment here. Both of them are clearly in the range of the concern of a church historian. In the first I was closely associated with him, and it happened that I agreed with him. In the second I looked on from a distance, and it happened that I did not agree with him. In both of these happenings Dr. Fry showed his genuine zeal for his church and exercised in a positive way his amazing talents for leading men, his special skill in organization, his photographic memory and rare foresight, his prodigious diligence and contagious affability. This was a combination of qualities which, if it had been devoted to the service of his nation, might have brought him to the highest office in the land.

I

The first event to which I call attention was in the area of the modern ecumenical movement. Some of the Lutherans in America had become involved in this movement before Franklin Clark Fry arrived on the ecclesiastical scene. When Dr. Fry became F. H. Knubel's successor as president of the United Lutheran Church in America in 1945, Dr. Knubel and I had been engaged for nearly a decade in a struggle in the ecumenical movement to secure recognition of the principle that an ecumenical council, whether worldwide or American, must be constituted entirely of member churches and be directly responsible to them. This position had two facets. One was the so-called representative principle, which maintained that an ecumenical council is composed of churches, not of various kinds of ecclesiastical organization, and that it represents and speaks for the churches only in those matters which the member churches have committed to it. This principle was opposed to the common practice of "co-option," by which leaders who were already "in" were free to invite other "expert" individuals to come in. In short, the "representative principle" insisted that an ecumenical council represents churches, not individuals or autonomous groups of churchmen. A second facet was expressed in the term "confessional representation," which urged that an ecumenical council should apportion representation according to the various ecclesiastical or confessional positions which are still struggling with one another toward Christian unity, and not merely according to geographical regions.

We Lutherans in America who were involved felt that the practice of co-option was intolerable in any "council of churches," and we insisted that the churches themselves must choose their representatives in these councils. I became involved in this struggle because the ULCA sent me as one of three delegates to the Edinburgh Conference on Faith and Order in 1937, where the first concrete move was made in the direction of forming a World Council of Churches. That conference chose me to be one of the fourteen men who with fourteen alternates were charged with responsibility for all details in actually setting up a World Council. This gave me opportunity to plead for the recognition of the representative or confessional principle in the constitution of the WCC and to be the mouthpiece for Dr. Knubel, Dr. Ralph H. Long, and other American Lutherans. It was a long process because the war years prevented progress in the building of a World Council.

When World War II came to an end in 1945, the work of constructing a World Council of Churches was renewed with high speed. Dr. Fry had become president of the ULCA in January of that year, and he gave his full support to the campaign for the confessional or representative principle. He talked with key individuals in America, Lutheran and non-Lutheran, and helped persuade many of them. Through his executive board he called a conference in September, 1945, of representatives of nearly all the Lutheran churches in America "for the purpose of achieving a common understanding with reference to the World Council of Churches." This group strongly endorsed the idea of confessional representation.

With the Lutheran churches of Europe also Dr. Fry exercised his power of persuasion and helped to secure their endorsement of our idea concerning representation. Some of their leaders were not easily persuaded, partly because as state churches they regarded regional representation as sufficient, partly because most of them had no easy way to choose representatives beside themselves, but largely because they were at that time involved in church-state obligations that handicapped them in external relations as church bodies. But Dr. Fry had helped to reorganize and strengthen the Lutheran World Convention (afterwards to become the Lutheran World Federation) so that most of the Lutherans of the world could speak with united voice. The result was that in 1946, when the committee preparatory to the World Council was told by some non-Lutherans that this idea of ecclesiastical or confessional representation in the council was harbored only by "a little group of Lutherans in America," I could present documents to prove that most of the Lutheran churches in the world would insist upon such representation. After a very spirited debate and with the aid of Dr. Samuel Cavert, chairman of that committee, the proposal of the American Lutheran on the committee was adopted and the provisional constitution of the proposed World Council was changed accordingly.

This guaranteed Lutheran participation in the World Council, and for many years Lutherans constituted the largest and most active confessional group in the council. At the organization of the Lutheran World Federation in 1947, Dr. W. A. Visser 't Hooft, the general secretary of the proposed World Council, publicly indicated his acceptance of confessional representation, and at the organization meeting of the World Council in 1948 he told me that he now saw that without this principle he could not have gathered delegates for the assembly. Soon thereafter we find Franklin Clark Fry operating at the center of the World Council and applying his great skills to the very heart of it, first as vice-chairman of both its central and its executive committees (1948-54), and then as their chairman (1954 to his death in 1968).

This was a highly important process within the ecumenical movement, and without it there would probably have been no Lutheran participation in the World Council and possibly no World Council at all.[1]

II

The second area of Dr. Fry's achievement on which I want to comment here is the structure of the Lutheran Church in America. It was conceived in his mind and born of his planning. If it is true that "The University of Virginia is the long shadow of Thomas Jefferson," it is also true that the LCA is the long shadow of Franklin Clark Fry. When the editor of the *American Lutheran,* a Missouri Synod man, in the issue of January, 1958, page four, presented a brief account of events among Lutherans of America during the preceding year, he referred to the beginning of plans for union of the Augustana Lutheran Church and the ULCA. He noted that there would be some obstacles, and then he commented: "But there appeared to be a will in both bodies to remove whatever obstacles exist. Leaders of the ULCA were said to be eager for the merger, since such a move would permit the framing of a new constitution obviating some of the difficulties inherent in the present articles, many of them dating from 1917 [when the ULCA constitution was written]."

The editor's use of the plural "leaders of the ULCA" was a euphemism, and his phrase "some of the difficulties" was purposely vague. In the negotiations for merger the expected difficulties disappeared. This was largely because the organizational structure of the Augustana Church was very much like that desired by "leaders" in the ULCA. The Augustana group was organized as a "synod" in 1860 and became loosely attached to the General Council in 1870. When the General Council decided in 1917 to merge with the General Synod and the United Synod South, the Augustana Synod quietly seceded and began an independent career. It established "conferences" within the synod but gave them no basic powers. Gradually more powers were given to the president, and in 1948 more centralized authority was set up in the constitution and the name was changed to Augustana Lutheran Church. In the merger negotiations for the LCA a decade later the new "Augustana Church," once a seceded synod, had equal representation with the entire ULCA, and the proceedings moved smoothly and swiftly. The result was a fairly complete reversal of the sources of power in this part of American Lutheranism.

I think I can pinpoint the moment of conception of this monolithic ecclesiastical structure. During the years of discussion about the basis of membership in the WCC I had been asked to draw up a precise definition of a "church" that could qualify for membership. The result could be epitomized in three words: self-governing, self-propagating, and self-supporting (the last to be interpreted loosely). This was to apply both to membership in the Lutheran World Federation and to membership in the World Council of Churches. When we received an application for membership in the LWF from the Federation of Evangelical Lutheran Churches in India, we insisted that the individual churches must apply, and this was done. But Bishop Sandegren of India raised the question as to why we were accepting into the WCC the Reformed organization called the "Swiss Protestant Church Federation."

Dr. Fry and I decided to interview Dr. Alfons Koechlin, the president of the Swiss organization, to inquire about the nature of this so-called federation. For by definition the WCC was not to consist of federations, alliances, associations, councils, and so forth, but of churches. It was during the first week of August, 1946, at Cambridge, England, at one of the special conferences set up by the Provisional Committee of the WCC, that we had our first opportunity to confer with Dr. Koechlin. He had been active in the ecumenical movement before either Dr. Fry or I had been, and he was a bit irritated by the approach of the American Johnny-come-latelies. He retorted to us somewhat as follows: "Go and examine yourselves. Dr. Fry, what are *you* president of? What kind of church do *you* have? Is not the ULCA merely a federation of territorial churches called synods, which govern themselves, have their own budgets, levy their own assessments, propagate themselves through ordination and through missionary operations on their own territory, and do not the synods use the ULCA in New York as a mere bureau through which they can do some things better by cooperation than as individual synods? What's in a name? Our so-called federation is more closely organized than your so-called ULCA." We were embarrassed; for once we had no answer. We went no further with our inquiry about Swiss ecclesiology. Now I cannot be sure, but I firmly believe that it was at this time that Dr. Fry began to ponder seriously a radical change in the essential nature of the ULCA so as to secure something on the order of the glorified synod called the Augustana Lutheran Church. It was not long after that event that Dr. Fry talked to me about the relative weakness of the ULCA compared with Augustana.

Over the decade that followed, power in the ULCA gradually flowed to New York. This was due partly to the general change in culture. In civil life power flowed to Washington, and now huge colossi began to sit astride the nation, like the military-industrial complex, and states' rights within a "federal union" have largely disappeared. In church life also the territorial synods were confronted with tasks of national and international scope and gradually yielded their powers to the bureaus centering in New York. Organic mergers of church bodies became fashionable and always resulted in greater accumulation of power at the top levels.

The ULCA was no exception. The natural flow of power from the congregations and the synods to the higher levels of authority in the church was perceptible and could easily be traced. A long step in the process was taken at Toronto in 1954. The President's Report to that convention openly disclosed Dr. Fry's dissatisfaction with the distribution of power in the ULCA, particularly as between the synods and the church. At the same convention a ponderous report was received from a commission appointed by the president. It was called the Commission on Organizational Structure. It proposed numerous changes in the constitution of the LCA. Nearly all of the proposals were adopted. They were far-reaching and constituted, among other things, a substantial increase of power reposed in the hands of the president, giving him, for example, greater authority over the secretary of the church and over the bureaus called "boards."

But the great leap came when the merger of the Augustana Church with the ULCA and two smaller groups was constructed. It afforded the opportunity for radical changes in the distribution of power in the ULCA, the opportunity that "leaders in the church" had long desired, at least a decade long. Power now suddenly flowed in a stream to top echelons. This is not the place to set forth in detail the sharp contrasts between the distribution of power in the ULCA and its antecedents on the one hand, and that in the LCA on the other. From his point of view Alfons Koechlin was right: The ULCA was, in its constitution at least, a federation in which the synods were the *sources* of the powers vested in the top levels. But the structure of the LCA has by its constitutions reversed all that. The synods now have only such constitutions and such remnants of power as the president of the church and his executive council and the conventions of the LCA give to them.

I know of no Lutheran church of considerable size in the whole world in which the president or bishop has such sweeping powers. I know of no group of persons in any Lutheran church of considerable size in which the constitutions vest such great powers in a president and an executive council as is the case in the LCA. In this remarkable turnabout of polity the most crucial factor was the personality of Franklin Clark Fry.

This kind of ecclesiastical structure, if it is long continued, will, in my judgment, prove to be a definite disservice to Lutheranism in America. It can probably not be proved, as some newspapers asserted two or three years ago, that the decline of benevolence contributions in the LCA exceeds the decline in other church bodies, and that this is due to the extraordinary personal pressures as exerted by the president upon the colleges and seminaries of the church. But it can be proved that other large Lutheran bodies in America will never consent to become subject to such high and deep powers as now reside in the presidency and presidium of the LCA, and thus the good cause of cooperation and unity among all American Lutherans is being delayed.

The towering monolith of church polity that was born with the creation of the LCA could come about only through ignorance of the congregational polity traditional among Lutherans, or through misunderstanding or conscious violation of the polity implications of the Lutheran confessional writings. To this writer it seems to grow out of an inexact theological conception of what the church really is. Some years ago there came from New York (not from Dr. Fry) a pronouncement to the effect that anyone who opposed the terms proposed at the top level of the ULCA was really opposing the Holy Spirit. The speaker did not realize that in the Lutheran conception of the church, the Spirit of God is quite as fully present and active in the smallest battalion of a Christian congregation as it is in the ponderous overheadquarters of the commander in chief.

In my view as a student of history there is considerable danger in such a concentration of ecclesiastical power. And there are others who think so. Such dangers have not yet been realized, although some rulings from the president's chair at conventions and some "interpretations" of the LCA constitution by the president have aroused misgivings in some quarters.

But there are signs of change ahead, in the church as well as the state. From many quarters come the accents of dissent both in the nation and in the Christian organizations. There is a growing demand for a "new federalism" that will change the direction of the power-flow. The monolith must disappear. The "church in each place" must come into its rights again.

And indeed a student of historical trends can already discern manifest signs of change in this respect, both in Catholic and in Protestant churches.

See, for example, the NEW YORK TIMES of August 10, 1969, pages 1 and 64, where the reporter-analyst of church trends shows that a much larger portion of benevolence contributions of church people is now being retained by the territories and localities. This, the reporter explains, is due to the fact that a much larger portion of the activities of the church bodies is now in the area of welfare and social services, and that these services can be best applied by a new federalism in the churches. This development in benevolence giving, the analyst suggests, is a real threat to what he calls the present "massive build-up of large national bureaucracies" so characteristic of some Christian bodies. The reporter describes the growing "concern for decentralizing all sorts of . . . powerful hierarchies," the increase of resistance to quotas and apportionments of moneys to be distributed by the Establishment, the quiet "revolution against excessive authority," and the call for the "redistribution of wealth and power." In all of this he includes by name the Lutheran Church in America.

And so it is. In our church a relaxation of the paper autocracy and oligarchy seems to be in process. It may not come through a relentless tide of dissatisfaction, nor a crippling collapse of benevolence giving, nor by constitutional amendment. It may come by intentional neglect of authoritarian restrictions and controls, or it may come simply through changes in leadership. It is probable that if Dr. Fry could have lived a normal span of years, with his clear perception of trends and his foresight in planning, he would have started to lead us through this transition so clearly indicated by trends in almost every aspect of American culture. For he was a great leader, indeed.

---

[1] All this is set in larger framework in the author's *Basic History of Lutheranism in America* (Philadelphia, 1964 edition, especially pp. 356-371), and presented in much greater detail by Professor Dorris A. Flesner in his microfilmed Hartford doctoral dissertation on "The Role of the Lutheran Churches of America in the Formation of the World Council of Churches," 1956, 359 pages, based largely upon the personal correspondence of Knubel and Wentz.

The LCA Minutes of 1964 contain a statement of "Sound Principles for LCA Interchurch Relationships" (pp. 401-402), defining the "evangelical principle" and the "representative principle." Cf. the LCA Executive Council Minutes, 1969, pp. 584-594, on LCA Inter-church Relationships.

For other views, see the memos by Reed (No. 2), Cavert (73), H. P. Van Dusen (79), and Niles (86) in this volume, and Cavert's discussion in his *Church Cooperation and Unity in America*, pp. 274-276.

26

Theodore G. Tappert

Professor Tappert raises a theological question about Dr. Fry's ecclesiology.

F. C. Fry on Church Polity

I do not intend to elaborate here on the admiration I had for Franklin Clark Fry's many gifts: his phenomenal memory, his astonishing parliamentary skill, his rare talent for analysis, his sharp discernment of the ecclesiastical implications in an issue, his intense loyalty to his church, and so forth. Others will deal with such matters at length, I am sure, and I will undoubtedly concur in all that they say.

I propose simply to make a modest suggestion that may contribute to an understanding of this man's work. I have in mind a theological implication in his ecclesiology. He was not a "professional theologian," as he often conceded, but he had more than a little acquaintance with theology and knew how to value what professional theologians were about. However, he was vocationally preoccupied with ecclesiastical structures and their practical operation. The consequence was, perhaps inevitably, that the search for arguments to buttress some form of polity or other caused him at times to press his own theological convictions into strange shapes.

A case in point is the notion that the church must be in the form of an ellipse with two foci, the church at large and the local congregation.[1] It is of course possible to draw a diagram of an organization in this way. But actually the church exists wherever the Word of God and true faith are, as the Lutheran confessions put it. This means that not only part of the church but the whole church exists in every local assembly of Christians "among whom the gospel is preached in its purity and the holy sacraments are administered according to the gospel" (Augsburg Confession, Article VII). This is not to deny that the so-called church at large has important functions to perform which local congregations could not perform effectively, or perform at all, by themselves. Nor does it imply that the

---

(b. 1904) Joining the Philadelphia Seminary faculty in 1931, Dr. Tappert has been professor of church history since 1938, and for over two decades editor of the Lutheran Church Quarterly and its successor, the Lutheran Quarterly, and briefly of the LWF's Lutheran World Review. He served on the reconstruction and relief staff of the LWF in Germany 1947-48. He has been a member of the Board of Publication of the ULCA and the LCA since 1944. He has played a leading role in several scholarly societies, and in inter-Lutheran and Reformed-Lutheran negotiations.

ideal form of church organization is congregational, as some have hastily concluded. In fact, there is no permanently ideal form of church organization at all. It is ever incumbent on Christians to rely on their reason to fashion those structures of church and ministry which will best serve the proclamation of the gospel and the cultivation and expression of faith in their own time and place.

Dr. Fry was successful to a high degree in fashioning such patterns of organization for his day. His practice was exceptional, but some of the arguments he employed to support it were at best vulnerable. I am suggesting that his great achievements should not be judged—as if anybody would be tempted to judge him so!—by his random theological opinions. I would add a related question that should be worth exploring at length: What really were his ecclesiological convictions?

---

[1] 1958 ULCA Minutes, pp. 37-38. Cf. LCA constitution, Article IV, on the nature of the church.

27

Martin J. Heinecken

Professor Heinecken analyzes Dr. Fry's concern with theology: his views of its function in ecumenical and inter-Lutheran relations, and in church pronouncements on important subjects; his conservative theological foundation and its effect on his churchmanship.

Dr. Fry's Concern With Theology

Although Dr. Fry did not, to my knowledge, contribute in writing to the field of theology, it would be a great mistake to conclude that he had no interest in theology or no insight into the problems and that he made no theological contribution. A man of his giant intellectual powers and critical acumen could not fail to have a vital interest in theology. His own judgments were always theologically based judgments. Consistently he stressed the importance of the best possible theological education for the ordained ministers and other leaders of the church as well as the importance of theology for every one of the priesthood of believers. He vented his characteristic spleen on more than one occasion upon a minister of the church who blithely made crucial theological judgments and then ended up by saying either triumphantly or disparagingly, "Of course, I am not a theologian." "Imagine," Dr. Fry said in effect, "climbing into the dentist's chair and watching him line up all those ominous-looking tools and then just before having him climb into your mouth, hearing him say, 'Of course, I am not a dentist.'"

For Dr. Fry the very being of the church, its message and mission, depended upon its theology. No decision was ever made except on a theological basis. In ecumenical relations theological considerations played the major role. The influence which Dr. Fry exerted upon the shaping of the World Council of Churches and later as chairman of its Central Committee is well known and should not be underestimated. Not only did he insist upon a council of "churches," rather than a geographical confederation, but he formulated both the "representative" and "confessional" principles, which have upheld the necessity of theological integrity.

(b. 1902) Dr. Heinecken has been professor of systematic theology at the Philadelphia Seminary since 1945. He has been a member of numerous committees and commissions appointed to draw up church statements on various theological and practical subjects. From 1956 to 1962 he served on the ULCA Commission of Adjudication. He was a delegate to the LWF assemblies of 1957 and 1963.

With this it may come as a surprise to many how conservative a Lutheran Dr. Fry really was. In the informal discussions held between representatives of the Lutheran Church–Missouri Synod and the Lutheran Church in America shortly before his death, for example, he stated that he had never received communion except in a Lutheran service from a Lutheran minister and had never participated in a service of intercommunion. It should also be said that the progress made with the Lutheran Church–Missouri Synod in those informal talks was one of the things that brightened the last few agonizing months of his life. At the last of these informal meetings he attended, although he was in extreme pain, he was in the highest of spirits. Whereas at one time he had been very disdainful of friendly relations with the Lutheran Church–Missouri Synod, there was decided change in the last year or so and nothing would have gladdened his heart so much as to have lived to see the accomplishment of Lutheran unity. On one point, however, he was adamant: There were to be no additional official confessional statements drawn up as the basis for unity. The common acceptance of the Lutheran confessions is a sufficient basis and there has to be mutual trust as to the integrity of this confessional subscription. Hence he initiated the informal conversations in order that thereby mutual confidence might be achieved—*as indeed it was.*

As for the nature of Dr. Fry's own theological predilections in the ongoing theological debate it would be difficult to make a judgment. To my knowledge he did not have any intimate theological advisers. In any case, if he did, the present writer was not one of them. Although he listened to and respected my judgment, he never entered into intimate theological dialog. Perhaps there were others with whom he did. It is significant, however, that he gave active support to the theological statements accepted by the church during his administration, e.g., "The Doctrine of the Ministry," 1952, "The Statement on the Sacrament of the Altar and its Implications," 1960. It is also significant that he was critical of the 1966 LCA statement on the doctrine of the ministry.[1] This is not to suggest that Dr. Fry agreed with every detail of these documents, but certainly he did agree with their general tenor. Whether or not he agreed with the underlying theology, in this he was absolutely consistent: Whatever the church in convention decided upon he carried out most meticulously and to the last detail, even when, on occasion, it ran counter to his own judgment—perhaps then more meticulously than otherwise in order to prove to the church the consequences of its folly.

If I were to venture a guess I would say that the basic theological position to which Dr. Fry adhered was that which he learned from his teacher, H. E. Jacobs, as set forth in his *Summary of the Christian Faith* (1906). Of course, it would be naive to suggest that Dr. Fry did not recognize the "datedness" of this theology (e.g., the "dogmatic" finality of the question-and-answer form with the attendant proof passages). Nevertheless, the whole classical structure of this theology must have appealed to his orderly mind and it is my considered judgment that in all essential matters his basic theology was shaped by this summary of the seventeenth century dogmaticians rather than by the theology that emerged from the Luther renaissance, the Barthian revival, and the more recent Bultmann controversy and the subsequent reaction to it in a new emphasis upon history. Much of this must have seemed to him as a private sport of the professional theologians, while the life of the church continued to be shaped by something more basic and more stable. There is no question, at least, about his interest in the Lutheran liturgy and the preservation of it both for the sake of its classical theological structure as well as for its esthetic appeal in the language of King James. He had no love for meddling with the liturgy for the sake of popular appeal any more than for theological dispute carried on for its own sake.

Finally, his violent reaction to the criticisms of the institutional church and his militant opposition to the enthusiasm for the unstructured church must have been obvious to everyone. This was to be expected of one who used his genius to build a structure for the church which would enable it most effectively to *be* the church and to carry out the mission of the church. It would be a great mistake to suppose that his interest in the writing of constitutions was merely the indulgence of a private whim or the occasion for the display of his own brilliance. The church simply had to have the right kind of form in order properly to channel its dynamic. In this he was consistently Lutheran—whatever one's judgment might be as to the structure that emerged.

To some, perhaps, Dr. Fry—rarely, if ever, seen in public except in his clericals—may have appeared as the embodiment of the Establishment with all its "hang-ups" (the modern phrase that either sums up whatever impedes progress or else designates a person's own psychological confusions—in this case, the former). To me, however, he remains the embodiment of a humble servant of the Lord, who dedicated all his genius to the shaping and functioning of a church in and through which God's will might be accomplished. If there is such a thing as ecclesiastical pride which glories in the institution, there is also a more subtle form of pride, which means to identify its peculiar concern, whether this be racial injustice, the war on poverty, or opposition to the war in Vietnam, with the only genuine expression of Christianity. Of this pride Dr. Fry was not guilty. In these days of justified as well as unjustified criticism of the institutional church, Dr. Fry may well serve as a symbol of a balanced view which would never *identify* the true church with any institutional embodiment, and yet would recognize the necessity of a proper visible expression of the "hidden" reality of that church against which the gates of hell shall not prevail. So in this way he would serve also as a symbol of a "lived theology," for it is of the essence of a Christian theology that it exists only as enfleshed in human beings.

---

[1] See ULCA Minutes for the first two examples. For the third, see LCA Minutes, 1966, pp. 434-447; this statement failed to gain the church's approval, even after revision, at the next two biennial conventions. Cf. the memo of Henninger (No. 15).

28

Donald R. Heiges

Dr. Heiges concentrates on President Fry's concern for the church's mission in higher education, both secular and theological.

Dr. Franklin Clark Fry entered my life personally in 1945 when he became president of the United Lutheran Church in America. At that time I was serving as pastor to Lutheran students in New York City, and my visits to 231 Madison Avenue increased in frequency because Dr. Fry's door was always open to me. This availability continued until his death despite several occasions when I made decisions which were a great disappointment to him. I always regarded him as my "chief pastor," and he never disappointed me in that relationship.

When I became, in 1950, executive secretary of the Division of Student Service (later named the Division of College and University Work) of the National Lutheran Council, I discovered to my great amazement that Dr. Fry read every word of the minutes and other official documents of the division. Between 1950 and 1958 I received perhaps a dozen letters, memoranda, and notes (hand-written while in flight overseas) calling my attention to inaccuracies, conflicts with NLC policy or ULCA polity, and even infelicitous phrases. Obviously if he "combed" with such care the minutes and reports of my division, he did the same for all NLC documents, as well as for all the documents of the United Lutheran Church in America, the National Council of Churches, the Lutheran World Federation, the World Council of Churches, and many other agencies and organizations! This attention to detail required an enormous amount of time. Where did he find the time in his global schedule?

My reference to college and university work suggests some observations upon Dr. Fry's posture with regard to the church's mission in higher education, and especially to campus ministry and theological education, with both of which I have been closely related.

No church leader during his lifetime was more committed than Dr. Fry to the mission of the church in the colleges and universities. In fact,

---

(b. 1910) After serving as executive secretary of the NLC Division of College and University Work (1950-58), and dean of the Chicago Lutheran Seminary (1958-62), Dr. Heiges has been president of Gettysburg Seminary since 1962. Concurrently he served as president of Philadelphia Seminary (1964-70). He has been a councillor of the NLC (1958-66) and chairman of agencies on student work for both the LWF and the National Council of Churches.

he looked upon this mission as being among the church's highest priorities. This was made evident in several ways.

In the first place, every year he accepted an impressive number of invitations to preach or to speak on campuses in this country and abroad. This activity he frequently referred to with pride as his "university circuit." He told me that when a conflict occurred between an invitation to speak at a university and another type of invitation he usually chose the former. He did so not because on many such occasions honorary degrees were conferred upon him but because he viewed each invitation as a God-given opportunity to make his witness to Christ and his church in an arena of critical importance. And he was capable of making that witness with spiritual power and intellectual integrity. The invitations continued to come year after year because he merited the respect of the university community.

Secondly, his devotion to the church's ministry in private and public institutions of higher learning was unswerving even when at times he had misgivings about the leadership of the enterprise. To those of us directly involved in campus ministry his devotion and enthusiastic support were magnificent. This devotion and support were evidenced not only orally, and this he did with eloquence, but also by action. A hard-headed realist, he backed up his words with strong support of the church's financial investment in campus ministry.

During my eight years as executive secretary of the Division of College and University Work Dr. Fry threw his not inconsiderable influence back of every request I presented to the National Lutheran Council for increasingly large annual allocations to operating budgets and for capital funds. The knowledge that I could count on him, especially when the going became rough, created in me a confidence, indeed a boldness, to make, what seemed to some, unreasonable demands of the participating church bodies of the National Lutheran Council to undergird financially the campus ministry.

It must also be noted that Dr. Fry's willingness to support the church's ministry in the college and university world was matched by his insistence upon competence and faithfulness in the carrying out of this ministry. He had a holy impatience with less than perfection in performance even though he was painfully aware of human weakness and perversity. Following a visit to a university where he sensed either incompetence or less than full dedication on the part of campus ministry staff he did not hesitate to slap my wrist with the sharp rejoinder: "We are providing you with money to invest—not to squander!"

Closely related to Dr. Fry's devotion to the church's mission in the colleges and universities was his deep concern for theological education, especially in the Lutheran Church in America. During the negotiations leading to the formation of the Lutheran Church in America he had hoped that responsibility for the seminaries would be lodged in a strong Board of Theological Education as the instrument of the whole church. The eventual compromise which divided responsibility between the synods and the Board of Theological Education weakened the possibility of realization of his dream of three very strong LCA seminaries in the United States. To realize that dream he advocated more effective utilization of institutional resources. Thus he applauded the consolidation of four seminaries into the Lutheran School of Theology at Chicago; he used the authority of his office to help bring about the merger of Central Seminary with the LSTC; and he gave strong support to the BTE recommendations, as adopted by the 1964 LCA convention, urging the unification of the Gettysburg and Philadelphia seminaries, and the merger of the Hamma School of Theology with either the LSTC or the American Lutheran Church's Evangelical Lutheran Theological Seminary (Columbus).

Although I participated from 1958 to 1962 in the negotiations leading to the creation of the Lutheran School of Theology at Chicago, my major involvement has been with the two seminaries in the Northeast. On September 1, 1962, I undertook the responsibilities of the presidency of the Lutheran Theological Seminary at Gettysburg. On January 30, 1963, I attended by invitation a meeting of the Philadelphia Seminary's Joint Board—Faculty Long Range Planning Committee at which Dr. Jerald C. Brauer, dean of the Divinity School of the University of Chicago, presented an oral report of his exploration of potential places for the relocation of the seminary. Dean Brauer concluded his report by recommending that the Lutheran Theological Seminary at Philadelphia be relocated in Washington, D. C. Dr. Fry, also present by invitation, immediately responded with enthusiasm for the recommendation. In the discussion which followed a committee member asked me about the implications of relocation in Washington for the Gettysburg Seminary. I replied to the effect that such location on the territory of one of Gettysburg's supporting synods would, in my judgment, force the Gettysburg Seminary to re-examine its position as a separate institution. (The Philadelphia Seminary Board eventually rejected Dean Brauer's recommendation and voted instead to relocate the Seminary at the University of Pennsylvania.[1])

In June, 1963, Dr. Fry represented the LCA at the convention of the Central Pennsylvania Synod. During an inter-session recess we reviewed the January meeting in Philadelphia and subsequent events, and Dr. Fry indicated that (a) he still looked with favor upon the proposal to relocate the Philadelphia Seminary in Washington, and (b) he regarded university orientation as an issue of lesser importance in the Northeast than the unification of the seminaries, although he hoped that both could be achieved.

I have briefly described these events because they indicate that Dr.

Fry regarded the consolidation of the Gettysburg and Philadelphia seminaries as the *sine qua non* of first-rate Lutheran theological education in the East. All other factors were to him secondary in importance. In fact, the unification of these seminaries remained as one of the major unfulfilled objectives of his leadership of the Lutheran Church in America.

Dr. Fry's total commitment to the movement for the reduction in numbers of LCA seminaries reflected his passionate dedication to quality theological education, which he was convinced could not be achieved without consolidation of existing schools and resources. The mathematics of reduction was a means to a necessary end. He gave public expression to his concern for excellence on several occasions in the mid-sixties. What he had to say on two of these occasions is illuminating.

Speaking at the Lutheran Theological Seminary at Philadelphia on October 21, 1964, Dr. Fry called for a new "determination for the raising of the standards of education for the Christian ministry among us." He pointed out that "a perceptive observer at the recent convention of our Church in Pittsburgh remarked that it was perfectly obvious that every report at that convention consciously or unconsciously called for or demanded more highly educated men and women, beginning with the laity and reaching a pinnacle in the ministry of the Gospel." Dr. Fry went on to say: "Anyone who cannot recognize this need is blind or stubborn or has the unfortunate combination of both qualities. With the level of education rising about us in a way that should abash us and rebuke us it would be no less than devastating if theological education alone were to remain stationary." In appealing for the upgrading of theological education he contrasted the requirements of other professions and observed: "It is not that I am interested only in the prestige of the clergy, but there's no doubt about it that there has to be an integrity and dignity in the ministerial office in relation to all other vocations in order for the Church to occupy the place in men's minds and in their estimates that it richly and necessarily deserves." (Quoted from two unpublished addresses.)

In connection with the 125th anniversary observance of Concordia Seminary in St. Louis on December 9, 1964, Dr. Fry spoke as follows:

"The first thing that the church expects of a theological seminary in these days is that it shall wisely prepare men to be pastors of congregations as the congregations of the future are likely to be thirty years from now. . . . This means that the educational success of a theological seminary demands immense prophetic foresight and calls for the daring required to fit men to the radically altered context of a generation that is just now being born."

"Secondly, the Church has the right to expect its seminaries to equip men with theology that has feet. Feet to walk into, out into the actual world of men. . . . Theology needs to breed a faith that can interpenetrate every one of the disciplines of the mind. For that purpose a theological student ought to be fully equipped in physical science, in the humanities, in the social sciences. There needs to be immediate contiguity and constant interaction between theological study and every other part of university scholarship in these days. The place where minds are blindingly awake is precisely in the university." (*Educational Integrity and Church Responsibility.* Papers and Proceedings of the Fifty-First Annual Convention of the National Lutheran Educational Conference, January 9-11, 1965, pages 14-16.)

I should like to conclude these observations and reflections with a reference to a meeting of the Executive Committee of the Lutheran World Federation in the summer of 1957 preceding the LWF assembly in Minneapolis. As vice-chairman of the executive committee Dr. Fry played his usual no-nonsense role in the committee's deliberation of insisting upon facts, their accurate interpretation, and precisely formulated motions. At the beginning of the second day of the meeting it was Dr. Fry's turn "to lead in devotions." His role changed completely to that of a warm-hearted pastor and preacher. As he read as the lesson of the day the familiar story of the Prodigal Son, I had the feeling that those present began to sink into somnolence on the assumption that everything that could be said about the passage had been said hundreds of times—but not for long. Within minutes after Dr. Fry began his meditation every person in the room was wide-awake and indeed "hanging upon" each word as *the* Word sounded with authenticity and clarity. At the conclusion of the prayer and benediction a hush fell upon the room which the chairman was reluctant to break. After the morning session adjourned several committee members confessed to me that Dr. Fry's devotions that day had been one of the mountain peaks of their lives. When Dr. Fry is characterized as a giant the tendency is to think of his brilliance, his overpowering competence, his fantastic capacity for work (and all this and more is true), but let us remember that he was also a giant in the realm of the Spirit.

---

[1] This latter plan was eventually abandoned.

29

Harold Haas

Dr. Haas analyzes the attitudes of Dr. Fry toward the church's role in social issues.

It is not easy to record a few thoughts about Franklin Clark Fry. He was one of the rare persons one meets in a lifetime. This uniqueness was rooted in the complexity of his personality and character. Whatever one person can say about him, another can probably say something quite different, with both being quite honest about their recollections of actual experience.

My major area of contact with him was through service for a decade (1957-1966) on the staff of the Board of Social Missions of the United Lutheran Church in America and the Board of Social Ministry of the Lutheran Church in America. These were years in which the church was trying to formulate new theological and program responses to major social issues.

The attitudes and actions of Dr. Fry concerning this attempt are hard to evaluate. He supported the work of the Board of Social Ministry without reservation. He would periodically write and speak on some of the issues (e.g., race relations) with commitment, courage, and brilliance. There is not the slightest question in my mind about his *personal* commitment to eliminate social injustice of every kind—or his belief that every Christian should have such commitment. He was, however, wary about too deep an involvement of the church in such issues.

"Social action is a substitute for faith," he said on various occasions. This did not mean he was opposed to social action if it was based on fundamental theological grounds. He did, however, see the danger of a social action or secular city theology that had lost all the vital reference points of the historical Christian faith. Generally, in his role as president of the church, he needed some prodding by persons or circumstances before making a forthright move. When the move came, his words and actions made no uncertain sound. It is, however, my honest recollection that he

---

(b. 1917) Dr. Haas was executive secretary of the ULCA Board of Social Missions and then of the LCA Board of Social Ministry (1957-66). He has been active in the National Council of Churches, serving on its General Board from 1956 to 1965. After a period as dean of Wagner College, Staten Island, New York, he returned to church administration in 1970 as executive secretary of both the Division of Mission Services and the Division of Welfare Services of the LCUSA.

moved with some uncertainty in the area of social ministry as it was emerging in his last years. If this sounds negative, it should be pointed out that this remains one of the uncertainties of the church. The compulsions for involvement are increased; the dangers of collapsing the church into the world are even more acute.

On a more personal level, Dr. Fry was one of the easiest of all persons to work with. The dominance of his mind, personality, and experience sometimes made it seem from the outside that those working with him would be submerged or overwhelmed. I am conscious of no time in ten years that he ever interfered with the work the Board of Social Ministry (or Social Missions) or its staff was called upon to perform. He would regularly call all to account on the basis of the rules adopted by the church. Within those rules, boards and staff members operated with full support from Dr. Fry whether or not he agreed with decisions. He could sometimes be rough on staff incompetence. On the other hand, one could disagree with him directly and frankly. While he was always "on stage" in public, there was little pretentiousness about him. (Generally when he wanted to see me, he would call personally on the telephone and ask if he should come to my office.)

Quite apart from some of the major trends of our time, Dr. Fry was committed without reservation to the organized church and to the transcendental dimensions of the Christian faith. There was much more to his Christian commitment, but the rest was subservient to these primary aspects of Christian faith and life. The brilliance of his intellect, his remarkable articulateness, his clarity of concept of leadership, his fantastic energy and, above all, his unwavering Christian commitment, made him one of the unforgettable persons and church leaders of his time.

30

Minerva (Mrs. Charles W., Jr.) Baker

The late Mrs. Baker, a leader in Lutheran women's work, writes on Dr. Fry's approach to the place of women in the church.

My first acquaintance with Dr. Fry as a Christian leader began in Des Moines, Iowa, at a convention of the Women's Missionary Society of the United Lutheran Church in America. He was a young man at that time and was scheduled to give the closing devotions of the convention. The convention, however, had gone overtime, and another convention was moving in. A request came to the presiding officer to omit the closing devotions that had been assigned to Dr. Fry.

I happened to be sitting beside his mother. She said to me, "Franklin will never stand for this. He has always been ten steps ahead of me since the time he was a child."

Just them he walked to the platform and asked that everyone in the back be seated. At once there was perfect quiet. He proceeded with his closing devotions, speaking as only he could speak. The members of the incoming convention listened as attentively as if they were a part of our convention. From that day on, I recognized Dr. Fry as a man of promise, a man with a compelling personality who commanded respect and generally succeeded in getting what he wanted and what he thought was right.

It was while I was serving as vice-president and president of the WMS of the ULCA that I learned to know him really well. My honest feeling was that Dr. Fry was not too happy about our women's organization, mainly because the women decided just how and where their funds should be allocated. There was a time when some members of the WMS resented being told what they should do as an auxiliary of the church.

Dr. Fry said once, "Too many women want to dictate rather than cooperate." His idea was that the women of the church should cooperate from the local level all the way to the top in carrying out the whole program of the whole church at home and abroad.

(1896-1970) A high school guidance counselor and Lutheran pastor's wife, long a resident of western Pennsylvania, Mrs. Baker was president of the ULCA Women's Missionary Society, later called the United Lutheran Church Women, 1946-52. She participated briefly in postwar relief work in Europe. She was a member of the ULCA Executive Board (1956-62) and the LCA Executive Council (1962-66). She was a councillor of the NLC for six years, a delegate to the 1963 LWF assembly, and a member of the LWF Commission on Stewardship and Congregational Life.

Dr. Fry felt, nevertheless, that there was definitely a place for the women's organization in the work of the church. He was particularly interested in their having a leading role in the ministry of mercy, and in his messages to them he always stressed this aspect of Christian service, for which he thought they were peculiarly fitted.

He was always ready to help the women's group, too, in any way that he could. The time came when the WMS needed a new constitution and bylaws. I recall an extremely hot day in July (before the days of air conditioning) when Dr. Fry spent the entire day with our board, guiding us in the preparation of a proper document. As we floundered in confusion at what should be placed in the main constitution and what should be put in the bylaws, he was always able to clarify the situation. When we wallowed in a slough of words and ideas, he was never at a loss for the exact, concise phrasing which pulled us out of our trouble. It was a marvelous display of learning and balanced judgment, and he took pleasure in giving freely of these gifts.

At the time of the merger out of which the Lutheran Church in America was formed, I was asked to be the moderator for the organizational meeting of Lutheran Church Women. This was going to be a difficult task which I did not wish to assume. I asked Dr. Fry's opinion about serving in this capacity.

He said, "Have you a right as a Christian woman to refuse? Pray it over." Then he continued, "I can promise you that I will be sitting there in the front row to assist you in any way I am needed."

He told me once that he had memorized Robert's Rules of Order. He said, if at any time a parliamentarian needed him, just to ask him for help.

Dr. Fry was sure, however, that the women at the organizational meeting of the LCW would not ask many questions or have long discussions from the floor. I told him that he did not know women as well as I did, and that I expected we would be pressed for time and might have to resort to a question box. At the close of the meeting, that was the one time that Dr. Fry said to me, "You were right and I was wrong."

Dr. Fry gave a pleasing report of the newly organized LCW to the first meeting of the Executive Council of the LCA (to which I had been elected). "At the beginning," he said, "you could cut the tension with a knife, but when it was over and the officers were elected, one from each of the merging groups, the women were walking out, arm in arm." He was well satisfied with the new organization. He was favorable toward the new plan which provided that the women place their contributions in one fund rather than allocating them to different boards and causes.

From time to time I had many serious discussions with Dr. Fry in regard to the place of women's work in the church. I said that if at any time I was named by him to serve in a certain position merely because I was a woman and he was appointing me only to give representation to women, then I would not wish to accept that appointment. On the other hand, if he felt that I had something to contribute as a Christian and a member of the church, I would be glad to serve. He agreed with me on that point of view.

My first contact with the National Lutheran Council occurred when Dr. Fry requested me by wire to go to Chicago to substitute for one of the men who was unable to attend the NLC meeting. When I attended this meeting as a substitute, it was apparent that a number of the other men were not particularly receptive to the idea of having a woman at the meeting. Dr. Fry kindly explained that I was there at the request of the ULCA. He had a very special way of putting one at ease under trying circumstances, such as these. The following year I was mentioned by the ULCA as a member of NLC.

When the Lutheran World Federation met in Hannover, Germany, following the Second World War, a special division was given over to women's work. Dr. Fry did not regard this plan favorably. He suggested to me, as a participant in the women's division, that a request be sent to the floor of the general meeting of LWF that we no longer have a separate division for women, but that consideration be given to the proposal that women be included in some of the main committees. This plan was adopted.

For all his learning and intellectual ability, Dr. Fry possessed very human qualities. He was an ardent baseball fan. The general convention was being held in Atlantic City at the time the Pittsburgh Pirates were playing their final game with the New York Yankees. He asked a page to hand him regular reports on the progress of the game. He said to me at the opening of the afternoon session, "You Pittsburgh fans have my sympathy—the Pirates are not in the running." But at the end of the game, he said, "They won by accident." A great fan, but a poor loser!

Because I was conscious of Dr. Fry's brilliance, keen insight, impulsiveness, and determination to hold to his convictions, I once feared him and stood more in awe of him than of any other person in the ULCA. Many of his co-workers felt the same way about him. There were times when he could be very critical and even sarcastic.

When I was on a program and I knew he was in the audience, sometimes it would be difficult for me to speak with ease. I said to him on one occasion, "I get butterflies and weaken when I know you are listening."

His answer was, "Any speaker who is so sure of himself that he does not have butterflies will never be worth hearing." He assured me that he was a most sympathetic and understanding person and that he himself had had to conquer, to a great degree, that same feeling from the time he was a young man.

It was then that I began to understand how tender-hearted he could be. When you really knew him, you discovered that he was gentle, kind, and considerate. In spite of his busy schedule when he went to other parts of the world, he always remembered the members of the Executive Board of the ULCA and later the members of the Executive Council of the LCA with cards or greetings.

When you came to know him better, you discovered, too, that his criticism was usually constructive. Even what appeared at first to be sarcasm could prove to be a soul-searching experience.

Dr. Fry knew that there was some opposition to him at times because he was so frank, and even blunt, in the statements he made. He did not wish to stand in the way of progress nor prevent the fulfillment of his cherished dream to bring the churches together. He told me once that if he felt he was a stumbling block to the merging of the churches, he would be willing to step out of the scene at any time.

Time has proven that he was not a stumbling block. Rather he was the great guiding spirit who was able to help bring the merger to reality and to lead and direct our church in its formative years.

In 1962 the merger of the Lutheran Church in America took place, and Dr. Fry was elected its president. Memos 31 to 40 focus on *the process of merger and aspects of the life of the new church.* Five of the writers were members of the Joint Commission on Lutheran Unity.

31

Malvin H. Lundeen

As chairman of the Joint Commission on Lutheran Unity and leader of the Augustana delegation, Dr. Lundeen writes of Dr. Fry's role in the origin and progress of the merger negotiations.

Franklin Clark Fry—A Man for Specifics

The date was March 28, 1955; the place, Chicago, Illinois. The Commission on Ecumenical Relations of the Augustana Lutheran Church had invited representatives of the various Lutheran bodies in the United States to confer with it on the question of "what constitutes essential conditions of Lutheran unity in America."[1] During the morning of that day a conference was held with the Lutheran Church—Missouri Synod representatives. In the evening it was the committee of thirty-six representing the four bodies which in 1960 organized the American Lutheran Church, with which the meeting was held. There were polite conversation, repetitious presentations of the traditional points of view, and the usual indecisive conclusions.

In the afternoon of that same day, a meeting was held with the Committee on Relations to American Lutheran Church Bodies of the United Lutheran Church in America with Dr. Franklin Clark Fry as its chairman. During the early part of that conference the discussion followed pretty much the same pattern of generalities as were seen in the other discussions. But suddenly there came an electrifying change. President

(b. 1901) Dr. Lundeen was successively president of Augustana's Iowa Conference (1946), vice-president of the Augustana Lutheran Church (1951) and president (1959-62), and secretary of the LCA (1962-68). He was chairman of the JCLU 1956-62. He served on the NLC Executive Committee (1955-66), and became the first president of the Lutheran Council in the USA (1967-70). He was a member of the General Board of the National Council of Churches (1964-70), and a delegate to the 1963 LWF assembly and the 1968 World Council of Churches assembly. Since 1968 he has been assistant to the president of the LCA Minnesota Synod, and a member of the LCA Court of Adjudication.

Fry asked permission to present a communication on behalf of the ULCA, the gist of which was in these words:

> In behalf of The United Lutheran Church in America which has declared "its desire to merge with any or all" Lutherans in America, and has authorized this commission "to participate in drafting a constitution and in devising such organizational procedures as may seem wise in effecting union," we respectfully invite the Augustana Lutheran Church to appoint a commission of equal number to meet with us for that purpose and to join with us in issuing invitations to all other Lutheran church bodies to appoint like commissions. May the blessing of God our Saviour rest upon this endeavor to reveal openly the unity which we have already received as His precious gift.[2]

Dr. Fry called attention to the following five basic and specific points of consensus which

> impressively exhibit our already existing unity of faith and spirit.
>
> Like you in the Augustana Lutheran Church, we in the United Lutheran Church in America subscribe to all the confessions of the Evangelical Lutheran Church without any reservations of heart or mind.
>
> Like you, we hold that no further definitions of doctrine, in addition to the historic confessions of our Church, are necessary for Lutheran union, and we set up no other standards or tests apart from the confessions or alongside them.
>
> Like you, we desire all negotiations looking toward Lutheran union in America to be open to all Lutheran church bodies, and we extend pulpit and altar fellowship without exception to all.
>
> Like you, we fulfill ex animo the constitutional purpose of the Lutheran World Federation to foster Lutheran participation in ecumenical movements both internationally and nationally.
>
> Like you, we believe in and practice a large degree of local and regional autonomy in our church polity as a consistent application of the Lutheran principle.[3]

This invitation inspired, written and presented by Dr. Fry, was the "spark" which moved both the Augustana Church and the United Lutheran Church in America off dead center as far as a larger Lutheran unity was concerned. It can also be said that Dr. Fry's proposal brought Augustana back into the mainstream of its historical tradition. From 1870 to 1918 Augustana had been a member of the General Council. This relationship was terminated when the Augustana Church decided not to join with the Council, the General Synod, and the United Synod South to form the

United Lutheran Church in America in 1918. But with this invitation and its acceptance Augustana was again identified with that segment of American Lutheranism from which it had received so much during just slightly less than one-half of its century-long history.

The invitation was enthusiastically accepted by the Augustana Church at its ninety-sixth annual convention held in Gloria Dei church, St. Paul, Minnesota, June 13-19, 1955. On December 16, 1955, the following joint invitation was issued to all Lutheran bodies in America, "In gratitude to God for the unity in the Gospel that He has given to the Lutherans of America, and in the conviction that this unity ought now manifest itself in the organic union of our separate church bodies,

The United Lutheran Church in America
and the Augustana Evangelical Lutheran Church

respectfully invite your honorable church body to designate duly authorized representatives to meet with the commissions of our two Churches, and with similarly empowered representatives of other Lutheran church bodies, to consider such organic union as will give real evidence of our unity in the faith, and to proceed to draft a constitution and devise organizational procedures to effect union.

For the United Lutheran Church in America
Franklin Clark Fry
President
For the Augustana Evangelical Lutheran Church
Oscar A. Benson
President."[4]

As is now well known, only the American Evangelical Lutheran Church and the Finnish Evangelical Lutheran Church were able and willing to answer the invitation affirmatively. On December 12 and 13, 1956, representatives of these bodies together with those of the ULCA and Augustana met in Chicago, Illinois, and organized the Joint Commission on Lutheran Unity (JCLU). Much time was given over at that meeting to a consideration of the polity and the official doctrinal declarations of the four bodies represented. And, again it was Dr. Fry who moved the commission from the generalities of its discussion to the specifics which were so necessary if there was to be a proper beginning of the tremendous task which was being undertaken. He introduced the following statement which was unanimously adopted:

> After hearing the reading and interpretation of the doctrinal statements of the four churches here represented, the Commission rejoices to note that we have among us sufficient ground of agree-

> ment in the common confession of our faith, as witnessed by the Lutheran confessions, to justify further procedures in seeking for a basis for the organic union of our churches, including the formulation of a proposed constitution for a united church having in it articles on doctrine and practical matters of organization.[5]

And so, the work was launched which led to the formation of the Lutheran Church in America on June 28, 1962, after five and a half years of planning. In that short span of sixty-six months, many were the occasions when Dr. Fry moved the work along by this specific proposal and that. One remembers, not least of all, his service as chairman of the Committee on Constitutions, in the writing of each of which his incisive mind and ready command of language were clearly in evidence.

Many persons, of course, both within the JCLU and outside its membership, were involved in bringing into being this new ecclesiastical entity now known as the Lutheran Church in America. But without a doubt it was the presence on the commission of Franklin Clark Fry, a churchman deeply committed to his Lord and to the cause of Lutheran unity, that provided the impetus which moved the preparatory work along so rapidly, for, just as nature abhors a vacuum, so Dr. Fry abhorred time-consuming generalities. As a substitute for these, however, he was always ready creatively to suggest specific goals and procedures.

Just as this ability made him invaluable in bringing into being the LCA, so, no doubt, it was this same passion for the specific proposal which enabled him to contribute so richly to the Christian world generally.

Franklin Clark Fry was a man who "got things done," for he was a man for specifics.

---

[1] Report of the Ninety-Sixth Synod, Augustana Evangelical Lutheran Church, p. 440.
[2] *Ibid.*, p. 442.
[3] *Ibid.*, pp. 441-442
[4] Report of the Ninety-Seventh Synod, Augustana Evangelical Lutheran Church, p. 426.
[5] Report of the Ninety-Eighth Synod, Augustana Evangelical Lutheran Church, p. 459.

32

Conrad J. I. Bergendoff

Another veteran Augustana statesman discusses President Fry's role in the JCLU, particularly in the negotiations on membership of the clergy in secret societies. Then as a former LCA board secretary he assesses Fry's manner of leadership in the new church, in contrast with that of Archbishop Söderblom.

It had been my privilege to attend the Philadelphia Seminary a few years before Franklin Clark Fry arrived there. This meant that we had common memories of some of the leaders of the United Lutheran Church in its early years. Though he was a little younger I always felt in his presence that he was the older. For he did inspire respect by the variety of his gifts and his mature personality.

My most ineradicable impression of his leadership derives from an encounter during the proceeding of the Joint Commission on Lutheran Unity, when the merger of 1962 was being worked out. We had reached a point where sharp differences appeared between the representatives of the Augustana Lutheran Church and of the United Lutheran Church. In retrospect I view the episode as critical in the negotiations—indeed it might have been the occasion for the failure of the proposed merger.

The Augustana group had anticipated opposition. Its members knew that their church would not accept the stand of the ULCA on the question of membership in secret societies. Historically Augustana had held that a Christian could not consistently belong to organizations which, as far as known, professed a deism not in accord with the Christian faith. It had not been altogether willing to exclude from its congregations members of such organizations, though some of its pastors had carried this logic to such a point. In the merger it was clear that the ULCA would not accept the Augustana position. How then should we proceed?[1]

The Augustana group, knowing the practice of the congregations, had agreed beforehand that no attempt would be made to write into the proposed constitution a prohibition of lay membership in lodges. But it would

---

(b. 1895) As a young man a secretary to Archbishop Nathan Söderblom, Dr. Bergendoff became an eminent educator, theologian, and statesman in the Augustana Lutheran Synod (later Church). He was president of Augustana College and Seminary, Rock Island, Illinois, 1935-48, and continued as president of the college until 1962. From 1962 to 1964 he was the first executive secretary of the LCA Board of Theological Education. His many services include those of consultant to the American Military Government in Germany (1948), and member of several commissions and committees of the National Council of Churches and the LWF.

not yield on the point of membership of pastors in secret organizations, for on this the synod had a consistent record of a hundred years.

The debate in the commission was as heated as at any time in all the many sessions. Objection was raised by the ULCA to making a differentiation between pastors and laity. This argument did not impress Augustana, for in its thinking the pastor, by his unique place in the congregation, exercised influence by his example. There is no reason to recall the discussion here except to emphasize that we had reached a stage where Augustana, for all its interest in merger, was ready to break off.

Franklin Fry was chairman of his delegation. Obviously he did not side with Augustana. But when he saw the seriousness of the impasse, he asked for a separate caucus. As this took place we wondered if the merger was now possible. I have never heard what happened in the caucus. But when we resumed the chairman announced the reluctant agreement of his delegation. The result was Article VII, Section 4 of the constitution which denied ordination to members of "any organization which claims to possess in its teachings and ceremonies that which the Lord has given solely to His Church" (to the best of my knowledge this wording came from the pen of Dr. Fry).

It was the only time that I had to face Fry in direct opposition. My estimation of his character was deeply influenced by the encounter. In opposition he was courteous, firm, but not unyielding. For the sake of a higher goal he subordinated his own opinion and was ready to try to reach a conciliatory position. Incidentally, the episode illustrates the power he wielded in his own delegation, which was a strong one and unafraid to speak its mind.

There were occasions when the commission as a whole did not accept his guidance—few though these were. He wanted a smaller number of synods than was finally fixed. He argued for a centralization of church boards in New York—many preferred a wider diffusion. In general, I thought of him as conservative and I was surprised when he agreed to an unusual name of the church, "The Lutheran Evangelical Church"—a decision reversed at a following session![2]

During my two years as executive secretary of the Board of Theological Education—a position he persuaded me to take—I had many contacts with the president of the church. Both in personal conferences and in board meetings I had opportunity to see something of the quality of his leadership. I never ceased to wonder at his mastery of detail. He knew what was going on everywhere in the church. We were told in the days of the merger that he wrote the bylaws while in bed recuperating from illness. After the formation of the LCA he made it his business to follow through, and no church body could ever have had a more devoted leader, anxious to bring together the diverse strands of the union. He spent himself in countless meetings and innumerable travels to show his concern for every part of the new church. He wanted order, and clarity, and harmony. He was not a legalistic interpreter of the rules of the church body, but he was a superb administrator.

With his thorough knowledge of the church he could be pardoned, I think, a certain dictatorialness. He didn't have much patience with the fumbling and uncertainty that goes with the democratic process. Usually he had already pretty well concluded his position before discussion proceeded far. I recall once when he fixed on the word "dynamic" as a proper adjective for the church. And certainly that designation fitted his own style.

He had his idiosyncrasies. His gay laughter at some of his own expressions, his slapping of his knees in his glee, his looking around to see the reaction of his hearers to some declaration of his, amused those who were of more sober temperaments. I was sometimes surprised at the frankness of his criticisms of other churchmen—for instance, when he remarked about a prominent figure in the World Council, that this man was too hungry for power, or when, as often, he expressed his dismay at Lutherans who dragged their feet on the issue of unity. And for all his remarkable memory he could forget—as happened when the LCA delegation neglected to bring a present to the diocese of Uppsala on the observance of its 800th anniversary in 1965. We agreed on the desirability of reducing the number of seminaries, but I am not sure that he shared my optimism in regard to church colleges.

He could be jovial, as once when a small group celebrated a birthday of Dr. Luther Reed. Two hobbies often came to the surface—the fortunes, or misfortunes, of the New York Yankees and of the Democratic party. But on the whole I got the impression that he paid the price of loneliness for being the leader far out in front. Often he spoke of the one week a year he spent with his family at a private spot. The other fifty-one weeks left little leisure and unengagement for the cultivation of deep fellowships.

Yet I had abundant reason to count him as a friend. I owed to him my appointment to the delegation of the National Council of Churches to the Russian Church in 1962. He had some part in naming me to various inter-Lutheran theological commissions. He gave me the assignment of writing the preamble to the constitution of the LCA. It may be, therefore, that I am prejudiced in my writing of him, but my memories of him are those of a large-hearted, respected, and cherished friend and colleague.

I heard him speak on many occasions, on many subjects. It was my feeling that he could hardly find time to do much reading amid the many organizational duties that descended on him. I watched his close attention to the emergence of the constitution of the LCA. I remember his part in the restructuring of the National Council of Churches. We all know of his great role in the World Council. When could he read, and reflect? I heard him at community services, commencements, at conventions, and on television. His talent lay, I judged, not in probing deeply, but in seeing clearly and widely. And who had more vital contacts with men and women all over the world? Surely this meant broadening thought and deepening compassion. His monument is less in words than in the agencies he helped create. What other churchman has so spent himself in countless journeys across the nation, and the earth, in the cause of unity?

His genius was one of administration, and at a strategic time in the history of the church those gifts of his bore worldwide fruits. The Lutheran Church in America owes more of its character to the achievements of Franklin Clark Fry than anyone of us can measure.

* * *

The Lutheran church has known another great leader in this century, and I am tempted to contrast Franklin Clark Fry and Nathan Söderblom, especially since both have enduring significance in the annals of the ecumenical movement. I have watched both at close range in their offices and am impressed how different the qualities can be which the Lord uses in guiding the church. In Söderblom there was something of the bold visionary and daring dreamer, calling for a meeting of the churches in the midst of a world war. He could master detail, but only as it was necessary for carrying out large plans. His command of languages dazzled an international conference, and his genial countenance and artistic interests made him a center for wide circles of friends. Fry, too, could dominate an assembly, but more through skill of parliamentary procedure and clarity of means by which a desirable result could be achieved. From experience in building I would suggest that Söderblom had the gift of the imaginative architect, Fry the skill of the expert engineer. How necessary both are is realized by anyone who has observed how poor engineering can destroy a good plan or how handicapped is the engineer who lacks such a plan. I do not imply that Fry could not see visions as well as Söderblom, but in my mind Fry's talent was the shaping of a free church in a free state while Söderblom enthused men and women in many lands to see something they had not seen before and inspired them to action. Fry studied every joint and seam of a church fabric and impressed his people by his sure sense of direction in which they should move. It is meaningless to try to decide which is the greater gift. It is meaningful for the church to thank God for both of these great bishops who have had much to do with the shape of the church in our day.

---

[1] In the ULCA *Pastor's Desk Book*, June, 1959, Dr. Fry published statements by Dr. Bergendoff and ULCA's Judge Henninger on the "Lodge question."

[2] See *Pastor's Desk Book*, February, 1960, on the selection of a name for the merged church.

33

O. V. Anderson

An influential Augustana leader writes particularly of Dr. Fry as an architect of the structure of the LCA.

Among my many reminiscences of Dr. Franklin Clark Fry, gathered over a period of many years, some of the most significant are those that cluster around our associations in the sessions of the Joint Commission on Lutheran Unity looking toward the merger of four Lutheran church bodies into the Lutheran Church in America, as well as from the meetings of the Executive Council of the LCA. In all of these sessions the stature of Dr. Fry's churchmanlike leadership was constantly in evidence.

Despite the very great numerical disparity in the membership of the four former church bodies now constituting the LCA, the representatives of the Suomi Synod and the American Evangelical Lutheran Church, with only about 50,000 members together, were very nearly twice as many as in the United Lutheran Church in America delegation headed by Dr. Fry and representing some two and one-half million members. The historic backgrounds of the four churches merging to form the LCA were German, Swedish, Finnish and Danish. Among the JCLU representatives from the ULCA one could have expected a preponderance of persons of Germanic background. However, Fry had seen to it that half of his delegation bore Scandinavian names. The rest were mainly key men from the large synods in the east, where favorable action concerning merger was essential.

Some might conclude from this that it was simply an evidence of Fry's "astute ecclesiastical engineering," of which even those envious of his leadership abilities had to concede he was a master. But, in more fair and understanding judgment one could discern his keen insight in arranging so that fear of overwhelming size was dispelled and persons of common background and interest could "feel at home" in a greatly enlarged fellowship.

It is pretty generally known that Dr. Fry was the "architect" for the

---

(b. 1903) Dr. Anderson was president of the Illinois (later Central) Conference of the Augustana Church (1954-62). He was a member of the JCLU committee which wrote the new LCA constitution. He was chairman of the Augustana Book Concern, member of the Augustana Board of American Missions, and a representative to the National Council of Churches. Since 1962 he has been pastor of Bay Shore Lutheran church, Milwaukee. He was a member of the LCA Executive Council from 1962 to 1970, and has been a representative to the LCUSA since its founding (1967).

structure and constitutions governing the life of the LCA on the national, synodical, and congregational levels. During a period of recuperation in the hospital he had drafted many of the documents with exquisite legal and linguistic care for just the correct statement. We were six on the constitution committee carefully reviewing the documents and studying the implications of the various sections in order to be able to explain and defend the wording before the entire JCLU, composed of some fifty representatives of the four merging church bodies.[1]

A representative of one of the smaller churches had a most difficult time to keep abreast of Fry's agile mind and all-encompassing grasp of the functioning of a very large ecclesiastical organization. This good brother always seemed to be "tagging along" behind Fry's fast pace, finding himself in the wrong document, or on the wrong page, thereby frequently requesting to go back to review a previously made decision and generally slowing down progress when deadlines had to be met.

From Fry's "puckered-up lip" it was obvious that the slow progress was most annoying to him. Frank Fry was struggling in self-discipline to act patiently, kindly and courteously with a less gifted brother. And he did so! The man who had enormous capacity to remember statistics, faces, names, and a whole array of complicated arrangements had difficulty at times to remember that few men had been as richly endowed as he. To illustrate, at meetings when routine business left a portion of our minds free for other things, a number of us liked to solve the crossword puzzles in the NEW YORK TIMES, which usually provide a good mental workout. Dr. Fry's time to do so was often but four or five minutes while others of us required perhaps ten times as long.

While respect and tribute are due Franklin Clark Fry as ecumenical churchman, masterful parliamentarian, and courageous leader, many will remember him especially as a sincere and dedicated pastor, and perhaps particularly as a wise counselor and pastor to pastors. A friendly word in conversation, a telephone call, a postal card or note in his fine hand from some distant land indicated when circumstances called for it a warm personal concern. His was a pastor's heart! Most appropriately the Fry Memorial Fund[2] has been established to provide study grants for pastors who need financial assistance to help prepare them for a more effective ministry. From youth to his concluding days Dr. Fry gave himself unstintingly in fulfillment of the ministry entrusted to him by our Lord.

---

[1] Proposed constitution was published in *Official Documents of the Lutheran Church in America,* Philadelphia, 1960. See also the *1958 Report of the Joint Commission on Lutheran Unity,* Philadelphia, 1958. Abridgments of the 1958 JCLU "Statement of Agreement on Unity" and of the LCA constitution are printed in R. C. Wolf, *Documents of Lutheran Unity in America,* Documents 226 and 227.

[2] See 1970 LCA Minutes, pp. 251-252.

34

Raymond W. Wargelin

Dr. Wargelin describes President Fry's relations not only with the Suomi Synod but also with the Christians of Finland.

Dr. Franklin Clark Fry and the People of Suomi

The outreach of Dr. Franklin Clark Fry's contacts and influence among the people of Suomi extended around the world. This was typical of his life's work with everything. The Finnish people, though being a less numerous ethnic group, have, nevertheless, managed to spread into many parts of the world. The Finnish Missionary Society in Ovambokavango, Southwest Africa; the Finnish Missionary Society in China; the Finnish Evangelical Society Missions in Japan, the ethnic Finnish concentrations in Australia and Brazil, were all well known to Dr. Fry through his service on the various commissions of the Lutheran World Federation and through his contacts as president of this ecumenical body.

However, it is not in the above terms that this writer desires to share insights concerning Dr. Fry and the people of Suomi, but rather in terms of the United States, Canada and Finland.

A Plan of Cooperation

Possibly the earliest contact that the late and revered Dr. Franklin Clark Fry had with Finnish Lutherans extends back to approximately 1921, the year when the Plan of Cooperation in home missions work was approved. The plan authorized the Immigrants Mission Board of the United Lutheran Church in America to make an annual grant to the Home Mission Board of the Suomi Synod in order to increase the latter's mission outreach to unserved areas in the United States and Canada. The plan also included scholarship grants for theological students at the Suomi

---

(b. 1911) Succeeding his father in the presidency of the Suomi Synod 1955-62, Dr. Wargelin as vice-chairman of the JCLU led his church into the LCA merger. He served in the same period on the Executive Committee of the NLC, and from 1966 to 1970 as representative to the National Council of Churches. He had previously been president of the Lake Erie Conference of the Suomi Synod (1947-55). He was a delegate to the Minneapolis and Helsinki assemblies of the LWF. Since 1962 he has been regional secretary of the LCA Board of American Missions, serving a territory from Upper Michigan to the Dakotas, and has been president of the LCA Finnish Interest Conference since its founding.

Theological Seminary, Hancock, Michigan. Dr. F. F. Fry, father of Dr. Franklin Clark Fry, was at the time a member of the ULCA Executive Board, and subsequently became the executive secretary of the Board of American Missions. The elder Fry was a frequent visitor at the annual conventions of the Suomi Synod. These conventions were conducted in the Finnish language, which meant that everything had to be conveyed through an interpreter for the official representative of the ULCA. It is obvious that experiences of this nature were shared by Dr. F. F. Fry with his intimates including his son, Franklin Clark, who was a student of theology at the time.[1]

The Plan of Cooperation proved to be helpful and fostered mission development in many ways within the Suomi Synod. It made possible a level of structured programming not previously experienced in the Synod; it also served to sow the seeds of future merger. The Plan of Cooperation was terminated by the ULCA by action taken at the 1930 biennial convention in Milwaukee, Wisconsin. The Suomi Synod had not agreed to the proposal to merge into the ULCA; the plan was phased out by 1935. Dr. Franklin Clark Fry's opinion concerning the ultimatum presented to the Suomi Synod was one of regret.[2]

Lutheran World Action Grant for Finland

In the meantime, by 1942 the Suomi Synod had joined the National Lutheran Council. In the setting of the challenging inter-Lutheran activity of World War II years, representatives of the Suomi Synod did have some opportunities to meet and associate with the rising young leader. On June 15, 1945, Dr. Fry addressed the fifty-sixth annual convention of the Suomi Synod, having been elected president of the United Lutheran Church a few months earlier in Minneapolis. It was an occasion to remember and there are many who still do. He stood straight and tall yet very much at ease; his resonant voice was heard to every corner of the church without any difficulty. He was well informed and what he said was undergirded with the essential of evangelical Christianity. That he was youthful was undeniable, yet his maturity was the holding impression. His incisive message that day centered on the monumental task of relief work to be commenced in Europe because of the Allied victory. He answered many questions which, interestingly, were questions on church structure and polity. Item 54 of the convention minutes records the following: "Dr. Franklin Clark Fry, the president of the ULCA, brought the greetings of his church to the convention, and encouraged everyone in a heart warming manner to greater commitment to the work of the Lord in these difficult days of trial."

World War II had been particularly difficult for Finland; the nation had been drawn into a defensive war against the Russians, who had attempted several times during the course of the war to overrun Finland. Northern Finland had been devastated by a German army of occupation; homes, farms, cities, churches, and rectories were completely destroyed. There was damage elsewhere following the repeated air raids by the Russians. The nation had to pay crushing war reparation payments in specified industrial materials. The colossal losses in human lives, the task of resettling more than ten percent of the population, because of the loss of eastern Finland to Russia, were enough to make a nation fall prey to communism and fall behind the Iron Curtain. Finland is the only European country bordering on Russia which did not fall behind the Iron Curtain.

The tremendous material relief, both to the people as well as to the church, in the form of Lutheran World Action undoubtedly was one of the decisive factors in preserving the morale of the people of Finland. A million dollars in assistance in LWA funds was to be the commitment by the Executive Committee of the National Lutheran Council. Items and concerns of this nature engulfed the attention of the newly-elected president of the ULCA. Deputation teams were soon on their way to Europe to determine strategy and fact-finding. This writer has a photograph produced by the News Bureau of the National Lutheran Council which depicts the departure, on July 7, 1946, by ocean liner bound for Sweden, of a deputation team consisting of Dr. Ralph H. Long, executive director of the National Lutheran Council; Dr. Franklin Clark Fry, president of the ULCA; Dr. Abdel Ross Wentz, president of Gettysburg Seminary; and Dr. J. A. Aasgaard, president of the Norwegian Lutheran Church of America. This inspection trip was the first opportunity Dr. Fry had to become acquainted with Finland proper. He made a host of friends there, among them leaders of the church such as Archbishop Aleksi Lehtonen, Bishop (later Archbishop) Ilmari Salomies, Bishop Eelis Gulin, and Dean Ahti Auranen, who was to serve subsequently on the staff of the Lutheran World Federation. Dr. Fry was later to cement a particularly warm and meaningful relationship with the present archbishop, Martti Simojoki, who served a term as a vice-president of the Lutheran World Federation.

An interesting sidelight of the $1,000,000 grant to the Church of Finland for relief work is provided by Dr. John Wargelin:

> The Council was sympathetic to the grant for Finland. But when it was learned that the Church of Finland planned to buy coffee with the money and to sell it with the approval of the Finnish government (the price of coffee was and is high in Finland, but the people love their coffee in spite of the high cost; by this method the one million dollars would bring six million dollars),

> some of the members of the Council objected on ethical grounds, saying that it was gambling. Then Dr. Fry spoke. He said that he knew the Finns to be sincere Christians. If they wished to increase the value of this grant through this legal act, it was for them to decide. Dr. J. A. Aasgaard made the motion to give the Church of Finland one million dollars, the motion was seconded by myself and the motion was unanimously adopted.[3]

Dr. Jacob W. Heikkinen, a pastor of the Suomi Synod, was the liaison representative of the NLC in Finland during the allocation period (1947). The reconstruction work and relief work came at a most meaningful and critical period in the life of the nation. In addition to the reconstruction of churches and parsonages, plus the material relief of the people, the funds were also used to establish important lay training institutes. One of them, the Järvenpää Lay Institute, outside Helsinki, has immortalized this Lutheran help from America with a large plaque of inlaid wood, adjacent to the "America Hall."

Appreciation From Finland

Eelis E. Gulin, a retired bishop of the Church of Finland, in a letter written to me after the death of Dr. Fry, describes his reaction to Dr. Fry as an individual: "I read your beautiful article about our noble and mutual friend, Franklin Clark Fry. We are rich when we have had such leaders as he was. I especially remember him as the leader of the Harrisburg convention, October 1956. How spirited, how capable, how brilliant! And in the midst of everything he had the time and the friendship for the least of us. I can never forget his friendly countenance which, in itself, encouraged one to new dedication to the Lord."

The Church of Finland, acting through the theological faculty of the University of Helsinki, had a splendid opportunity to express their appreciation and thankfulness to Dr. Fry prior to the convening of the 1963 Helsinki assembly of the Lutheran World Federation. The setting was academic; all of the ceremony surrounding the granting of doctorates of theology with all of the rich traditions of the centuries was resurrected for the occasion. The Finns had gone to this length only three times previously during the twentieth century, and this event outdid all the others. The official promoter, Professor Aarre Lauha, addressed these words to Dr. Franklin Clark Fry in the great hall of the university before the university community and the president of the republic:

> Our faculty wishes to give recognition to you for the exceptionally abundant work which you have performed in the common endeavors of the Lutheran churches. In this field you have great and

fruitful merits in your country, but also internationally your share in this matter has been of central importance. Since the founding of the Lutheran World Federation, you have held demanding positions in it, the highest of which is the federation president's responsible post during the last six years. Your merits in effecting unity among the Lutheran church bodies are of historic stature. Your contribution as one of the leaders of the ecumenical movement will always be remembered. For this came at a time when Christendom was seeking the possibilities of brotherhood and co-operative efforts in order to put God's will into effect. Our faculty is happy that it has the privilege, by granting you the doctor of theology degree, of assuring you of its deep respect for your far-reaching work and incomparable personality.[4]

The Finnish nation apparently had granted special honors to Dr. Fry on previous occasions unknown to this writer. It was, however, apparent that Dr. Fry wore two such decorations at the above-described promotion.

It is of interest to isolate from the mass of materials of the Helsinki assembly that which Dr. Fry had to say about the setting, the people and the church who were hosting the assembly. In the Foreword to the *Proceedings of the Fourth Assembly of the Lutheran World Federation* (page 9) he wrote:

Within all of this pulp, there was a juice that only we who were at Helsinki could taste. The brilliant and penetrating Bible study, the intercessions and the daily celebrations of Holy Communion flooded us with a radiant sense of the presence of God. *The flavor of Finnish piety and the sturdy Christianity of the national life of Finland were an elixir for the soul. Who could forget the altogether superb address of the President of the Republic above all?* [italics ours] Even dry questions having to do with the structure of the federation elicited an animated interest and a feeling of mutuality as never before.

In a press interview before the assembly Dr. Fry said:

Secondly, we wish to express our heartfelt greeting to our hosts. Peace be unto this city. We rejoice when our churches decided that we were to go to Helsinki, even as ancient Israel rejoiced as the people of God went up to Jerusalem. God's Word has been guarded here in its purity through many generations. This land has raised a band of fearless witnesses for our dear Lord. The Church of Finland and the Finnish people are in high regard in our midst and we wish to receive for ourselves something of that which is their best.[5]

Further Thoughts on Finnish Christianity

Perhaps some additional light can be thrown on what Dr. Fry meant by the words, "receive . . . something of that which is their best." The Suomi Synod observed its seventieth anniversary June 24-26, 1960, in Virginia, Minnesota, and Dr. Fry had agreed to preach at the Sunday service of the great festival day. This festival drew a great deal of attention in the mass media and Dr. Fry was kind enough to grant an interview. One of the reporters asked him about Finnish pietistic theology.

> Dr. Fry quickly admitted that there really is such a thing. "The piety of the Finns is a definite quality. The Finns and the Hungarians oddly are the only two peoples we know of who have managed to undertake the pietistic movement successfully. . . . You know, there is a danger involved with pietism. It can very easily become a form by itself, without meaning. And that is the danger of it. But the Finns and Hungarians have been able to survive these dangers and their churches have been able to live with the movements and to foster them and become stronger for God because of it." . . .
>
> Asked if some of this so-called "Finnish pietistic theology" is being introduced by Suomi Synod theologians now teaching at Maywood Seminary, Dr. Fry stated, "Definitely. They have brought into our thinking the values of Finnish pietism. Dr. Walter Kukkonen and Karlo Keljo of the Suomi Synod have brought decided nourishment to the ULC seminary at Maywood."[6]

For what it is worth, this writer, quoting himself, feels that a mutual understanding and appreciation existed at this point between the Finns and Dr. Fry.

> He was not only a skilled church diplomat, parliamentarian, a student of history and church law, but also an inspired proclaimer of the Word. His proclamation was biblical and Lutheran; it was incisive preaching of the law and the prophetic message. The gospel was not left unproclaimed; it rang forth purely and without qualifications. The homogenizing of all things and the approval of all things were not his characteristics. Shortcomings were laid bare boldly and directly. But the doorsill to the storehouse of grace was left low enough for the "poor miserable sinner" to surmount. To many of us it appeared that Dr. Fry understood the dimensions of Finnish Christianity very well.[7]

This article written after Dr. Fry's death was published by public demand in several Finnish language publications, both in the eastern as well as in the western parts of the United States and Canada.

The Era of the Joint Commission on Lutheran Unity

Without question Dr. Franklin Clark Fry was the leading figure in the merger discussions which were productive in the creation of the Lutheran Church in America. As a participant in the process and as president of the Suomi Synod, there was never any question in this writer's mind or, for that matter, in "our" collective mind, as to what was actually taking place. As representatives of one of the two smaller bodies in the Joint Commission on Lutheran Unity, the members of the Suomi delegation were continually amazed at the equal representative power that they possessed with all of the other bodies, regardless of the size of the bodies. This same representative principle prevailed in all of the sub-committee functions as well as in the eventual "little JCLUs" in the districts, conferences, or existing synods of the four bodies. As a result, each body had the distinct conviction that its voice had been heard and that each had had the opportunity to make its unique contributions where it was deemed right to do so.

The Joint Commission on Lutheran Unity, at the commencement of its task, was several years behind the Joint Union Committee which produced the American Lutheran Church. It was sensed that the JCLU should attempt to create a corporate entity as nearly simultaneously as possible to the organizing of the future American Lutheran Church. This was not articulated, but it gradually became the understanding. The amount of work to be done was tremendous and the coordination and development of the process were nothing short of a miracle. At one time it was assumed that it would be necessary to hire a full-time coordinator. Tremendous credit falls therefore to many key leaders, such as Dr. Malvin Lundeen, chairman of the JCLU. However, continually, it was Dr. Fry who kept the commission moving ahead clearly towards the fulfillment of its task by key suggestions, by wise deployment of talent, by the assembling of suitable alternatives which were fruitful in achieving needed compromises, and by the assumption and fulfillment of certain tasks which were bewildering by virtue of their size and complexity. During the course of the negotiations, Dr. Fry had a serious illness and was hospitalized for several weeks. When this writer offered him his commiseration, it became evident that the hospitalization had been just what he had needed to complete the first draft of the proposed constitution and bylaws! The vast materials assembled and the numerous principles evaluated by the many sub-committees went through his computer-like mind and emerged in a balanced presentation of the defined powers and functions of the future constitution of the LCA. By the time that the American Lutheran Church was formally organized (1960), our four merging bodies had already agreed on our documents of consolidation.

A very important policy decision was made by the JCLU in regard to the matter of pulpit and altar fellowship with other Lutherans, which subsequently has become the official policy of the Lutheran Church in America. The counsel of Dr. Franklin Clark Fry in this matter was prophetic and far-sighted. The possibility of developing conversations with the Lutheran Church—Missouri Synod on possible membership in a reorganized National Lutheran Council had surfaced in the waning years of the 1950s, mainly because it was evident that a council of two major bodies was not a very bright prospect for cooperation. It was Dr. Fry's counsel that the subject of pulpit and altar fellowship should be answered with the affirmation that the churches of the JCLU consider themselves to be in fellowship already with all Lutheran churches by virtue of acknowledging the Lutheran confessional books, and that all possible attention, prayer, and work be devoted to the prospect of reorganizing the NLC so that it might include other Lutheran bodies, particularly the Lutheran Church—Missouri Synod. It is God's grace that there is now in existence a Lutheran Council in the USA constituted in membership in the above manner.

For the Suomi representatives on the JCLU, the experience gathered during the negotiations was productive in much broadening of understanding but particularly in achieving confidence. It was in the spirit of confidence that the Suomi Synod came to the constituting convention at Detroit in June, 1962; it is in the same confidence that the people of Suomi function in the Lutheran Church in America even though to their deep sorrow the towering figure of Dr. Fry is no longer among them.

A Special Interest Conference: Suomi Conference

Dr. Fry was particularly helpful to this writer in developing the proper constitutional language needed to secure the authorization for the special interest conference activity known as the Suomi Conference. The basic authorization for special interest conferences is stated in the bylaws to the LCA Constitution, Section IV, items 1, 2 and 3. The definition of the powers and functions requested by the Suomi Synod for the Finnish special interest conference were specified in Resolution 37 (Minutes of the Constituting Convention, LCA, 1962, page 232).

Dr. Franklin Clark Fry managed to schedule and conduct the convening and constituting meeting of the Suomi Special Interest Conference on Sunday afternoon, 1:30 p.m., July the first, 1962; the same afternoon he and the other newly-elected officers of the Lutheran Church in America were installed with solemn festivities at Cobo Hall, Detroit, Michigan. That he managed this was typical of his willingness to expend himself for the church. We had made arrangements that a special driver would drive us from the Bethlehem Lutheran Church of Detroit following the organization meeting of the Suomi Conference to the great festival of consecration at Cobo Hall. It was my privilege to conduct the installation rites specifically for him. Needless to say, it was an unforgettable moment for this writer.

Dr. Fry continued to manifest particularly gracious interest towards the functioning of the Suomi special interest conference. Annual reports on the activities of the conference were submitted to him and the executive council regularly. Each year he responded with a personal note of appreciation and encouragement. In 1967, while returning from the Executive Committee meetings of the Lutheran World Federation held in Waterloo, Ontario, Dr. Fry paid a special visit to the annual festival of the Suomi Conference gathered in Toronto, Ontario, at St. Ansgar's Lutheran church. Through a breakdown in communication, he had not been properly informed of the location of the meetings. The length to which Dr. Fry went to acquire this esoteric information was enough to bow our heads in permanent shame. Yet his words were particularly warm and gracious and the elderly Finns from the United States and the youthful Finns recently migrated into Canada were distinctly touched.

The other special guest at this Toronto festival of the Suomi Conference was Martti Simojoki, archbishop of the Church of Finland. He was a particularly close friend of Dr. Fry. Remarkable in understanding and vision, this churchman in all three of his messages to the Suomi Conference underscored the task of the Finnish Lutherans in the United States and Canada as ceasing to be a diaspora on this continent and finding their rightful place in the indigenous Lutheran churches of the land as soon as possible. Obviously, this had been the program and policy of the Suomi Synod in becoming a part of the Lutheran Church in America. The chief objective of the Suomi Conference is to maintain fellowship activities for the benefit of the elderly and the first generation Finns. The Toronto festival was such a manifest success in numbers and the archbishop's admonitions were so challenging in this writer's mind that he undertook to write Dr. Fry asking whether the Suomi Conference was "over-acting" its role. The following quotations from Dr. Fry's letter of July 11, 1967, were most reassuring: "No wonder you found Archbishop Simojoki so bracing and admirable. . . . No, we have to reckon with facts. Many of your first-generation people and a few others (there will always be some) with a first-generation mentality have to be met in a friendly, constructive spirit at their own level. Not only met there but patiently led up from it. That is precisely what you are doing. I for one think of it very positively."

Perhaps the thing that torments those of us who knew Dr. Franklin Clark Fry and had opportunities of associating with him, is that fact that we never had an adequate chance to say to him the deep appreciation that we felt in our hearts. He was taken from our midst too rapidly for this. For this reason, this writer has a feeling that the numerous words of appreciation addressed to him at the close of the Helsinki Assembly, as he stepped down from that high post, contained a premonition of his impending death, even though he was the picture of strength and the epitome of self-control. However, the words spoken by the Resolutions Committee, by the newly-elected president of the Federation, Dr. Fredrik A. Schiotz, and by Bishop Bo Giertz,[8] approached the grandeur that befitted his life.

---

[1] From the private papers of President John Wargelin: "President Fry told me that when his father returned from the Suomi Synod Conventions, he had much to say about his new friends and their leaders. He had not had any contacts with the Finns before this time."

[2] *Ibid.*: "Sitting at dinner in Atlantic City with Dr. and Mrs. F. C. Fry, he said that the action of the ULCA, in his opinion, had been unwise."

[3] Private papers of Dr. John Wargelin. See R. W. Solberg, *As Between Brothers*, Minneapolis, 1957, pp. 108-110.

[4] *Teologiska Fakultetens vid Helsingfors Universitet doktorspromotion*, 1963, p. 21.

[5] SUOMALAINEN, Hancock, Michigan, September 1963, p. 3.

[6] MESABI DAILY NEWS, Virginia, Minnesota, June 27, 1960.

[7] *Suomi Konferenssin Kirkollinen Kalenteri*, Hancock, Michigan, 1969, p. 34.

[8] *Proceedings of the Fourth Assembly of the Lutheran World Federation*, Berlin, 1965, pp. 410-413, 431-433.

35

Johannes H. V. Knudsen

Dr. Knudsen writes of President Fry and the American Evangelical Lutheran Church.

My major recollection of Dr. Fry has its sources in the lengthy discussions of the Joint Commission on Lutheran Unity. The comradeship that was developed there had a great personal value, and although Dr. Fry was a man of major power and authority, he was essentially "one of the boys" who treated all with friendly consideration. In the involved negotiations he was amazingly competent and consistent, with a mind for detail matched by no one. He did not always win his point and he was willing to negotiate, taking his defeats gracefully. The latter were remarkably few, for he had great power of persuasion, and he operated with foresight and with plans laid well in advance. I suspect that he anticipated most of the opposition and had calculated which items were expendable from the United Lutheran Church point of view in order to retain the continued cooperation of other parties. When the head-on clashes came, he was firm but fair, insisting on a vote and yielding if the vote went against him. On one occasion, when we had debated the issue of secret societies with some fervor, he stood firmly on the position which he knew represented ULC, but I suspect that he was not displeased at the opposite stand taken by a majority. One long session tested his composure as well as that of others, namely, the deciding balloting on board secretaries. He remained firm, for I believe that he felt he had given enough ground, but there were no outbursts, and when the decisions had been made, no breaks had occurred.

The later years of strain and undermined health probably affected composure as well as judgment, but I was then no close observer of the scene. On only one occasion was I near the center. The Standing Committee on Approaches to Unity reported at the Kansas City convention

---

(b. 1904) The treasurer of the JCLU was a prominent educator and churchman of the American (formerly Danish) Evangelical Lutheran Church. Dr. Knudsen was president of Grand View College (1942-52) and dean of the Seminary in Des Moines, Iowa (1942-54), then professor (1954-71) at the Lutheran School of Theology at Chicago and for most of that period dean of graduate studies. He has been a member of the LCA Committee on Approaches to Unity (1962-70) and of many church agencies and committees, and a leader in Danish-American cultural relations.

(1966) and Dr. Fry was pressed hard to accede to Missouri's request for negotiations about pulpit and altar fellowship, not so much out of consideration for Missouri as to strengthen the hand of the American Lutheran Church. Dr. Fry was adamant that we should not negotiate what had already been granted in our own constitution. As other members of the committee did, I conceded this point, and I still believe that the principle was right. But I also had an uncomfortable feeling that the sound argument had motivations in personal relations, and I was unhappy that the resolution was rushed through the convention, for most of the delegates did not know what the issue was. Some of those who knew were sharp in their criticism.

I cannot reveal any major insights into what was happening on the Lutheran scene, but I would like to make a testimony of what I felt was a considerate and consistent attitude toward individuals and small groups. My church, the American Evangelical Lutheran Church, was tiny, but we were always treated with understanding and respect. Dr. Fry had the perspicacity to recognize our strength, and his eloquent foreword in Enok Mortensen's history of our church, *The Danish Lutheran Church in America* (Philadelphia, 1967), is a true and touching tribute. In this connection I must tell of an incident which occurred in the mid-fifties. Our church had rejected a committee proposal that we join the ULC as a synod. The vote had shown a majority in favor but not the necessary two-thirds. Upon returning to Chicago I called Dr. Fry at his hotel to talk about the vote. I had been in favor of the committee report, although I am now convinced that subsequent developments offered a better solution, and I voiced my regret to Dr. Fry. His answer, which I cannot quote verbatim, ran like this: Don't be sorry! Now the AELC can join ULC and Augustana in planning a merger. It is always good to have a third party at a negotiating table. (This was before it was known that the Suomi Synod would also join the merger committee.) The tactic in this instance was shrewd, but it was also a recognition of the significance of a minority group.

Personally I have experienced numerous examples of consistent friendliness. My move in 1954 from Des Moines to Maywood, where I took over the administration of graduate studies in the seminary, depended upon the support of this work on the part of ULC. Dr. Fry made no overt commitment to this support, for he could not do this officially, but he let me know that he favored my presence on the Maywood faculty, and he never failed this "covert commitment." I trusted him and he never failed me. On one occasion he showed a personal concern over and beyond the necessary. He attended a meeting at Nyborg Strand in Denmark, which was close to the scene of my grandfather's participation in Danish church life. I therefore wrote him a letter telling him about the significance of events and places. I did not expect any response, but it happened that the Central Committee of the World Council of Churches was invited to the local folk school. When Dr. Fry was to respond to an official greeting, he brought greetings from me. This he told me in a two-page letter, closely written in his precise script, in which he related the entire event. I was pleased that a man as busy as he would take time for this friendly note. A postcard with "Greetings from Denmark" would have been more than I expected.

His sense of humor is well known, and he relished stories of which he was the target. He enjoyed the telling of a joke almost as much as its content. In 1957 I was standing outside the assembly hall at the Lutheran World Federation assembly at Minneapolis with my teen-aged daughter when Dr. Fry came by. He stopped to exchange remarks and he told a funny story, slapping himself on the leg and guffawing heartily. When he turned to go my daughter turned to me with a puzzled expression and said: "Is he something!" My impulsive answer was: "He is about as much as he can be!" Dr. Fry enjoyed my report of her remark, but I did not tell him of my reply. If I had, he would have responded with genuine humility. The judgment of its truth is now up to history. I for one shall cherish his memory.

36

George F. Harkins

Dr. Harkins confines himself to a single topic: Dr. Fry's principles of church union, as exemplified in his attitudes toward the Joint Commission on Lutheran Unity and the interdenominational Consultation on Church Union.

Anyone who was ever in Franklin Clark Fry's presence for more than five minutes learned that he was a man of deep conviction; more than that, that he had strong feelings and established opinions about almost every subject of importance that could be mentioned.

For instance, he held firmly to the view that church union should be based solidly on agreement concerning the fundamentals of the Christian faith, and that any foundation less than that would be inadequate. To the delight of everyone who attended the first meeting of the Joint Commission on Lutheran Unity, the group which prepared for the four-way consolidation that eventuated in the Lutheran Church in America, consensus was reached promptly that there existed among the four churches sufficient agreement in the faith to warrant proceeding toward the formation of a new church body. Should such agreement have been lacking (unthinkable!), I am confident that he would not have been willing to participate further in the negotiations. Because such agreement existed, he and all the other members of the JCLU moved forward in preparation for the new church with alacrity. In this, as in every other matter of theological consequence, he adhered firmly to the position of the former United Lutheran Church in America.

When the proposal was made in San Francisco (1960) that a number of denominations begin exploring the possibility of forming a new church body which would be "truly catholic, truly reformed and truly ecumenical," none of the Lutheran church bodies in North America was invited to participate in the explorations,[1] That was more by design than by oversight because both Dr. Eugene Carson Blake and then-Bishop James A.

(b. 1913) Dr. Harkins was intimately associated with Dr. Fry since 1949, as assistant to the president (1949-60, 1962-68), and secretary of the ULCA (1960-62). Since 1968 secretary of the LCA. Long active in interchurch agencies, he has held among other posts those of president of the NLC (1965-66) and vice-president of the LCUSA (1970-   ), president of the USA National Committee of the LWF (1967-70), and a member of the National Council of Churches' General Board since 1964.

Pike recognized that three Lutheran bodies in North America had just completed a merger of their own, and that four other Lutheran bodies were well on the way to forming the Lutheran Church in America.

Another reason, however, came to the minds of a number of Lutherans: it was clear from the day of Dr. Blake's sermon in San Francisco that the negotiations were to focus primarily on factors other than *consensus doctrinae,* a basic ingredient in the merger producing the Lutheran Church in America and, matchingly, the basis for any other merger in which Dr. Fry would have been interested.

His commitment to the full text of John 17, and not just to the five words "that they may be one," would not permit him to settle for union without oneness in the faith. Our Lord's words, "even as we are one," meant significantly more to him than oneness in desire or oneness in general understanding. Our Father and our Savior, to Franklin Clark Fry as to Lutherans everywhere, are one in purpose, one in proclamation, one in understanding the terms of salvation, and one in fervency for the salvation of men. He would not have deviated from that position.

---

[1] The "Blake-Pike Proposal" led to the formation of the "Consultation on Church Union" (COCU). For a brief account of the movement see Cavert, *Church Cooperation and Unity in America,* New York, 1970, pp. 337-342. See also the memos of Beazley (No. 76) and Marshall (38).

37

Martin E. Carlson

Dr. Carlson writes of his association with President Fry as a member of his staff.

Franklin Clark Fry: The Man for Whom I Worked

It was intermission time at the Ford Auditorium, Detroit, in 1962. I had my friend of several years, Dr. George F. Harkins, cornered in an isolated hallway. "George," I asked, "is it possible for one to work closely with Dr. Fry and still be your own man?" The question was unnecessary—for I knew that George had worked closely with Dr. Franklin Clark Fry for at least a decade and that he was his own man. But still I had to ask it.

Dr. Fry had just been elected president of the Lutheran Church in America. Earlier that same day he had asked me if I would serve as one of two assistants to the president. This I felt I could do only if that question could be answered to my satisfaction. Who could better answer it than one who had worked in that relationship with Dr. Fry for so long? I had known Dr. Fry since about 1947, had frequently seen him "in action," and during Joint Commission on Lutheran Unity days had occasionally worked very closely with him. But there were always those who said, "It's not possible to work for him and be yourself. It has to be his way." I had to assure myself that this was not true.

The only job description I ever had came when he invited me to join the staff. "I have asked George to be the liaison between the president's office and the boards and commissions and to be responsible for ecumenical affairs. I would like you to be responsible for budgeting and fiscal affairs and for relationships with synods." That was all. I suspect he felt that if one was not able to create a job within those broad areas, one didn't belong on the president's staff. Of course, there were specific assignments he would ask us to take, but it was primarily our responsibility to sense what was required and do it. This left staff remarkably free to create their own jobs. He expected initiative from staff. He was open to new ideas and new ways of doing things.

(b. 1910) From 1949 to 1962 executive director of the Board of Finance of the Augustana Lutheran Church, Dr. Carlson has been assistant to the president of the LCA since 1962. He has been a representative to the LCUSA, and has served as chairman of the National Council of Churches' Department of Stewardship and Benevolence.

Dr. Fry frequently sought the counsel of staff. Seldom was it a search for facts—those he knew! But rather, "What do you think of this?" When he sought counsel privately or in staff meetings, he was open to changing his mind assuming, of course, that one had the facts correct and that one's logic was impeccable. He was never very patient with either muddle-headedness or incompetence. At the same time he took staff into his confidence in a remarkable way. There was a recognition that the president's office—and the church—were frequently judged by the way in which staff might interpret issues and deal with specific situations. He never wanted staff to be caught in the trap of ignorance. For that reason staff undoubtedly knew much more about situations involving the president's office than most people realize. Frequently he would say, "We work as a collegium in this office." There was no doubt in anyone's mind as to who was president, but there was a strong sense of partnership.

After an area of responsibility had once been assigned to staff, he did not take it back in specific instances nor did he second-guess decisions made. It was not at all uncommon for him to say to a board or commission executive, "Martin has responsibility for that. Whatever decision he makes is final as far as the president's office is concerned." And when decisions were in error, he always sought to preserve the integrity of the one who made it. How well I remember the time I advised a synod convention erroneously on a procedure. I knew it was wrong, but it appeared to be the lesser of two evils. The convention was bent on making a decision in an area in which synods, in the polity of the LCA, have no competence. When we discussed it afterwards in the office, he pointed out still another way (constitutional, of course) that it could have been done—and I had never thought of it. "But if it will embarrass you in any way, Martin, we'll let it rest right here. There's no harm done."

Twice in my lifetime it has been given to me to live and work in the shadow of a truly great man. Dr. Fry was one of these. He was a giant of faith and intellect, he had convictions that ran deep and a singleness of dedication to his Lord and his church. He had an uncommon sensitivity to the changing times and changing issues. To be in the proximity of such a man for six-and-a-half years does not leave one untouched.

38

Robert J. Marshall

Dr. Fry's manner of leadership and his personal relations with Dr. Marshall are discussed in this memo, along with Dr. Fry's position on the Consultation on Church Union and other inter-religious organizations.

Dr. Fry was elected president of the United Lutheran Church in the year that I was ordained. A layman from my first parish was a delegate to that 1944 convention in Minneapolis and gave a firsthand report. Two years later as a delegate in Cleveland I saw Dr. Fry demonstrate his ability as he presided for the first time at a convention of the church. Naturally, a young pastor would respond to such leadership with considerable awe. My mind perceived the link between the president's personal dynamism and the church's growth in membership, finance, ecumenical participation, world relief, and missions.

I did not meet Dr. Fry personally until I was teaching at Muhlenberg College. He took part in the centennial of the college, and spoke of the importance for a Christian to use his head as well as his heart. In 1948 the convention of the church met nearby in Philadelphia. Dr. Fry delivered a special address for Lutheran World Action. Without a single note and without any of the exaggeration that belongs to superficial oratory, he held the large crowd at noiseless attention for a full hour.

After that, I did not attend a convention of the church until I was a delegate in 1960 at Atlantic City. Then merger negotiations were well along. Arrangements were completed for the adjourned convention two years later in Detroit. It would be difficult to unravel which was most impressive at Detroit—the sense of history while Dr. Fry presided at the last convention of the United Lutheran Church and later was elected and inducted as the first president of the Lutheran Church in America, or the unusual sight of him seated as a delegate during the constituting convention.

Later in 1962 I needed Dr. Fry's assistance while I was suffering from the shock of having been elected president of the Illinois Synod. Since

---

(b. 1919) Dr. Fry's successor as president of the LCA, Dr. Marshall was formerly professor at Chicago Lutheran Seminary (1953-62) and president of the LCA Illinois Synod (1962-68). He has been a member of the LCA Executive Council from 1964. Since 1968 he has been a member of the WCC Central and Executive Committees, since 1969 a member of the LCUSA Executive Committee and of the General Board of the National Council of Churches, and since 1970 vice-president of the LWF.

Dr. Malvin Lundeen was the representative of the Lutheran Church in America at the synod convention, I relied upon him for counsel at the moment. I sought out Dr. Fry at the earliest possible time, however, which happened to be the organizing meeting of the Commission on Evangelism. He was presiding at that meeting as the election of officers was delayed until the end of the day. I asked for time during the lunch hour and expected him to be in a great rush. As I sat in his office, I made two starts at rising in order to leave him free for his other responsibilities. Each time he sat immovable, solidly in control of the situation. Since I had serious doubts that my election was the wisest, I would not have been surprised if he had expressed similar reservations. Regardless of what he thought, he spoke encouragingly. I remember saying, as we parted, "With your help, I will stay on the job and do my best, and I'll talk to you again a year from now." During the conversation, he recalled how Dr. Charles Cooper, an Old Testament professor like myself, had been elected a synod president, and Dr. Fry asked, "What is it about you Old Testament professors?" I said, "I guess it's the Law." He gave one of his characteristic guffaws. He had turned us to joking, as though there were nothing to worry about. While I do not remember many of the words that passed between us during that conversation, I do remember his attitude which gave me support during the days ahead. It was this kind of affirmation which Dr. Fry had been able to spread throughout the church and so create a sense of purpose and mission.

I was never sure whether he consciously controlled such situations. In a meeting of the executive council where there had been particularly tense debate and where the decision went against his own opinion, he turned to joking. The person next to me said, "Have you ever noticed how funny he becomes after he has lost?" I really had not, but I do know that he could use humor to restore an environment of cooperative effort. In the most difficult circumstances he was able to look beyond his own very clear and strong convictions to the welfare of the whole group.

In fact, Dr. Fry could move to make his own creative contribution as the viewpoints of others led him into a new position. This was true with regard to the Consultation on Church Union.[1] Since he was convinced that the Lutheran Church in America would not be well advised to participate in the consultation, he at first opposed our being present even as an observer consultant. When it became apparent that the executive council disagreed, he eventually championed the suggestion that the presence be arranged through the Lutheran Council in the USA, so that all member churches would have the benefit of a unified presence.

In another ecumenical development, Dr. Fry was confronted by the growing desire for official participation by congregations or synods in inter-religious organizations that included more than Christian churches. He feared that such organizations would exalt religion with a small "r" and pose an insidious threat to true faith. With regard to a particular organization which involved the Illinois Synod, he proposed a clarifying statement to indicate that the organization would deal only with community service and not with propagation of faith. Other members of the organization readily adopted the statement as an improved understanding of purpose.

In the campaign for funds to build the Lutheran School of Theology at Chicago, I imposed upon Dr. Fry as countless others had done through the years. He was patient even when some of the plans did not work out well. He visited congregations and succeeded in securing commitments in excess of any other worker. I remember the drive from Rockford to Chicago when my wife was at the steering wheel. Most of the conversation became an exchange between the two of them. Because of my wife's childhood in Japan he told of his visit with the emperor. My small part in the discussion allowed me to say to him, "This flat country can't possibly be as beautiful to you as to me." He retorted, "You have an accurate perception." When my wife followed with her enthusiasm for Chicago, he admitted to appreciation for anyone who liked those paper-strewn streets.

When Dr. Fry represented the church at the convention of the Illinois Synod in 1965, I arranged to fly with him from Chicago to Rock Island. He grumbled a little at taking an earlier flight than necessary, and I had to admit to imposing upon him for a personal reason. Three times in the preceding month, at widely separated points, I had been introduced at speaking engagements as a possible successor to the president of the church. I wanted to stop such talk but what should I do? Dr. Fry advised bluntly, "Do nothing." He only said enough besides to make it necessary to change the subject, "It is encouraging to think there might be one to carry on—at least one." We never spoke of the matter again.

I wished we had, when just three years later news reached me of his resignation. The earlier report of his hospitalization had arrived on the first day of the 1968 convention of the Illinois Synod, but had not disturbed me because, as someone wrote later, we had thought of Dr. Fry as indomitable. Word of the resignation came to me on May 31 through Dr. Reuben Swanson, president of the Nebraska Synod, who reached me for another purpose by telephone in Cape Girardeau, Missouri. Since he had heard secondhand, I advised him not to spread the report until it was confirmed. I confirmed the news by calling the synod office as I changed planes in St. Louis. Once arrived at my parents' home for one day of the Memorial Day weekend, I heard the television reports. It turned into a morose holiday. The suddenness and finality of Dr. Fry's decision was reenforced on the following Sunday by his absence from Augustana College where he was scheduled to deliver the commencement address. Within the week, while I was serving as LCA representative at the convention of the Western Pennsylvania–West Virginia Synod, television newscasts reported Dr. Fry's death.

My last visit with Dr. Fry came on May 14, less than a month before his death. Four representatives from the Lutheran Church in America held the first of the informal discussions with a similar panel from the Lutheran Church–Missouri Synod. The night before the discussions, the LCA group met with Dr. Fry. I was the first to arrive at his room. He told me he had been seriously ill. I asked him whether it was the same trouble he had suffered so frequently. He replied, "No, this is different." Then another member of our team arrived and we pursued the matter no further.

The next day Dr. Fry allowed one of the members of our team to carry his baggage. During the meetings at the headquarters of the Lutheran Church–Missouri Synod, he took aspirins and drank coffee–two things I had never seen him do before. He was perspiring profusely at times. Yet he was still the dominant spokesman in the discussion. He spoke of the tests the church would be facing in the near future, of the need for Christians of like faith to band together as a strong front. His mind was as keen as ever. He was sympathetic at some points, jovial at others. He ate a hearty lunch.

After the discussions, when we were waiting for a taxi, Dr. Fry was joking about how this headquarters was the Vatican of the Lutheran Church–Missouri Synod, a seat of power such as he had never been able to create in New York. I replied with, "Oh, I don't know!" and he laughed his robust guffaw. When we arrived at the St. Louis airport, we thoughtlessly let him pay the taxi fare, as he had always done, even though we should have been taking care of him. The care of all the churches had been his so long, we could not think of him in any other way than in the role of leader.

---

[1] See the memos of Harkins (No. 36) and Beazley (76).

39

Earl J. Treusch

Dr. Treusch comments on President Fry's interest in Canadian Lutheranism.

Concerning the late Dr. Fry, it is my intention to attempt to recall from personal experience only those things which impinge upon the Canadian Lutheran scene.

In Canada, as is surely the case elsewhere, there was constant amazement at his concern for every detail. Distribution of the minutes of any meeting would inevitably elicit a reply from Dr. Fry which detailed the varied breaches of constitution of which one was guilty.

Of course, as is so well known, identical concern was shown for proper parliamentary procedure. At the 1950 convention of the Canada Synod (United Lutheran Church in America), several motions with attendant amendments became hopelessly snarled. A synodical president asked Dr. Fry what proper parliamentary procedure at the moment should be. He expressed surprise at the question, saying, "I haven't seen any concern for parliamentary procedure for the last hour and a half."

The following, perhaps, can also be looked upon as concern for detail: It was in 1945 (I believe) that Dr. Fry and Dr. Clarence Stoughton constituted a visitation team to the Canada Synod on behalf of stewardship. They conducted meetings in a number of centres, including one in a parish neighbouring to mine which consisted of a small congregation in open country. To some this may appear as the proverbial ten-ton truck to deliver a tin of peas, but to me as I met Dr. Fry on this occasion for the first time it was at least a symbol of his interest in all.

Insofar as Canada itself is concerned, there are no specific comments which come to mind. However, landing at the airport in Saskatoon, Saskatchewan, in June 1951, in the midst of a snowstorm, he was heard to comment, "I don't believe that God meant this country to be lived in."

But what of his interest in Canadian Lutheranism,[1] specifically in an indigenous Lutheran church in Canada? On the one hand he appeared to look upon such with favor. For example, in his introduction to V. J.

(b. 1915) Dr. Treusch was president of the Saskatoon Lutheran Seminary in Saskatchewan 1950-55. Since then he has been general secretary of the Canadian Lutheran Council and its successor (1966), the Lutheran Council in Canada. He was a delegate to the LWF assemblies in 1957 and 1970. Active in ecumenical work, he is presently vice-chairman of the joint working group of the Canadian Catholic Conference and the Canadian Council of Churches.

Eylands' book, *Lutherans in Canada* (Winnipeg, 1945), he wrote: "There is a stirring in the tops of the mulberry trees in the Lutheran Church in Canada and it can be heard rustling in these pages. A Canadian Lutheran Council is in early prospect. A vigorous, self-reliant, united Canadian Lutheran Church may be waiting a little further in the mists ahead. God speed the day!"

He also indicated interest in Lutheran outreach to the French Canadian, and pointed out that, in his estimation, Canadian Lutheranism would not reach full maturity until it also found its place in French Canada.

On the other hand, he felt it unwise to interfere in Canadian Lutheran affairs. Although the constitution of the former United Lutheran Church in America called for its president to serve ex officio on all boards and agencies of the church, there was a direct conflict with the constitution of the former Canadian Lutheran Council which required that all councillors be resident in Canada. This was resolved by Dr. Fry through the selection of a "permanent proxy," resident in Canada, who would serve on the council in his stead.

In 1961, discussing the LCA–Canada Section which would soon be brought into being and which thereafter would be related directly to the Canadian Lutheran Council, he said to me as its executive director, "You'll be getting letters from me for another year but after the Canada Section comes into being you can make any mess in Canada that you want to and I won't be able to do a thing about it." This was stated facetiously, but it indicates how he endeavoured not to interfere.

Nevertheless, his attempts were not always successful. At the abortive attempt in 1947 to organize the Canadian Lutheran Council, Dr. Fry had been selected by the National Lutheran Council to serve as its representative to the new Canadian agency supposedly about to be born. Representatives of other Lutheran bodies, however, saw in his presence only the president of the United Lutheran Church in America, and questioned why he should be there to "interfere" when presidents of other church bodies had remained in the United States.

Sometimes this "lack of interference" was interpreted as disinterest in Canadian Lutheran affairs, particularly with reference to an indigenous Lutheran church in Canada. It was felt by some that, although speaking favourably, he would proffer no help in this direction, and even when requested for assistance would confine himself to pointing out difficulties along the way.

Yet, in spite of the foregoing comments, Dr. Fry at all times maintained the deep respect and loyalty of the Canadian wing of his church.

---

[1] Documents of negotiations in Canada, 1944-59, are found in R. C. Wolf, *Documents*, chapter 24.

40

William H. Lazareth

Professor Lazareth analyzes the multi-faceted personality of Dr. Fry, commenting (among other things) on his role in the selection of the second general secretary of the World Council of Churches, and his involvement in the church's social policies.

The official stationery read imposingly, "Office of the President—The United Lutheran Church in America." Yet in July, 1961, between ecumenical trips abroad, that international leader took time to send a handwritten greeting to the one-week-old son of one of his pastors. One sentence is particularly revealing of the multi-faceted personality of Franklin Clark Fry: "I want to welcome you, Paul: welcome you to the love in your home, to the adventure of living in an age bursting with the incredible, to the company of the one worthy Master, to the light of faith."

1. "The love in your home" is a reminder that Franklin Fry could be personally compassionate as well as professionally callous. Both qualities were likely determined by a single-minded devotion to his singular calling as Christian pastor turned world churchman.

Dr. Fry was an exemplary presiding officer at church gatherings. He was generally extremely courteous, just and helpful to friend and foe alike. When not in the chair, however, he was not above annihilating adversaries through a pyrotechnic display of intellect and wit. While debating important issues, he freely employed any lethal weapon available at the moment. Obtuse church bureaucrats were humiliated by a sarcastic review of the niceties of English grammar; pompous civil officials were bound in logical knots through parliamentary legerdemain; verbose academicians were silenced with untranslated Greek quotes memorized from the New Testament. Sometimes these tactics were prompted by intellectual arrogance; more often they seemed to be dictated by a holy impatience with anything less than man's best for the work of the church of Jesus Christ.

(b. 1928) An authority in Christian social ethics, Dr. Lazareth joined the Philadelphia Seminary faculty in 1955 and has been professor of systematic theology since 1962 and dean since 1965. He has been a representative to the NCCCUSA (1954-57), a member of the LCA Board of Social Ministry from 1962 on, a member of the Faith and Order Commission since 1967, a delegate to the World Council of Churches (1968) and the LWF 1970 assemblies, and a participant in many church study conferences and commissions.

Behind the public scene, Franklin Fry could also be a kindly man in personal and pastoral relationships. To be sure, he was never a champion of the maudlin, the sentimental, the moralistic, or the trite. Yet in daily life he acted lovingly in a countless number of quiet ways. Friends would unexpectedly receive well-timed notes and phone calls of encouragement or consolation; colleagues were offered words of correction and criticism in studied understatement; pastors and others in trouble were counselled with gentle wisdom and sincere empathy. He had a deep love for the parish ministry and often spoke movingly of earlier pastoral experiences. Many a casual acquaintance was pleasantly surprised by his fantastic ability to recall seldom-seen names and faces. He was also unexpectedly at ease with children, especially if they were bright enough to know something about current events, the Bible, or the New York Yankees!

2. "The adventure of living" helps one recall that Franklin Fry could be socially exhilarating while also linguistically pedantic. Both characteristics were probably rooted in his conviction that an unshared life was not worth living.

Any person who would take advantage of a brief hospital confinement to write a new church constitution (Lutheran Church in America) obviously had an incredible passion for words. Precise language fascinated Dr. Fry. He could thrill over a refined bylaw or a gracefully-shaded expression in ways that would continually exasperate less fastidious men. He could, and often did, squeeze all the "oratorical juice" out of any parliamentary motion as he painstakingly and methodically honed every word, reshaped every phrase and perfected the language with picayune scrupulosity. (That sentence, for instance, would have appalled him!) Never will I forget how embarrassed I was the first time the president of the church sat through a public speech of mine while noisily paging through the entire NEW YORK TIMES and even triumphantly completing the "double-crostic"—only to have my shame compounded into shock as he then sparked the audience reaction in a subsequent discussion period on the basis of detailed information gleaned simultaneously from the speech through one strategically-cocked ear!

Though generally too overpowering a presence to be a very good listener, Dr. Fry was a delightful storyteller himself. He loved to gather a circle of friends about him and re-create his latest trip or reenact a recent experience with great relish and not a little embellishment for dramatic effect. His zest for life was contagious, even if not all his rather esoteric jokes deserved quite all the raucous laughter he generously devoted to them himself. His dark eyes would alternately flash and bulge, an omnipresent Dutch Masters cigar would be deftly waved like a symphony conductor's baton, as he recounted colorful anecdotes about both the celebrities and common folk whom he encountered throughout the world. Though he often spoke familiarly of famous persons, it was never in the spirit of sophisticated name-dropping. In fact, to watch him page through his highly-prized autograph album was to share in the boyish enthusiasm of an overgrown Bethlehem Lutheran P.K. whom God had amazed by granting a highly exciting life.[1]

3. "The company of the Master" calls to mind the fact that Franklin Fry was ecclesiastically conservative as well as ethically liberal. Both commitments were based on his keen appreciation of the distinction between law and gospel in the interrelated realms of God's creation and redemption.

Dr. Fry's dialectical stance as a world ecumenical leader rooted in a confessional church deserves special emphasis. His self-imposed lot was often a lonely and misunderstood one. In Lutheran isolationist circles, he would court unpopularity by pleading for a deeper loyalty to the ecumenical breadth of the church catholic. Turning to ecumenical circles, he would then freely raise non-denominational hackles by insisting that "ecumenical" should properly mean interconfessional, in defense of the Lutheran church's evangelical and representative principles. Through dogged determination, he single-handedly dragged American Lutheranism into the mainstream of twentieth century Christianity, while at the same time preserving the ecclesial integrity of both the National and World Councils of Churches. No mean feat!

It was Dr. Fry's distinctive understanding of this "evangelical catholicity," in my judgment, which alone can explain his ambiguous role in the controversial choice of a second general secretary of the World Council of Churches, to succeed Visser 't Hooft.[2] As an avid ecumenist, he wanted a Protestant who would expand the council's growing ties with Roman Catholics and the Orthodox (hence, one who could claim episcopal succession and a firsthand knowledge of Russian language and culture). As a staunch confessionalist, he also wanted a man who could appreciate theological integrity and ecclesiastical discipline (hence, one who was schooled in the Faith and Order Commission, who would view a general secretary of a council of churches as the responsible and accountable agent of the elected officials and representatives of the autonomous churches comprising the Council and its Central Committee). In short, I believe that Dr. Fry wanted an ecclesiastical career diplomat, an ecumenical civil servant, to become World Council's second general secretary in order to have Geneva avoid both the temptation and the charge of developing into a "Protestant super-church."

The liberal quality of Dr. Fry's political and social philosophy is well established as a matter of public record. What deserves fuller recognition, especially among Social Gospel-oriented critics, was his equally strong insistence that Christian social ethical involvement have a solid theological foundation.

A graphic illustration of this conviction took place in the spring of 1964 at a crucial stage of the civil rights struggle. Dr. Fry stormed late into the final meeting of the Board of Social Ministry prior to the LCA biennial convention. Inwardly I winced under his icy glare because we both knew that the main item on the agenda was board endorsement of a draft text on "Race Relations" to be proposed for national convention adoption. Beyond its scathing denunciation of racial prejudice and segregation, the text also included two significant innovations for social ethical thinking on American Lutheran soil: corporate church involvement in social action and moral justification for civil disobedience to unjust laws. Dr. Fry soon proceeded to subject our board in general, and me in particular, to a grueling, eight-hour critique of every single phase of that draft statement. Over an hour was spent in debating the improvement of one crucial sentence alone. He spared no words, to say nothing of mercy, in posing every biblical, theological, legal, social, and political counterargument that he could muster. In the heat of discussion, I began to wonder whether he was not secretly a refined racist, after all! It was only after the last sentence was officially approved that he smiled broadly, extended his hand to me, and quietly suggested that it might now be time to have a drink together. A few weeks later the entire statement was adopted in substance by the church, not least of all because it had already survived its most exacting "ordeal by fire" as the president of the church served secretly and selflessly as the devil's alvocate in a godly cause.[3]

4. "The light of faith" prompts the personal judgment that Franklin Fry was respectful of theology while also dedicated to piety. Both attributes should not be unexpected in a man who loved God with all his mind.

Dr. Fry never tired of insisting that every thinking Christian should be a theologian, especially as a pastor. Fellow clergymen were constantly challenged to study, read, think. Yet in the physical presence of a professional theologian, he would often speak self-depreciatingly as one "called to squeeze an oil can on the church's squeaky machinery." (Fortunately neither he nor his listeners ever took that kind of talk too seriously!) Though he obviously was a master in church administration, he also took genuine delight in theological discussion. Nor was he too proud to request theological guidance for taxing administrative duties: "Help! Would it be at all possible for you to suggest the wording that you think would be required . . ." (January, 1967). In fact, he once remarked that he would gladly have become a professional theologian if he had ever been exposed to more than arid Lutheran scholasticism in his own seminary training. His vigorous support of Lutheran seminary mergers was rooted in his commitment to theological excellence. Perhaps his theological temperament was more akin to that of a Melanchthon than to a Luther; he served the Lutheran church's theological task best by clarifying and organizing the more creative but less systematic efforts of a Martin Heinecken or a Joseph Sittler. It should also be said openly to his credit that, during his administrations, no ULCA or LCA theologian was ever allowed to be subjected to the pressures and even harassment that had to be endured by colleagues in other American Lutheran bodies during those same years of biblical and theological upheaval.

Yet for all of his pride before men, Franklin Fry appeared to be humble before God. He preached a simple gospel centered in the saving righteousness of God in Christ. He was well versed in the scriptures, especially the Pauline epistles. Never was that great bear of a man more lovably human than when reverently singing all seven verses of an old German hymn—very slowly, very loudly, and very much off key in his painfully flat, Ohio nasal twang. If he was all too prone to pray for the whole family of God before his own beloved clan, he also quite matter-of-factly expected God to care for those whom official duties often compelled him to neglect both as a husband and as a father. He knew how to sacrifice for the Lord of the church and felt few qualms in asking other strong Christians to do the same.

Franklin Clark Fry will be missed—and remembered—as one of the first ecumenical astronauts to explore God's universal church.

---

[1] P.K. is an American colloquialism: "preacher's kid."

[2] Other writers on this subject are listed with the memo of Lilje (No. 58).

[3] LCA Minutes, 1964, pp. 491-493.

Memos 41 to 47 deal with *the wider range of Dr. Fry's churchmanship* —international Lutheranism and ecumenical Christianity.

41

Paul C. Empie

Dr. Empie analyzes President Fry as a church statesman and a person, devoted to ecumenism as well as Lutheranism. He illustrates with incidents from the National Lutheran Council, from Dr. Fry's relations with the American Lutheran Church and the Lutheran Church–Missouri Synod, and from the Lutheran World Federation, the National Council of the Churches of Christ in the USA, and the World Council.

How does one go about the process of reflecting objectively about a person like the late Franklin Clark Fry? He aroused such a range of reactions from those he dealt with—from adulation to dislike—that the truth seems elusive. The search almost resembles the plight of the proverbial seven blind men, each of whom described the shape of an elephant by the part of its body he happened to touch!

Even his critics must concede that he was one of the truly great men of his generation. I was privileged to work with him for a quarter of a century. I learned more from him in the process than from anyone else I have known, and shall always be indebted to him. At times the tuition was painful but the lesson was always worth it.

He once told me that friends were life's greatest treasure, and that he had few real friends. I think I was one of them but can never be quite sure. It seemed as though in his working relationships he bent over back-

---

(b. 1909) Along with Franklin Clark Fry the most distinguished leader of cooperative and ecumenical Lutheranism in America, Dr. Empie joined the NLC staff in 1940, and from 1948 to 1966 served as its executive director. He helped organize Lutheran World Action (1940) and Lutheran World Relief (1945); he has directed LWA since it began, and from 1952 to 1970 was chairman of LWF/World Service. He is termed by Dr. Wolbrecht (No. 53) the person most responsible for getting under way the "Inter-Lutheran Consultation" which led to the creation of the Lutheran Council in the USA in 1967; he served as co-secretary of the consultation. From 1967 he has concentrated his attention on international Lutheran matters, as general secretary of the USA National Committee of LWF and, since Dr. Fry's death, president of Lutheran World Relief. Meanwhile he has participated intimately in the affairs of the National Council of Churches, and in the 1960s he helped organize national theological consultations between Reformed and Lutherans, Catholics and Lutherans, Orthodox and Lutherans.

wards not to be partisan to his friends and often was harder on them than on those he disliked. At times he would open up with a frankness that was almost embarrassing, revealing his contempt or disgust with individuals of fairly high standing and reputation. It was almost as though he were saying, "Look, I have to get this off my chest to someone, and that's one of the things friends are for! Naturally they will respect my confidence."

At other times he would open up to friends in the most intimate way, disclosing insights and pearls of wisdom. And above all, he was *loyal* to his friends to the end.

In his early years as president of the United Lutheran Church in America he was brash and had supreme confidence in his own judgment. At times this made him all too impatient with those who did not quickly recognize that he was right and concur with his opinions. For example, following the successful conclusion of the 1946-47 $10,000,000 Lutheran World Action appeal, the National Lutheran Council Executive Committee debated at length the size of the 1948 LWA goal. Some wanted to continue at the $5,000,000 annual level. Dr. Fry insisted that $3 million must be the limit. Over his protest the goal was set at $4 million. Whereupon, in an outburst of frustration, he berated the entire committee, saying in effect, "Now that you have seriously disrupted the plans of the ULCA in 1948, you'll have to bear the consequences." Then for the first time he mentioned the ULCA's projected $6,000,000 Christian Higher Education Year appeal, something which had at no time entered the debate. Actually both the LWA goal and the CHEY appeal were oversubscribed.

My point in relating this incident is merely that he had expected the rest to go along with his judgment without even giving his reason. He mellowed considerably in this respect in his later years. I once said to him, "Dr. Fry, God didn't see fit to endow everyone with the gifts you possess. The rest of us far outnumber you, and you'll have to learn to put up with us!" He laughed and made no comment.

When Dr. Fry erred, he was quick to apologize. Once at an annual meeting of the NLC at Atlantic City I presented an oral report explicating and supplementing my written report circulated in advance. Dr. Fry, as was often the case, sat in front working on double-crostics. At the conclusion of my report, he asked for the floor and sharply criticized something in my written report, which I had considerably modified orally. After the session, I went to him and said, "Dr. Fry, we can't go on like this. You practically called me a liar, even after I had clarified the point you raised in my oral statement." He accepted my word instantly. "I'm sorry, Paul," he exclaimed, "I'm truly sorry. I wasn't listening at that point. I beg your pardon." And he meant it!

Dr. Fry had neither respect for nor patience with those who acted like doormats. He despised "rubber-stamps." At one time during a meeting of the NLC Executive Committee, he expressed a harsh opinion of some one or something. I don't remember the issue. Whereupon Dr. Julius Bodensieck sprang to his feet, pointed his finger, and exclaimed, "That's wrong and unkind, Dr. Fry, you should repent for saying that—you should repent!" Despite this public rebuke—a rare experience for Dr. Fry—he always respected and honored Dr. Bodensieck, speaking of him with affection.

During the ill-fated attempt of Dr. P. O. Bersell in 1949 to persuade the churches to transform the NLC into a federation, hopefully to include the Lutheran Church—Missouri Synod, the stubbornness of Dr. Fry in refusing to accede to Dr. Behnken's stipulation—no doubt wisely—brought the meeting to naught (so I was told—I was not there). Dr. S. E. Engstrom later told me that he had asked Dr. Fry to sit with him in the coffee shop and had said to him in effect, "Dr. Fry, you're a big man, but you're not big enough to stand in the way of progress toward Lutheran unity." Dr. Fry was unmoved, but continued to hold Dr. Engstrom in high esteem. When the latter died, he made a special effort, in the midst of a crowded schedule, to fly to Minneapolis for the funeral.

It is fair to say that Dr. Fry always acted with consistency and integrity according to his own light, regardless of opposition from friend or foe. I believe that history will judge him kindly in this respect. He had little use for the policy of "selective fellowship" among Lutherans, and insisted that upon the basis of the Lutheran confessions, full pulpit and altar fellowship was called for without further delay. At the 1963 Helsinki assembly of the Lutheran World Federation, both the LCA and the American Lutheran Church sponsored morning communion services. Many ALC delegates attended and communed at the LCA service. Dr. Fry attended the ALC service, but conspicuously—consistent to the last!—sat firmly in his seat during the administration of the sacrament. "Anyone who rejects my church rejects me," he told me; "I'll be no exception to anybody's rules!"

Again, he may have been right in thus forcing the issue. I always learned to ponder, not about what Dr. Fry intended by a particular move, but about what would be his fourth or fifth move thereafter. He played tactics like a game of chess, enjoying it to the hilt, and usually to the ultimate benefit of the church.

In considering a draft of the constitution of the National Council of Churches, Dr. Fry had stated that forty-two changes would be necessary to harmonize it with "the representative principle" and "the evangelical principle," if the ULCA were to become a member. All the changes were made. He told me with considerable glee how at the next meeting of the constitution committee Mrs. Harper Sibley began the discussion by saying, "Mr. Chairman, what do the Lutherans want this time?"

One of my greatest debts to him is related to his insistence on being precise in the use of words. Time after time he would ask in meeting what a particular statement meant, or would attack it. When the intention of the author was explained, he would reply, "Well, that's not what the words actually say, and I can only go by what is stated in the text." Listening to him expound on the proper use of language was an education in itself.

One of his superb gifts was that of instantly putting his finger on the key point of any issue. This gift was used continuously in his capacity as president of Lutheran World Relief, during the board meetings of which extremely complicated policy problems constantly arose. Here his fabulous memory served him well, bringing before us previous incidents or precedents which illuminated the issue at hand. These discussions often led him into detours in the course of which he would reminisce at length about people and world problems in an altogether fascinating way. In small intimate groups of this sort, he was at his best, for he felt completely uninhibited. He loved to challenge the lawyers, professing to be a layman in the field, but often revealing unusual depth in his understanding of the fine points of law.

In the efforts to bring the Lutheran Church–Missouri Synod into the discussions for the establishing of a new joint Lutheran agency, a critical point had been reached.[1] In my report to the National Lutheran Council in 1958, I had pointed out that the pending mergers of eight Lutheran bodies into two created a new situation which called for reassessment of the NLC, and that any new plans should involve the Missouri Synod. My specific recommendation was that acting under a constitutional provision, the NLC study the desirability of restructuring from scratch, and invite the Lutheran Church–Missouri Synod to participate in the discussions from the very start.

Dr. Fry then arose to make a motion which would alter the procedure from my proposal, though aiming toward the same goal. He moved that the NLC, with permission from the participating bodies, invite the Lutheran Church–Missouri Synod to an exploratory meeting in order to examine present cooperative activities in American Lutheranism and the possibility for extension of such activities. I was worried that this direct approach might fail, and had believed that the LC-MS could more readily be induced to begin with a smaller step of sitting in on discussions where it would have full voice and might help frame proposals which thereafter it could sell to its constituency.

At first it seemed that I had been right. Dr. Behnken replied with his well-publicized "state of flux" letter, to the effect that since the eight NLC bodies were in the process of merging into two churches and thus their theological positions were in a state of flux, it would be an inappropriate time for the LC-MS to consider the proposal. The invitation was rejected.

Some of the NLC church body presidents were furious, regarding the letter as an insult to the confessional integrity of their churches. The proposal seemed dead. But (according to friends of mine in the LC-MS central office) Dr. Behnken was deluged with telephone calls, telegrams, and letters protesting this arbitrary and summary action. Whereupon he wrote me another letter, to the effect that perhaps he had misunderstood, and that if the proposed discussions would include doctrinal matters, the LC-MS would be willing to participate.

This letter aroused my ire! Dr. Schiotz and I had met with Dr. Behnken and Dr. Grumm at the St. Louis airport and had made it quite explicit that conversations could and should include theological considerations. Whereupon I drafted a long letter reviewing our correspondence and conversations, making it quite evident that there had been no misunderstanding, but accepting the change in Missouri's stance. Fortunately I held the letter for review by the NLC Executive Committee meeting scheduled a few days later. Dr. Fry was not present, being seriously ill, confined in bed, and suffering great pain. Between sessions Dr. F. Eppling Reinartz, at that time the NLC president, went to Dr. Fry's bedside and read the text of the proposed letter. "Heavens, no," Dr. Fry exclaimed, "that's just the wrong thing to say!" Despite his intense pain, he then dictated to Dr. Reinartz a brief, four-sentence letter which began with the words, "We have received your letter with a welcoming spirit. . . ." His tactics were perfect, mine had been stupid! It was one of his major contributions to the ultimate establishing of the Lutheran Council in the USA.[2]

Another incident discloses a completely different side of Dr. Fry's character. When we traveled together in 1950 for our first contact with Lutherans in Yugoslavia, we had a long and fascinating interview with Marshal Tito at his island retreat of Brione. Later we proceeded to Belgrade where Dr. Fry had arranged to meet with the leader of the Serbian Orthodox Church. A reporter came to our room at the Moskow hotel, for an interview. He spoke English fluently. At the conclusion of the interview, he closed his notebook, and turned to Dr. Fry saying, "May I ask you a personal question?" Told to proceed, he said, "You are intelligent and sophisticated men. How then can you be Christians and serve in the church?" An eager look came over Dr. Fry's face as he quickly and succinctly expounded the gospel, in contemporary terms and in a twentieth century context. The reporter was visibly moved. When he had left, Dr. Fry turned to me and exclaimed, "This is one of the high points of my whole trip! There is no greater function in the church than the pastoral one, and *how I miss it!*"

Actually, of course, his pastoral concern was evident all through his brilliant ecclesiastical career. He loved to meet with world-renowned public figures and get their signatures in his autograph book (he got Marshal Tito to sign—typically I have a beautiful color-slide of the three of us), yet his heart never lost its sensitivity to the spiritual needs of the congregation.

Yes, he was a great man, to whom the whole Christian church and I personally will always be indebted. His faults were in fact made more conspicuous by the massive scale of his virtues. I often have said, and continue to say publicly and privately: "Thank God for His gift to the twentieth century in the person of Franklin Clark Fry."

---

[1] See F. K. Wentz, *Lutherans in Concert. The Story of the National Lutheran Council 1918-1966*, Minneapolis, 1968, pp. 171-174.

[2] Document 245 in Wolf, *Documents of Lutheran Unity*, prints abridgements of several of the aforementioned communications of 1958-59: The NLC resolution, three letters of Dr. Empie to Dr. Behnken, and two letters of Dr. Behnken to Dr. Empie.

42

O. Frederick Nolde

Dr. Nolde comments chiefly on Franklin Fry's entrance into leadership in the ecumenical movement and his devotion to it, with a glance at other aspects of his personality.

In his life of public service Franklin Fry contributed so much and from his contributions so much can be learned that any brief accounting is misleading and indeed presumptuous. It is only with the understanding that this present venture is preliminary to further assembling and analysis that I mention a few factors which in my opinion must find place in any more final evaluation.

From where I was in a position to observe, his dedication to the ecumenical movement must find high place. During the first meeting of the central committee following the Amsterdam assembly in 1948 while plans were being laid for the newly-founded World Council of Churches, Dr. Visser 't Hooft commented to me: "That Franklin Fry has much to give in depth to the ecumenical movement and he'll be in a better position to make his contribution if he holds a high office. He is going to be named vice-chairman of the central committee and we are convinced that in due course he will become chairman."

Franklin Fry and Visser 't Hooft had not always seen eye to eye prior to that occasion, nor did they always agree subsequently. But commitment to a common Lord and devotion to a common cause brought them at the end of the road to a deep friendship with mutual respect.

Thirteen years later—when Fry had completed a distinguished seven-year term as chairman—the decision was reached to invite him to continue in office for a second term. Prior to the election by the central committee,

---

(b. 1899) A schoolmate of Dr. Fry at Philadelphia Seminary, Dr. Nolde served his alma mater in the department of religious education from 1923 (professor 1931) to 1969, and as dean of its graduate school 1943-62. He was also an associate professor at the University of Pennsylvania (1925-43). Becoming a specialist in international affairs, he was an associate consultant for the Federal Council of Churches to the United States delegation at the formation of the United Nations (1945). Associate director (1946) and then director of the World Council's Commission of the Churches on International Affairs (1948-68), he is widely credited with having drafted the article on freedom of thought, conscience, and religion in the United Nations' Universal Declaration on Human Rights (1948). He was vice-chairman of the Carnegie Endowment for International Peace 1959-69.

I was talking with Hilda Fry at the Jampath Hotel in New Delhi. She remarked that requirements made of Franklin had progressively increased and that mounting fatigue made necessary a limitation upon further commitments. Nevertheless, whatever the cost, his services would be available to the World Council of Churches.

In his public life and in his personal practice, Franklin Fry elevated the pastoral office. Many people saw him only as a competent and fair administrator. Some regarded him as difficult to get along with and few found themselves really comfortable in his presence. Yet my inclusion of this characteristic is prompted by reports from those who observed it or who, as I myself, personally experienced it in time of bereavement.

One cannot omit reference to Franklin's multiple competences. A single illustration must suffice. A most able chairman, he seemed almost to scoff at ordinary human beings who got themselves involved in complicated procedural disorders out of which he extricated them while at the same time doing most complex acrostic puzzles.

Franklin had few diversions or convincingly distracting hobbies. He was for years an ardent New York Yankee fan—in fact receiving the scores periodically while chairing a meeting during baseball season, particularly during the world series.

Perhaps his lot might have been easier if he had been disposed to find outlets in small talk and small affairs which distract lesser men. However, Franklin Fry never sought an easy life.

43

Stewart W. Herman

Dr. Herman vividly recounts President Fry's early experiences in postwar Europe: the promotion of material relief and reconstruction, aid to orphaned missions, problems of church reorganization in Germany including the personalities of Bishop Marahrens and Martin Niemoeller, and the relation of ecumenism and Lutheranism in Fry's churchmanship.

Before his first year as president of the United Lutheran Church in America had ended, Franklin Clark Fry was thrown by virtue of his high office into the maelstrom of European postwar relief and reconstruction. Within the years 1944-1948 he rose in a breath-taking spiral of ecclesiastical escalation, from the position of an ecumenically obscure parish pastor to the vice-chairmanship of the Central Committee in the newly formed World Council of Churches. It is on this period that my memory of him most vividly focuses.

The end of World War II coincided with the beginning of an arduous challenge to all Christians, but especially to Lutherans. Two needs loomed large: first, the provision of material aid to both friends and enemies in war-ravaged Europe,[1] and secondly, the reconstitution of interchurch ties for the resumption of Christian mission. Lots of apparently insurmountable obstacles littered the bombed-out roads.

In retrospect, some of the obstacles now seem inconsequential. Writing back to us in Geneva from Copenhagen in mid-December, 1945, Dr. Fry was characteristically lavish in his appreciation of our hospitality, then added,

> Yes, my passport was found. We finally had to break open the lobby desk—with the concierge's permission—and there it was in

---

(b. 1909) A graduate student and then pastor in Germany during the 1930s, and during World War II a member of the US Office of Strategic Services, Dr. Herman served on the WCC Geneva staff of Reconstruction and Interchurch Aid (1945-47), and was the first American civilian church worker to enter Germany after the war. Next he became the first executive secretary of the LWF Service to Refugees (1948-52). During these periods scores of his articles on the European situation published in the church press helped to arouse the concern of Americans for fraternal aid. He became secretary of the LWF office on Latin America (1952-63) and executive secretary of the Division of LWF Affairs for the USA National Committee (1956-63). He was the first president of the merged Lutheran School of Theology at Chicago from 1964 to 1971.

> the top drawer. Quite evidently it had never been given to the [Swiss] police. Alas, I left a small bundle of soiled wash in the cabinet in my hotel room. Will you please retrieve it when you can? Send it over with Michelfelder when he comes to America in a couple months—if he will carry it. The Swiss frontier guard picked up my extra ration coupons, demanded them!
>
> Here's the pay-off! The Visitors Bureau [U. S. Military] clean forgot to send a car to Basle for me. Luckily I was able to ride all the way with a captain [U. S.] from the leave command in Berne. It was an uneventful journey except for a slipping clutch, trouble with lights and *two* flats. The second left us sitting in the frigid night for one hour and a half from 9 to 10:30 p.m. out in the country. I arrived too late in Frankfurt to get out to the Guest House so I holed up in the freezing Carlton Hotel.

"Uneventful journey"—but only in comparison with various adventures during the previous month when we had skidded off the icy autobahn at night while going back and forth across the cold and hungry country to talk with military and church leaders.

Food and clothing were urgently needed after the war, but Bishop Oxnam who led the party consisting of Bishop Sherrill and Dr. Fry took the position that there would be "no mass starvation" in Germany that winter—certainly not in the U. S. Occupied Zone. This raised a small storm of public protest at home. Then came an account of the visit to President Truman in the White House on January 16, 1946, as excerpted from Dr. Fry's letter to me a few weeks later.

> Then it was my turn. I rehearsed the encouragement which we had received from General Clay on this point and was met by hesitation. When I pressed further, the answer came back from our representative among the Big Three that, of course, nothing would be shipped into the American Zone or into any part of Germany until there was an inter-Allied agreement among all four powers. It was an affair for the Allied Supreme Council. As a gentle refutation, I then produced our letter from the British Army of the Rhine sanctioning our shipping all kinds of materials there. The President missed the refutation but reacted vigorously. He pounded the desk that no supplies could be sent anywhere else in Germany until the needs of the American Zone were met first.
>
> "But, Mr. President, according to your own statement we are not allowed to ship into the American Zone and won't be for the foreseeable future. Why then can't we send the clothing which has been accumulated already to the Christians of North Germany [British Zone]?" To that the President said in perplexity, "You

don't think for a moment that we are going to have to wait for the other Allies, do you? Just be patient and we'll have the American Zone open."

"Oh, that's wonderful. Can we tell our people that the permission will come soon?" "No, I don't know when it will be. It will be indefinitely delayed."

At that Oxnam, give him credit, broke in. "But, Mr. President, our concern is for this winter. We are anxious for the stuff to get there without delay."

The final Presidential reply was the piece de resistance. "Don't you worry. We'll have the inter-power agreement and the relief supplies will arrive long before the winter is over."

I know that the whole thing sounds as if I am crazy. I'm not! The conversation is accurately reported in substance. A later phase of the interview, about Myron Taylor at the Vatican,[2] made, if anything, even less sense. We all came out shaking our heads, groping, hoping that we would wake up. As for me, I declared to my fellow-visitors I was going out "to build fires."[3]

Build fires he did! When the smoke cleared away CRALOG (Committee of Relief Agencies Licensed to Operate in Germany) had been established, and Lutheran World Relief, of which Dr. Fry was president until his death, was ready to send its representative and the first relief shipment before the end of March—but to the American Zone.

Dr. Fry was equally interested in the fate of the "orphaned" missions.[4] I had written to him at length regarding a rather tense meeting between representatives of the German mission societies and of the International Missionary Council at Baarn, Holland, in May, 1947. The Germans —men like Freytag of Hamburg, Ihmels of Leipzig, Hartenstein of Basel, Berner of the Rhineland—hoped soon to resume a full share in the great world mission enterprise. Almost two years since VE-Day![5] Two paragraphs from Dr. Fry's immediate response to me in Geneva:

> A copy of my recent letter to Grossjann of the Syrian Orphanage [in Jerusalem] Committee will be the most eloquent evidence (not that you need it!) that we American Lutherans are not conspiring to seize permanent possession of the German mission field. We would feel a swimming in the head and a sinking in the pit of the stomach if we were confronted with any such mammoth responsibility. Selfishly as well as theologically and fraternally, we want to hand over the immense burden as speedily as possible. That goes for the American Lutheran Church in New Guinea,[6] I am sure, although it has assumed from the start that the Germans will not be readmitted to that territory and it has probably proceeded in a way that is seemingly more oblivious to German inter-

ests than any other American sponsoring agency. Don't forget, though, that the American Lutheran Church is still only the agent of the American Section [of the Lutheran World Convention] in New Guinea and that the American Section's undeviating policy about the return of German missions rules there too.

It is distinctly to the credit of the Germans that they have set their wills against believing that they will be debarred from many areas of the earth's surface for years to come. They still cannot comprehend the revulsion and suspicion with which they are regarded in so many quarters. It is probably good for their sanity not to realize the disfavor in which they stand to the full. At the same time I sympathize with them at hesitating merely to train up missionaries for foreign societies. Pastor Niemoeller made that offer unequivocally here in America and even as he did it, I made a mental remark that such an action would have to rest upon an almost superhuman magnanimity.

In a matter of weeks the Lutheran World Federation was to be established in Lund, Sweden, and in the following year the World Council of Churches would gather for its first assembly at Amsterdam. Dr. Fry had become key figure in the Lutheran effort to sort out relationships and priorities ever since that first visit to Germany when he sidestepped Bishop Meiser of Bavaria's obvious appeal to support the proposal for a United Lutheran Church of Germany (VELKD) in opposition—at that time—to the proposal of the *Bekennende Kirche*[7] for an Evangelical Church in Germany (EKID) based on the Barmen Declaration of 1934. As it turned out, both organizations were formed and still exist—but the acute antagonisms which once informed them have virtually evaporated.

Personalities were very much involved. On the same first trip Dr. Fry and Dr. Ralph Long, executive secretary of the National Lutheran Council, stopped to see Dr. Marahrens, bishop of Hannover, also president of the Lutheran World Convention.[8] Fry's letter from Copenhagen on December 14, 1945, already cited, says:

Long gave Marahrens both barrels about M's dealings with the Nazis and the handicap which he has become to the church but the old man mountain didn't budge an inch. I am almost despairing about him! Meanwhile I wrote long memos to Lilje about all that was said at Geneva.

Another personality, of course, was Dr. Martin Niemoeller. He had emerged from concentration camp as a hero and it was proposed almost immediately that he should visit the U. S. as a guest of our churches. Would the Lutheran churches co-sponsor the visit of a man who was known to be hostile to the idea of a United Lutheran Church and strongly in favor of the EKID? From Dr. Fry's letter of June 18, 1946:

> Let us consider the Niemoeller incident in particular because I surmise that Doctor Cavert's report of our attitude may have ignited the spark. A purist like you will tell me instantly that you cannot ignite a spark, that you only ignite the punk—but I hate to call myself a punk! Doctor Cavert reported the true facts but I fear that his terse statement, as he has repeated it to me, may have aroused some serious misconceptions. Our American group did unanimously, with the full concurrence of Wentz and Bersell, come to the conviction that a visit by Niemoeller last spring would have been unfortunate. You may be surprised at the reasons. You may even be astonished when I tell you that they had nothing to do with our view of Niemoeller's ecclesiastical, to say nothing of confessional position in Germany. I *hope* that you will believe me anyway. In all of our discussion and in the deep recesses of my own mind there were only two considerations. We felt first that excessive American adulation of Niemoeller might have unwholesome repercussions in Germany when he returned. In a word, I was afraid that they would make him look like a Quisling. If I wanted to compromise him, there would have been no shrewder device that I could recommend. It is because we emphatically did not want to compromise him that we cautioned delay.

A few months later he wrote:

> Good reports have reached me through Dr. Cavert about the reception that Pastor Niemoeller has received widely during his tour. An unfortunate note was struck by an RNS [Religious News Service] release which announced that we Lutherans were dissociating ourselves from the sponsorship of our mutual friend. It was a distortion of a simple little statement to our own church press that we were leaving the scheduling of his itinerary exclusively to the Federal Council. It had already taken it over!

Of course, the key to the issue in Germany at that time was the word *Kirche*. That was the important—and ambiguous—term in the title of both the VELKD and the EKID. Were these agencies to be regarded as churches or merely as federations of churches? The EKID was to become—and did become—the representative member body from Germany in the World Council of Churches. Strong exception was taken to this because EKID was composed of autonomous Lutheran, Reformed, and Union church bodies, but the main argument in favor of a single membership was that postwar Germany desperately needed this symbol of Christian unity.

Dr. Fry's ability to analyze complex issues is well remembered. He had no difficulty in distinguishing between literate ecumenicity and alphabet soup, between true councils and councils masquerading as churches. In spite of the ambiguity surrounding EKID, he took his position solidly on the side of the World Council of Churches. His declaration of ecumenical loyalty in a letter of March 8, 1946, is significant in the light of what he would be writing a few weeks later:

> As for my statements to the other Lutherans of America, every one of them has been calculated to sustain confidence in the World Council and to encourage them to persevere in joining it—if! . . . Through it all, the issue of confessional representation has remained paramount, of course, as has been from the beginning.
>
> As soon as 't Hooft's reassuring letter about Germany [no further pressure "for an interconfessional solution"] arrived I immediately heralded the joyous news to all my fellow-presidents as a welcome, further proof of the good faith of the World Council and of the rightness of our joining it. Since then the United Evangelical Lutheran Church (nee United Danish) has taken the first decisive steps. That is a conclusive proof of the spirit of the leadership that I have consistently striven to give. All the others, not counting Missouri, are firmly in line.
>
> I hope that I have allayed your misgivings about my own position. It will be another act of true friendship on your part if you set the misapprehensions of others in Geneva at rest. On my honor, every criticism either thought or spoken, in my heart or on my lips, has arisen from my utterly sincere desire that the World Council will succeed and that our church can have an eager and constructive share in it. Although I don't formally belong to their number in America, I claim to be a friend of the World Council second to none.[9]

But his letter of April 16 shows strong hesitation regarding possible developments in Germany if the mood of the EKID leadership should prevail.

> Niebuhr and others here sense the theological implications of the tussle within the EKID. The Confessional Church with its *Bruederrat* typifies embattled Barthianism to our friend from Union Seminary, who has been reporting a fact which has been familiar to us for a long time that "the Confessional Movement in Germany is almost completely under the influence of Barth and his followers." Many here are none too happy at the threat that this tendency may prevail.

Two months later, June 18, he comments on an article I had written regarding the need for a more generous Lutheran approach to the ecumenical movement:

> If the Bekennende Kirche is rightly free to advance its views in a vigorous, organized way in favor of a common faith and against "historical characteristics" of provincial Churches, are the Lutherans entirely wrong in seeking some united voice? Mind you, I have declared myself in season and out of season in many groups of American Lutherans against the early formation of a United Lutheran Church in Germany because I dread that it might be divisive when the Lord and the times clearly call for united action. But is even a passive resistance against any of the views of the Bekennende Kirche a sign of guilt? Within the past decade the accusation has been made that a nation which has been solely on the defensive has been responsible for the war that is waged against it. I know that the simile is not perfect as it is applied to the Church situation in Germany. But is there not at least a hint that the Lutherans there are in somewhat the same predicament? Frankly several of us have been disquieted by accents which seem to be coming increasingly from Geneva in favor of all-out unionism. The minutes of the meeting of church directors on April 28th and April 1st are full of them. For instance when Doctor Cockburn [Director of Reconstruction at WCC] is quoted as saying that it is "essential that denominational differences should be sunk" in church extension, we hesitate. But why go on? We are in danger of getting not only into disagreement but into acrimony. And that I would deplore. All that I want to add is that just today an influential Presbyterian and an equally influential Methodist voice have been raised here in New York to speak the same caution.

Those who knew him will recognize in these few excerpts from personal correspondence the authentic voice of Franklin Fry, champion by turns of wide-ranging confessional and interconfessional convictions, who by turns could be both ingratiating and imperious in his progress toward unity in truth.

---

[1] The story of Lutheran overseas relief and reconstruction is told in R. W. Solberg, *As Between Brothers*, Minneapolis, 1957; see also F. K. Wentz, *Lutherans in Concert*, Minneapolis, 1968 (history of the National Lutheran Council). The wider context is seen in H. E. Fey's account of Church World Service, *Cooperation in Compassion*, New York, 1966. More briefly: Fey, ed., *The Ecumenical Advance* (vol. 2 of *History of the Ecumenical Movement:* 1948-68), London, 1970, chapter 8; and Cavert, *Church Cooperation and Unity in America*, New York, 1970, chapter 10. Memos in this volume by Sherrill (No. 78) and Confer (44) also deal with this early period of interchurch aid.

[2] President Roosevelt had appointed Myron C. Taylor his "personal envoy to the

Vatican" in 1940. President Truman's determination to continue this arrangement greatly exercised American Protestants. The Federal Council of Churches protested vigorously. See Cavert, *American Churches in the Ecumenical Movement,* New York, 1968, pp. 170, 214. Several times between 1947 and 1952 Dr. Fry reported on the subject in the *Pastor's Desk Book.*

[3] Bishop Sherrill's memo (No. 78) also alludes to the visit to Germany by the Federal Council deputation of Oxnam, Sherrill, and Fry in December, 1945, with Stewart Herman as guide. Their report appeared in the FEDERAL COUNCIL BULLETIN, January 1946, pp. 6-7. See also the LUTHERAN, January 9, 1946, pp. 4-7, and Solberg, *op. cit.*, pp. 36-38. The LUTHERAN of January 30, p. 4, briefly reported the interview with President Truman by the delegation of Oxnam, Roswell Barnes, and Fry; see also pp. 4-6 and February 6, p. 4.

[4] Lutheran aid to orphaned missions, through the National Lutheran Council's Commission on Younger Churches and Orphaned Missions (CYCOM), is recounted in Solberg, *op. cit.*, and F. K. Wentz, *op. cit.* For the larger context see K. S. Latourette and W. R. Hogg, *World Christian Community in Action,* New York, 1949. See also the memo of Schiotz (No. 50).

[5] "Victory in Europe Day" was May 8, 1945.

[6] The (former) American Lutheran Church cooperated with the Leipzig Mission Society and the United Evangelical Lutheran Church of Australia to serve the mission in New Guinea.

[7] The *Bekennende Kirche,* which rallied around the famous Barmen Declaration, was the outstanding organized movement of German church opposition to Hitler. Cf. A. C. Cochrane, *The Confession of the Church under Hitler,* Philadelphia, 1962. The name was earlier translated "Confessional Church"; subsequently the more accurate translation "Confessing Church" has gained wider acceptance, for it distinguishes the movement from the "confessional" Lutherans and Reformed.

On the early development of the EKID and the VELKD, both of which were established between 1945 and 1947, see R. Rouse and S. C. Neill, *History of the Ecumenical Movement:* 1517-1948, 2nd ed., London, 1967, pp. 466-468.

[8] The memo of Lilje (No. 58) also alludes to the episode. On the period of transition from the Lutheran World Convention (founded 1923) to the Lutheran World Federation (1947), see Solberg, *op. cit.*

[9] A group of American contributors to the WCC organized themselves in the early 1940s as "Friends of the World Council."

44

Bernard A. Confer

The long-time executive of LWR observes not only Dr. Fry's political and tactical sagacity in the cause of overseas service, but also his readiness to spend himself for it.

Dr. Fry over the years showed a keen sense of the importance of political considerations. In and out of the church some people have spoken in deprecating fashion of some of the things he did or said which were more or less obviously tactical moves. I must say that I never felt in sympathy with his critics at this point. I have only admiration for the way Dr. Fry understood human nature and was willing to take the little political steps which led to securing larger goals which he had set. Too many very capable people are willing to go out on a limb for large objectives but do not want to take the time and exercise the patience to achieve the little steps which make the large accomplishments possible.

Over and over Dr. Fry demonstrated that he was a master at the political. A little incident will demonstrate his technique. About a year after Dr. Bengt Hoffman assumed the directorship of the Department of World Service of the Lutheran World Federation I mentioned to President Fry that Dr. Hoffman for many months was not adequately responsive to me or my colleagues in Lutheran World Relief. Dr. Fry said that he had word that Dr. Hoffman would visit the United States in several months' time and he would see what he could do about this.

In connection with Bengt's visit Dr. Fry invited the senior Lutheran World Relief staff and their wives to his home for dinner and the evening, with Bengt Hoffman as guest of honor. In an atmosphere of friendliness and conviviality he with no apparent intention or plan left no doubt as to his confidence and trust in the staff of LWR. As far as I know he never said a word to Bengt about the problem I had brought to his atten-

---

(b. 1914) Administrative secretary (1946) and then executive secretary of Lutheran World Relief, Inc., of which Dr. Fry was president, Mr. Confer has been for more than two decades the chief administrator of the Lutheran program of overseas material relief, in which the Missouri Synod has shared since 1953. He was chairman of the Council of Relief Agencies Licensed for Operation in Germany (CRALOG) from 1950 to 1956. Since 1955 he has been an officer of the American Council of Voluntary Agencies for Foreign Service, chairman 1968-70 and now honorary chairman. From 1956 he directed the NLC Department of Lutheran World Service; from 1957 he has served on the board of directors of Church World Service, currently as vice-chairman.

tion. I do know that following that evening in the home of Dr. and Mrs. Fry, Bengt was ever so much more friendly and understanding as he considered proposals and requests from the executive staff of LWR.

Dr. Fry was a master of tactics generally. I shall never forget the incident of the pope's tiara.

The NEW YORK TIMES carried the story of the New York luncheon at which Cardinal Spellman, who had just returned from Rome, revealed that the pope had given his tiara to the cardinal in appreciation for the generous help sent to Europe after World War II, by the Catholic church in the United States and by Americans generally. A couple of days later I had a phone call from Bishop Edward Swanstrom, the director of Catholic Relief Services, extending an invitation in behalf of Cardinal Spellman to a luncheon at his residence to discuss how the agencies together might use this diamond-studded tiara in a cooperative way for the benefit of overseas needy. In addition to the chief elected and chief staff officer of CRS and LWR there would be similar representatives of Church World Service and the American Jewish Joint Distribution Committee.

Since the luncheon was only days away I sought to reach Dr. Fry, the president of Lutheran World Relief, at once by telephone. I was able to get him out of the National Lutheran Council Executive Committee meeting in Chicago. Dr. Fry's response was instantaneous. He had another appointment for lunch that day. He suggested that I sign up Pastor Edwin Nerger, secretary of LWR and a clergyman of the Lutheran Church—Missouri Synod, to go with me. I suggested this luncheon might be pretty important to inter-group relations, but Dr. Fry said that was the very point—the subject was a sensitive one and that possibly the greatest potential problem might be within the Missouri Synod. If the luncheon revealed that some cooperation would be necessary it would be best for LWR if an officer from the Missouri Synod had had a strong role leading to the decision.

It seemed to me that Dr. Fry took a great deal of satisfaction in the fact that within Lutheran World Relief there was represented cooperation across a very broad spectrum of Lutheranism in the United States. As presiding officer he took great pains to give the board members from the Missouri Synod every opportunity to make their views known, and our guests from the Wisconsin Synod to speak as freely as they felt inclined.

During the late forties LWR did not have the Missouri Synod's cooperation nationally. When later there were some indications that cooperation might develop, the board of directors designated Dr. Paul Empie and me to visit with the national officer of the Missouri Synod with offices in New York City, Dr. O. C. J. Hoffmann. Dr. Hoffmann received our visit favorably. He said that some key men from his synod would be attending a meeting in New York City, and in connection with that meeting he would endeavor to set up a conference.

Dr. Hoffmann made appropriate arrangements with Dr. Lawrence Meyer, synodical planning counselor, and Mr. Boehne, an influential member of the synodical board of directors. It would be a dinner meeting. Dr. Fry, Dr. Empie and I would attend. When the day came, Dr. Carl Lund-Quist, general secretary of the Lutheran World Federation, happened to be in the city, and we took him along too.

The time for the meeting was very inconvenient to Dr. Fry, who was in the midst of a regular meeting of the United Lutheran Church Executive Board. He wisely arranged for a presiding officer in the event he would return late. He came to our meeting with a heavy cold. Had I been in his shoes I would have been inclined to send excuses. But Dr. Fry did come, and played a key role at the meeting. I am confident he saw not only the potential for a stronger and more effective LWR program, but also the long-term implications for relationships among Lutherans.

Many persons have looked on Dr. Fry as unquestionably an egotist. Some of the things he said and did support that point of view. But my relationships with Dr. Fry indicate that he had a trait of humility which every now and then came to the fore. His keen sense of the political and of the tactical led him to expect that due respect should be shown to a church president by virtue of his office. The combination of the presidency with awareness of possession of a tremendous intellect fostered an appearance of egotism. His readiness to complain when he was discriminated against did nothing to detract from that appearance.

Two or three stories may help add balance to the record. When I first came with Lutheran World Relief in the late forties there was a tremendous focus on needs in Germany. LWR already had a working agreement with two German-American groups, one of which was the Plattdeutsche Volksfest Verein of New York. One day I received a visit from the chairman of the PVV Relief Committee. He explained that the relief committee had secured a prominent spot on the program for the annual festival and asked that I intercede with and prevail upon Dr. Fry to be the chief speaker. When I later approached Dr. Fry he accepted the invitation with alacrity.

After the Sunday afternoon and evening affair had taken place I heard from a mutual friend what these affairs were like: a lot of beer is guzzled, singing breaks out in various parts of the hall, and the speaker at one end of the hall must compete with the operation of the bar at the other end. That the president of Lutheran World Relief was subjected to such treatment was very embarrassing to me.

Came the next meeting of our board of directors and I apologized to President Fry in the presence of the board. His response was typical of him.

"Bernie, don't let it worry you. You did the right thing. For many of those people it was the only time in the year when they hear a pastor speak."

One time the United States Government Advisory Committee on Voluntary Foreign Aid invited the American Council of Voluntary Agencies for Foreign Service to send a delegation to a meeting of the committee to discuss mutual concerns in the area of government–voluntary agency relationships. Charlotte Owen, the executive director of the American Council, assembled a delegation of the officers and invited me to be on the delegation. I already had a conflicting appointment. More important, President Fry had some deeper convictions than I in one of the areas of concern—the growing pressure for increasing the flow of government resources through voluntary agency channels. With Miss Owen's consent I asked Dr. Fry to go in my place, but explained that she insisted he could only go as my representative. He agreed, cleared his schedule, and went to the Washington meeting. I thought he might find this representative arrangement a bit uncomfortable, but not so—the first time he spoke, I am told, he started by making clear that he was present as the representative of Mr. Bernard Confer!

Another incident may be of interest here. For many years I have held that President Nasser of Egypt would be a key to the solution of the Arab refugee problem and Middle East tensions generally. Though Dr. Fry did not specifically concur with this view he never expressed difference with it, and I suspect he thought the judgment might just possibly be right. So he was not surprised when, even though we had no program in Egypt, I proposed he try to visit with President Nasser since he had to make a plane connection in Cairo anyway. Upon my approach, a mutual acquaintance, the ambassador of the Arab League at the United Nations, said he felt the conference could be arranged and he would like to set it up. Dr. Fry cooperated by scheduling more than a day in Cairo.

By the time Dr. Fry left New York the ambassador did not have a reply and at my request sent a follow-up message. The ambassador remained confident and asked that Dr. Fry get in touch with the head of the secretariat of the president upon arrival.

Upon his return to New York Dr. Fry telephoned to say that the visit with Mr. Nasser never materialized. Since he and I liked to take digs at each other, I adopted rather a stern voice and said, "But a man has to show patience in these cases." He thought I was serious and outlined at great length how he had telephoned the head of the secretariat upon arrival, referred to the ambassador's request, and left the name of his hotel and room number and stayed in his hotel until the evening. The next morning he again called the head of the secretariat and renewed the request to see President Nasser and then stayed in the hotel, taking his meals in his room until the plane left that evening. I admitted that was going pretty far. Said Dr. Fry, "Of course I had plenty to do, working out of my brief case; but it would have been nice to have been out-of-doors a little." I knew, too, he had friends in the Coptic Church and at the university he would have enjoyed seeing.

I am sure Dr. Fry could have been a success in just about any field he might have chosen. He could have been a brilliant lawyer. Had he gone into industry, I think he'd have become a giant. He was a born leader. He understood administration.

But he belonged in the organized church. And his record confirms what many of us knew him to be—the top church statesman of our time.

45

Bengt R. Hoffman

A European-born colleague analyzes Dr. Fry's style of leadership: his way of handling people, the "European" and "American" qualities of his political nature, his sensitivity to many tensions in the world service enterprise—national interests in the international program, the churchly focus and the fundamentally human focus in programs of aid to the "third world," Fry's Lutheran and ecumenical loyalties. Dr. Hoffman then brings his observations around to personal factors: Dr. Fry's spirituality and his friendliness.

Franklin Clark Fry in Europe

I

The Lutheran World Federation was unfolding its glories under the blue skies of Hannover, Germany, when I first met Franklin Clark Fry. The year was 1952 and the occasion was the second general assembly. Carl Lund-Quist, the general secretary, stood on the terrace, beckoned to me and said: "Bengt, I want you to meet Franklin Fry." Well, I was not so sure that FCF would feel like meeting another person from the crowd, a visiting worker from the World Council of Churches, secretary among many secretaries. But Carl insisted and so I was introduced. I remember him well from that first encounter in the milling crowd among the coffee tables: a large person with an *eloquentia corporis*—which he utilized—and very observing eyes. Oh yes, FCF knew about me and my work. I had been in China, hadn't I, hailed from Sweden and I was now "Referent" for the WCC's reconstruction work in Germany and Austria. All his information was neatly stored on the first floor of his mind. But he was peering at me from the second story, taking my measurements with the nimblest of mental movements, like a sort of super-tailor taking you in from top to toe before the yard tape is applied. I had the feeling he was all over me but in a friendly fashion. The second floor of his mind had a large window toward divination.

(b. 1913) Swedish-born Dr. Hoffman directed the LWF Department of World Service from 1956 to 1961. For more than a decade before that he was engaged in work with war prisoners in Great Britain, Canada, and the USA under the auspices of the YMCA, with students in Europe and China for the World Student Christian Federation, and with interchurch aid in Germany and Austria for the WCC. After teaching a year at Concordia College, Moorhead, Minnesota, he became professor of ethics and ecumenics at Gettysburg Seminary in 1967.

I said to Carl, a little awestruck: "He knew me!" Carl said: "Of course, that's Frank's specialty, to know people and remember them."

There was that peculiar sensitivity with FCF, really the ground for his memory of persons and his strength as a church politician. I sat in his New York office several years later and talked about some personnel problems in the World Service operation of the LWF which I then headed up. He said: "Those personnel questions are often hard for me. I have been endowed with a measure of sensitivity for what people are. It's something I have had to harness. It's a little of an extra burden. Useful, of course, but sometimes it gets in the way, negatively and positively."

He could be generous in admitting that the sensitivity apparatus might fail him, as it occasionally fails all of us. I made a certain field-staff appointment early in my directorship, mainly because the person was close at hand and a delay would have badly disrupted the operation and added another headache to a beginner's list of afflictions. But also because I sensed a latent capacity with the appointee. FCF had let me know indirectly—he had his ways—that in his judgment it wouldn't work. He knew, because the person belonged to his church. But the move proved successful. A year later FCF conceded, with a little slap on his right thigh: "I'll have to hand it to you. You were right; I was wrong."

Perhaps he was more outspoken about his impressions of people when away from his New York office. In Geneva he might have felt a little less inhibited. He would on occasion virtually spit out his views of a person whose qualities he questioned. It was always amusing although fairly devastating. Perhaps persons with a keen psychological perception have a special need for this kind of catharsis.

No question about it, FCF was a superior leader not least because he possessed a sixth sense for a person's number. His footwork was so swift that many people could not follow it. Many of us resent that kind of thing; it makes us feel uncertain. Psychological pedestrians in high places rather resented FCF's swiftness. They claimed it emanated from "a cold intelligence." I believe it came from "feeling." FCF mastered a meeting so well because he sensed the emanations from the participants, read their personalities, so to speak. He played on a committee as one plays on an instrument. And, of course, sometimes he used his mastery in discordant ways.

II

There was thus another side to FCF's feeling-intuition. It became a tool in his church politics. Some people object inwardly to that possibility. Perhaps they would deny that there is or should be politics in the church, especially since it gives individual ambition too much leeway. But personal ambition and advancement of causes are intertwined in the business of church politics. I don't see why we should not realistically acknowledge this within the household of faith. What we should guard against is letting our church politics occur as though (a) church politics did not exist and (b) no one is really aware of the ambiguity of church political maneuvering. FCF was in part brought up on the idea that one should not talk about Christian church politics. He acted sometimes as if he never thought that somebody might think: "Is he really unaware that some can see through?" I suppose few of us helped him to think in realistic incarnational terms about the fact of personal ambition and skill and the fact of power politics and their interconnection.

FCF not infrequently harbored an ulterior motive of a more or less political character behind an engaging cordiality. For those who knew that his jokes and "confidences" were sometimes designed as campaign material, deliberately planted, it was not always easy to take it all as ingenuous spontaneity. He often spoke and wrote of "friendship." "Overflowing friendship to all," I read in a handwritten letter to me on staff matters of May 3, 1960. He meant it. He did embrace many with a very knowledgeable and imaginative friendship. But these friends were also more or less useful in his schemes and being a realist he could never forget that. Some of us who used to meet him rather frequently heard him say more than once: "In my position I can have no real friends." I believe his "no-friendship" statement was more than the mere routine slogan to which high office holders sometimes subscribe: the loneliness of the heights and all that. FCF really suffered a little from having had to sacrifice some of the genuine for what he considered necessary prestidigitation. The child in him wanted to give and receive loyalty. The "realist" in him said that all are out for themselves anyway.

His realism was in the good old European tradition. Europeans probably understood FCF better on that score than many American church leaders who may find it hard to acknowledge that they are involved in politics as churchmen. That is to say, Europeans were not as perturbed as many Americans obviously were about power maneuvers that looked "cut and Fry-ed"—a witticism which FCF knew people were employing with respect to his political deftness. He slapped his right thigh when he quoted that one.

Unconsciously he seemed to have taken to a more "realistic," "European" stance concerning lapel-twisting and personal persuasion campaigns.

This europeanism was often discernible in FCF's americanism. It was the americanism of an easterner, a little suspicious of anything that came from west of New York and Pennsylvania, a certain awareness of belonging to the seasoned East in contradistinction to the supposedly unseasoned Midwest and West.

Yet, underneath it all was a goodly portion of the American faith. He had no patience with ethnic separatism. To the extent to which he detected ethnic assertiveness in the European churches his remarks could indeed be scorchingly anti-Danish or anti-Swedish or anti-German. I remember his treatment of the question of German pastoral care for German immigrants in Canada. Canadian Lutherans were part of the church over which he presided. The proposal was made from Germany in the second half of the fifties that the Department of World Service of the LWF[1] integrate with its annual budget the support of German-speaking ministry in Canada. The money was to have come from Germany. FCF worked determinedly against the idea. I met him several times to discuss this matter. The Lutheran churches of the new world should serve the newcomers in the language they normally used and that was English. Since the church at the receiving end, on FCF's insistence, did not approve the request, the World Service program accordingly never included the proposed item. The Germans doubtless continued to provide some pastoral care in German for non-English-speaking Germans. (It seems they had a case, seeing that many newcomers knew no English.) But FCF prevented the international channel from relaying the necessary funds.

FCF followed with keen interest all reports of our discussions in the LWF Commission on World Service about the place of national Lutheran interests in the overall program. Some national money drives emphasized rather heavily the elements of pride and self-congratulation in rising contributions. Their leaflets and flyers often underlined the fact that the national church in question was solely or primarily responsible for a given project. One was, metaphorically speaking, flying the national flag over aid projects. The commission sometimes faced rather insistent demands for inclusion of undertakings, in themselves worthy but too narrowly confined to the principle of national sovereignty, translated into church language. (The latter of course being more pious than the worldly tongue, hence less recognizable at first blush.)

There were actually two concerns which made most commission members hesitant with respect to these demands. First, there was always the fear that the addition of a "national project" would entail administrative long-term obligations, eventually falling on the general, international budget. Second, did a project which was the exclusive interest of one national group have a rightful place in a program where interchurch cooperation is the lodestar?

Compromises were certainly made, as was proper. For one thing, the initiatives and the dedication involved in "unilateral" national aid undertakings were frequently admirable. But on the whole the commission sought to implement the principle that interchurch efforts to assist humans in need should be based on joint international sharing of economic and administrative responsibility. FCF supported this principle and followed with sympathy the attempts to uphold it. In conversations about the matter he clearly showed that he had understanding for the department officials who were targets of sometimes unpleasant attacks in their defense of the supranational essence of the aid work. Once when I attended an LWR board meeting in New York where the sensitive matter was the object of some comments, FCF gave me a friendly nod from the chair, smiled and said as an aside: "I know what Bengt is up against. Some people give him a rough time on this account. But he is right." For once I had been on the side of the angels.

III

"The third world," the Asia and Africa of the have-nots, became the concern of Europeans in the fifties. It was in part a result of guilt feelings vis-à-vis the millions whom colonialism had exploited. In part it was a sign of the social equalization process in Europe. In part it reflected the theological tidal change by which *the humanum* came to the fore.

The churches began to feel the pressure from those who had become convinced that new forms of development work in Asia and Africa should be part of the Christian task. Some leaders sensed that many who lived on the outskirts of church life were prepared to accord existential significance to the institution if it would undertake such extended socio-economic assistance. (Thereby adding to an already established tradition of "practical" mission work, emergency aid, and refugee service.) We LWF/WS workers registered the new willingness. We received letters from some churches urging us to provide coordinating administrative machinery. I, for one, believed that this was a job for the LWF as far as the Lutheran churches were concerned. A process of information began, with a view to eventually integrating socio-economic development projects with our coordinative duties. Since the idea was new some exploratory initiatives had to be taken. I cannot say that all of the Mission and World Service leaders were immediately amenable to the thought. Some said that Mission should not overextend itself in the social field, since eventually mission boards would have to pick up the bill. They also said that Christian mission was direct propagation of the gospel in the first place; the needs of the underdeveloped nations should be handled by secular organs created for the very purpose of socio-economic development, for example the World Bank. But we doubtless faced an opportunity of relevant service in relation to European church people, often including the large uncommitted fringe. They wanted to help and they wanted the church to assist rather than secular organizations. We also had an opportunity to undergird the social outreach of the younger churches and strengthen their stewardship power.

A journey through eastern and southern Africa which I made together with Sigurd Aske of the Mission Department and Wolfgang Hessler of the News Bureau persuaded us that the time had come for a new move.

It was important to apprise the LWF president of the plan not least because it would come before the executive committee as a novel aspect of Lutheran World Service commitment. I discussed the matter with FCF several times in 1960 and 1961. He appeared noncommittal at first. For one thing, he was among the instigators and a staunch defender of the American Lutheran stewardship idea with respect to foreign benevolence. That is to say, giving should not be geared to individual projects or special sob stories. That would cause unevenness of support and confusion in the minds of donor and recipient alike. (The other side of the coin is that to some degree this system removes Lutheran church members in America from a sense of personal participation in the alleviation of specific needs.) Secondly, FCF always had in view the danger that the LWF might become too big an operation, thereby perhaps taking wind unnecessarily out of WCC's sails. As leader of both bodies between 1957 and 1963 he had to keep confessional initiative and interchurch interests in some sort of a balance. (However, as the WCC had taken the fundamental stance that it would not administer service projects, the nature of the WCC and the nature of the LWF interchurch aid and service to refugees in one important regard were not of the same denominator.)

It was gratifying to me when FCF came out for the new kind of service. But in the process he altered my thinking on one important point. I had originally thought of a new agency which would assume responsibility in behalf of the churches not only for information gathering and forwarding of project proposals but also for administration. FCF thought that would be too far-reaching a commitment. In retrospect I can see that his realism led us aright. When the new development service was finally approved at the Executive Committee of the LWF in Warsaw, June 1961, it was FCF's formulation that prevailed. The new activity would consist of "validation" and "coordination," not responsibility for administration of individual projects. Indigenous churches would be involved in the latter. During the sixties the development service of the LWF/WS grew substantially in range and depth. It may not be very widely known that FCF gave to it its name and course of action.

The name given the new venture was "Community Development Liaison and Validation Service." Later the title was shortened: "Community Development and Liaison Service"; the original task remains: "to validate social and economic development projects and recommend them to donor groups." This according to an article in *LWF Information,* No. 14, 1970, pp. 6-7. The same article reports the beginning of the activity as 1962. As indicated here, the inception dates further back—first as an exploratory enterprise and then as an official LWF undertaking finalized at the executive committee meeting in 1961.[2]

FCF was keenly aware of the danger of organizational hypertrophy. He was healthily skeptical of the tendency to proliferate international offices in response to various movements and demands in the churches. Arising out of decisions taken at the LWF Executive Committee meeting in Porto Alegre, Brazil, a discussion concerning interpretation arose in our "cabinet" which administered the federation during Carl Lund-Quist's sick leave in the spring of 1960. There was some lack of clarity as to the most adequate final formulation. In some branches of our work one insisted on elevation to a kind of department status and felt that Porto Alegre could be interpreted that way. On May 3, 1960, FCF sent me a handwritten letter in response to some queries from me on behalf of the "cabinet." It says in part:

> Dear Bengt, I hope I am not too late with this comment on the Porto Alegre minutes. As usual, I have been out of New York on a gruelling speaking-itinerary, day after day and in aggregate week after week.
>
> Yes, I would approve a footnote to the Personnel Practices, consisting of the words "including the senior secretary" (lower case letters) of the News Bureau. Omit the parenthetical insertion from the footnote itself, of course, and attach it to the words "unit heads" at the first place where they appear.
>
> Do we need to think through the situation of the editor of the Rundschau[3] as a parallel case? By the way, I have received a *very* unhappy letter from—— in reply to my notice to him of the gist of the Porto Alegre decisions. . . . Frank

IV

In the Chapelle des Pèlerins in Geneva we Lutherans heard FCF preach one Sunday in the end of the fifties. The sermon was delivered extemporaneously, it seemed. It dealt with the power and the glory of the world and the right proportions into which they fall under the gospel of Christ. As usual it was a masterful performance linguistically. The quotations from poetry came as though they were read directly from a printed page. But that is all external. What struck me most forcibly was that FCF was addressing himself in a very special way. There was an elegiac tone. From the positions of prominence which he had no doubt worked hard to attain (besides being self-evidently chosen), he looked at his life and said in effect: when one has achieved all this there may still be emptiness; there may still be, in fact there *is*, a deep dissatisfaction. Here was a man preaching of loneliness as a cry from the heart (not, I repeat, just the conventional confession that seems to belong to all public evaluations of high office). He was telling us how difficult it is to say genuinely: "So you also, when you have done all that is commanded you, say: 'We are unworthy servants. . . .'"

After a journey to the Near East FCF turned up in Geneva. In a meeting for quite a few WCC and LWF workers in our home he held forth entertainingly, acidly, perceptively. We asked and he answered, increasingly coaxed by our questions. The colors of his tales sparkled. He enjoyed it all, slapped his right thigh frequently. He saw the king, yes (he was fond of seeing kings, presidents, prime ministers, archbishops, popes, cardinals, and church presidents, and liked to put them down in his story a couple of notches by some deft and naughty words, the effect of which he savored for some triumphant seconds before continuing). He met with church congregations and refugees. Had he visited the Chapel of the Sisters of Zion with the partially excavated courtyard of Fortress Antonia, the place where Pontius Pilate held sway, the slab stones where Jesus the Christ stood *that* morning facing the last trial? Yes, FCF had. He grew pensive. His gaze had a far-off look. He said: "You stand there but your soul falls prostrate, your soul falls prostrate."

When I came to Gettysburg as a professor at the seminary in 1967 I sent him some lines reporting my appearance within his church. Back came a handwritten note. Never did he dream that I would land as a teacher in his old home area. How strange and how gratifying. I was thrice welcome, to the church, to the seminary, and for old friendship's sake. He thought my road had been an unusual one. "Career" was probably not the right word, he wrote. But whatever the word, should he assume that this was the definitive station? He wasn't sure in my case. That "Cordially, Frank" note is the last one I have from him. It is more personal than church-political; in fact I don't think it is political at all. FCF's life influenced mine politically, no doubt about it. (That is another story, though.) But it also touched me personally—and that's how I prefer to end this account.

---

[1] The story of LWF/World Service (established 1953) and its antecedents is told in R. W. Solberg, *As Between Brothers,* Minneapolis, 1957. Cf. F. K. Wentz, *Lutherans in Concert,* Minneapolis, 1968. See also memos of Herman (No. 43) and Muetzelfeldt (69).

[2] See also *Reports 1963-1969*. LWF, Geneva, 1970, pp. 33-47.

[3] *Die Lutherische Rundschau,* German-language organ of the LWF.

46

Edmund F. Wagner

An inscription in the Interchurch Center in New York stands for Mr. Wagner as a tangible reminder of Dr. Fry's influence in Christendom.

It was my privilege to share in many ventures of great interest to Franklin Clark Fry. One of these was the formation and building of The Interchurch Center—the nineteen-story building at 475 Riverside Drive, New York City, and covering the entire block from 119th Street to 120th Street, Claremont Avenue to Riverside Drive.[1] It took over three years to bring the early plans to a successful completion. When Dr. Fry originally asked that I sit in with the organizing group, he assured me it would not take much time—three or four meetings. Over the years I had occasion to mention this disparity of estimated time and in typical Fry fashion, with that glint in his eye, he would say, "Ed, I cannot help it if it took you so long to do such a simple job." He loved The Center and all it stands for.

Entering the west lobby through the glass doors that look out over the Hudson and the Palisades, one is greeted by the inscription of St. Paul's words on Christian unity:

There is onc body
and one spirit
just as you were called
to the one hope that belongs
to your call
One Lord—One Faith—One Baptism
One God and Father of us all
Who is above all
and through all and in all

These inspiring words from Ephesians 4:4-6 are incised in gold on a gently curving wall panel of patina rose marble from Morocco.

(b. 1898) Edmund Wagner, a New York real estate and banking executive, was president of General Realty and Utilities Corporation 1944-58, and has been an officer or director of several other large corporations and a director of the Better Business Bureau. He served as treasurer of the ULCA and then the LCA from 1952 to 1966, president of the church's Common Investment Fund 1954-68, and member of the LCA Executive Council until 1970. He was the first president of the board of trustees of the Interchurch Center, dedicated in 1960, and continues to serve in that capacity. He is current president of the American Bible Society, and a former trustee of the National Conference of Christians and Jews.

This tribute to Dr. Fry was made possible by gifts from a group of friends.

My friendship with Franklin Clark Fry is one of my most treasured possessions. The memory of it will be a joy to me throughout my lifetime. Franklin was a leader among men, yea, a leader among leaders.

I shall always be grateful for the only too few opportunities that came to us when our families could be together. These were rare occasions when this man had the available time to spend with his family and friends. I know I shall miss him, and the memory of his tremendous qualifications of leadership and devotion to the work of the Lord will forever provide a challenge to all who worked with him.

---

[1] See Cavert, *The American Churches in the Ecumenical Movement, 1900-1968,* New York, 1968, pp. 212-214.

47

Erik W. Modean

A prominent religion news editor relates two incidents from 1961, regarding Dr. Fry's position in the World Council of Churches.

It was between sessions of the National Lutheran Council's annual meeting at Detroit in 1961. Dr. Franklin Clark Fry, then president of the United Lutheran Church and destined a year later to head the new Lutheran Church in America, was holding court before an array of the nation's leading religion reporters.

"Dr. Fry," one of the reporters asked, "who seems likely to succeed you as chairman of the Central Committee of the World Council of Churches?"

It was a pertinent and timely query in that the WCC was scheduled to hold its third assembly in New Delhi that coming November. No officer of the council, by tradition, was ever elected to succeed himself.

"Well, now, let's see," responded Dr. Fry, "who are the possibilities?" Then he proceeded to discuss, dissect and discard at least a score of arrived, up-and-coming, and potential church leaders in Europe, Africa, Asia and America.

When he had completed his shrewd, perceptive, almost uncanny analysis of the strengths and weaknesses of the possible candidates, one unspoken but inescapable conclusion remained:

The only man qualified to succeed Dr. Franklin Clark Fry as chairman of the powerful, policy-making Central Committee of the World Council of Churches was Dr. Franklin Clark Fry.

He was, of course, absolutely right. Even though they criticized his magnificent ego—he was quoted as saying that modesty was a virtue reserved to those who had something to be modest about—the reporters acknowledged, almost in awe, the genius on which it was founded.

(b. 1911) Beginning a journalism career in 1928, Mr. Modean joined the NLC staff in 1945 and since 1948 has been director of the NLC News Bureau, now the LCUSA News Bureau. He headed the English news staff at the last four LWF assemblies (1952-70) and the last three assemblies of the World Council of Churches (1954-68). A leader in the Religious Newswriters Association since its founding in 1949, Mr. Modean was recently made its first life member. He also served for three years as president of the National Religious Publicity Council. He is a layman of the Lutheran Church in America.

At New Delhi the World Council, as usual, elected six presidents. If the Lutherans were represented on the presidium, it had to be by Dr. Martin Niemoeller, the famed U-boat commander of World War I, whose credentials as a Lutheran had long since been repudiated by his German peers.

"What gives?" we asked Dr. Fry in words to that effect. "Erik," he replied impatiently, as though lecturing a naive child, "it simply means that the chairman of the central committee has to be a Lutheran."

When the new central committee met later in closed session to elect its officers, it was reported to the press that a contest seemed likely to develop for the chairmanship of the committee. Reporters almost laughed themselves into hysteria over the sheer implausibility of it.

And thus it was that Dr. Fry was named to an unprecedented second term as chairman of the WCC's Central Committee, a post, it must be added, that he filled with supreme distinction from 1954 to 1961 and then until his untimely death in mid-1968, just as he did everything to which he turned his hand, his heart, and his vast resources of mind and spirit.

Part Two

Memos from the American Lutheran Church *and* the Lutheran Church—Missouri Synod

Memos 48 to 56 are written by Dr. Fry's colleagues in sister Lutheran bodies in America, men associated with him chiefly through church negotiations and through the National Lutheran Council and its successor (1967), the Lutheran Council in the USA. The memos are arranged in approximately chronological order.

48

Julius Bodensieck

Dr. Bodensieck shares a few recollections of inter-Lutheran negotiations in the early 1940s, the postwar reconstruction period, and the first decade of the LWF.

Whoever has studied a report which Dr. Fry wrote for his synod or committee knows that he was a "perfectionist." He always knew what he wanted to say and said it in the most lucid and terse language possible. Whenever he was on the program in international or interconfessional meetings we knew that he presented his case in the most comprehensive and intelligible manner. We never had reason to feel ashamed of him, and he was the best representative that our church could have chosen.

(b. 1894) Dr. Bodensieck was professor (1921-30, 1948-49, 1954-64) and president (1940-47) of Wartburg Seminary (of the former American Lutheran Church), Dubuque, Iowa. He was active in postwar reconstruction, first as commissioner to Germany from the American Section of the Lutheran World Convention (1946), then as liaison for the Federal Council of Churches between the American military government and the German churches (1946-48), and from 1950 to 1953 as a commissioner of the USA National Committee of the LWF. He was a councillor of the NLC (1943-46, 1949-50), a delegate to the LWF assemblies of 1947 and 1952, and the editor of the three-volume *Encyclopedia of the Lutheran Church* (1963), an eleven-year LWF project.

At Hannover, in 1952, when it was my honor to conduct the final mass meeting of the Lutheran World Federation at the football field of the city, Dr. Fry had been chosen as the speaker to represent American Lutheranism. For several evenings prior to the event, he and I met to put his speech into really correct and pleasing German, because he wanted to use the language of the people for his address. (He told me once that his father did not know much German, and in fact, surprised a German-speaking couple that wanted to get married by reading the section called *Trauerfeier* (Burial Service) in his German *Agende* instead of *Trauung.*) We went over his speech, I do not know how many times, and I indicated the syllables to be stressed so as to avoid a mutual friend's mistake in putting the stress in the word *Verantwortung* on the *wort* syllable.

I remember the same exactitude in the drafting of the resolutions adopted at the Minneapolis convention of LWF (1957) where the small committee which he had appointed met in the basement of the Leamington hotel night after night for eight days (with "beer and trembling," as TIME put it, because it was too late to get coffee served after 1:00 a.m.).

I observed the same almost fierce energy in committee meetings at Uppsala (1946) prior to the founding of the LWF and at many of the committee meetings preparing for the Hannover and the Minneapolis conventions.

If I may add another personal note, I should express my admiration for Dr. Fry that he never remembered my somewhat emotional outburst at an intersynodical committee meeting in Chicago in the early forties when I proposed an all-Lutheran union, then and there, and Dr. Fry brushed the idea aside as premature and preposterous (in view of Missouri's attitude) and I challenged his right to dispose of the matter in such a cavalier fashion. I think I said that he should repent for what he said. He got up from his chair and declared that he had three things to say in reply, but he was so angry at the moment that he only said two and then sat down, saying that he had forgotten the third thing.

But no one could have been more helpful to me a few years later at the meeting in Uppsala in preparing for the organization meeting of LWF.

And I think it was really he who was instrumental in persuading the then Federal Council of Churches of Christ in America to appoint me as the Protestant liaison representative between the U. S. military government and the Protestant churches in Germany, and he continued to be vitally interested in the manner in which I tried to live up to my responsibilities in that position. And generous as he was, he named me a member of the drafting committee at the Minneapolis convention.

I admired Dr. Fry as a truly Christian gentleman, as a matchless Lutheran leader, as a powerful preacher, and as a true friend.

49

Edward C. Fendt

A veteran ALC leader analyzes Lutheran intersynodical developments over two decades, eventuating in the LCUSA (1967).

President Fry in Intersynodical Fellowship Discussions

Both by natural endowment of leadership qualities and by an inflexible adherence to well defined goals, President Fry usually became the dominant figure in any intersynodical group discussing fellowship between Lutherans or eventual union of Lutheran churches in America. He knew what he wanted and he understood what others wanted. If there was a conflict of views or even contradiction of goals, his method was not to resort to compromise but to elucidate and defend his own position again and again. He was convinced that he was right and that time would prove him to have been right all along.

His assertions and clarification of issues were always characterized by winsomeness and candor. It was difficult to disagree with him. He made it so easy to follow his lead and agree with his observations. At times when he looked directly into the eyes of other members of the committee, as he spoke with precision and conviction, his "eye power" and his disarming smile at the end of his statement made further comment superfluous and unnecessary.

Dr. Fry did not always win in every intersynodical discussion on closer affiliation between Lutheran synods. He wanted a union of his own United Lutheran Church and the former American Lutheran Church in the late 1940s. But he did not want this on the basis of the Pittsburgh Agreement[1] nor did he want it after a prolonged period of altar and pulpit fellowship. He then regarded the union of these two church bodies as the best immediate approach to eventual overall Lutheran unification in America.

Shortly after Dr. Henry F. Schuh became president of the American Lutheran Church in 1950, the ALC committee on intersynodical fellowship invited its counterpart of the United Lutheran Church to a meeting to

---

(b. 1904) A member of the faculty (1929), then dean (1946) and later president (1959-71) of the Evangelical Lutheran Seminary (of the former ALC), Columbus, Ohio, Dr. Fendt was for many years a member of his church's Committee on Interchurch Relations, the Joint Union Committee, and (since the 1960 ALC merger) the Inter-Lutheran Consultation. He was a delegate to the LWF Minneapolis assembly in 1957.

discuss a mutual declaration of altar and pulpit fellowship. The ALC delegation did not insist on reviving the Pittsburgh Agreement as the basis for such fellowship, but regarded a declaration of fellowship as long delayed after both churches had adopted the Pittsburgh Agreement. About ten years earlier President Fry did not want to stop with a declaration of fellowship. He wanted the two churches to begin union negotiations.

Such a step was impossible for the ALC which had unanimously voted in its 1950 convention against a union of the churches in the National Lutheran Council (which included the ULCA) and had instead limited union negotiations to begin with churches in the American Lutheran Conference (not including the ULCA). As a result neither group could report any important developments coming from this meeting.

Dr. Fry in his earlier years as a church president was particularly pessimistic about the Missouri Synod ever coming into genuine cooperation with the churches comprising the National Lutheran Council. He had tried and lost several times in expanding that cooperation. When at long last the Lutheran Church–Missouri Synod decided to participate in discussion of the Theology of Cooperation with representatives of other Lutheran churches, as a necessary basis for forming a cooperative agency involving all of the major Lutheran churches in America, Dr. Fry was dubious about the outcome. He made up his mind and announced that he would not say anything in the first two meetings of the twenty-seven-member delegation. He kept his promise to himself and his associates, but in the third meeting after there was evidence of a common desire to seek closer affiliation he definitely took a leading role in the discussions that eventually culminated in the formation of the Lutheran Council in the USA (which began operations in 1967).[2] No man made a more significant contribution than Dr. Fry in formulating the constitutional statements of policy and procedures of this organization.

Dr. Fry was a cooperative and resourceful member of any sub-committee to which a particular task was assigned. It was here in the smaller group rather than in the chair presiding over the larger groups that the real Dr. Fry became known and appreciated. He was genuinely kind and benevolent in his attitude and suggestions.

One example will illustrate this characteristic helpfulness. He and President Behnken of the Lutheran Church–Missouri Synod were seated side by side around a table seating six. The task was to formulate the common resolution to be submitted to the negotiating churches authorizing the committees to arrange for doctrinal discussions preliminary to making plans for a cooperative agency. The other four members of the sub-committee knew that Drs. Fry and Behnken might not agree on every statement. Both presidents surprised the group by being overly generous to each other's viewpoints. Once toward the close of the meeting President Behnken suggested a wording that caused President Fry to exclaim: "We cannot accept that. The Missouri Synod will never buy that, John." His neighbor, Dr. Behnken, reached for Dr. Fry's knee under the table and said: "Thanks, Frank."

Dr. Fry's outstanding contribution to Lutheran unity in America is hard to assess fully at this juncture of confessional and ecumenical developments in Chistendom. Two factors stand out in bold relief. (1) He was a leader in the forces uniting Lutherans in loyalty to the holy scriptures as the sole basis of faith and life in their common acceptance of the Lutheran confessions, refusing to add anything further as a requirement for Lutheran church unity; (2) he was and is recognized as a gift of God to the church, whose prophetic insights and consecrated churchmanship endeared him and won respect for him in the other two major Lutheran groups in America as well as in his own church.

---

[1] The "Pittsburgh Agreement" (1940) of the ALC and the ULCA on the inspiration of the scriptures is printed in *Doctrinal Declarations*, St. Louis, 1957, pp. 69-70. See also memos by Ruff (No. 14), Henninger (15), and Krauss (16).

[2] Several other writers in Part Two also comment on the Inter-Lutheran Consultation (1960-66) which designed the Lutheran Council in the USA; see also the memo by Empie (No. 41). Cf. R. C. Wolf, *Documents of Lutheran Unity*, chapter 26.

50

Fredrik A. Schiotz

From over two decades of close association, a distinguished ALC executive discusses Dr. Fry's manner—both ingratiating and caustic—his leading and his following, his precision of mind and his devotion to the gospel.

Some Personal Observations

My first meeting with Dr. Fry occurred on the side lines of a football game at St. Olaf College in October, 1944, a few days after his election as president of the former United Lutheran Church in America. It was at the convention sessions in Minneapolis that the United Lutheran Church had responded affirmatively to the proposal by the American Lutheran Conference that the National Lutheran Council be requested to accept responsibility for the student ministry of the conference churches and the ULCA.

At the annual meeting of the National Lutheran Council in early February, 1945, the council voted to assume responsibility for the student work of all the council participating bodies. Thereupon I was elected to serve as the first executive secretary of the united work. One further action was required before the election would be a completed action, namely, the approval of the Executive Board of the United Lutheran Church.

I had two other calls at the time, and I was not at all sure that one who had been involved in the student ministry of an antecedent group should head up the united work. I sought out Dr. Fry to counsel with him. It became immediately evident that Dr. Fry was not going to "guess" at what the executive board would do. The matter was something for the executive board alone to decide. Since its meeting was six weeks away, I

(b. 1901) After serving as executive secretary of the American Lutheran Conference's Student Service Commission (1938-45) and then of the NLC Commission on Younger Churches and Orphaned Missions (1948-54), Dr. Schiotz became the last president of the Evangelical Lutheran Church (1954-60) and the first president of the new American Lutheran Church (1961-70). He has been a participant in all five LWF assemblies, chairman or vice-chairman of its Commission on World Missions since 1949, director of its Department of World Missions (1952-54), and member of its Executive Committee since 1955. He was president of the LWF 1963-70, and since then has been an honorary member of the executive committee. He served on the Executive Committee of the NLC and its successor, the LCUSA, from 1955 to 1970. He has been a member of the World Council Central and Executive Committees since 1961.

decided at once that the National Lutheran Council ought to begin its student ministry with a new man.

The consultation with Dr. Fry revealed him to be a man who was careful to follow proper administrative procedures. Important actions had to have their justification in constitutional or church resolution authorization. This careful concern for procedure spilled over into areas of protocol. At the Lutheran World Federation's Helsinki assembly in 1963, a formal university convocation preceded the opening assembly session. Ambassadors had been invited as honored guests. A member of a given diplomatic corps had been detained by important official telephone calls. When he arrived late, he was quietly ushered to his seat. Later, in a small group, Dr. Fry vehemently objected to the diplomat's late arrival. In his judgment, if the diplomat could not be there on time, he should not have accepted his seat at all.

Behind concern for proper procedure and protocol was an orderly mind that could articulate with remarkable clarity. This made him a favorite draftsman for resolutions that were to be reported out of committee sessions. And few were the times when someone else reported that editorial revisions were not offered by Dr. Fry

Dr. Fry owned a strong, manly personality. But this manliness was not inhibited from showing compassion and sympathy when the occasion prompted it. I recall an experience in late November, 1948, when this quality became very visible for me.

Dr. Fry was the chairman of the Commission on Younger Churches and Orphaned Missions of the National Lutheran Council and I served as its executive secretary. I had been on a visitation trip among some of the younger churches of Asia. This included the Batak Church of Indonesia. Because of the struggle against the Dutch for Indonesian independence, Bishop Sandegren of South India and I had to pass through the military lines of both armies to reach the area where consultation could take place with the Batak Church officers. Reports had gotten back to New York that our lives were in danger. When I returned, immediately upon seeing me Dr. Fry embraced me as a long lost son. No man had given me such an affectionate welcome since the time I was a small boy and would be embraced by my father returning from the day's work.

In personal confrontations, particularly in his first meeting with people, whether it would be in private or in public, Dr. Fry exuded unexcelled warmth and graciousness. It would not be an overstatement to say that he was a charming man to meet. Who of the World Council of Churches delegates at the New Delhi assembly (1961) will forget the aplomb and the grace with which he welcomed Prime Minister Nehru? The whole assembly was seized by the atmosphere of friendship which his appropriate words generated.

But this gracious man could also cut to the quick. Such words or actions were usually provoked by his own strong convictions of what was right. The American Lutheran Church and its antecedent bodies had practiced *de facto* fellowship with the former United Lutheran Church in America. When the American Lutheran Church began discussions with the Lutheran Church–Missouri Synod and the Synod of Evangelical Lutheran Churches without first declaring official fellowship with the Lutheran Church in America, it disturbed Dr. Fry immensely. He showed it by action and speech. At the Helsinki assembly (1963), he made a point of not going to the communion table (although present at the service) when the assembly service was under the auspices of the ALC.—At the convention of an LCA synod where one of the ALC district presidents was a guest, Dr. Fry was asked by a delegate how he assessed the possibilities for Lutheran union. In the course of his reply, he expressed little hope for the ALC. He envisioned getting together with the Lutheran Church–Missouri Synod before it would occur with others and concluded that the Lutheran Church–Missouri Synod and LCA would flow past the island community of the ALC, converging below the island.

There is no question but that individuals and groups were sometimes hurt by Dr. Fry's words and actions. Early in our associations, he told me of an incident that became for me a key to understanding his occasional caustic remarks. In the course of his telling, he spoke of his dislike for a certain individual. It was done with the same cutting edge that might be directed at associates and sister churches. This volatility in his nature was a cross that he had to carry.

Gifted, informed, and perceptive as Dr. Fry was, he could be wrong. At the meeting of the Executive Committee of the Lutheran World Federation at Strasbourg, France, in October, 1958, a recommendation from the Commission on World Mission was before the committee. The recommendation proposed the erection of a short-wave radio broadcasting station at Addis Ababa in Ethiopia. It was proposed that the station should be powerful enough to cover all of Africa, the Middle East, and Southeast Asia. Dr. Fry spoke cautiously against the proposal. He expressed the judgment that the Ethiopian government, however friendly, was in danger of being overthrown by revolutionary forces. Nevertheless, the executive committee voted to accept the risk and to proceed.

Several years later the broadcasting board needed a chairman with ecumenical depth experience. In this situation, despite his earlier judgment about the "Radio Voice of the Gospel," Dr. Fry willingly accepted the additional burden imposed by the chairmanship.[1]

In 1960 discussions got under way looking toward finding a theological basis for Lutheran cooperation.[2] The objective was the organization of a Lutheran Council that might include most Lutheran constituencies in the

United States of America. Dr. Fry thought the project was stillborn, but he consented to go along in the exploration. During the first two meetings he said nothing, not wanting to be blamed for the presumed failure of the consultations; however, thereafter he became increasingly active and supportive. And when the time came to draft the documents that were to govern the work of the new Lutheran Council in the USA, he became an enthusiastic participant, often making determinative suggestions.

When Dr. John Behnken relayed the first response of the Lutheran Church–Missouri Synod to the proposal to organize what has become the Lutheran Council in the USA, it was a cautious "no"; but he countered with the assurance that the Lutheran Church–Missouri Synod continued to be ready to discuss the possibility of altar and pulpit fellowship on the basis of scripture. The letter was read at the annual session of the National Lutheran Council, meeting in Milwaukee in February, 1959. The NLC did not have the authority to act on fellowship discussions. But the proposal for altar and pulpit fellowship discussions was accepted by the American Lutheran Church. In the first meeting of representatives of the two churches on February 10, 1962, it was agreed to invite the Lutheran Church in America to participate in the discussions. The first invitation was transmitted in writing. It was repeated several times in subsequent conversations. But to each proffer Dr. Fry maintained a courteous but firm refusal to enter discussions. He adhered to the principle that churches committed to the Lutheran confessions should officially endorse the practice of fellowship without preliminary theological discussions.

As contacts with the Lutheran Church–Missouri Synod became increasingly cordial in the Lutheran Council associations, and after the New York convention of the Missouri Synod in July, 1967, Dr. Fry consented to an "unofficial" meeting of individuals from LCA with individuals from the Lutheran Church–Missouri Synod. His heart hungered for fellowship, but his mind held steadfastly to the Lutheran principle on fellowship. The first "unofficial" meeting was held in St. Louis May 14, 1968. On the plane en route home, he penned a note to me wherein he said in part:

> . . . I do want you to hear at once that the four of us from the LCA . . . had an open-hearted and very fraternal time of it with our LC-MS hosts today. The unprogrammed conversation was not only exceptionally polite, but it was candid and pointed. . . .
>
> Unobtrusively but I think effectively I did have a chance, one that arose very naturally, to press the urgency of evangelical Christians' pooling of strength as we face a time of diminution of church membership and influence, intellectual and otherwise. I

pleaded for as close an approach to each other to the limit to which conscience permits.

No one who knew Dr. Fry could other than admire his prodigious capacity for work and the abandon with which he gave himself to the church's service. This was demonstrated in a remarkable degree when he carried out his promise to attend the Black Lutheran Clergy Conference held in Chicago May 7-10, 1968.[3] The presidents of the three large Lutheran bodies were scheduled for a panel discussion the forenoon of May 9. During the course of a question-and-answer period, Dr. Fry volunteered to be available until noon but said that he would have to leave then. There was some audible murmuring at this statement. Quietly he replied, "I got up from a sickbed to come and I must leave." No one in that meeting realized at that time that less than a month later Dr. Fry would have concluded his service to the church militant.

Of all the gifts with which God had endowed Dr. Fry, I cherish most the recollection of his faithful witness to the gospel. This was present, no matter what the setting might be. His preaching was marked by its emphasis on grace. Through the years—on two different occasions—I heard him speak with evident feeling about the believer as an empty cup, a cup which God wanted to fill with His love to the point of overflowing.

---

[1] On the Addis Ababa radio station, "Radio Voice of the Gospel," see *Proceedings of the Fourth Assembly of LWF*, pp. 177-181; the LWF *Reports 1963-1969*, Geneva, 1970, pp. 87-107; Fey, ed., *The Ecumenical Advance*, pp. 396-397. RVOG began regular broadcasting in 1963. It shares its facilities with the Near East Christian Council, the East Asia Christian Council, and the WCC Division of World Mission and Evangelism. Dr. Schiotz himself was the first chairman of the broadcasting board. Cf. the memo of Schmidt-Clausen (No. 68).

[2] On the Inter-Lutheran Consultation (1960-66), see the memo of Empie (No. 41), and the note accompanying the memo of Fendt (49).

[3] A conference of about seventy pastors, from all three major Lutheran bodies. *A Consultation of Black Lutheran Clergymen, Chicago, May 7-10, 1968*, Chicago, n.d., gives the statements by Dr. Schiotz, Dr. Fry, and the first vice-president of the Missouri Synod, Dr. Roland P. Wiederaenders.

51

Oswald C. J. Hoffmann

A Missouri Lutheran leader in Lutheran cooperation sketches several episodes in Dr. Fry's relations with the Missouri Synod, including a misunderstanding in 1945, and the subsequent inter-Lutheran collaboration in producing films.

At the Valparaiso University commencement in the spring of 1967, Dr. Fry was granted an honorary degree, probably the first that he ever received from an educational institution of the Lutheran Church–Missouri Synod. Dr. O. P. Kretzmann made a point of the fact on presentation that he himself had recently received an honorary degree from a Roman Catholic institution, and the action of bestowing this honor upon Dr. Fry did not seem to be out of place.

Our son Paul was being graduated that year from the university, and I was asked to deliver the commencement address. The only importance to be attached to this fact is that our whole family was invited to have lunch before the commencement exercises with the university administration and the honored guests, among whom was Dr. Frederick L. Hovde, president of Purdue University, also receiving an honorary degree.

Our son was accompanied by his fiancée, also a student at the university but attending the nurses' training school at Lutheran hospital here in St. Louis, associated with the university. There were six of us in all, and seven places at our table.

Without invitation Dr. Fry set himself squarely down at our table, giving the definite impression, although he did not say so outright, that he wanted to have a little fun instead of a deep philosophical conversation with some of the educators about the problems of the church and the future of American education.

He started out handsomely, as he always did, with a great deal of to-do with our son about the two of them now becoming alumni of Valparaiso University. Every now and then during the conversation he would come back to this subject. "As a fellow alumnus . . . ," and so forth. He brought up the subject with a certain glee, as if he had now accomplished something for which he had been striving his whole lifetime.

(b. 1913) Dr. Hoffmann was director of Public Relations for the Lutheran Church–Missouri Synod (1948-63), and for many years secretary of Lutheran Church Productions and Lutheran Film Associates. Since 1955 he has been the speaker on the international radio program, "The Lutheran Hour." He has been a member of the LCUSA Executive Committee since 1967, and president of the Council since 1970.

At one point during this boisterous luncheon Dr. Fry said, "I guess I should not be saying this to a young man who is planning to enter the seminary, but I managed to get through my whole theological training without a word of Hebrew." He went on to say something about Hebrew being a fine thing, but he wondered whether most pastors really needed it. He didn't say it in just that way, because he did not leave the impression with our son that he was making a mistake in fulfilling the Hebrew requirement for Concordia Seminary in St. Louis.

* * *

When the Lutheran Council in the USA was formed in January of 1967, the presidents of the participating church bodies were appointed to the executive committee. There had to be a few others, and I became one of them. Much of the business of the Council, and the determination of its early policies, were laid at the door of the executive committee.

At the first meeting, I chose an inconspicuous spot at the far end of the table facing the chairman. One of the reasons was that I wanted to smoke my pipe and not disturb anybody else. Dr. Fry came into the meeting right on the dot, as was his custom, and firmly chose the only other place at my end of the table. After that, the same thing occurred at every other meeting of the executive committee. I soon discovered the reason. He liked to pass his witticisms, repeat them if they did not elicit an immediate response, and slap his knee loudly when they did. He could always laugh two or three times at the same sally, after each repetition.

In all of the meetings of the Lutheran Council it became apparent that he was restraining his incisiveness, which could at times be brutal, to further the peaceful progress of the new organization. He showed special deference to representatives of the Lutheran Church–Missouri Synod, probably because he realized the whole situation was new and tender to them. Furthermore, he had had a good deal of experience in the old National Lutheran Council with representatives of the American Lutheran Church. I take it he knew them, as they knew him.

* * *

One of the blackest moments in inter-Lutheran relations occurred right after World War II. There was a great need for physical relief in Germany at that time. Feeling against Germany was still running high, but certain Lutherans chose to risk unpopularity in order to do what they regarded to be right, under the circumstances. They set out to help.

It became apparent that action of this kind ought not to be unilateral. Therefore, arrangements were made for a delegation from the National Lutheran Council and from the Lutheran Church–Missouri Synod to meet in Germany before deciding finally upon a course of action. There were differences of opinion about what should be done, with Missouri Synod emphasis upon individual action by its members (relief packages, etc.) and NLC emphasis on corporate action, with which it was more familiar.

As I recall it, representatives of the NLC were Dr. Ralph Long, Dr. Aasgaard, and Dr. Fry. Representatives of the LC-MS were Dr. John Behnken and Dr. Lawrence Meyer.

As things worked out, the Missouri Synod representatives received their travel documents from the State Department, and proceeded to Germany. Apparently there had been some mix-up, and the documents for the NLC representatives did not come through. As a result, the Missouri Synod representatives went to work in Germany, meeting church leaders like Bishop Theophilus Wurm, Bishop Hans Meiser, and others in order to work out a program.

Finally the NLC representatives received their documents, and proceeded to Europe.[1] They met with the Missouri Synod representatives, somewhat by chance, in a hotel lobby in Frankfurt. Dr. Fry proceeded to excoriate Dr. Behnken for what he regarded as the part Dr. Behnken had played in seeing to it that travel documents for the NLC representatives were delayed. I understand he insisted the Missouri Synod representatives made statements to the State Department that they were to be the only Lutheran commissioners working on this project.

Dr. Behnken was mystified by the whole business, especially by Dr. Fry's rather violent reaction. Apparently, as Dr. Behnken always insisted, he had no knowledge of the reason for the delay in the coming of the NLC representatives, and assumed that they had decided to come later on. Even that assumption illustrates the nature of the relationships which existed at the time.

The meeting in Frankfurt broke up, apparently without any resolution of the conflict. After Dr. Behnken's return to the United States, he asked Dr. Arthur Brunn, vice-president of Synod, to meet with whomever he could in order to compose the dispute. I happened to be along on the occasion when Dr. Brunn had lunch with Dr. Walton Greever, at that time the secretary of the United Lutheran Church in America. Both of us knew Dr. Greever very well, because all of us were members of Koinonia, a Lutheran clergy discussion group in New York City. Dr. Brunn assured Dr. Greever that Dr. Behnken knew nothing of the circumstances which had caused the problem issuing forth in the painful meeting at Frankfurt. I can still see those two men walking ahead of me across 37th Street back to the headquarters of the ULCA, with their arms around each other.

Apparently Dr. Greever was able to convince Dr. Fry of the purity of Dr. Behnken's intentions. I was told by Dr. Behnken himself that on his next meeting with Dr. Fry, nothing at all was said about the Frankfurt meeting. However, Dr. Fry went out of his way to be kind, generous, deferential. Dr. Behnken said, "Dr. Fry treated me as if I were his father."

A year or two later I happened to meet Frances Knight, who headed the Passport Division in the State Department. We were riding together in an elevator. I introduced myself and she replied with a laugh, "I sure made a mess of those Lutheran permits to enter Germany, didn't I?"

* * *

Lutheran Church Productions, Inc., was formed to produce the film "Martin Luther."[2] I don't remember the exact date the meeting was held, but it must have been about 1951. Lutheran cooperation was minimal at the time. The Missouri Synod was invited to participate in the project, and agreed to do so. The climate at the time was such that acceptance of the invitation was regarded with great suspicion. Some of the other Lutheran representatives were not hesitant to say that they thought Missouri was entering the project simply in order to kill it.

As things turned out, the suspicion was not altogether unfounded. Missouri Synod representatives saw to it that whatever thought there was along this line never came to the board of directors of LCP, Inc.

When the constitution was being drawn up, Dr. Fry exercised his vaunted ability to help his confreres arrive at the proper phraseology. At one point, he offered a suggestion for changing a paragraph. I ventured the opinion that the original proposal was as good as his amendment. Thereupon he said, "Well, in that case, I'll move it." The chairman, Dr. Paul Empie, asked for discussion. There was none. Paul seemed to have run into this situation before, and the color began to rise from his collar-line. Finally, he had to call the motion, and the vote was almost unanimously in favor of Dr. Fry's amendment. In the hush that followed, Dr. Empie asked for any "no" votes. There was one, mine, delivered in a somewhat stentorian voice. The hush that followed was like the silence of the grave.

The meeting went on for about fifteen minutes, and then adjourned for the day. Dr. Fry went quietly for his hat and coat, picked up his brief case, proceeded to the door of the meeting room, wheeled around, and called out with a loud voice, "Ossie. . . ."

Always correct, he never addressed anyone in the room except by his official title. Everyone in the room turned around, somewhat startled, and Paul Empie smiled. I don't remember whether he winked at me or not.

* * *

Dr. Fry always struck me as an impulsive man with enormous ability. Indeed, his incisive mind caused him to be severely impatient with people who could not see a point as quickly or as clearly as he could. I must say that I never held this against him. Without putting myself in the same league as Dr. Fry, this is a failing of mine, too. It is a failing. I could understand how his feeling boiled up within him when discussion went on and on without arriving at the plain solution that he could see right at the outset.

Dr. Fry was a man of deep feeling. At times his feelings got away from him. Even in this, you could see him grow over the years. He matured personally and professionally, a process that you could see taking place. It never stopped. Perhaps, this is a mark of the greatness of the man.

---

[1] The Missouri delegation reached Germany in October, 1945. Dr. Fry and his colleagues arrived in December. See also the memo of Stewart Herman (No. 43), which deals with another aspect of this same trip of Dr. Fry.

[2] Released in 1953. See also the memo of Endress (No. 18).

52

E. Clifford Nelson

An ALC church historian analyzes the evangelical, catholic, and theological factors of Dr. Fry's churchmanship, in three areas: church structure, ecumenical relations, and social-cultural life.

Churchmanship sub specie evangelii

I feel under no compulsion to give a report on Dr. Fry's many and well-deserved accolades. What I say will hardly make more notable the Fry escutcheon which already exhibits more than thirty honorary degrees and reams of eulogies. Rather I would use this opportunity to view him from a distance—I was never close to him—and note certain things which I, as an alleged historian, judge ought not be overlooked in some future evaluation of the man's leadership in the church.

The key words, I think, are evangelical, catholic, theological, and ecclesial. And the last is really first: his churchmanship was evangelical, catholic, and theological. All of these together help us to understand how he measured his role in the church, the body of Christ.

I think it is true that Fry did not conceive of the body of Christ in static "essential" terms. The Pauline phrase described the church in dynamic, lively, functional terms. Its dynamic was the gospel; its life was the Spirit of Christ; its function was mission. Therefore, Fry always saw its instrumental character, its unity in Christ, and its relation to culture *sub specie evangelii.*

I wish to mention three areas where I think I have detected this understanding of churchmanship.

First, there was his fabled skill as a parliamentarian and writer of constitutions. He saw with theological astuteness the significance, for a doctrine of the church, of the famous Lutheran cliché, "in, with, and under." In, with, and under the earthly, historical, politico-sociological

---

(b. 1911) Dr. Nelson was professor (1952-66) and dean of the faculty (1961-65) at Luther Seminary (ELC), St. Paul, Minnesota, and since 1966 has been professor of religion at St. Olaf College, Northfield, Minnesota. He was adviser on religious affairs to the United States high commissioner for Germany 1951-52. He was the director of the Minneapolis LWF assembly in 1957, and a speaker at the Helsinki assembly (1963). Recently he has done extensive research on Lutheran church polity and Lutheran relations.

forms in which people must live, he saw the church as the body of Christ functioning in its evangelical, catholic, and missionary task.

The corpus of stories and jokes, the mass of truthful legends and myths which grew up around his amazing constitutional abilities testify in the final analysis to what some have called the profundity of his "incarnational theology." He saw clearly the need to look for the church where it is to be found, namely, in the world under human forms, a creature of the Holy Spirit through the gospel living out its purposes in the midst of men's all too obvious humanness. Therefore, he worked with constitutions and Robert's Rules of Order to make the body of Christ visible and audible to the *saeculum* for whose life the body was given. Tirelessly, and often imperiously, he worked to relate the empirical church to the ecclesial witness of the New Testament and the Lutheran confession.

Second, Fry was convinced that the true church was a catholic church. Once upon a time, he wrote a preface to the American edition of a British book called *The Catholicity of Protestantism.*[1] Enthusiastically recommending the book, he said, "Lutherans will be interested, and humbled, to see how widely" the catholicity of Protestantism "rests on the insights . . . of Martin Luther." It was an unshakable belief of Franklin Clark Fry that Lutheranism at its evangelical heart was catholic. Its very nature demanded participation in the ecumenical movement. One task of the catholic church, he said, was to manifest to the world the unity it already possesses in Christ. Because he was convinced of this "givenness" in catholicity, he devoted most of his years as a churchman not to *achieving* unity but to *manifesting* it. This is why he labored vigorously in the World Council, in the Lutheran World Federation, and in the councils of American Lutheranism. In order that the world might know that the Father had sent the Son, the unity of the body must be made evident. Therefore, Fry was not much interested in a "spiritual" unity, a disembodied oneness.

Sometimes his voice was listened to, sometimes not. One time when he was heeded was at a consultation prior to the formation of the World Council of Churches. The year was 1946, the occasion was the meeting of the Executive Committee of the Lutheran World Convention in Uppsala. He wrote about it in THE LUTHERAN OUTLOOK (January, 1947) under the title, "A Crisis in Lutheranism." The question, he said, was Lutheran membership in the soon-to-be-established World Council. Before the war, in fact long before Fry became active in ecumenical circles, his predecessor F. H. Knubel, together with Professor A. R. Wentz and later Bishop Hanns Lilje of Germany, had prepared a statement on Lutheran participation in the ecumenical movement.[2] Large segments of this statement were lifted bodily out of the United Lutheran Church's "Washington Declaration" (1920),[3] whose chief author was C. M. Jacobs, professor of historical theology in Philadelphia. It was this 1936 statement—which stipulated that ecumenical assemblies be constituted only of official representatives of church bodies—that lay behind Fry's account of the Uppsala (1946) decision to urge "confessional representation" as a main guiding principle for allocation of seats in the World Council. Prior to this the architects of the World Council had thought of geography as the primary determining factor: so many were to be chosen from Great Britain, so many from Germany, so many from the USA, etc. The assumption was that the most significant ties were regional rather than confessional. Thus, through the Uppsala action, the roots of which were imbedded in the 1936 statement, the Lutheran churches were assured that their confessional convictions would be respected in the World Council of Churches, in whose inner and outer workings Fry was to play such an influential part as a confessional Lutheran deeply committed to the ecumenical movement. He saw clearly that confessional links were far stronger than geographical ones; yet only in physical proximity could Christians learn to manifest the catholicity of the church.

On another occasion Fry was not listened to. Since World War I attempts had been made within American Lutheranism to bring about a greater degree of organizational union. The mergers of 1917, 1918, 1930 were examples of this.[4] The work of the National Lutheran Council fostered inter-Lutheran understanding. Always, however, there was this problem: what is necessary for church unity? Augsburg Confession (Article VII) had stated simply that it was sufficient to agree in the doctrine (proclamation) of the gospel and the administration of the sacraments according to the gospel. All Lutherans affirmed the Augsburg Confession. However, this affirmation did not remove the fragmented character of American Lutheranism. Dr. Fry and his church (the ULCA and later the Lutheran Church in America) rested the case for unity in this confession.[5] Others, notably the Missouri Synod, deemed as necessary a subscription to extra-confessional statements to guarantee the sincerity and doctrinal rectitude of those who sought fellowship. In the fifties it was clear that the National Lutheran Council, of which Missouri was *not* a member, was divided in part over the same issue. The mergers of 1960 and 1962 reflected this.[6] When negotiations to bring the Lutheran Church—Missouri Synod into fellowship were undertaken, Dr. Fry and the LCA said, "There already exists a basis for fellowship. No further statements are needed." To avoid an impasse the president of the American Lutheran Church sought a compromise: doctrinal discussions *without* the issuance of an extra-confessional doctrinal statement. Missouri interpreted this according to its tradition; the LCA according to its. Result: doctrinal discussions between the ALC and the Lutheran Church—Missouri Synod *and* the approval of an extra-confessional doctrinal statement. The ALC president reported to the Denver convention of the Missouri Synod (July 14, 1969), that commissions of the two bodies concluded their doctrinal discussions "with the adoption of a *Joint Statement and Declaration.* This has been *approved by our respective church conventions* (italics added) in 1967 and 1968." This was, as Fry said, a denial of the *satis est* of Augustana VII and the *predicted* outcome of the ALC—Missouri discussions. In other words, Fry's voice had not been heeded. Fellowship, therefore, was only partial by 1969: (1) the LCA considered itself to be in fellowship with all Lutherans, respecting the sincerity of their confession; (2) the ALC was in fellowship with the LCA and LC-MS—with the former on the basis of Augustana VII, with the latter on the basis of an extra-confessional statement; (3) the Lutheran Church—Missouri Synod was in fellowship with the ALC but not the LCA. Question: if Lutheran church B is in fellowship with Lutheran churches A and C but the latter two are not in fellowship, does this mean that things equal to each other are not equal to each other?

For one sitting on the side lines it seems that Fry was theologically right but socially inept. He would have been well advised to sit down across the table from Missouri to remove the image of the "city slicker versus the country bumpkin." Then in friendly conversation he could also have insisted intransigently on the *satis est* of the Augsburg Confession which all the discussants theoretically affirmed. Fry was famous for a speech delivered in Strasbourg (1958) in which he stressed the necessity of a proper balance between "truth and unity." Some Christians tended to emphasize a concern for "truth" to the virtual exclusion of "unity"; others tended to emphasize "unity" with a minimal concern for "truth." Actually both were needed. These two, said Fry, are "the twin imperatives."[7] Perhaps Dr. Fry ought to have added a third imperative: *agape,* selfless love. Truth, unity, love, these three in proper balance *sub specie evangelii,* might have prevented the schizophrenia of the Denver convention in 1969.

The *third* area in which Fry exhibited ecclesial concern was the relation of the Body of Christ to culture and/or society. I return for a moment to reiterate his ecclesiological stance: the Pauline term "body of Christ" described not so much the essence or the nature of the church as it did its *dynamis,* its function. The human body is healthy when it functions properly. Likewise the church as "body" is the functioning instrument of Christ in the world. In a radio program taped shortly before his death, Fry discussed the social crises of our day, particularly our "callous disregard" toward the victims of poverty and racism. He said, "If I am loyal to my God . . . I must in conscience labor for their welfare, for justice to them, and for some prospect that they will achieve the manhood that God desires for them."[8] Few could have said this more trenchantly.

One of the most eloquent and evangelical words about the relation of Christianity to the world of academe was spoken by Dr. Fry in the Aula at the University of Helsinki in 1963. Unfortunately no record of the address has been found. Apparently he had no manuscript. Inquiries in Helsinki, Geneva, and New York have failed to produce so much as a listener's jotted notes, to say nothing of a taped record. I was there, but in my rapt attention failed to make notes for later reference. Let me try nevertheless to record at least my impressions of the event.

The occasion was the presentation by the University of Helsinki of honorary degrees to a number of dignitaries in attendance at the fourth assembly of the Lutheran World Federation. Fry, as president of the LWF and as one of the honored recipients, gave the response on behalf of those who had received their doctor's hat. It was a brilliant performance and perhaps the best thing uttered at Helsinki, surely worthy of recall. The words which flowed easily and eloquently from the speaker were a vivid illustration of the commandment to "love the Lord thy God with all thy mind." A mind dedicated to the gospel of grace does not abide the pitting of piety against learning. It does not tolerate intellectual sloth or the relaxation of mental discipline in the face of the world's challenges. There is no safety in retreat to the "spiritual" or the "religious" realm. The fact is that the Creator God of biblical faith has endowed us with brains. Our intellects are given not to declare our independence from God, but to serve God in the freedom of faith, hope, and love. The human arm has freedom of motion in the lubricated joint of the shoulder, but its motion is in response to the head. In like manner, intellectual enterprise is an arm of the church, the functioning body of Christ, not to build another Tower of Babel but to glorify God as Creator, Redeemer, and Sanctifier: the Lord and Giver of life. The dedicated Christian mind says: *Credo ut intelligam* (I believe in order to understand); the church's faith is always *fides quaerens intellectum* (faith seeking understanding). Man does not reach faith by reason; God is not identified by the mind. The glory of God is not discovered by a rational penetration of heavens. Rather, faith is a gift of the Spirit which does not cancel out the mind but regenerates, reorients, and illuminates it. *Post fidem* the mind understands that the heavens declare the glory of God and the firmament shows his handiwork. This was Fry at his best. But, alas, my recall does not do the address justice. A later discovery of his manuscript would reveal how impressionistic the above recital is. But faulty and inadequate as it is, the event belongs in the collective memory of the church.

In summary, Dr. Fry always looked at the church and his role in it under the aspect of the gospel. The church, as a creature of the Word, lives in, with, and under earthly forms to be an instrument of the Word. Furthermore, its unity is nothing apart from Christ, and as Christ is not divided, so his church is not divided. For the sake of the word of the gospel, this unity must be made evident. Finally, the church as the dynamic, functioning body of Christ is positively and hopefully oriented toward the future of society and culture, which like all else, however, must be viewed *sub specie evangelii.*

---

[1] Edited by R. Newton Flew and R. E. Davies, Philadelphia, 1951.

[2] LWC Executive Committee statement: "Lutherans and Ecumenical Movements," in *Lutheran World Almanac 1934-1937,* New York, 1937, pp. 36-38.

[3] *Doctrinal Declarations,* St. Louis, 1957, pp. 15-23; abridged in R. C. Wolf, *Documents of Lutheran Unity in America,* Document 148.

[4] Reference is to the formation of the Norwegian Lutheran Church of America, the ULCA, the National Lutheran Council, the (former) American Lutheran Church (and the American Lutheran Conference). See A. R. Wentz, *Basic History of Lutheranism in America,* Philadelphia, 1964.

[5] See the "Savannah Resolution," 1934, in *Doctrinal Declarations,* pp. 58-60. Cf. the memo of Erb (No. 24).

[6] The (present) American Lutheran Church was formed in 1960, the LCA in 1962. See Wentz, *op. cit.*

[7] Dr. Fry's presidential message to the LWF Executive Committee at Strasbourg in October 1958 dealt with the responsibility of a confessional organization like the LWF. The address is not recorded in the minutes, but a lengthy news release (LCUSA News Bureau 58-126) datelined November 5, 1958, gives a synopsis with a number of direct quotations. LWF *Report to the Member Churches, 1958,* p. 4, also gives a synopsis.

[8] In "Protestant Hour" program of 5-19-1968, "Being Christian in a Violent Society," with William S. Ellis and FCF. LUTHERAN, 6-19-1968, p. 17.

53

Walter F. Wolbrecht

A former Missouri executive gives impressions of Dr. Fry in a variety of settings, but chiefly from experiences with the Inter-Lutheran Consultation and the LWF Helsinki assembly.

Although I had met him years earlier and had seen and heard him repeatedly, most of my recollections of President F. C. Fry date to the time of the Inter-Lutheran Consultation and the pan-Lutheran interplay as preparatory work for the establishment of the Lutheran Council in the USA, and derivatively for the Lutheran Council in Canada.

The Inter-Lutheran Consultation brought together representatives of the Lutheran Church in America, the American Lutheran Church, the Synod of Evangelical Lutheran Churches (Slovak), and the Lutheran Church—Missouri Synod over a period of years. Dr. Paul C. Empie, executive secretary of the National Lutheran Council, became the prime mover and deserves the lion's share of the credit for getting the crucial consultations under way.

It is no secret that both Dr. Fry and Dr. Behnken approached the first meetings of the Inter-Lutheran Consultation with great reluctance and considerable skepticism. Some of their wartime contacts had not been too peaceful. For this reason, one particular incident deserves to be put into writing, since it indicates once again upon what slender threads mighty developments can be based, and also, as I suddenly realize, because only two of the participants in the incident survive. The incident arose in this way. Dr. Empie and I had been chosen to serve as joint secretaries for the consultations. We soon looked for an opportunity to bring the two church body presidents together. Almost everyone who knew him realized that Dr. Fry loved to tell a story, enjoyed his own stories immensely, and in his glee would not only slap his own knee, but would often reach over to slap his neighbor's knee. It was not so commonly known that

---

(b. 1915) Dr. Wolbrecht was president of St. Paul's College, Concordia, Missouri (1951-54), then assistant executive secretary (1954) and executive secretary (1955-61) of the Board of Higher Education of the Lutheran Church—Missouri Synod. He was executive director of the LC—MS Board of Directors 1961-71. He was co-secretary of the Inter-Lutheran Consultation (1960-66) which designed the LCUSA, and since 1970 he has served on the Council's Executive Committee. In 1972 he was elected president of the Lutheran School of Theology at Chicago.

Dr. Behnken's right knee was arthritically painful and sensitive. In a four-cornered private conference which had just begun, Dr. Fry was manifestly trying earnestly to thaw out the situation. As he told a story, he was led energetically to slap Dr. Behnken's knee which in turn almost sent Dr. Behnken to the ceiling in pain. As it turned out, this may have been the finest thing that could have happened, because Dr. Fry would never deliberately have caused physical pain for anyone, and, in his solicitude of Dr. Behnken's reassurance, much of existing tensions melted away, apparently permanently.

For the Inter-Lutheran Consultation, various sub-committees advanced the preparatory work. I particularly came to appreciate the keen analytical mind and the passion for precision in words and wording which characterized Dr. Fry, but strangely enough perhaps to some, my chief memory of him is not as the constitutionalist, but rather as the group worship leader. His scripture reading and his prayers were always carefully prepared, prayed through and shared. At one conclusion, he extemporized some editorial judgments about English language Bible translations. He had chosen a chapter from Ephesians and felt constrained to point out the superior virtues of the *New English Bible* (New Testament, 1961) over the (to him) obviously inferior *Revised Standard Version.* I wonder what he would have said about the American Bible Society's *Good News for Modern Man* (1966)?

Most of the meetings were held in Chicago along the lake front, but several were held in the offices of the National Lutheran Council then at 50 Madison Avenue in New York. On one gloomy day when we were seated next to each other, I got my first information from him that his permanent state of health was not good. He had returned from one of his many trips to Europe, including Yugoslavia and Geneva, I believe. He was steeling himself against persistent pain and leaned over to whisper to me that it was trite, but to him increasingly true that one should wear out rather than rust out. The larger context at the time, incidentally, was a discussion of mandatory retirements and limitation on terms of office in confessional and conciliar organizations and an impending presidential election in the LCA.

He was a great example in high speed and sustained utilization of available time. I caught occasional glimpses of how he would plow through a brief case bulging with important reports and communications which came to him as church body president, as LWF president, as chairman of the Central Committee of the World Council of Churches, and as committee chairman for the National Council of Churches and who knows what else. But I learned from him also the virtues of the very brief and even the terse one-sentence letter of reply or comment.

He found a strange kind of relaxation in working favorite and difficult crossword puzzles, particularly in moments of boredom and sometimes as an exasperating act, as evidenced by occasional questions put to him to which he responded promptly, fully, and with great clarity, and yet with pencil in the crossword puzzle.

Once I unintentionally and accidentally gained particular favor in his eyes when I commented on a trip my wife and I made to visit friends on Lake Canandaigua, farthest west of the Finger Lakes, New York, and then learned that he thought that the Finger Lakes were probably the closest point of earth to heaven.

As unlike as they may have seemed to the casual observer, President Oliver R. Harms of the LC-MS and President Fry almost instinctively liked each other and came to be great and good friends. At one time, the latter had perhaps made fraternal visits to Missouri Synod delegate conventions out of a sense of duty. His visit "in his own back yard" at the New York convention in 1967 seemed to be a great pleasure. It gave several of us another glimpse into his way of working. As he came several hours before his time to appear on the platform, he sat in a remote corner and listened intently while scribbling a series of words and phrases which in his platform presentation he combined into an inspiring and memorable greeting.[1]

At the LWF assembly in Helsinki there were some contacts between the assembly president, Dr. Fry, and the LC-MS group of observers which deserved more extended and more comprehensive treatment, but no one who was there can ever forget the great desire he had to make it possible for the self-conscious federation to make every possible accommodation to any reasonably valid stricture on the part of Missouri over against the form and content of the constitution of the LWF. Despite his countless chores in connection with the assembly meetings, satellite gatherings, and social functions, he also found it possible to spend many hours with the special joint committee which worked on drafting and redrafting proposed changes.

About this time, too, he became greatly involved in the stirrings of Pope John XXIII and the convening preparations for and conduct of the Roman Catholic ecumenical council. He engaged in a steady correspondence with his fast friend, Archbishop Ramsey of Canterbury, and with the Eastern Orthodox patriarch of Constantinople to see what they and others could do to help make the Second Vatican Council indeed an ecumenical one.

It has become fashionable to develop various typologies of leadership. In my judgment, Dr. Fry was a great gift of God to the Christian church because he was first gifted with an entire range of leadership competence and he used these gifts fully all his life.

A few afterthoughts: At one of our last meetings, we engaged in wide-ranging table talk. As I remember, although he was a crusading Democrat, he was most displeased with certain things that President Lyndon B. Johnson was doing and advocating. He was certain that the only proper location for the Lutheran Council was in New York. He was a sworn enemy of a class of clergymen known as "floaters" attempting to shift easily from one church body to another, or to remain in both. He spoke warmly of the ecumenical impact of contemporary exegetical scholarship, and discouragingly of systematic theology, particularly as he had been "over-exposed" to it in his seminary days at Mt. Airy.

---

[1] Dr. Fry's remarks were taped and transcribed. See the *Source Register* in this volume.

54

Oliver R. Harms

The former president of the Lutheran Church–Missouri Synod testifies to mutual growth in understanding, especially through the Inter-Lutheran Consultation and the Helsinki assembly of the LWF.

It is difficult to describe Franklin Clark Fry. He was an experience, and it is almost impossible to convey an experience through description.

Dr. Fry was a gifted writer. He was an articulate speaker. Through either gift he was entitled to tributes which are normally reserved only for those who truly excel. What Dr. Fry wrote and what he said reflected what he was, a man of high intellect and great spirit. What he was always was much more, however, than could be sensed either through the spoken or the written word.

I learned to know Dr. Fry rather well through our associations in the Inter-Lutheran Consultation. These associations were frequent and they were extensive. They led to the formation in 1967 of the Lutheran Council in the United States of America. Largely through Dr. Fry's contributions we were able to translate words and ideas into structures and action. This new Lutheran agency stands alongside many others as living proof that Dr. Fry was willing to move from theory to action. He was willing to practice what he preached.

Our acquaintance grew into a friendship. I hold that acquaintance is a prerequisite for genuine friendship. While our friendship was rewarding to me personally, it also served the welfare of our church bodies. As friends we were able to find a way to help one another and our churches as they sought ways to draw near to one another. Our church bodies both were committed to the pursuit of Lutheran unity. However, our church bodies were also committed to principles of procedure which seemed to make it impossible for either of us to pursue our goal.

It was at this crucial moment in history that Dr. Fry agreed with me that a way must be found to explore pathways out of our dilemma. We

---

(b. 1901) Dr. Harms was president of the Lutheran Church–Missouri Synod 1962-69. He had been an officer of the church's Texas District from 1938, president 1948-50, in the course of a twenty-four-year pastorate in Houston. He then served as fourth vice-president of the synod (1956-59) and first vice-president (1959-62). Since 1970 he has been counselor and consultant on Resources and Development for the synodical board of directors. He was a member of the LCUSA Executive Committee 1967-69.

were able to arrange for informal conversations which later proved extremely fruitful. I cite this instance to demonstrate how Dr. Fry was always willing to let important pursuits like Lutheran unity have the place of preeminence, and that he was willing to invest his many personal relations in a way that would produce dividends for the welfare of the church.

I suspect that all of the large significant churchly institutions of the world heard Dr. Fry give witness to his personal Christian faith. Personally, I will always treasure the occasion when Dr. Fry gave such a testimony to the Lutheran World Federation assembly in Helsinki, Finland, in 1963. While many persons present on that occasion seemed to doubt the capacity of the Lutheran World Federation to articulate the doctrine of justification in a meaningful way for our time, no one was left in doubt that Dr. Fry was able and willing to articulate his own personal faith in God's justifying grace. None of us can readily forget that clear and moving confession of faith during the discussion of Bishop Lilje's presentation.

There are many who did not share the privilege of knowing Dr. Fry as some of us did. Our knowledge and our experience enable us to understand and to interpret him more adequately. Some believed Dr. Fry to be caustic. We knew also that he could be gentle and forgiving. There were those who felt him to be unnecessarily demanding. We knew the high standards which he set for himself. Some felt he was aloof and indifferent. We knew him to be intimate and considerate. There were some who disliked his candor about people and issues. We knew him to be equally honest about himself.

Recollections of Dr. Fry will always produce a broad range of impressions of the man. He was a man of many facets, many qualities, and many moods. Yet I find the key to unlock this powerful personality. He was driven by constraint to magnify his Lord Jesus at all times and in all ways. By his presence the gospel and the church were always lifted to a new and high plateau. He demanded, as he gave, the best for his Lord and his church. He shared, as a good steward, all the joy and blessing that God showered on him. It was my privilege to count Dr. Fry as a friend and to share through him and with him all the treasures of God's grace.

55

William Larsen

The late Dr. Larsen has reported on Dr. Fry's view of the relation between confessionalism and ecumenism.

When the annual meeting of the National Lutheran Council was held in Hollywood, California, in February, 1965, Dr. Paul Empie requested Dr. Franklin C. Fry to speak on the question of the role of confessional groups within the ecumenical movement. This was a particularly appropriate subject at that time because a number of questions had been raised here and there about the purpose of confessional groups and even why such groups as the Lutheran World Federation should exist at all. Dr. Fry was the right person to speak on this question, both because of his involvement in the ecumenical movement, as chairman of the Central Committee of the World Council of Churches, and his involvement in the Lutheran World Federation, of which he had been president. Dr. Fry was at the annual meeting of the NLC as president of the Lutheran Church in America. From notes that were taken on the comments by Dr. Fry, some light may be shed on his views concerning Lutherans and their relation to other churches.[1]

He began by pointing out that the developments in the Christian world in recent years had magnified the role of the confessional bodies. The participation of the Orthodox churches in the World Council of Churches and the gradual involvement of the Roman Catholic church in ecumenical activities had brought Christendom to a new situation. He continued his remarks by making reference to the wide chasms between some Protestant bodies. Protestants must find ways, he said, to give expression to the unity that they have, and Lutherans must look again at their common confessions to see if they are filling their confessional role.

(1909-1971) President of the United Evangelical (formerly United Danish) Lutheran Church 1956-60, Dr. Larsen was chairman of the Joint Union Committee (1959-60) which achieved the merger of his body and the former American Lutheran Church and the Evangelical Lutheran Church to form the American Lutheran Church in 1960. He then became its secretary (1961) and vice-president (1967-68), and executive director of its Board of Theological Education (1967-71). From 1946 to 1956 he was engaged in NLC student ministry. He served as vice-president of the NLC (1965-66) secretary of the LCUSA (1967-69), and president of the USA National Committee of the LWF (1970-71). He was a delegate to the WCC assemblies of 1961 and 1968.

From the time of the Reformation until 1923, when the Lutheran World Convention was formed, there were no international bonds among Lutherans. It was miraculous that Lutherans were able to recognize one another after this lapse of time. The Lutheran confessions were undiluted, and they served to help Lutherans to recognize their kinship with one another. "I refuse," said Dr. Fry, "to recognize as Lutherans at all those who use the Lutheran confessions as a shibboleth, or as a rallying ground. . . ." Dr. Fry stated that the Lutheran church is both confessional and ecumenical. The confessions were set down as a defensible understudy of the gospel, a guide to what is true about our faith; they are ecumenical in character.

It was declared at the Lund assembly (1947) that one of the functions of the Lutheran World Federation was to assist Lutheran participation in the ecumenical movement. Dr. Fry noted that churches from other confessional traditions have developed more participation in the World Council than have Lutheran churches. This calls for some self examination by Lutherans.

The program of the Lutheran World Federation came into being because of the distress following World War II. We got generous because we were feeding Lutherans, according to Dr. Fry. The program of LWF began on a sectarian basis but now operates on what Dr. Fry called the "enlightened humanitarian basis." The question was raised as to the appropriateness of a confessional group being involved in business of this kind. He said that a confessional group must constantly examine its program to ascertain whether or not there is encroachment on what might be ecumenical functions. He cited the Tanzania Christian Refugee Service, which was initiated by the LWF for the WCC, as an excellent example of organizing Lutheran work in relation to the effort of other Christians.

Every Christian has an obligation to cooperate with other Christians on the broadest basis possible so long as there is no violation of conviction and principle. Unity, said Dr. Fry, is a command of God and not an option. We are utterly disloyal to the Giver of the Good Gift if we fail to act on areas of agreement as energetically as on areas of disagreement. Those of us who are preoccupied with disagreements are missing something which has been given to the church.

The situation in which we find ourselves has been transformed profoundly from what prevailed in 1947. New patterns have to be faced, and enemies of the church have gained an ascendency that we did not comprehend. The church is under attack in every part of the earth. A church beset cannot afford divisions and differences which are not rooted in the heart of the gospel.

Dr. Fry expressed the conviction that Lutherans need not be on the defensive. He said, "My brethren in the faith live under many names." The people who esteem the Lord and acknowledge him as the Son of God are of different hues both in confessional background and in their color. The ecumenical movement dissolves many barriers, some of which are walls that are constructed from our own prejudices and misunderstandings. Lutherans must find their place in relation to the family of God on earth and witness in such a way that the impact is not divided.

The comments by Dr. Fry on the role of confessional churches in the ecumenical movement give us insight into his concern that Lutherans be faithful to their responsibility in the ecumenical movement and at the same time be aware of their responsibility to one another. The balance which Dr. Fry strikes in his discussion may be helpful to all of us—which is the main reason that I make this presentation.

---

[1] A summary appears in the NLC Minutes, February 10, 1965, pp. 49-50. See also Fry's ULCA presidential report of 1956, referred to by Tiemeyer (No. 21). For the wider context see the *Report of Secretaries of World Confessional Families*, Geneva, 1967, and Fey, ed., *The Ecumenical Advance* (Vol. 2 of *History of the Ecumenical Movement:* 1948-1968), London, 1970, chapter 5. See also the memo of Cavert (No. 73), where other writers on this subject are listed.

56

C. Thomas Spitz, Jr.

The general secretary of the LCUSA probes for the attitudes behind Dr. Fry's role in the origin of the new Lutheran cooperative agency.

Franklin Clark Fry was president of the largest church body participating in the Lutheran Council in the USA. He had played a principal role in drafting the council's constitution and bylaws. Those documents designed the council as a servant to the churches, to be governed by the constitution they adopted.

Few men have better understood or more diligently applied the authority and power of constitutions, governing body resolutions and parliamentary procedure. But he used them more often to enable action than to limit it.

When dealing with representatives of other churches, he made it a point to know and to understand, at least intellectually, the limitations and special needs which circumscribed their positions equally as well as he knew his own. In the early days of the council and in the years immediately preceding it, he displayed a distinctly pastoral concern and approach to the problems and questions confronting the people with whom he was engaged, even at times of sharp difference of opinion and controversy.

Knowing that the tradition of the Lutheran Church–Missouri Synod would make it possible for that church body to participate in the Lutheran Council in the USA only if the new relationship included continuing theological discussions, he insisted on the hard constitutional language which requires each participating church body to take part in the Division of Theological Studies while leaving their cooperation in other areas optional.[1]

Knowing that the other churches participating in the council hoped to continue their support of stateside military service centers within the new agency, but confronted by his own church's decision not to support such ministry, he permitted a last minute and totally unintended redefinition of

(b. 1921) Dr. Spitz, a member of the Lutheran Church–Missouri Synod, was chosen the first general secretary of the Lutheran Council in the USA (1967-). He had previously served on the staff of the Missouri-supported "Lutheran Hour" from 1953, and as its director of broadcasting (1959-65). He was chairman of the synodical Board of Missions for North and South America 1958-65.

"projects" to be undertaken by the council in order that the other churches might realize their hopes under that rubric while at the same time keeping intact the council's record for having all the churches cooperating in all of the regular work of the council.

Knowing that the Synod of Evangelical Lutheran Churches (Slovak) would be without presence in meetings of the executive committee should its one member on that committee be unable to be present, he formulated the action authorizing an executive committee member to designate an alternate if that were ever necessary to assure that each participating church had at least one member present.

The importance of these decisions and actions is not the point. Important was the attitude which they reflected, also in his discussions with President Oliver R. Harms of the Lutheran Church—Missouri Synod leading up to the council's role as observer-consultant at meetings of the Consultation on Church Union and in his willingness to meet with representatives of the Missouri Synod so that President Harms might fulfill a convention resolution requiring the exploration of altar and pulpit fellowship with the Lutheran Church in America. "Our constitution has already said what we think of fellowship with Missouri,"[2] Dr. Fry said, "but we must find a way of making available to Missouri the information it needs to decide what it thinks about us."

He told me more than once that a major responsibility for the church administrator is "to make it possible for proper things to happen."

When Franklin Clark Fry walked around from behind his desk to sit in the chair next to yours and, above all, when he lit a cigar, you knew he had time to listen and to talk. And you were never made to feel that the time had been taken from more pressing things. For those minutes, your concerns and your presence were the most important items on his agenda. They seemed sometimes to be more important to him than they were to you.

Others may have seen different applications of his power as a church body president, his knowledge of constitutions, and his peerless skill as a parliamentarian. In my experience, they were strengths which he contributed positively to the realization of the council's potential and to the solution of the problems I shared with him.

Too few people had opportunity to know Dr. Fry like that. Those who did were fortunate.

---

[1] The Constitution of the LCUSA, drawn up in 1964, is abridged in Wolf, *Documents,* Document 250. Specific reference here is to Article II, 3.

[2] Reference is to the LCA Constitution, Article II, 5.

Part Three

Memos from Lutherans outside America

Memos 57 to 70 represent international Lutheranism—fourteen Lutheran World Federation associates of Dr. Fry from Europe, Asia, Africa, and Australia. After Bishop Giertz's general remarks, the memos follow a basically chronological order.

57

Bishop Bo Giertz

SWEDEN

A Swedish bishop reflects on Dr. Fry's "American" characteristics, and his concern for the Christian message.

Encounter With an American

When we Europeans meet America's church leaders and collaborate with them, we experience the deep difference between a church life built up by voluntary energies, chiefly during the last century, and one which was built on ancient institutions and has remained a part of the nation's life for many centuries. The difference gives us Europeans much food for thought.

What strikes us first is the amazing efficiency of our American colleagues. During a six-year period it was my privilege to be one of Franklin C. Fry's most intimate colleagues within the Lutheran World Federation. I often say that I have him to thank for the most valuable things I have

---

(b. 1905) Theologian, novelist, and from 1949 until his retirement in 1970 bishop of Gothenburg, Dr. Giertz was formerly a worker in the Swedish Student Christian Movement, pastor, and chaplain to the king. He has served as vice-president of the Lutheran World Federation (1957-63) and member of its Executive Committee (1963-70).

learned about the art of conducting and leading a meeting, how to get an organization to function, and how to put resolutions into a form consistent enough to be effective. Fry and his American friends had a capacity for work which often left us Europeans breathless. After long days of taxing negotiations, sub-committees often had to work into the late hours of the night. The next morning, Dr. Fry appeared seemingly rested and efficient, and with a sheaf of airmail letters in hand which he had written during the early hours of the morning and at the breakfast table. When we came home from a week of such meetings, we felt that we had earned a few days of relaxation. Dr. Fry traveled on to the next conference and continued in the same way.

This efficiency is certainly in part a consequence of the fast pace of American society. It also reflects the way in which the American churches customarily accomplish much work with small means and few fellow-workers. If all salaries are to be paid from offerings, it is necessary to appeal to people's will and ability to give their best and do their utmost. One is able to take a slower tempo in an old folk church in which the pastor has long been considered a public official and has accustomed himself to work in that manner.

I believe that here both sides may have something to learn from each other. There are advantages for a pastor to have time for the members of his congregation and for his own family. It is important that the people do not get the impression that he is so continually in a hurry and pressed for time that they cannot in good conscience bother him. But for us Europeans, it is something of a challenge to see our American colleagues work, to see how they use the time and seize the opportunities—and still have time to be friendly and helpful. A European does not say half as many friendly words during a day as a normal American does. Frank Fry was also a model in this respect. Many times I have stood beside him and marveled at his ability, in a situation where he must have been dead tired, to exchange friendly words with a person whom he had met long ago, and in whom, humanly speaking, he had no reason to remain deeply interested.

The ability to speak in terms directly and basically Christian in the middle of bureaucratic and administrative routine also belongs in the picture. I have heard Dr. Fry speak during a break in such a hard working day, when he addressed a few words to the personnel at a church center and yet did so with a depth and cordiality which edified everyone. We Europeans find it difficult to be so direct and to give such spontaneous expression to our faith. Table prayers are an example of this. In America anyone may be requested to say a prayer almost anywhere. It is not unusual that Europeans, even bishops, feel somewhat embarrassed or confused if they are unexpectedly placed in this situation in a restaurant. We

Europeans sometimes feel that the American attitude is a little naive. We should rather feel that our own sophisticated formality is a form of unbelief. Is this not perhaps related to the fact that our churches for centuries have been established in society and have become accustomed to maneuver with caution among the children of the world?

Franklin Clark Fry did not hesitate to commend his fellow-workers when he was pleased with them. Personally, I experienced this in a special way every time I preached. This response came also to several of my Scandinavian friends. It was always the same thing which Dr. Fry appreciated—a basic Christian proclamation of atonement and justification. We Scandinavians preach with a somewhat heavier style than one generally uses in America. We are not so clever at telling stories. On the other hand, we have perhaps more dogmatic substance. It was entirely clear that Dr. Fry personally appreciated such sermons and was thankful for them. The message about the God who never tires of forgiving, and the Savior who is the friend of sinners, was just the message that he had learned to appreciate with the years. It was just this Nordic preaching tradition, which had preserved that trait of inwardness and depth, that he appreciated. I believe that we have here one of the points at which an exchange between Europe—in any event Scandinavia—and America can enrich one another. Franklin Clark Fry was in such instances sufficiently great and sufficiently independent to be willing to learn. This quality we need, both in Europe and in America.

58

Bishop Hanns Lilje

GERMAN FEDERAL REPUBLIC

With no colleague outside America did Dr. Fry have a longer or more intimate association than with Bishop Lilje. Recalling a number of episodes, the bishop comments on Dr. Fry's gifts of leadership, his development, and a few of his personal qualities.

I

In every respect, Franklin Clark Fry was a great man.[1] This may be said first of his outward appearance. His imposing figure in black clerical garb, his impressive stature, and his masterful leadership of meetings made him a striking person. Even between conferences and sessions he made the same impression on spectators and observers. Almost always he wore his clerical garb and his beautiful pectoral cross—at first a handsome piece by African artists, later an official cross suggestive of the European episcopal cross, which his church had presented to him as an outward symbol of his presidential office.

His most characteristic role was that of chairman of a great assembly. In this respect Dr. Fry's talent was incomparable. It was, above all, his nimble intellect which served him well here. Scarcely ever did he find himself embarrassed while chairing meetings. His replies were quick, and in general they always had a certain objective and conceptual pungency. As chairman of the Central Committee of the World Council of Churches, however, it was always evident that in view of the unique importance of this position, he took pains to avoid the kinds of pungency and aggressive-

---

(b. 1899) Dr. Lilje began his ecumenical career as general secretary of the German Christian Students Association and vice-president of the World Student Christian Federation (1927-34), then became general secretary of the Lutheran World Convention (1937-45), surviving wartime imprisonment by the Nazis. He was bishop of the Lutheran Church of Hannover from 1947 to 1971. He was a leader in organizing the LWF in 1947, and served on its Executive Committee from then until 1970. He was the Federation's second president (1952-57). Bishop Lilje has been vice-chairman of the Council of the Evangelical Church in Germany (EKD, 1949-69), presiding bishop of the United Evangelical Lutheran Church in Germany (VELKD), chairman of the German National Committee of the LWF (1955-69), and a member of the Central Committee of the WCC (1948-68). Since 1968 he has been a president of the World Council, and since 1970 honorary member of the LWF Executive Committee.

ness in which he liked to indulge in other situations. This bridling of his temperament contributed to the clarity and singleness of purpose of his leadership as a moderator.

Two other important features deserve special mention in this connection.

His photographic memory, famous among all who knew him, enabled him in a fairly astonishing manner to retain the names of conference participants. Furthermore, he always pronounced the exotic names correctly, even those which sound strangest to European ears—a masterful achievement which did honor to his linguistic instinct. Still more important was the fact that from the moderator's podium he could immediately recognize and acknowledge by name every person who asked for the floor. In an international assembly, in which all members have difficulty, at first anyway, to recognize one another accurately, this genial trait brought an element of ease and affability into the proceedings.

To the special traits of his skill in handling meetings, however, belonged also a perfect familiarity with parliamentary rules. In this point he was unrivaled, and there were only one or two in such a great assembly who could match him. These latter, to be sure, could make things tense even for him. The rest of us pedestrians never took the time to challenge Fry's handling of the rules of procedure, especially since we Europeans never felt with the same ardor that we were tied to these rules. Although Fry was in the position to administer the rules inexorably, and although he could use the rules with quiet skill in special situations in order to avoid unpleasant decisions, he increasingly took pains always to give a fair chance to those of us who were inexperienced or insufficiently experienced in Anglo-Saxon parliamentary procedure. He consequently exercised as much restraint in applying these rules as the situation permitted, and he helped to work out a modified edition of parliamentary rules for the meetings. On the whole, his manner of handling meetings prevented the suspicion from arising that anyone was manipulating affairs. On the other hand, when others undertook to manipulate things for their own advantage with the help of parliamentary maneuvering, he was in the position skillfully to oppose them on their own grounds.

This talent of Dr. Fry came to the fore again and again in the normal debates, and ordinarily he remained the victor. I experienced only one exception. Dr. Bersell, president of the Augustana Lutheran Church, at a meeting in New Haven, Connecticut, asked how a recently passed resolution was to be interpreted. Bersell apparently acquiesced in the explanation which Dr. Fry gave him. But on the next day Dr. Bersell raised a question over a similar point, referred to the resolution of the previous day, and asked the chairman to explain how the resolution just passed could be reconciled with the former one. None of us had paid much attention to this inconsistency, and still less had it occurred to anyone to impale Dr. Fry on this incongruous statement. Dr. Bersell, himself a master of parliamentary procedure, did not shun this gentle, friendly clash. Dr. Fry indeed was visibly shaken, and it was apparent that a correction of this kind was unpleasant to him, since it did not happen often.

In general, however, Dr. Fry administered this office of moderator in a masterful, and I should prefer to say, princely manner. In his bearing he reminded me again and again of a great ecumenical pioneer, Dr. John R. Mott, who was in his own right a master parliamentarian and in his manner of leading a great assembly was a truly princely figure. With a similar if not quite so old-fashioned and patriarchal bearing Dr. Fry administered the important office of chairman of this great body for many years. In 1954 he was elected chairman of the Central Committee of the World Council of Churches, as the successor of Dr. Bell, bishop of Chichester, and until his death, shortly before the assembly at Uppsala, 1968, he administered this office with such consummate skill that no one entertained a doubt of his re-election.

This is no merely formalized statement. The presiding officer of the Central Committee of the World Council is like a pilot; he must guide the ship through the waves with great skill, with a worldwide vision, with firmness and with kindliness, especially when discussions become unclear and confused. In the time of Dr. Fry, who had at his side throughout his term of office so towering and distinguished a figure as Dr. Visser 't Hooft, there never arose in the meetings a feeling of unclarity or vague leadership. For such a complicated structure as an ecumenical conference this is a real blessing, for such a meeting is threatened by many dangers: the confusion of languages, the often very profound differences in the formation of ideas and judgments, not to mention the confessional, national, and cultural backgrounds. This plethora of complexity Dr. Fry's leadership always had under control.

Along with his unsurpassed human ability it is very significant that in these affairs he was also thoroughly competent theologically. To portray this side of Dr. Fry's leadership is not simple; the question itself is difficult and complex. Dr. Fry, moreover, had a definite limitation in this area. Though his gift of comprehension was acute and though his ability to think his way into theological questions was great, he was not really an original theologian in the creative sense. For his task, however, this was perhaps a real blessing. He was protected from the temptation to press too insistently for an opinion of his own in complex and controversial questions. A case in point, I should say, is the criticism which he received in one instance, namely, the result of the assembly of the Lutheran World Federation in Helsinki, 1963. The great final report was unable to command a clear majority approval.[2] I am still of the opinion that Dr. Fry, who presided over this final session, could have passed relatively easily over a series of objections, which indeed deserved to be ignored, especially since they obstructed the coherence of the statement in a regrettable way. Refraining from any effort to present a theological position of his own, however, and dutifully subjecting himself to the rules of parliamentary procedure, he abstained from pressing his own opinion and thereby he also prevented the achievement of a unified statement at the end of this great assembly. To this day I am convinced that this better result could have been attained if Dr. Fry had been prepared to abandon his restraint. That he did not do so, however, reflects credit on the strict objectivity of his parliamentary style.

In smaller meetings his theological ability came much more immediately into evidence and often gained its point. For in these sessions of smaller scope there was greater opportunity to present one's own position in all candor than in the larger assemblies, where a subjective attitude of the chairman, or even an attitude which could be construed as subjective, would doubtless have led to many more controversies.

One final positive point regarding Dr. Fry's parliamentary ability lay in his extraordinarily broad knowledge of the ecumenical world. He was a world traveler in the grand manner, and in the many lands which he visited he always gathered very precise observations, so that he could quickly and for the most part very competently survey problems—even of a complex nature—from the various regions of Christendom, and therefore could be helpful in his parliamentary leadership.

II

This great cybernetic capacity in the larger ecumenical bodies was supplemented by a masterful leadership of affairs in the smaller bodies, especially in the Executive Committee and the Central Committee of the World Council of Churches. The smaller the circle, the more skillful and calm was the leadership of negotiations by Dr. Fry. Here his ability to turn controversies into friendly conversations came to full advantage. Although he was a man of outspoken likes and dislikes, with quick positive and negative judgments, his feelings almost never obtruded into the objective discussion of problems, and he did not indulge in sharp controversies of this kind.

There was one exception. That was the question of electing a successor to Dr. Visser 't Hooft.[3] Dr. Fry's plan was good. At the end of the session of the executive committee in Rochester, 1963, he unfolded his plan. All members of the central committee were invited to present suggestions for a possible successor. Dr. Fry himself had the good idea to hold conversations with the members of the Geneva staff before a decision was to be reached. As often happens in such periods of transition, so it happened here: tensions arose, which grew larger and sharper with time. After careful reflection by Dr. Fry and after his conversations with the members of the Geneva staff, the executive committee, which had been delegated by the central committee to nominate the successor, had agreed unanimously on Patrick C. Rodger to succeed Visser 't Hooft. This decision met remarkably stubborn resistance. The members of the staff in Geneva acted strangely. The report which Dr. Fry had to give of his conversations was not altogether pleasant and revealed the internal difficulties within the staff. Most important, however, was the objection to Patrick Rodger which came from Visser 't Hooft himself. And when many regarded it as awkward that Dr. Visser 't Hooft should try to influence directly the choice of his successor, the position of the central committee was definitely to support this attitude of Visser 't Hooft. In Enugu, Nigeria (1965), this discord came into the open. The proposal of the executive committee, which (as said above) functioned as the nominating body by order of the central committee, was rejected by the latter. A new proposal was made, presenting the name of the present general secretary, Dr. Eugene Blake. Blake was elected, not without long internal difficulties and tensions. The actual election, indeed, took place only at the next session in Geneva, but the situation had not thereby become easier for Dr. Fry. It was clear to him that it would be awkward to have two Americans at the head of the Council, one as chairman of the central committee and the other as the new general secretary. This problem was indeed difficult, and such a choice was not desired. But the central committee voted for Blake by a large majority. Dr. Fry thereupon immediately offered his resignation in order to remove the difficulty. After earnest and deeply moving discussion the central committee resolved to request Dr. Fry under all circumstances to retain his office until the next assembly, planned for Uppsala.[4] In the meantime death took him away. The assembly of Uppsala then elected as Dr. Fry's successor Dr. M. M. Thomas from India.

These events deserve notice because they make clear that Dr. Fry's leadership did not consist in an arbitrary leveling of all opposites. He did not shun controversies, and in them he did uphold his position with integrity. The central committee's confidence in him, meanwhile, was always secure.

This fact is all the more noteworthy, in that Dr. Fry traveled a remarkable course from strict Lutheran to ecumenical leader. I still remember the moment when immediately after the end of the war he came to Germany with a little delegation from the Lutheran churches of America. Its task was to inaugurate a program of American relief, which in the following years streamed into Germany in so magnificent a way and performed incalculable service for the Lutheran churches. On this occasion a meeting also took place with the president of the Lutheran World Convention, Bishop Marahrens of Hannover.[5] The delegation came unannounced—which is the way things happened at that time—to the opening worship service of the first synod of the Church of Hannover after the war. When the service, led by Bishop Marahrens, was ended, this little delegation under the leadership of Dr. Fry went to Dr. Marahrens in the sacristy. No one of us was included; they engaged in a private, confidential consultation with Marahrens. It later became clear that Dr. Fry with considerable vehemence called on Dr. Marahrens to resign his presidency of the Lutheran World Convention. Dr. Marahrens as president and I as the general secretary of the LWC had remained in our offices because we were convinced that during the war we should not, by submitting resignations, create a difficult situation which at such a time no one could have resolved. In this decision we were expressly confirmed by the member churches of the Convention. When the war had ended, however, our American brothers regarded the moment to have arrived for Dr. Marahrens to be asked to resign. It is beyond all doubt that Dr. Fry—to say it mildly—delivered this demand with great vigor. It is reported that when the presidential election in the United Lutheran Church in America was impending, Dr. Fry proceeded similarly with his immediate predecessor, Dr. Knubel. At all events, it remains a part of the picture of Dr. Fry that in such situations he could develop a certain hardness, and that his behavior was not always characterized exclusively by conciliatory politeness.

At that time he was still a strict Lutheran, *Lutheranissimus,* and the Lutheran churches of America in that period still kept a very perceptible distance from ecumenical alliances. This aloofness came to light in many areas, and it must be accounted one of the astonishing achievements of the ecumenical movement that it succeeded in winning over so important, influential, and convinced a man as Dr. Fry. This was primarily the personal achievement of Dr. Visser 't Hooft. When the problem arose in Evanston in 1954 to find a successor for Bishop Bell, Dr. Visser 't Hooft urged the nomination of Dr. Fry, on good grounds and in a completely honorable and candid manner. Dr. Visser 't Hooft had a sure eye for the quality of this personality, and he was aware, furthermore, what strategic importance representatives of the Lutheran church of America would have in the ecumenical partnership, not least in the financial realm. For it is remarkable that the Anglican church saw leadership in the emerging ecumenical movement almost as its self-evident privilege; the distinguished and in his own way unique Archbishop William Temple was the first born leader of ecumenical organizations, and above all the bishop of Chichester, Dr. Bell, was indisputably a leader-figure. It was a significant and bold decision to draw Dr. Fry into this position and thereby to discard an assumed privilege, an actual or merely imagined prerogative of the Church of England, by the election of a Lutheran. That Dr. Fry fully justified these expectations has already been stated.

The transition from narrowly confessional Lutheran to ecumenical leader, however, was completed by Dr. Fry in a credible manner. There has never been any dispute over this question. None was necessary, for two reasons: first, because of the unusually shrewd way in which Dr. Fry administered his office, and secondly, because with the entrance of the Orthodox of Moscow into the World Council, the "confessional" problem came to be experienced as an altogether self-evident question. The Orthodox Russians have seen to it that a confessional consciousness henceforth would not be viewed with suspicion. And that stream within the ecumenical movement which must be regarded as fundamentally dangerous, namely, the tendency toward more or less unrestrained assimilation, has been ended by the simple fact of Orthodox membership.

In this new situation Dr. Fry moved with natural ease. He displayed a candor which was surpassed only by his capacity for human openness, and this convinced Lutheran never created a situation in which offensive rivalries arose between the confessions.

Not even the ever-present political tensions did that. Not that occasions were lacking, to be sure, and the entrance of the Russians into the ecumenical movement in 1961 at New Delhi had equally strong consequences in the political realm as in the confessional. For it was part of the very nature of ecumenical work that the sensitive points of world politics would come into the picture again and again, and thus also the separation of East and West—and all this affected the great decisions of ecumenical policy. It must be said to Dr. Fry's credit that on this point he never lacked a resolute bearing. He had to take care as moderator of discussions to let objectivity prevail and to avoid splintering; but it is only a further sign of his skill that he succeeded in this without leaving traces of asperity. Indeed, even the Russians willingly accepted the skill of his leadership, especially since it was clear that he did not use his chairman's position against them.

One final, rather complicated glance at the character of Dr. Fry: that he was a vital, convinced, and warm Christian shone forth in his sermons and above all in his devotional meditations. They had a serene power of faith, and his sermons had in addition a lofty rhetorical quality. Many people, however, have doubted his capacity for warm personal intimacy. In fact, it was obvious that the circle of his immediate and intimate friends was not very large. I could mention the names of several individuals with whom he felt a bond of warm and loyal friendship, and whose friendship was important to him because he felt dependent on them. To be sure, this scarcely came to expression in an outward way. One could harbor the impression that he was indeed greatly respected, perhaps even feared in his judgments, but not really well liked. In view of his strong personality and his capacity for leadership, in view also of his quick and precise (to the point of harshness) manner of forming his judgments, this is not surprising. But just for this reason it must be emphasized that within that more intimate circle of friends which attended him, there was connected with his *noblesse* an almost tender capacity for masculine friendship, and that it could touch him deeply if in this close circle of friends suspicions and doubts about him should emerge. Even if he did not often show it and did not practice it to a great degree, he was also a master in the realm of affectionate friendship. This dare not be forgotten.

One further word, finally, on the significance of Dr. Fry in the political conversation of the *Ecumene*. The sovereign skill with which he represented the central committee showed itself also to the general public. Twice I was with Dr. Fry in a country with a totalitarian regime. The first time was in 1956 at Galyatetö in Hungary; the second was in Russia, 1964, in Odessa, Moscow, and Zagorsk. In both cases it fell to Dr. Fry to say a word of greeting or of thanks in behalf of the executive committee on the occasion of official receptions. It is characteristic of dictatorial states that when they deign to grant the church the opportunity of an international gathering, they act on a grand scale and arrange an elaborate banquet. One of the official functionaries makes a speech, and this ecumenical body must respond through some spokesman with a word of thanks. In Hungary Dr. Fry performed this office himself. He did so in a masterful manner, simply pointing out that the World Council of Churches consists of purely voluntary members, any one of which can also withdraw at any moment if it wishes—a very beautiful, quiet reply to a political system which permits such a withdrawal neither to its citizens nor to its allies. And in Russia itself he had the wisdom to delegate the expression of the greeting to Sir Francis Ibiam, then governor of East Nigeria, the later so hotly contested Biafra. The fact that an African, a government official of a newly independent African state, delivered this greeting, nipped in the bud all suspicions that the ecumenical movement is another form of colonialism. And the brief words which Dr. Fry added made clear its concern for the complete spiritual independence of Christian churches in the world. These two scenes came off without great rhetorical or dramatic display, but about what actually happened no one could have the slightest misunderstanding.[6]

---

[1] Bishop Lilje also contributed a chapter in *Mr. Protestant*, pp. 38-45.

[2] Reference is to "Document 75" on the doctrine of justification. *Proceedings of the*

Fourth Assembly of LWF, Berlin, 1965, pp. 478-482. The document was received and referred to the Commission on Theology for discussion, final formulation, and publication. The retouched document was published under the title "Justification Today," as a Supplement to LUTHERAN WORLD, 1965, pp. 2-11. See also Weissgerber's memo (No. 65).

[3] Other writers touching on this subject are Lazareth (No. 40), Beazley (76), Smith (80), Payne (85), Niles (86), Tomkins (87), Goodall (88), Ibiam (91), and Chandran (92). The problem is briefly noted in Fey, *The Ecumenical Advance* (Vol. 2 of *History of the Ecumenical Movement:* 1948-1968), p. 49.

[4] Dr. Fry wrote an account of this episode as information for LCA pastors in *Ministers Information Service*, April 1966.

[5] See also the memo of Stewart Herman (No. 43).

[6] See memos of Sherrill (78) and Niles (86). Others who write about this talent include Endress (18), Schiotz (50), Manikam (62), Smith (80), Payne (85), and Chandran (92).

59

Bishop Anders Nygren

SWEDEN

A long-time Swedish associate discusses elements of Dr. Fry's influence in the Lutheran World Federation and the World Council of Churches.

When one becomes acquainted with a man and gains an impression of his qualities and his personal character, one generally proceeds from the outward features to the inward. One sees him in certain situations and observes how he handles them, and so one gradually understands his personality and his significance.

My acquaintance with Dr. Franklin C. Fry developed in the opposite way. The first time we met, we were to work together at the level of the inner, basic Christian faith. I had been commissioned to produce, with Dr. Fry's help, a basic Christian document in English. I asked myself how this could be done, since at that time he had not mastered the German language nor I the English, yet we were instructed to conduct our discussions in these two tongues. I discovered, however, with what astonishing intuition he grasped the foreign language in all its finest nuances. I also observed how, master of words that he was, he succeeded immediately in putting the document into proper form in polished English. For me this was a mystery, and I had to think of the miracle of Pentecost when everyone heard the Word in his own tongue. It was as if something very similar was needed when the Lutheran churches of the world were striving for unity. It was the one Spirit who overcame the diversity of tongues. This first cooperation with Dr. Fry became for me a taste of the "manifestation of the Spirit," of which I Corinthians 12:7 speaks.

Later, I often had to think of the word about the variety of spiritual gifts (I Corinthians 12) in connection with Dr. Fry. To each is given a special gift. Dr. Fry was a man of many gifts. With his basic Christian and Lutheran anchorage he was able to serve the churches with the gifts which were given to him. It is not possible to give examples here of the many areas in which he brought his gifts lavishly to play. Of one of the many gifts of the Spirit given to him in supreme measure, the gift of

---

(b. 1890) At Lund University (1924-48) Dr. Nygren earned a reputation as one of the world's leading theologians. He was chosen the first president of the LWF (1947-52), and bishop of Lund (1949-58). He served on the WCC Central Committee (1948-54), and was for decades active in Faith and Order.

leadership, I gained a new understanding from him. In Lutheran or ecumenical work we often faced almost insuperable difficulties. Then a word from Dr. Fry could be a word of spiritual leadership for the perplexed assembly, and could direct the question into sound channels and produce unity. Here he had a function of greatest usefulness to exercise for his own church, for world Lutheranism, for the *Ecumene*, yes, for the whole church of Christ. One notices the importance of this office especially, now that he is no longer among us, and his words of guidance are missed.

It had been planned that Martin Luther King, Jr., should speak at the opening service of the World Council assembly at Uppsala in 1968, and that the arrangements should be left in Dr. Fry's hands. Neither of the two lived to experience this conference. One cannot help but think what the meaning of Uppsala 1968 might have been if these two men had been able to exercise their influence on the conference. Especially there was such spiritual guidance as theirs needed.

60

Bishop Lajos Ordass

HUNGARY

A well-known Hungarian bishop, preacher at the opening service of the LWF assembly in Minneapolis (1957), recalls his intimate experiences with Dr. Fry between 1947 and 1957.

One of Those Whom I Have Met Along the Way[1]

The year was 1947. It was shortly after the end of the second, bloody World War. Europe lay in ruins, Hungary perhaps the most devastated of all. Here we were raising questions about the future of the church. In our forsakenness the first encouraging word reached us from the side of the churches. We were invited to take part in the session of *Hilfswerk*, the postwar relief agency of German Protestants, at Geneva, Switzerland, in March, 1947. At the same time we received another invitation. In July, at Lund, Sweden, the Lutheran World Federation was to be formed. To this meeting also the representative of the Hungarian Lutheran Church was invited.

The Lutheran Church of Hungary sent me to both conferences. I was at that time in my second year of service as a newly-elected bishop.

Many difficulties had to be overcome before I was able to set out on my journey in February, 1947.

In Geneva I was very kindly received by the representative of the Lutheran churches of America, Dr. S. C. Michelfelder. We came into frequent contact, and it soon became clear to both of us that I ought not return to Hungary after the Geneva meeting, because it was highly uncertain whether I would again obtain an exit pass after so short a time. It would be better if I were to spend the time between March and July in the United States of America. Dr. Michelfelder put me in touch with the National Lutheran Council and the United Lutheran Church in America. He also supported my application to the American embassy for an entrance visa.

(b. 1901) Consecrated Lutheran bishop of Budapest in 1945, Dr. Ordass was deposed and imprisoned in 1950, restored in 1956, and deposed again in 1958, over the protests of the WCC and the LWF. He was vice-president of the LWF (1947-52), honorary member of the executive committee (1952-57), and vice-president again (1957-63). He now lives in retirement in Budapest.

Thus in April, 1947, I traveled to the United States. I felt that I was in a rather difficult situation. For many years we had had no connection at all with our brothers of the faith in America. This meant that I would be meeting strangers. Most difficult, however, was the realization that I would appear as a beggar from a totally impoverished church. Even to this day I can feel how fearful I was when I was notified of the date when I would meet Dr. Ralph Long and Dr. F. C. Fry. In a long and humble prayer I implored the Lord to make this an encounter with brothers.

We met for the first time in the United Lutheran Church headquarters on April 21, 1947. Ralph Long, Dr. Fry, and the young Carl E. Lund-Quist were present. I had difficulties with the English language and Lund-Quist, who spoke Swedish, was able to give me good assistance.

Thus I met Dr. Fry for the first time. It was a great relief to me to find these churchmen so sincere and candid. They had received me most kindly.

The church leaders gave me plenty of time to report on the situation in our church. I sensed their sincere sympathy. So it was not too difficult for me to say that we needed assistance. At their request, then, I related how I had conceived of my visit to America. First I wanted to visit all the Hungarian Lutheran congregations. I knew, of course, that these were for the most part poor congregations and that their members had relatives in Hungary whom they wished to help, but I hoped nevertheless that they would also be willing to aid our church. Then I mentioned that as a young student I had studied in Sweden, and therefore would like very much to visit the Swedish settlements. Their former mother country, Sweden, had suffered no damage from the war, so I could perhaps hope to find among them some understanding of our distress.

Then Dr. Fry spoke. I learned that the Lutheran churches of America intended to raise ten million dollars in two years, to help the damaged churches in Europe. He assured me that the Hungarian church would not be forgotten. He then proposed that I should indeed visit the Hungarian and Swedish churches, according to my plan, but that I should also help promote our common campaign with addresses. I should explain the European situation at several synod conventions. In this way I could make a contribution to the success of the campaign.

Dr. Fry's words greatly eased my mind. Now I had the feeling that I was not in America as a beggar, but that I could regard myself as a co-worker in the relief work for all of Europe. That filled me with great joy. This joy I gained from Dr. Fry's words. As I happily gave expression to my joy, I also remarked to Dr. Fry how greatly surprised I was that he had become the leader of the great United Lutheran Church at so early an age. He responded with that loud and unaffected laughter which later became world-famous, and merely observed, "Well, one has to begin sometime!" Then followed an intimate conversation about our families. With a warm glance he looked at the photographs of my family and told me that he himself had three children. We discovered that we were of almost exactly the same age. Then he embraced me warmly and said to me—as I recorded that very evening in my diary, "I have already heard a great deal about you, and loved you before I met you. And I have prayed for you. Now I am infinitely glad that we have become acquainted." From that day on to the present I have remembered Dr. Fry in my daily intercession.

On the following day Dr. Fry took me to the National Lutheran Council, where I met Dr. Empie and A. R. Wentz.

Dr. Fry saw to it that my travel arrangements were promptly prepared for six weeks. I was to visit the Hungarian congregations, then the Swedish. He put me in touch with the president of the American Lutheran Church, Dr. Poppen, and divided my time among several synod conventions. In this way I saw a great deal of the church life of America. At most of the synod meetings I met Dr. Fry again. Before my departure from America Muhlenberg College in Allentown granted me an honorary doctorate. This too was the work of Dr. Fry.

We parted, to meet again in Lund.

* * *

At the founding of the Lutheran World Federation Dr. Fry played an important role. He was the leader of one of the study sections. It was remarkable how much consideration he gave to those who experienced difficulties with the English language used at the assembly. In his lectures and addresses he took pains to speak so clearly that everyone could easily understand him. So it happened that a German delegate expressed his thanks to Dr. Fry in the plenary assembly for having spoken like a precise language teacher.

It was a festive moment when, in the presence of the entire assembly, we bestowed on Dr. Fry the honorary doctorate of the Hungarian Theological Faculty.

Among my recollections stands also the first working session of the newly-elected executive committee in Lund. We had to elect officers, including two vice-presidents. One was A. R. Wentz. It took a longer time to decide about the other post. Dr. Fry proposed me. The suggestion was accepted. When I subsequently thanked Dr. Fry, he answered, "We wanted to strengthen your position."

When I returned home, the church situation had greatly worsened. The church's struggle for its rights and freedom was brusquely frustrated and ended with my imprisonment and sentence to hard labor. At that time it really made me happy that by this action not only a bishop of the Hungarian church was condemned, but also the vice-president of the Lutheran World Federation. Dr. Fry was right. Though in a different sense, I was truly strengthened.

* * *

My time in prison meant not only humiliation and suffering. It meant that, too. But it was also a time of inner quietness, in which the fellowship of faith could be nourished. I always had the perfectly certain conviction that the prayers of my brothers in the faith surrounded me. And that was a great source of strength, which gave me the joy of the faith.

Long years followed, in which every outward contact was made impossible. Dr. Fry sent greetings as often as he could. I believe that he did not miss a single opportunity. He himself rose higher and higher in the world church, and worked prodigiously. On him lay the burden of much labor. I tried to support him in prayer.

* * *

The Central Committee of the World Council of Churches held its meeting in July and August, 1956, in Galyatetö, Hungary. At the same time the Hungarian government also reviewed the false sentence by which I had been condemned in 1948. Dr. Fry, weighed down with work, still found time, in company with Bishop Hanns Lilje, to deal with the Hungarian government regarding my case. So, together with Dr. Lilje and Dr. Carl E. Lund-Quist, he visited me in my residence. Of this day I have a small but significant reminiscence of Dr. Fry. It shows how deeply Dr. Fry could become absorbed in his work so that he forgot everything else. My wife offered coffee to the guests. Lund-Quist was astonished to see Dr. Fry drink coffee. He never drank it at other times. Indeed, he even accepted a second cup. Lund-Quist later told me that on the return journey he mentioned this point to Dr. Fry. Fry answered, "But I did not drink any coffee!" Lund-Quist assured him that he had drunk two cups. Fry merely replied, "I don't remember it at all!"

* * *

In 1957 the World Assembly of the Lutheran World Federation was held in America, at Minneapolis. The preparatory session took place at St. Olaf College. Here we met with Dr. Fry fairly often, but always merely in passing. After the executive committee session had ended, however, we had a good opportunity for conversation when we rode by auto to Minneapolis. Among other things we spoke about the presidency of the LWF. It was already clear that Dr. Fry would be elected. He told me how many important decisions in his life were being made at Minneapolis. He felt it as a distinct burden that he would be made president. He regretted that according to the statutes of the World Federation the same man could not be elected a second time. For it was his conviction that Dr. Hanns Lilje was the right man to be re-elected. He felt that Lilje did his work with joy and with great ease. It did not appear that the responsibility overburdened him.

The World Federation did elect Dr. Fry with great unanimity. At that time I spoke with one enthusiastic woman, who told me: Not only would Dr. Fry be a good president of the LWF, but he ought to be elected president of the USA. The good woman did not know what she was saying. She was giving voice to the infinite enthusiasm for Dr. Fry. In this she was right. Many of us had a similar enthusiasm for him.

* * *

I met Dr. Fry once more before my return from America.

August 30, 1957, was his fifty-seventh birthday anniversary. He spent the afternoon of this day in New York with our six-man Hungarian delegation. With great delight he showed us the new buildings of the United Lutheran Church Center. His minister son was with him. Afterward the father and the son drove our whole delegation to his home in New Rochelle, where we shared in his birthday celebration in the circle of his family. All this we experienced as a great privilege and honor.

* * *

At that time I hoped to be able to cooperate with Dr. Fry through the years as vice-president. I was pleased at the prospect.

Events turned out differently, however. The political situation in Hungary again made it impossible for me to work in the church, and thus also in the Lutheran World Federation. I could only observe its work from a distance.

* * *

Then to my surprise came the sad news of his early death. With deep emotion I thanked God that he had allowed us to meet on the way of the discipleship of Jesus, and had united us in love.

In my daily devotions the selections had just come in these days to Hebrews 12, to the words:

"Therefore, since we are surrounded by so great a cloud of witnesses, let us also lay aside every weight, and sin which clings so closely, and let us run with perseverance the race that is set before us, looking to Jesus the pioneer and perfecter of our faith."

From that time I have thanked the Lord God daily for the assurance that Dr. Fry is in that cloud of witnesses, and that God gives me the sure hope that we shall meet again in eternity.

---

[1] "The way" refers to the discipleship of Christ, writes Bishop Ordass. It is his custom to remember his deceased associates with thanks to God for their encounter on the way.

61

Bishop Niklot Beste

GERMAN DEMOCRATIC REPUBLIC

Bishop Beste of East Germany came to know Dr. Fry through their membership in the Lutheran World Federation Executive Committee.

I am happy, of course, that a memorial book for President Dr. Franklin Clark Fry is being compiled. Unfortunately, I fear that I cannot contribute anything of a personal nature to it. I first made President Dr. Fry's acquaintance in 1947 in Lund, at the founding of the Lutheran World Federation, and thereafter met him frequently at the meetings of the LWF Executive Committee. In this way I gained the opportunity to have several conversations with him and I became aware, again and again, how responsively and sympathetically he gave attention to the problems of our church and life in our land. He always treated me with overwhelming brotherliness. We also had some jolly times together. After 1957 I was no longer a member of the LWF Executive Committee, and consequently I saw Dr. Fry more seldom. However, the ecumenical assemblies and a visit from Dr. Fry in Berlin provided opportunities at least to greet him briefly. I met him for the last time in Helsinki in 1963, where he guided the difficult proceedings with great energy and vigor.

For many years we also exchanged greetings at Christmas, and during my visits to the United States to attend conferences at Evanston (1954) and Minneapolis (1957) I saw Dr. Fry in both cities and in New York, and received a kind welcome from him.

You may be assured that I greatly admired and liked Dr. Fry. I have two reasons for this esteem: one was the joy of a man who lived in Christ, a joy which animated him and radiated from him. The other was the clarity of his thinking, a clarity determined by the gospel.

(b. 1901) Head of the Lutheran Church of Mecklenburg (1946-71), Bishop Beste served on the Executive Committee of the LWF (1947-57), for many years as a member of the Council of the Evangelical Church in Germany, and as presiding bishop of the recently formed United Evangelical Lutheran Church of the GDR from 1969 to his retirement in 1971.

62

Bishop Rajah B. Manikam

INDIA

This late Indian leader, who was once a schoolmate of Dr. Fry in Philadelphia, has reflected on his friend's position in world Christendom, and particularly on the tension between Lutheran and ecumenical concerns.

My association with Franklin Fry began years ago when we were contemporaries in the Mount Airy Seminary, Philadelphia, Pennsylvania. Dr. Fred Nolde was also then at the seminary. Somehow we three, Fry, Nolde, and Manikam, were a trio at many of the ecumenical councils and committees. Frank was a very close personal friend of mine. He took a lively interest in me as a fellow Lutheran from Asia. When my wife was very seriously ill after a heart attack, he remembered to write me an air letter from a plane flying back to the States from Europe. We were deeply touched that after presiding over strenuous World Council meetings in Europe, he should have remembered us and written to us from a fast flying plane instead of resting his weary limbs and tired mind. This was indicative of the man!

I have marveled at his capacity to discern the complexity of issues and to come forward with a solution which ended controversy almost instantaneously. I remember especially the marvelous reply he gave Dr. Radhakrishnan when the Indian philosopher spun out his theory of the equality of all religions, at the World Council of Churches assembly at New Delhi.[1] About this capacity of his, I need not write more, because others abler than I will have written about it.

I have often wondered how much of a conflict he would have endured between being a staunch Lutheran and an ecumenical person, because I have myself gone through the same struggle. But I had always believed that Frank was at heart a very conservative Lutheran and there-

---

(1897-1969) Lutheran bishop of Tranquebar and president of the Tamil Lutheran Church in India (1956-67), Dr. Manikam earlier served as a secretary, then executive secretary of the National Christian Council of India (1937-51) and East Asia secretary of the WCC and the International Missionary Council (1951-56). He was a member of the provisional committee which founded the WCC, and a member of the central committee (1961-68). He was also president of the Federation of Evangelical Lutheran Churches in India (1954-67), a vice-president of the LWF (1957-63), and a member of its Executive Committee thereafter until his death.

fore his long period of chairmanship of the Central Committee of the WCC would have meant a more poignant struggle in his heart of hearts.

I have often wondered how really keen he was on church union, whether he would have had the courage of his convictions to have led his Lutheran church into union with another non-Lutheran church. These are struggles that a true churchman must needs experience in the ecumenical movement.

I must confess that at times I had felt that Frank was something of an astute politician and that he had really missed his profession in life. The way he could handle troublesome people, the diplomatic word he would utter on very difficult and tense occasions, the winning of his supporters, etc.—these made the great intellectual giant and saint that he was, a human being too.

To the younger churchmen he was particularly kind, and he encouraged us to have our rightful place in the councils of the ecumenical movement. He was singularly untainted by colour or race prejudice. He was a true internationalist, and we Asians loved him. In his death I have lost a real friend, nay, a brother in Christ, but his life will ever be an inspiration to me as it would be to very many in the world, especially in Asia.

---

[1] Both Dr. Goodall and Dr. Payne declare, on the basis of their detailed diaries, that Dr. Fry made this reply to Sri Rajyapal (Governor Munshi) of the United Provinces, at the Central Committee meeting at Lucknow on January 1, 1953. Miss Sarah Chakko was in the chair when Dr. Radhakrishnan visited the Central Committee on January 7, and Bishop Bell expressed the thanks of the company to him.

Dr. Fry recounted the episode in the ULCA *Pastor's Desk Book*, February 1953: "My longest-to-be-remembered chore was another response, this one to Governor Munshi. When that self-assured worthy spoke, he took it on himself to lecture the World Council on the impertinence of evangelism. 'Cultural imperialism' is how the Gospel looks to him. Jesus is one among many human sages. The Sermon on the Mount is full of echoes of the Bhagavad-Gita! As the governor's host, my answer had to be filled with dignity and courtesy. As a Christian, it did not dare to give an uncertain sound. It didn't! I hit the notes squarely without any tremolo. 'Salvation,' I said, 'consists of forgiveness, issuing in inward peace, soaring into joy, the whole based on faith. Above and beyond all hospitals and schools, "salvation" (which the aristocratic Hindu had publicly resented) will always be the most precious gift.'

"Munshi, a friend from two years ago when he was in New Delhi as food minister, took my testimony without wincing and received me as cordially as ever in Government House as his luncheon guest five days later."

See also Payne's memo (No. 85).

63

Bishop Stefano R. Moshi

TANZANIA

Bishop Moshi writes of Dr. Fry's rapport with African Christians.

We, all his friends in this area, were very sad about Dr. Fry's death. To us he was a great man whom we did not deserve to have (Hebrews 11:38a).

His name, Fry, was so simple—almost suggesting that, apart from being a great man, he also was such a simple person that nobody would hesitate to approach him.

I met him for the first time at the Hannover Lutheran World Federation assembly, 1952. I admired not only his stature, but also the respect he commanded from other people.

In 1955 I met him a second time when he attended the Marangu All-Africa Lutheran conference. He showed his humility and ecumenical spirit. It was the time when in some areas of Africa the people began to feel that they should be regarded as an indigenous church, no longer as mission fields, and that Africans should be trained for church leadership, which was much delayed by the missions.[1]

Many missionaries regarded such claims as rebellion against white people, but Dr. Fry was one of those few who were sympathetic to this ambition. He encouraged us and defended that feeling. We admired his spirit of justice and humility.

I remember him sitting with some African leaders at the Marangu conference, mentioned above, explaining to them what "World Council of Churches" would mean; he encouraged those indigenous churches who would feel ready, to join the WCC.

It was not long after that, that some African churches joined the WCC. In LWF meetings one could sense how he always encouraged the spirit of *Ecumene*.

Other fine qualities I remember were frankness, insight, and cheerfulness. He was so frank to speak out his mind for or against, but always

---

(b. 1906) Dr. Moshi became president of the Northern Diocese of the Lutheran Church in Tanganyika in 1959. The following year his title was changed to bishop. Since 1964 he has been president of the Evangelical Lutheran Church in Tanzania. He has served as chairman of the Christian Council of Tanzania, as a president of the All-Africa Conference of Churches, and as vice-president of the LWF (1963-70).

with good spirit. I never heard him complain outside the meeting about anything he did not speak of plainly in the meeting.

He had a very sharp insight; you could hear him giving warning to the meetings of what would be the consequence if certain decisions were made, and giving many examples of what had happened before as a result of such decisions. He had a very good memory which helped him to give such clear guidance.

He was very cheerful in any situation; he was not a man of despair. This made his influence of leadership so strong.

I end this brief observation by thanking God for giving us this great man. Dr. Fry died, but his work did not die.

---

[1] See *Marangu,* Geneva, 1956, the record of the conference.

64

Chitose Kishi

JAPAN

An elder statesman examines Dr. Fry's relation to Christianity in Japan.

It was in his own office that I met Dr. Franklin Fry for the first time. That was in 1948. My first impression of him was that he was a person who would be ready to meet anyone in debate at any time, as well as meet anyone in ordinary conversation. He reminded me of a legendary prince of Japan, Shotoku Taishi, who is said to have been such a wise counsellor that he could give appropriate and concise answers to the appeals of ten people at one and the same time. The impression of his complicated facial expression still remains with me. His glaring, piercing eyes indicated the keen mind which could read what others are going to say even before they speak.

At a later time we met in my office at the Japan Lutheran Theological Seminary in Tokyo. He glanced over the constitution and bylaws of the Japan Evangelical Lutheran Church which was in the process of reformation at that time. He scanned the document, pencil in hand. At that moment it was a great surprise to me that he bluntly mentioned some points of confusion in the documents, which, he said, would fatally affect the healthy development of the new church.

The points he mentioned were related to the structure of the executive board. Thereupon I, together with some other members of the executive board, tried to revise the structure in such a way as to create a better working system for the sake of the future of our church. We succeeded to a certain extent in accomplishing this, but still today we feel much more has to be done to improve the structure of our church's administration.

Dr. Fry was blunt when he had something important to say. He

(b. 1898) Imprisoned during the war on the charge of "preaching for peace," Dr. Kishi subsequently has served as president of the Japan Evangelical Lutheran Church (1947-49, 1953-68), and president of the Lutheran seminary in Tokyo (1949-69). He has been a moderator of the National Christian Council in Japan (1961-65), vice-chairman of the Japan Bible Society, and chairman of the Japan Ecumenical Association. He is the editor of Luther's Works in Japanese. He has been active in the LWF, and a delegate to the 1957 and 1963 assemblies. He was a vice-chairman for Asia in the preparation of the Montreal (1963) Faith and Order conference.

spoke with such confidence every time I heard him that I felt no one could escape from becoming the target of his terse remarks, no matter what they might say.

Dr. Fry's outlook was broad and understanding. It was proper that he should be the central figure in most of the meetings he attended. He was in command of whatever item came up for discussion. He was always ready to treat any item from various angles of consideration. This surely made him a valuable leader for the church.

Dr. Fry was a leader in ecumenicity and worldwide churchmanship. While we do not belittle his efforts in this regard, at the same time we hoped that sometime he might actually live for several months here in Japan with us in order to see the problems of our churches in Asia, particularly Japan, at the grass roots level. For he did not always understand our problems as they actually existed. Although he was a leader in world ecumenicity, perhaps he did not have a firsthand grasp of the actual problems of missionary work. We wish that he could more realistically have seen things as they actually are in the so-called "younger churches." But in making such a statement perhaps I am asking too much of even that great man, Dr. Fry.

65

Hans Weissgerber

GERMAN FEDERAL REPUBLIC

Dr. Weissgerber, a former LWF staff official, assesses Dr. Fry's influence in the LWF, particularly at the Minneapolis assembly in 1957.

When Franklin Clark Fry made his last trip to Europe in autumn 1967, Bishop Hanns Lilje gave a reception in his honor. About a hundred participants, representing church, state, and different institutions of our society were introduced to him. When I came to shake hands with him and Bishop Lilje his eyes twinkled, as they usually did, and the surprise was quite on his side. "Now, this must be Hans Weissgerber or a twin brother of his whom I have never seen before." Well, I don't have a twin brother and I tell this episode only because it shows that Franklin Clark Fry hardly forgot a man whom he had once met, even after many years.

The last time I had seen him was at the Lutheran World Federation assembly in Helsinki, 1963, when I was assigned to the staff that had to do the preparatory work for the documents of the assembly. In the middle fifties, when I worked for the LWF headquarters in Geneva, the cooperation between him and us was very close, since he represented one of the important Lutheran churches in the USA—it was long before the mergers had come up—and also played a leading role in the National Lutheran Council.

In Helsinki as well as in the annual meetings of the World Council of Churches Executive Committee meetings he again and again proved his outstanding abilities in leading and guiding conferences. Sometimes not very far from manipulation, he always guided the assemblies under his chairmanship in those directions in which he thought they should move. But he was always convincing, and that made it easy for an assembly to follow him. His qualities as church leader and ecumenical manager are well known. His theological contributions to both the ecumenical scene and world Lutheranism, however, are less in the mind and conscience of the public. Whoever is going to write the history of world Lutheranism and of the movement of Lutheran unity cannot bypass the role which

---

(b. 1929) Assistant director of the LWF Department of Theology from 1955 to 1958, Dr. Weissgerber was associate director of the Evangelical Academy of the Lutheran Church of Hannover at Loccum 1963-70. He is now secretary for information of the Evangelical Church in Hessen-Nassau.

Franklin Clark Fry played in the theological work that was accomplished at the Minneapolis assembly in 1957.

Of all the past assemblies, I would maintain, Minneapolis did the most profound and thorough theological work. The themes concentrated on were unity and Christian service to the world. It is regrettable that the results of this assembly did not receive the attention that was achieved, for example, by the failure of the Lutherans to reformulate the doctrine of justification at Helsinki in 1963.[1] Yet, the Minneapolis assembly turned out to be the first serious attempt of world Lutheranism to cope with the challenge to answer the questions of modern times. Unity was then—and still is—one of the key words of both ecumenical movement and theological research. And it was also clear that the world looked to the church and expected solutions of these problems which had already come up or were about to appear. The pursuit of Christian service to the world, even though in some parts of Lutheranism then characterized as "typically American activism," proved to be one of the most important contributions which Christians were able to make to the present and future tasks of society in the second half of the twentieth century. When pointing out the need of giving concrete answers and of providing solid measures of assistance and support to the worldwide social problems, the assembly was certainly not aware of the fact that it anticipated issues which proved their specific, even burning relevance only one decade thereafter. The sections of the Minneapolis documents referring to Christian world service did not receive the attention they deserved; at this moment their timeliness had not been recognized, the *kairos* had not yet appeared. So when the world conference on Church and Society in Geneva (1966) and the fourth assembly of the World Council of Churches in Uppsala (1968) took up the very same questions, they seemed to be brand-new to many observers of the ecumenical scene.[2] Actually they were not. I wish, however, to focus on FCF's contributions to the Minneapolis assembly.

I myself, a theological *Assistent* at LWF headquarters in my late twenties, was assigned the secretarial tasks of the preparatory commissions for the theological studies. It was planned that on the basis of the work of the Commission on Theology, on the five lectures to be presented in the plenary assembly, and on the results of the group discussions, some statements were to be published. A small committee was formed, consisting of Ernst Kinder (Germany), Krister Stendahl (Sweden), Julius Bodensieck, and Franklin Clark Fry. We had an initial preparatory meeting in Geneva, and then met twice before the assembly, once in New York and once in Minneapolis itself, Franklin Clark Fry chairing the last two sessions. I do not remember details. We had set up some drafts that were later completely altered and re-worked on the basis of the plenary and group discussions (we were very far from manipulating the assembly or causing it to accept prefabricated results). But if these drafts accomplished something like a combination of European and American theology, it is on account of Franklin Clark Fry's contributions. We European theologians were often inclined to be satisfied with theologically correct statements, but Dr. Fry always asked whether the statements and answers we were about to outline had some relevance to everyday life. I do not suggest that American theology as represented in FCF was interested only in the practical side of dogmatic statements—quite the opposite is true; but it was the combination of thorough systematical study and everyday-life application which he always pursued.

When we started work in our small group, it was almost clear that FCF was to be elected the next LWF president. It was also clear that in his person a great church leader and ecumenical strategist was to take over one of the key positions of present-day ecumenical structures. It was less known, however, that this man also gave a most substantial contribution to the theological work of the Minneapolis assembly. Franklin Clark Fry liked to quote his grandfather, Jacob Fry, one of the theologians of the pioneer era of American Lutheranism, who tried to transplant the heritage of European theology into American church life. Franklin obviously had learned more from his grandfather than a number of quotations. He learned that theological work is a dialog—a dialog between various partners: different theological schools, different generations, and different continental and ethnic groups which in their situation and tradition tried to preserve and actualize the Lutheran heritage.

Admittedly, the published "Minneapolis Theses"[3] had hardly anything in common with the drafts we set up in Dr. Fry's New York office; admittedly, further, his talents were later seen most clearly in the area of ecumenical and ecclesiastical strategy. Yet his contribution to the theological side of the Minneapolis assembly, though hardly known, must not be underestimated. I have been witnessing how FCF brought his theological insights into an assembly that had to deal with both the theoretical and practical aspects of Christian unity and service in the world.

Nobody, after all, should be surprised about this combination. You cannot develop any church strategy if you do not have a solid theology to substantiate it.

---

[1] The assembly debated but did not adopt "Document 75" on justification. *Proceedings of the Fourth Assembly of the LWF,* Berlin, 1965, pp. 352-357, final form 478-482. See also the memo of Lilje (No. 58).

[2] Accounts of these two conferences, and bibliographies, appear in H. E. Fey, ed., *The Ecumenical Advance* (Vol. 2 of *History of the Ecumenical Movement:* 1948-1968), London, 1970.

[3] *Proceedings of the Third Assembly of the LWF,* Minneapolis, 1958, pp. 84-91.

66

Bishop Friedrich-Wilhelm Krummacher

GERMAN DEMOCRATIC REPUBLIC

An East German leader comments on Dr. Fry's brotherliness and his ecumenical loyalty.

On May 27, 1949, I met Dr. Fry for the first time in the "Church House" in East Berlin. It was an unforgettable day. Dr. Fry was one of the first emissaries of peace and reconciliation from the Lutheran churches of America to come to us in the east of Berlin after the catastrophe of the Second World War. Just at the time of his unexpected visit, our youngest son Christoph was born. How heartily he rejoiced with us, the happy parents!

Not until the decade from 1957 to 1967, however, did I meet him annually at the Executive Committee of the Lutheran World Federation: in Minneapolis and Helsinki, in Strasbourg and Warsaw, in Iceland, Porto Alegre, Tanzania, and elsewhere. I do not know whether I could have called myself his "friend" in these years. His organizational ability in the direction and handling of difficult ecclesiastical, structural, and financial questions was too great to permit this. Consequently, one could not wholly suppress a feeling of impersonal, cool distance from an important church organizer, who always found a solution, even in complicated situations. But then he would disarm me again by his humor and his hearty laughter! Even more, however, by the deep earnestness of his prayers; for here one came into immediate touch with the heart of a simple and devout brother in Christ.

Two points from my encounters with Dr. Fry seem to me to be of prime importance for our further progress on the road of ecumenism:

I think there was not one of the numerous conferences which we both attended, that he did not immediately upon meeting me inquire thoroughly, with full brotherly interest, about the situation of Christians in our land and in the socialist countries of eastern Europe—not from

---

(b. 1901) In 1955 Dr. Krummacher, formerly a high church councillor and then a general superintendent in the Evangelical Church of Berlin-Brandenburg, was elected bishop of Greifswald (Evangelical Church of Pomerania). He was a member of the LWF Executive Committee 1957-70. He has served on the WCC Commission of the Churches on International Affairs, and as chairman of the Bishops' Conference of the Evangelical Church in the German Democratic Republic.

political or church-political interest, but simply from the concern of a brother who is interested in others, even though he himself lives in an entirely different social system. Now, the question is this: will that power of brotherly concern and of common faith, beyond our political barriers, continue among us with such spontaneous vitality and credibility after Dr. Fry's death?

The second point is this: in all the years in which I met Dr. Fry as one of the leaders of the Lutheran World Federation, he was at the same time active in the World Council of Churches, in a position of responsibility. No one could entertain a doubt over his clear Lutheran confession, for it was his life and not merely a confessional heritage. I am convinced, however, that at the same time he also served the whole *Ecumene* with complete loyalty, beyond the confessional differences. For the further progress of world Christendom it seems to me a question of prime importance, whether there will be men and women who with passion for the truth and with inward fidelity will recognize their roots in the church family of their fathers, and yet will also be prepared, out of love and responsibility, without prejudice or reservation, to serve the entire ecumenical Christian fellowship beyond the traditional boundaries of the confessions. Will this legacy of our departed brother, Dr. Fry, continue to be realized and deepened among us?

67

Bishop Hermann Dietzfelbinger

GERMAN FEDERAL REPUBLIC

A leading West German bishop discusses the Lutheran World Federation, concentrating on the theological work at the Minneapolis assembly and the development of closer relations with Roman Catholics.

Perhaps the recollections of Franklin Clark Fry which I record here are too personal. However, the impressions which remain with me from my numerous contacts with him have a strongly personal side. I met him mostly at conferences, primarily in connection with the Lutheran World Federation, and relations at conferences easily become impersonal. But these meetings also had intermissions and excursions into the neighboring countryside which offered many opportunities for us to get to know each other more intimately as persons. Again and again the tall figure of the American gentleman in black clerical garb made a deep impression on us Europeans. While he spoke with reserve and restraint, he could survey the whole circle of listeners and transfix one after another with his piercing eyes, as if he wished to draw each person into the fellowship of conversation and challenge his thought. On these occasions the great problems of the church, and even the problems of international politics were discussed, but also our little personal interests, and Fry the grandfather would frequently talk about his grandchildren or tell stories and jokes in the American style.

The last letter which Dr. Fry wrote to me was dated May 15, 1968. It was a warm, brotherly greeting by the chairman of the Executive Committee of the World Council of Churches on my sixtieth birthday. When I received the letter in July, 1968, the writer was no longer alive, and we had been shocked to learn of his unexpected but eloquently faithful death. For this very reason I cherish the words of that letter as a special legacy of this man who combined a devout heart with great talents in ecclesi-

---

(b. 1908) Dr. Dietzfelbinger was consecrated bishop of the Lutheran Church in Bavaria in 1955. He had been the chairman of the German Evangelical Student Pastors' Conference (1942-49), and for a time director of the Lutheran Institution at Neuendettelsau. He has been a member of the LWF Executive Committee since 1957, and chairman of the Council of the Evangelical Church in Germany since 1967. He was the initiator of the Lutheran Foundation for Inter-Confessional Research, and first chairman of its board.

astical affairs, and a sincere concern for the whole *Ecumene* with the ability not to lose sight of the individual man.

I met him for the first time in the summer of 1957, when the Executive Committee of the Lutheran World Federation held its final preliminary discussions at St. Olaf College, Northfield, Minnesota, before the plenary assembly in Minneapolis. At that time president of the United Lutheran Church in America, he had been described to me as a master in the handling of conferences and discussions. This indeed he was, and continued to be as long as he held important offices in his own church, in the Lutheran World Federation, and in the World Council of Churches. We German members of the Executive Committee of the LWF marveled at his Anglo-Saxon parliamentary skill with its precision and its freedom. Each person had opportunity to express what was on his mind. Not seldom, particularly when regulations or structural ordinances were under discussion, it seemed to us that the manner of procedure was too slow and dry. But at the right moment Fry could intervene with unexpected quickness and steer the group toward the goal—*his* goal! All at once we stood in surprise before a scarcely expected solution, which nevertheless was very often the right solution.

But just at this plenary assembly of the LWF in Minneapolis, Dr. Fry also displayed much more than the skill of an adroit conference chairman. What won us to him in the work of the various committees was his great passion for the church of the Lutheran Reformation and for its gathering in the LWF. He knew what the Lutheran Reformation can mean in the whole *Ecumene*, and he wanted to give it its proper place. We considered it logical and self-evident to elect Dr. Fry president of the LWF at that time. "Christ frees and unites" was the great theme of Minneapolis. For the theological theses which were formulated in hard but fruitful effort we are especially indebted to his tireless, propulsive urgency. Though many other tasks have arisen in the meantime for the LWF and for the ecumenical movement, these Minneapolis Theses[1] ought not to be forgotten, but should receive more careful attention than hitherto in the broader ecumenical discussion.

Among the ecclesiastical and theological questions in which I myself had closest contact with Dr. Fry, our relation to the Roman Catholic church was the most prominent. In the Evangelical Lutheran Church in Bavaria, for which I was the spokesman, as well as in many other Lutheran churches of Germany, the discussion over these questions had been for a long time a bread-and-butter matter, so to speak. Accordingly, I received from the German National Committee of the LWF the instruction to present in Minneapolis the plan of an Institute for Interconfessional Research. At that time Fry was very cool toward these plans. For the Lutherans in the USA, he thought, this theme was not too urgent. Moreover, he maintained that their aloofness toward the Roman Catholic church was much too great. Nevertheless, he acquiesced in the plan that we should investigate what possibilities might exist in the framework of the LWF for dialog with Roman Catholic theology. To the commission charged with this work he devoted his careful attention. When Pope John XXIII a few years later called the Second Vatican Council and thereby brought the Roman Catholic church itself into closer contact with the ecumenical movement, Fry could exclaim in retrospect: "It was providential that the Lutheran World Federation prepared itself in advance for these conversations!" From that time he was one of the men who energetically promoted ecumenical dialog between Lutheran and Roman Catholic theology. For me as the commissioner of the LWF for relations with the Roman Catholic church it was a special joy when under his presidency the "Lutheran Foundation for Inter-Confessional Research" was established in 1963 by the assembly in Helsinki.[2]

On his personal stance toward the questions of the Christian faith I have seldom heard Dr. Fry speak. He was in fact a retiring kind of person, and it sometimes happens in the church, as elsewhere, that great responsibility makes the man who bears it all the lonelier. But I can remember to this day a sermon which he once preached to us on Luke 11:5 ff. There one friend asks another: "Dear friend, lend me three loaves." Dr. Fry lingered long in his sermon on the word "lend," and said: In the last analysis all that we have is lent to us for a while by God—our time and our power, human knowledge and theological understanding, the possibility to work to full capacity and the possibility of personal fellowship with one another. Often he repeated: "Lent—lent—lent by God!" To him God had lent unusually many gifts and powers, for his own church and for the great tasks of the ecumenical movement. Dr. Fry had worked as a good steward with what had been granted him, as it is expected of the servants in the parable of the pounds. Especially the Lutheran Christian knows that in our working everything depends on the grace of God. But the grace of God is so human that it makes use of our human working. From the work of Dr. Fry, too, it can bring forth fruit which abides.

---

[1] *Proceedings of the Third Assembly of the LWF*, Minneapolis, 1958, pp. 84-91. See also the memos of Weissgerber (No. 65) and Schmidt-Clausen (68).

[2] A research program had already been launched in 1960 at Copenhagen. In 1965 the "Institute for Ecumenical Research" was opened at Strasbourg. See the LWF *Reports 1963-1969*, Geneva, 1970, pp. 238-256.

68

Kurt H. Schmidt-Clausen

GERMAN FEDERAL REPUBLIC

The former general secretary of the LWF sketches Dr. Fry as an interesting friend, a helpful adviser, and an ecumenical leader. Then he analyzes Fry's role in the evolution of the Federation during the past decade, with special reference to relations with Roman Catholics and Reformed, the African radio station, the effort to strengthen the Federation's churchly status, and the move to re-elect him at Helsinki (1963).

Encounters With Franklin Clark Fry

There are very few men of my acquaintance who could be compared with Franklin Clark Fry in regard to versatility of talents or firmness of character, to tenacity of purpose and, indeed, to cordially sincere urbanity and humanness. That all these gifts were found together in a single person, however, and that they were combined with a singular instinct for doing the necessary thing at just the right time, gave Fry a unique dynamic and a contagious persuasive power which made him one of the most amazing phenomena of recent church history. One may well exclaim with Shakespeare: "He was a man, take him for all in all. I shall not look upon his like again."

I met Dr. Fry for the first time in late autumn of 1950, in Loccum. We candidates in the pastoral seminary had been invited to attend a reception given by the bishop of Hannover for an American church president whose name meant nothing to us. It was Fry. Along with Dr. Bersell and other Lutheran church leaders of America he was in Europe to participate in a meeting of the Executive Committee of the Lutheran World Federation, which had taken place at Tutzing, Bavaria. In connection with that, he was to undertake a tour of inspection in order to gain firsthand acquaintance with the various results of the generous programs of relief which the Lutheran churches of America had inaugurated in war-ravaged Europe after the Second World War. We expected an "executive," but

---

(b. 1920) Dr. Schmidt-Clausen joined the staff of the LWF in 1959, and served as its general secretary 1961-65. He became the secretary for missions and ecumenical affairs of the Lutheran Church of Hannover in 1965, and in 1970 head of the Osnabrueck Diocese *(Landessuperintendent)* of that church. He is chairman of the Ecumenical Commission of the VELKD, and since 1970 a member of the LWF Executive Committee.

we met a man. Unforgettable to me is the liberating effect of the contagious humor which radiated from Dr. Fry. Immediately all self-consciousness disappeared from us, and we found ourselves in the position of being able to hold a wonderful conversation, to the degree our knowledge of the English language sufficed. And here occurred another surprise: we conversed not about problems of church or Christian service or theology but about ancient Greece and the excavations by Americans who had contributed so much to the illumination of that epoch. It was clear to us all that we had met a remarkable man.

Two years later I met Dr. Fry in Hannover, at the second assembly of the Lutheran World Federation, at which I served as interpreter. Along with my work in the translators' booths at the plenary sessions, I often had the task to translate into German the addresses and interviews which took place outside the assembly, including three times for Dr. Fry, who was besieged by press and radio. No work was more pleasant, since Dr. Fry tactfully saw to it that the translator could easily follow. This says a great deal about a man whose command of language was as powerful as his. He could quickly empathize with another person's problems, and then he was a perfect partner. I experienced this first at Hannover, and again later many times in other situations and in more important kinds of collaboration.

How far his tactfulness went may be illustrated by a little episode from the Hannover assembly. Since I had learned the English language chiefly in England and not in America, there clung to me a noticeable English accent which led many Americans in Hannover to tease me for my "Oxford slang." Dr. Fry heard of this, came to me, and apologized for his countrymen, although it was at bottom only a harmless jest. He was always concerned for good relations between men, not only then but also in much more difficult situations, in some of which I shared later. Once he said to me, when after a particularly turbulent committee meeting I spoke to him about his successful efforts to moderate tempers: "If we do not try again and again, as Christians, to treat our fellowmen kindly and tactfully and to overlook their rudeness, then I have no idea why we are Christians at all." Of course, he himself did not always succeed in bridling his temper. He had an impetuous nature. So much the more did I marvel, again and again, at the iron discipline which he imposed upon himself in this and other respects.

My next encounter with Dr. Fry came in 1954, when I took part in the second assembly of the World Council of Churches in Evanston, Illinois. The humid heat of those summer days on the shore of Lake Michigan was indescribable. Many otherwise fastidiously well-mannered Europeans cast all restraints aside and shed coats and ties, to work in their shirt-sleeves. This I never saw, either then or later in tropical regions, on the part of

Dr. Fry. He possessed a certain natural dignity, which comported well with his warmhearted and good-humored temperament; he never attempted to deny them. Despite the heat, good work was accomplished in Evanston's McGaw Hall. On this occasion I had my first opportunity to marvel at the sure and adroit skill with which Franklin C. Fry could lead meetings. Not only did he have complete command of all rules of order and the strategies of conducting negotiations; he was also prepared down to the last detail in respect to the order of the day and its sometimes very complex matters. Even in comparison with other American or English moderators he was "in a class by himself," not to mention us continental Europeans, who even to this day have great difficulty to master the simplest rules of good parliamentary order. With Fry in the chair, everyone had his opportunity to speak and received his rights, and yet the items of business were taken care of thoroughly and punctually, no matter how large the assembly might be. Substantial results were always attained.

In Evanston Franklin C. Fry was elected chairman of the Central Committee of the WCC, as successor of the bishop of Chichester. This important position, which must be described as the key office of the World Council, he occupied with great success and prudence until a few days before his death. These fourteen years will go down in the history of the ecumenical movement and of the World Council as the foundational years. Here all the decisive patterns were set, which have established the lines of operation characterizing the ecumenical movement today: Union with the International Missionary Council took place; Eastern European Orthodox churches joined, and conversation with the Roman Catholic church became possible; worldwide social involvement of Christians got under way, in which the World Council together with other ecumenical organizations (the Lutheran World Federation and many others) was able to accomplish pioneer work in the sector of providing aid for the development of new nations. Last but not least, the Council succeeded in intensifying theological-dogmatic conversations and in bringing the concerns of world mission and of social service into one organic relation. All these developments were pursued with lively interest, promoted, and guided into practical channels by Franklin C. Fry, as I learned from experience in innumerable conversations.

In his hands the art of leadership, of organization, and of making practical arrangements became an extremely reliable, sensitive instrument in the service of promoting new and sound ideas. This became clear already in Evanston, when the problem was to integrate the fruitful impulses of the European, "eschatologically" oriented theology into the total ecumenical outlook. It was repeated later with infinite frequency, not for the last time during the long and arduous negotiations for the unification of American Lutheranism. These talents, however, were also used especially in the service of world Lutheranism, the advancement of which lay particularly on Fry's heart. Lutheranism owes him an infinite debt.

In this respect the encounter which I had with him during the third assembly of the LWF at Minneapolis in 1957 was typical. The executive committee had charged him with the difficult task of chairing the coordinating committee. This group was responsible for working out the theological theses, and consequently had to pour the findings of some twenty sub-committees into a significant and mature form. Since I also belonged to the coordinating committee, I had an excellent opportunity to observe Fry's manner of work at close quarters. What he accomplished was again striking. Most European theologians, before the work began, had not been able to imagine how an American church leader, whose abilities they thought they saw primarily in the field of organization and management, could handle the complex theological material at hand. They were quickly disabused. An altogether new Fry appeared before our eyes, a man with remarkable theological insights and a significant measure of systematic methodical power. He succeeded, in a fashion which scarcely anyone had regarded possible: a theological-dogmatic consensus[1] of considerable quality was hammered out, whose equal is not to be found in succeeding years; even in Helsinki nothing comparable was produced. Franklin C. Fry demonstrated that Lutherans can work out a theological-dogmatic consensus under the conditions of the modern age. Requisites are only appropriate methods and clear convictions.

With his election as president of the LWF Franklin Clark Fry was confronted with a task which corresponded to his abilities and convictions, and which at the same time was a task after his own heart. He was able to prove not only that loyalty to his church and confession need not run into competition with love for the ecumenical movement, but that loyalty to the church of the Augsburg Confession involves a comprehensive ecumenical outlook and commitment. Hence he considered Lutherans odd who shut themselves off from the ecumenical ideal; he not only regarded them as provincial and narrow-minded, but he doubted the relevance of their understanding of the Lutheran confession.

In the summer of 1959 I was asked to join the general secretariat of the LWF. I gladly accepted, although it meant a difficult departure from my congregation. I accepted because the prospect of collaboration with men like Fry, Lund-Quist, Vajta, and Sovik seemed to promise good possibilities for learning and working. I was not mistaken. Of course, there came a very bitter disappointment just at the beginning: the serious illness which had befallen Dr. Lund-Quist in 1959 scarcely permitted me to work under him. After a few months, to everyone's regret, he resigned the office which he had so admirably filled. In spite of my brief experience I was invited to assume leadership of the general secretariat. In this difficult situation Dr. Fry manifested to me a truly fatherly friendship, broad-mindedness, and helpfulness. Without his advice, which was always at my disposal but which he never thrust on me, my effort to settle into the new task with its many complicated problems of detail could hardly have succeeded. On every visit of Dr. Fry to Geneva, though his schedule was always crowded with appointments, he sacrificed many hours, sometimes in the daytime and sometimes at night, to help the neophyte general secretary of the LWF until the most important problems became familiar to me. He never took advantage of his superiority. He also knew how to combine necessary precision with that dose of geniality which spurs a subordinate to act on his own responsibility. At that time he also approved and defended those decisions which I had already made and in which another opinion could have been held. One can imagine no more agreeable superior and teacher; he never lost himself in pedantry. He was very demanding in regard to work and exactness. Since he imposed on himself the same burden and discipline which he expected of others, collaboration with him was easy.

Naturally, there were differences between us. In part they lay in the contrast of our ages and temperaments, but they were grounded partly also in our diverse experiences and convictions. One distinction never played a role between us: our different languages and nationalities. From the outset he wanted it clearly understood that Americans, in spite of their great material contributions to the World Council, possessed no "innate" claim to leadership, just as little as Germans should see themselves perpetually condemned to ecumenical discrimination on account of their Nazi past. This attitude was by no means self-evident to everyone at the end of the 1950s. For Dr. Fry it had long been self-evident. To him every kind of discrimination was odious. In this respect it was an achievement that at that juncture a German was entrusted with the leadership of an international organization for the first time since the Second World War. Without Dr. Fry, one may surmise, that might have become possible only much later. Without him it is also probable that the admission of the large and small churches from the eastern bloc into membership in the World Council, which took place at Delhi in 1961 against considerable opposition, could have happened only with great difficulty and perhaps not at all.[2] For distrust was very great at first.

After entering the general secretariat of the LWF I noticed that Fry exhibited a perceptible reserve toward the Roman Catholic church, which had just announced the forthcoming Second Vatican Council. My proposal to him in 1960, to inaugurate confidential contacts with the recently established Secretariat for Unity, with the purpose of introducing our theological and practical viewpoints into the future conciliar discussion, met with skeptical rejection at first. Nevertheless, he continued to listen with interest. The matter was by no means settled for him just because a young man had not been able to convince him at the first suggestion. A few weeks after this conversation I received a letter from him authorizing me to establish confidential contacts with the then Professor Willebrands, in order to probe the terrain. Out of these contacts grew the proposals of the Catholic secretariat to invite observers of the LWF and of other world confessional organizations to the Council.[3]

Fry did not hesitate to change his mind in another situation, too, and to acknowledge the fact openly. He regarded the Commission for Interconfessional Research, proposed in 1957 by the German National Committee of the LWF and approved by the LWF assembly, and the institute of the same name planned by this commission, established at first in Copenhagen and later removed to Strasbourg,[4] as a costly and completely useless whim of impractical European theology professors. He passed up no opportunity to pour out the vials of his derision and the irony so richly at his command upon this project and its advocates. Although Vilmos Vajta and I contradicted him at every opportunity as forcefully as we could and tried to win him over, our efforts made no perceptible impression. It was the helpful preliminary work before the Vatican Council and the guidance during the Council, through the careful publications of the institute and the coordination of the observers, that won him for the cause; he resisted the cause no longer, even though he did not exactly support it with enthusiasm. He acknowledged his change of judgment frankly and publicly.

Inhibitions and objections of both fundamental and practical kinds made him also oppose at first the plan to erect a Lutheran short-wave and standard broadcast radio station in Addis Ababa, Ethiopia.[5] He was concerned over the considerable cost, which might very well—as it appeared—exceed the abilities of the member churches of the LWF. He had practical fears, also, in view of the political developments in Ethiopia and the possible repercussions for the sponsor. After vigorous debates he grudgingly acquiesced. But the practical achievements convinced him. During the last years of his life he actually assumed the chairmanship of the sponsoring board of trustees. The cause had won him over.

He took a skeptical position at first, also, toward the plan set forth at Helsinki to engage in Lutheran-Reformed theological conversations on the international level with the Reformed World Alliance—assisted by the Study Department of the World Council.[6] The Department of Theology was almost at the point of despair, because its intrinsically excellent plan appeared already for the second time on the agenda of the LWF Executive Committee and again threatened to shatter on the opposition of Dr. Fry. His objection had good grounds. He did not wish to see the LWF maneuvered into a position where it would undertake binding doctrinal negotiations, instead of leaving these to the member churches, to which alone this prerogative belonged. When the cause and its immediate advantage for the whole of Christendom became evident to him, however, he himself proposed a compromise formulation which saved the cause: the member churches should be requested to send participants to this discussion on their own responsibility, while the LWF would merely offer technical assistance. In this way both the letter and the sense of the constitution were satisfied and at the same time an important project was made possible, which—as events have turned out—has proved thoroughly successful.

Promotion of the unity of world Lutheranism was very dear to his heart. This led him in 1963 into a conflict with a sizable minority of the delegates to the fourth assembly of the LWF, whose view was well represented also in the staff. The aim of this group was to "upgrade" the Federation ecclesiologically, i.e., to transform it into that which it can be according to its nature and according to the sense of the confession, namely, a single, though federatively organized, world-embracing church. Actually, this plan would not have ended the administrative autonomy of the member churches. That would be utopian, and not even desirable. It would, however, turn a federation of churches holding the same confession but lacking fellowship at the Lord's Supper, into a single communion with a unity of confession, proclamation, and sacrament. But this would have made it more difficult, if not impossible, for the Lutheran churches not belonging to the LWF—especially the Lutheran Church—Missouri Synod—to unite with it. Franklin C. Fry, who attached great importance to gaining the membership of the Missourians for the LWF, therefore attempted to prevent the proposed constitutional changes. He even succeeded, after consultation with the Missouri Synod's official observers at Helsinki, in putting through some constitutional changes which dispelled Missouri's misgivings.[7]

Although by theological conviction I counted myself at that time (and still count myself) among those who wish to see the ecclesiological significance of the LWF strengthened, I had to acknowledge that Fry was right in this situation. The constitutional changes which he proposed shunted the ultimate clarification of the churchly character of the LWF, which we desired, into the more remote future without making it impossible. They facilitated Missouri's entry, as its observers affirmed in all candor. The settlement of the ecclesiological nature of the Federation can still come—after the accession of Missouri—but then hand in hand with Missouri. It can only be hoped that the Missouri Synod will indeed vote to join. This would be an immense enrichment in insight and experience for all member churches of the LWF, and surely also for the entering church itself.

Another conflict, having to do with the person of Dr. Fry, was eased at Helsinki. There were a considerable number of delegates who would gladly have seen the re-election of the president, which according to the present constitution is impossible. If the constitution could have been changed, Fry would have been re-elected. In the situation at that time this would have been an undeniable advantage for the LWF and for the ecumenical movement. For a long time Fry decisively rejected this idea, which was urged on him by many people. He did not wish to remain president by the device of a constitutional change. Responsible leaders, however, had finally convinced him that in spite of all obstacles he dared not evade re-election. The executive committee, which would have had to submit to the assembly an appropriate proposal to change the constitution, was ready to do so by majority vote, but at this point some extremely unpleasant statements were made by the opposing group in the committee. Thereupon Franklin C. Fry withdrew his consent to stand as a candidate in the case of a constitutional change. Many persons have regarded this development as an unfortunate mistake which worked to the detriment of world Lutheranism and of the ecumenical movement.

The last time I met Franklin C. Fry was at the beginning of 1968 in Hannover. He was on his way to Göttingen to receive an honorary degree. He was as cheerful and resolute as ever, although signs of great weariness became perceptible during the conversation. At dinner we made great plans for the forthcoming assembly of the World Council at Uppsala. Occasionally he would remark: "I wonder whether I will be there. . . ." We took this remark as a passing expression of his great tiredness. A few months later I learned how right he had been. In the midst of final preparations for the assembly, death took the pen from his hand. No one will forget the shock and deep emotion which swept over the participants at the assembly when the unfinished address was read which Dr. Fry had prepared as his report for Uppsala.[8]

During the assembly and afterward I often asked myself how Franklin C. Fry would have judged the development of the ecumenical movement which took place in and since Uppsala. For all his appreciation of the social and political involvement of Christians and their churches, he would nevertheless have resisted energetically the efforts of those who wish to "refashion" Christianity into an element of the immanent political and social progress of the world, and hand in hand with this, to regard faith in the God manifest in Christ as an expendable relic of an unenlightened past. For Franklin Clark Fry the ecumenical movement was first and last an instrument in the hands of the living God for the purpose of encouraging Christendom to an ever clearer and more harmonious witness to the gospel. In his view of the ecumenical movement the Lutheran church and its confession had an indispensable service to render, namely, to hold it to this center, the gospel, and unweariedly to recall it to this center, again and again. Everything else which claims attention in the ecumenical movement—however eloquent and energetic—can possess only secondary importance in relation to the gospel. Will the Lutheran church do justice to this task pointed out to it by Frankin C. Fry, or will it change itself back into an instrument of activistic religion, which conspires to seize control everywhere in the world today? There are dangerous, alarming signs that this fanatical action-faith, camouflaged as limitless love for mankind, has already won a prominent place in the church of justification by faith. Self-justification by action, or justification by faith alone for Christ's sake? That is the question here.

I am grateful that in Franklin Clark Fry I encountered a preacher and bishop who, in spite of all other cares and tasks, never lost sight of the center of the biblical good news. "May he rest in peace, and may eternal light illumine him!"

---

[1] The "Minneapolis Theses," *Proceedings of the Third Assembly of LWF*, Minneapolis, 1958, pp. 84-91. See also the memos of Weissgerber (No. 65) and Dietzfelbinger (67).

[2] See *The New Delhi Report*, London, 1962.

[3] The development of these relations can be followed in Fey, ed., *The Ecumenical Advance*, chapter 12, and in the LWF organ, LUTHERAN WORLD.

[4] The "Institute for Ecumenical Research" was opened at Strasbourg in 1965. See also the memo of Dietzfelbinger (No. 67).

[5] On the "Radio Voice of the Gospel," see the memo of Schiotz (No. 50).

[6] The plan, inaugurated not by the LWF assembly but by the executive committee in 1963, has gone forward through the decade.

[7] *Proceedings of the Fourth Assembly*, pp. 325 f. The constitutional changes can be seen conveniently in the LWF's *Lutheran Directory*, 1963, Part II, pp. 192-201.

[8] Vice-chairman Ernest Payne read the unfinished report (*Uppsala Report*, Geneva, 1968, pp. 277-281), and brought it to completion (281-285). See also the memo of Payne (No. 85).

69

Bruno Muetzelfeldt

AUSTRALIA

The head of LWF World Service writes particularly of Dr. Fry's loyalties both to ecumenism and to Lutheranism, both to Christian truth and to Christian service.

"It is so dull to be tied to these rails," thought the railroad engine as it sped across the Australian desert. "I would much rather be free to jump the rails and chase a few kangaroos!"—Not altogether surprisingly, this rather amusing little illustration is still vivid in my memory, even though it is now many years since I heard it from the lips of Dr. Fry when he preached in Melbourne at the time of the World Council of Churches Executive Committee meeting in 1956. Since this was shortly before the Minneapolis assembly of the Lutheran World Federation, he spoke on the theme "Christ Frees and Unites." Adapting his analogies to the local situation in his inimitable style, he chose this example of the engine, the rails, and the kangaroos to provide a verbal sketch of the difference between freedom and licence: Even as an engine loses its freedom to fulfil its purpose and to reach its goal unless it considers itself bound to the rails, so true freedom in the Christian life cannot be achieved by following every whim and fancy: rather, discipline is of the essence.

Perhaps I remember this incident so clearly not only because of its aptness for the purpose of the point Dr. Fry wanted to illuminate, but also because it threw light on the man himself. Apart from the extraordinary keenness of his intellect and the brilliance of his oratory, it was the way in which he had disciplined his thinking which was one of the most impressive characteristics of this outstanding churchman.

His clarity of thought, which shed light on many perplexing questions of our time, left its impact also on the complex issues of ecumenicity—mission—service. Dr. Fry had been intimately associated with these issues from the very outset. Today it seems strange that barely twenty-five years ago it took considerable courage to advocate assistance to people in need

---

(b. 1918) Himself a German emigrant to Australia, Dr. Muetzelfeldt was president of the New South Wales District of the United Evangelical Lutheran Church of Australia when he took on added duties as Australian executive officer of LWF World Service, in charge of immigration affairs, in 1957. Since 1961 he has been director of LWF World Service, with offices in Geneva, Switzerland.

without regard to race, religion, nationality, and political conviction, especially when some of the destitute lived in former enemy countries. Dr. Fry was in the vanguard of this struggle for the acceptance in practice of a principle to which so often in Christian history only lip-service had been given. His disciplined mind could not tolerate the idea that the Christian response to the Lord's all-embracing command of love could be inhibited by emotive consideration of politics and popularity. He reflected on this subject in his president's report to the Lutheran World Federation Helsinki assembly in 1963 when he said:

> In a time when the unity of all humanity is being forged and people everywhere are coming to realize almost against their will that we mortals are all in one bundle of life, the Federation has been a pioneer to remind us of the biblical adage that we are to do good to all men, not only to those of the household of faith.[1]

His ability to see the issues clearly was also apparent in his stance on the involvement of international and national, interconfessional and confessional agencies in the field of Christian social responsibility and service. He held the view that confessional programmes and ecumenical practice, far from being mutually exclusive, ought to complement each other within the totality of Christian social concern. Therefore, though committed to the ecumenical ideal, he felt strongly that, in the face of the mammoth privations of man, there ought to be a maximizing of efforts by all who could be effective in this field with requisite co-ordination. This conviction led him enthusiastically to support and closely to be associated with the service endeavours of four agencies, viz., Church World Service, Lutheran World Relief, WCC/Division of Inter-Church Aid, Refugee and World Service, and LWF/World Service. The fostering of ecumenical objectives was one thing (and no one could question his ecumenical convictions), and the meeting of human needs was another. Where both could be accomplished within the same context: well and good; but to allow the one to inhibit the other, or vice versa, could be a denial of both.

A similar distinction between ideological concepts and organizational patterns was evident in his thinking on the much-debated issue of "Mission and Service." The often emotionally overcharged discussion on the interrelationship between mission and service seemed to him largely futile and sometimes annoying. For him it was so self-evident that the true disciple of Christ was totally committed to both. To elevate the one above the other, or merely to use the one to achieve the purposes of the other, could be a degradation of both.

However, the spiritual unity of these two elements of the Christian's life was to him no argument for an organizational merger. Pointing out that in government, in business, and also in the church various facets of equally valid and inter-related activities require distinctive organizational patterns for their effective implementation, he questioned attempts to merge the administrative structures of international programmes in mission and service. It is fascinating to note that a man who, because of his spiritual insights, the depths of his theological perception, and his extraordinary mastery of language, was himself so outstanding an exponent of the ministry of the spoken Word, was at the same time so forceful an advocate for the importance of the ministry of service to have organizational frames most suited for its specific task.

Thus, as I was privileged to discuss these vital issues with him and to learn from him, I came to know him as a man who would dismiss the plausible to accept the genuine, who would disregard the emotive to promote the valid.

How one can respect a man with so disciplined a mind! Yet, when I think of what brought forth in me not merely respect but a deep affection for this man of unusual stature among his fellows, then it would seem that it was the glimpse one gained when, ever so rarely, he lowered his guard to reveal a very human man; a man longing for understanding in the loneliness that is the burden of those whose great and rare gifts set them apart from others; a sensitive man who was often regretful that his quick wit had sometimes hurt rather than helped; a man deeply concerned for his family and friends, realizing that they had to share with him the burdens of his encompassing concern for the broader family of mankind and of his passionate dedications to the cause of the Lord; a man of profound depth and devotion. I think that it was this facet of Franklin Clark Fry which I treasure the most.

---

[1] *Proceedings*, pp. 36-37.

70

Archbishop Gunnar Hultgren

SWEDEN

The retired primate of the Church of Sweden shares observations of Dr. Fry in the 1960s, and relates an audience with King Gustaf Adolf.

Franklin Fry had already had a long career as an ecumenical leader when I, as a newcomer to ecumenical affairs, took my place on the Executive and Central Committees of the World Council of Churches. My first impression, which was a lasting one, was of a chairman who led the proceedings with brilliance and precision and found personal satisfaction in doing so. To his technique as a leader, and likewise to his personal disposition, belonged a frolicsome sense of humor with which he was able to break the tension even at a critical moment. Not only did he encourage shy newly-elected members to speak, but he also paid scant attention to verbose debaters. There was no doubt that even in very intricate questions, he had in mind the direction which the discussion should take, and was skillful in recognizing and seizing the critical moment to bring the matter to a vote.

No one could fail to recognize that Fry was passionately engaged in ecumenical affairs. Apparently he was fully interested in everything within that broad sphere. It seldom showed in his face or his voice when controversial questions were dealt with and essentials were at issue. Occasionally he did express his feelings when there was a question of a sensitive election, and later on when he became deeply involved in the battle against racial discrimination. Otherwise, he felt it incumbent on the chairman to control his feelings.

Fry was a Lutheran, and there were only a few of us from that confession in the executive committee. Obviously this fact created a bond among us. Yet not once in a ten-year period did Fry seek my support for a special Lutheran point of view. In one instance only did he attempt to influence me, and then the issue had no confessional significance. This

---

(b. 1902) Dr. Hultgren was successively bishop of Visby (1947) and Härnösand (1950) and then archbishop of Uppsala (1958-67). He participated in the 1963 LWF assembly, and was a member of the Central and Executive Committees of the WCC (1961-68). He is chairman of the Swedish Ecumenical Council, and co-chairman of the international Anglican-Lutheran discussions begun in 1970.

ecumenical breadth in Fry may be explained by the fact that he represented an open Lutheranism, solidly anchored in evangelical faith but free of dogmatism. It was only at Helsinki in 1963 that I had the opportunity to see him function as president of the Lutheran World Federation. There he played the same impartial role as a mediator between a more liberal and a more conservative Lutheranism. This confirmed the impression I had received at closer range by the manner in which he met the divisions within the Church of Sweden over the question of women ministers. Here he displayed a friendly understanding of both sides and yet made one of the parties aware of his personal sympathy.

Avoidance of a fixed position in such churchly questions of principle belonged to Fry's understanding of the objectivity which a leader should maintain. But did not this attitude have its roots in his position toward dogmatic theology? I have never heard Fry deliver a theological lecture. Theology was not very apparent in his speeches and sermons. However, his messages certainly showed knowledge of the Bible as well as exegetical insights. Fry was sufficiently theologically oriented and trained that he could display good judgment in interpreting the essential Christian articles of faith. Apparently he was conscious of his lack of charisma in these matters and therefore did not want to make pronouncements on his own, much less appear as a master.

If in the public sphere Fry preserved a noticeable distance toward his colleagues, he showed the same quality in private. He did not devote his free moments to social contacts, but rather used this time for his correspondence. I recall how irritated I became on one occasion when on a boat excursion, or perhaps it was while waiting at an airport, he spurned a golden opportunity for conversation in order to pursue his favorite hobby instead, the solution of crossword puzzles! In spite of many declarations that he counted me among his most dependable friends, I cannot remember many personal conversations at our many meetings. But on occasion he could charmingly relate episodes from his early studies of archeology in Greece, or discuss his plans for a longed-for vacation with his family.

The best memory I have of him comes from his week-long visit in Sweden in the spring of 1962. Both the official and the personal elements in his personality found their strongest expression at the audience which King Gustaf VI Adolf granted at the castle in Stockholm. It was a sight to behold, to watch the king and Fry together, both stately, both by nature dignified and refined. The king began with a polite question about where Fry had come from, and Fry responded that he had just arrived from Addis Ababa. The king related that he had visited the "abuna," the head of the Ethiopian church, during the thirties, but had heard that he had later become independent in his relation to the Coptic patriarch of

Egypt. Then Fry felt it expedient to change the subject to India, which he had recently visited. But it proved that the king, as crown prince, had made a long visit there as guest of his brother-in-law, the then Governor General Mountbatten, and the king was eager to receive information about the latest developments in the country. To this Fry responded brilliantly, if in a somewhat subdued manner. At the conclusion of the audience Fry seized his great opportunity and took from his pocket his little autograph book intended only for great men, and with these words, "You see, Your Majesty, I am still a child!" asked the king for his signature.

Franklin Fry was an eminent spiritual leader, a statesman of the church, who not only conveyed the impression of being a man of great wisdom, but really was one, yet at the same time was at heart a true man and a Christian, a child of great simplicity.

Part Four

Memos from American Christians of sister churches

In Parts Four and Five leaders in the ecumenical movement comment on their Lutheran colleague. The writers in Part Four (Memos 71-80) are Americans. Archbishop Iakovos and J. Irwin Miller offer general reflections. Memos 73 to 77 have their focus chiefly on church affairs in the United States, Memos 78 to 80 on international Christianity.

71

Archbishop Iakovos (Coucouzis)

Greek Orthodox

The Greek Orthodox primate of the western hemisphere ponders whether Franklin Clark Fry should be called a convinced ecumenist, or rather, what kind of ecumenism he espoused.

Frank Fry's Ecumenism

Was Fry truly a convinced ecumenist? There were many people who asked that question while he was still with us, and there are still a few even among his friends who find it very difficult to answer. Their difficulty lies in the fact that Fry wrote no books on the ecumenical movement, and, therefore, left with us no real ecumenical documents that would identify him one way or another.

Fry's role as a chairman of the Executive and Central Committees of

---

(b. 1911) Since 1959 Iakovos has been archbishop of the Greek Orthodox Archdiocese of North and South America, with headquarters in New York. Born in Turkey, he became dean of the cathedral in Boston (1942-54), then bishop of Malta (1954-56). He spent the years 1955-59 at Geneva with the World Council of Churches, as representative of the Ecumenical Patriarchate. He was a president of the WCC 1961-68.

the World Council of Churches did not permit him the luxury of time to put into print his personal thoughts and reflections on the question of Christian unity. My personal opinion is that Fry was an ecumenist, a convinced ecumenist, if I can judge from the dedicated and masterful way he presided and served the ecumenical movement over a period of twenty years.

It is true that Fry did not expound an ecumenism which could be identified as his own, for he did not share the romantic or the "public relations-oriented" ecumenism of so many. He could see unity in no other way but in its true light. He knew too well that "human nature"—this gigantic stumbling block—could not easily be removed so as to free the way towards unity. True to his personal beliefs and opinions, he preached many times on the need for renewal and reconciliation, but if I remember correctly, rarely did he preach on Christian unity.

Fry was both by nature and by conviction a pragmatist and he would go to great pains in prudent silence, rather than commit himself even oratorically to a cause which he felt demanded long and prayerful studious years before one would reach even the definition of the nature of the unity we seek. Being a theologian, a church administrator, and in addition, a churchman of distinction upon whom the eyes of the world are turned, Fry was in no way willing simply to accommodate or please his listeners.

Ecumenism is not a theory: nor is it a mood or an emotion. Ecumenism is a commitment which must be preceded by at least two other commitments: the commitment to an all-demanding God, and the commitment to an all-demanding church: His church. Personally, I know of no other such ecumenist, with the exception of one: Athenagoras I of Constantinople—not because he is an Orthodox, but because he has lived through a divided and hateful Christianity for over eighty years.

Fry was an American clergyman, and a Lutheran. As an American, he knew that you cannot easily erase the over two hundred sects and denominations we have here. As a Lutheran, or better still, as the leader of one of the three Lutheran churches in America, he could not ignore the cause of division still at work within all of us. His ecumenical views, therefore, could not be crystalized in any form; they are a matter of prayer and of continued study. Fry would prefer to be the exponent of a true Christianity rather than the preacher of an untenable ecumenism.

He believed, nevertheless, with all his heart in the imperativeness and usefulness of a sincerely motivated rapprochement as well as in the need and purposefulness of a dispassionate and objective theological dialog and encounter. He exemplified the first through his personal, very warm attitude; he encouraged the second with a visionary enthusiasm. He would favor any and all kinds of church mergers for he believed that a united church is closer to truth and to modern reality, and he would compromise his views with none who uphold the belief that church unity might come as a result of a "united front of social action." Fry believed that our actions must be dictated by our conscience and not only by circumstantial reasoning.

Being a gifted, a truly charismatic person, Fry could have been one of the most popular leaders of modern American Christianity. He preferred to be in the graces of the Lord rather than in the graces of men. A Christian leader who divests Christianity of its spirituality and sees it only as a "social gospel" subscribes to the kind of Christianity Judas preferred. Christianity is by its nature the revelation of God's will for man; not the revelation of man's idea of God. And for this reason Christianity must be the inspiration of man's actions, and at the same time, the ultimate criterion of man's morality.

Fry's ecumenism emanated from such a concept of Christianity. He lived with it and died with it. The moment he asked me, while he was lying on his deathbed just two days before his passing unto eternity, to pray for him, Frank was putting his "imprimatur" on his own concept of ecumenism: the earth shall never become a Christian *Ecumene* unless we learn to live together, to pray together, and endlessly expand and extend the present into the future. Fry believed "the earth is the Lord's and the fulness thereof; the world, and they that dwell therein." This was Fry's ecumenism; he lived and died for it.

72

J. Irwin Miller

Christian Church (Disciples of Christ)

A layman prominent in business, public affairs, and church expresses an appreciation of Dr. Fry's contribution to the ecumenical discussion in a time of testing.

It was my good fortune to know Frank Fry during a decade when the institutional church was tested as severely as it has been during this century.

We were usually, but not always, on the same side of the fence. Frank, however, was always the same person, whether the issue was the theological implications of an act of the National Council, the place of women in the church, the transfer of leadership in the World Council, or critical issues of race or national disagreement.

He stood on a personal foundation built of fearless conscience, strong historical sense (a rare thing nowadays), and a clear theology which controlled his actions.

His contribution to any discussion was incisive. His manner of thought and speech demanded a high quality of response. So in a very real sense he elevated every discussion in which he was a participant. To these discussions he brought a quality to which no one would apply the popular adjective, "relevant." Some would even have labeled him "old-fashioned." I would not agree with them, but would instead prefer "timeless." There was in Frank a timeless quality which abhorred fashion and which has always characterized the good advocates of any time. In a society which has too little sense of history it was good indeed to associate with such a man.

(b. 1909) Mr. Miller has been president (1945-51) and since 1951 chairman of the board of the Cummins Engine Company, Columbus, Indiana. Long active in ecumenical affairs, he has served as president of the National Council of Churches (1960-63), and as a member of the Central and Executive Committees of the World Council (1967-68). He has held a number of important posts in the business world, and has been appointed by presidents of the United States to several commissions on national and international problems.

73

Samuel M. Cavert

Presbyterian

Dr. Cavert (who could have written equally authoritatively about the international scene) has chosen to concentrate on the origin of the National Council of Churches, and the debate over the ecumenical principles which Dr. Fry upheld.

Franklin Clark Fry was an outstanding example of the Christian who combines loyalty to a particular confessional heritage with devotion to the church universal. A stalwart Lutheran, convinced of the permanent significance of the Lutheran witness, he was constantly conscious of a Christian community transcending the denomination.

Although Dr. Fry's extraordinary service to the ecumenical movement was most conspicuous in connection with the World Council of Churches, he also played an important role in the historical development of the National Council of the Churches of Christ in the USA. In one aspect of it his influence was so crucial, and also so revelatory of his churchmanship, that it deserves to be better known.

Dr. Fry came to the presidency of the United Lutheran Church just at the time (1945) when the discussions that led to the creation of the National Council of Churches were reaching a decisive stage. Representatives of the eight interdenominational agencies which were contemplating the merger that made the National Council possible had prepared a preliminary draft of the constitution for submission to the denominations. Up to this time the United Lutheran Church had sat lightly to organized efforts of cooperation or united action with non-Lutherans. It had defined its relationship with the Federal Council as only consultative rather than

---

(b. 1888) In many ways the title "Mr. Protestant" should belong to Dr. Cavert. His ecumenical career began during World War I, in the Federal Council of Churches' Wartime Commission. Joining the executive staff of the FCC in 1920, he served as general secretary from 1930 to 1950 and then as general secretary of its successor, the National Council of the Churches of Christ in the USA 1951-54. He was a leader in the provisional committee which designed the World Council of Churches and chairman of the committee on arrangements for its first assembly, 1948. He was active in maintaining communications among Christians during World War II and in promoting postwar reconstruction in Europe. He was executive secretary of the New York office of the WCC 1954-57, and director of the Interchurch Center in New York 1963-64. Besides making ecumenical history, Dr. Cavert has recently written two definitive histories of American ecumenism.

one of official membership. All who were committed to an advance in cooperative unity through the proposed National Council were greatly concerned about the policy which the United Lutheran Church would adopt with reference to the new interdenominational structure.

In the discussions that ensued Dr. Fry took a vigorous part, though less in formal conferences than in extended conversations with Dean Luther A. Weigle, as chairman of the committee planning for the National Council, Hermann N. Morse as its secretary, and myself. The net result was a modification of the original draft of the constitution at two critical points. They had to do with the way in which the so-called "evangelical principle" and the "representative principle" should be interpreted.[1]

Those who had drafted the constitution in its early form felt that they had adhered to both of these principles, but Dr. Fry was not fully satisfied with the flexible way in which the principles had been applied. To some of the members of the planning committee he seemed at times unduly tenacious of his own interpretation of what must follow from an acceptance of the general principles. Even from those from whom he differed most, however, he commanded the highest respect. His intellectual acumen, his clarity in analyzing a situation, and his penetrating insight into the issues at stake were recognized on all sides—so much so that after the formation of the National Council he served for six years (1954-1960) as chairman of its Committee on Policy and Strategy.

In applying the "evangelical principle" Dr. Fry insisted that all local and state councils of churches, if they were to be recognized as in association with the National Council, must officially declare themselves in agreement with its constitutional preamble acknowledging Jesus Christ as "divine Lord and Savior." This raised the serious administrative question as to how far the National Council could properly go in a centralized control over local structures of cooperation. Some of the state and local councils, concerned to protect what they regarded as a rightful autonomy, felt that Dr. Fry's stand involved the imposing of too much ecclesiastical authority "from the top." In the summer of 1951 Dr. Fry attended the annual conference of the Association of Secretaries of Councils of Churches, at Lake Geneva, Wisconsin, to discuss this point with them.[2] I think that it would now be generally agreed, even by those who did not then see eye to eye with him, that the adoption of his proposal has resulted in a more cohesive and stable conciliar movement than might have developed otherwise.

The "representative principle" raised a still more difficult question of application. Dr. Fry stoutly insisted that the only valid type of representation in the governing bodies of the National Council is *denominational*. Over against this view was the conviction of others that *geographi-*

cal representation of the Christian community is equally authentic in theory, and in practice essential to effective operation. The latter consideration induced Dr. Fry in 1950 to accept, though very reluctantly, an article in the constitution which provided that "the cooperative work of the churches in the various states, cities, and counties" should have a limited representation. He could not, however, be really satisfied with any arrangement which recognized any other group than the constituent denominations as entitled to designate members of the National Council's assembly or general board. Chiefly as a result of his urging, the constitution was subsequently amended by a provision under which state and local councils do not have representation as such. Instead, by a rather cumbersome scheme, the denominations are granted certain additional members who represent their "interests and concerns" in local and state councils. From Dr. Fry's standpoint this was a way of insuring complete denominational authority and control while meeting the practical need for established contacts with state and local councils. There is, however, still a minority view which holds that Christians gathered for mission in a community are quite as authentically an expression of the church as a denomination is. To Dr. Fry's insistence that a council is not "the church," this group would reply, "True, but neither is a denomination 'the church.' "[3]

In addition to fusing denominational loyalty and ecumenical vision, Franklin Fry embodied another blending of interests which is of high moment today—Christian evangelism and Christian social action. He never saw them as viable alternatives but always as two aspects of an indivisible whole. He was deeply committed, especially in his leadership of the World Council of Churches, to the mission of the church in secular society, but never at the expense of its witness to a transcendent Presence and Purpose that alone gives ultimate meaning to our existence.

[1] On these principles in ecumenical discussion, see the memos of A. R. Wentz (No. 25), E. C. Nelson (52), H. P. Van Dusen (79), and others.

[2] Text of FCF's address in the ULCA *Pastor's Desk Book*, July, 1951.

[3] See Cavert, *Church Cooperation and Unity in America*, New York, 1970, pp. 274-276. For the world context, see Fey, ed., *The Ecumenical Advance* (vol. 2 of *History of the Ecumenical Movement:* 1948-68), London, 1970, especially chapters 3, 4, 5. Other writers in this volume who deal with the confessional vs. regional issue in ecumenism include (besides Wentz, Clifford Nelson, and Van Dusen) Larsen (No. 55), Manikam (62), Schmidt-Clausen (68), Thomas (84), Niles (86), and Chandran (92).

74

Luther A. Weigle

United Church of Christ (formerly *Congregational)*

Another distinguished veteran of ecumenical leadership reminisces about Dr. Fry's influence in the shaping of the National Council of Churches, and about Fry's relation to the Revised Standard Version of the Bible.

In 1938 and again in 1945, at his invitation, I had a conference with the president of the United Lutheran Church in America which led to important decisions. The first was with President Frederick H. Knubel, who was interested in the proposed revision of the American Standard Version of the Bible which was then getting under way, and expressed the hope that one of the scholars of his church might be chosen as a member of the Revision Committee.[1] I welcomed his suggestion, and told him that the charter of the committee provided not only for the election of Old Testament scholars and New Testament scholars but also that "not less than three and not more than five of the fifteen members of the Committee be chosen with a view to their competence in English literature or their experience in the conduct of public worship or in religious education." I reminded him that I had myself been elected to the committee under that provision, as had Dean Willard L. Sperry of Harvard Divinity School and Dr. Walter Russell Bowie of Grace church, New York. After due consideration, Dr. Knubel informed me that he would like to propose Professor Abdel Ross Wentz of the Gettysburg Theological Seminary. I seconded that proposal; Wentz was duly elected, and proved to be a highly competent member of the New Testament section. His most important assignment was to prepare the first draft of the revision of the English translation of the Letter of Paul to the Romans. We owe to him for example, the rendering of Romans 1:17: "He who through faith is righteous shall live."

My conference with President Franklin C. Fry in 1945 was on a quite different subject. I had been president of the Federal Council of the

---

(b. 1880) Professor (1916) and dean (1928-49) of Yale Divinity School, Dr. Weigle was long active in the Federal Council of Churches. He was its president (1940-42) and chairman of the committee which planned the National Council of Churches of Christ in the USA (1941-50). From 1928 to 1958 he was chairman of the World Council of Christian Education. For over three decades (from 1930) he was chairman of the committee which produced the Revised Standard Version of the Bible.

Churches of Christ in 1940-42, and in 1941 was made chairman of a wider venture in inquiry, known as the Committee on Closer Cooperation of Interdenominational Agencies. That turned out to be a nine-year job; by 1948 we had progressed far enough that the vision of a National Council of the Churches of Christ in the United States of America had emerged, and we were definitely commissioned to be the planning committee for the organization of that Council. My conference in 1945 with President Fry and Secretary Reinartz was in the interest of so shaping the prospective National Council that it could in good conscience include Lutheran bodies as well as other Protestant and Orthodox churches.

Because I was recovering from a recent operation I was not able to be present at the constituting convention of the NCCCUSA, assembled in Cleveland, November 28 to December 2, 1950. The program had been prepared by the planning committee, and my place as its chairman was taken at Cleveland by Dr. Hermann N. Morse, who had served through the nine years as its secretary. Three Lutheran bodies were among the twenty-nine communions associated in the constitution of the NCCCUSA: the Augustana Evangelical Lutheran Church, the Danish Evangelical Lutheran Church of America, and the United Lutheran Church in America. At the invitation of the planning committee, Dr. Fry presided at the first plenary business session on the morning of November 29, and led in the formal service wherein the National Council of the Churches of Christ in the United States of America was officially constituted and dedicated "to the glory of God and the service of mankind." At the opening session of the general assembly on the previous evening, which was a service of worship, President Bersell of the Augustana Lutheran Church had led the congregation in the prayers of thanksgiving, followed by the united singing of the doxology.[2]

Among the standing committees appointed at this first convention of the National Council of Churches was the Constituent Membership Committee, with five members, Dr. Fry, Bishop Ivan Lee Holt, Dr. Ralph Waldo Lloyd, Dr. Riley B. Montgomery, and myself. I was named as chairman, and after one or two terms, was succeeded in that post by Dr. Fry. From 1954 to 1960 he was chairman of the important Policy and Strategy Committee of the National Council of Churches.

Dr. Fry was an effective debater, a competent administrator, and a pleasant companion and friend—sometimes with a hearty burst of laughter and a resounding slap on his thigh, sometimes with the quiet even voice that was incisive just because it was low-keyed.

He would occasionally tease me over some phrase in the Revised Standard Version of the Bible which he regarded as inept. He was particularly concerned over the use of "loaf" in Matthew 7:9 and I Corinthians 10:17, and the use of "ferments," "dough," and "yeast" in I Corinthians 5:6-7 and

Galatians 5:9. I had to admit that he was right with respect to these particular passages, and they were among the thirty or more "changes to more accurate or literal translation" which the Standard Bible Committee authorized at its meeting in June, 1959. These changes are referred to in a new paragraph which appears toward the close of the Preface to the Revised Standard Version of the Bible in all printings from 1960 on. It is perhaps well for me to remind readers that only those printings of the Revised Standard Version which have been made in 1960 and thereafter are fully accurate, embodying decisions made in 1959. There will be no further changes made at any time earlier than 1977, which will be the twenty-fifth anniversary of the publication of the Revised Standard Version of the Bible. *The New Testament Octapla* (New York: Thomas Nelson & Sons) may be relied upon as it was printed in 1962 and contains the text of the RSV as modified by the changes authorized in 1959.

President Fry was one of the half-dozen Protestant church leaders whom Dr. Gerald E. Knoff and I consulted after we returned in 1954 from a conference in London with officers of the Catholic Biblical Association of Great Britain. He heartily approved the proposed cooperation with the Catholic scholars, as did the others whom we consulted, including the archbishop of Canterbury. The cooperation thus begun has grown through the years, so that now we have not only a Catholic edition of the RSV but also a Catholic imprimatur for the Oxford Annotated Edition of the RSV. Six Catholic scholars have been elected to membership in the Standard Bible Committee—three of whom attended its session in 1968. There will be a full attendance of Catholic scholars at the meetings of the Standard Bible Committee which have been set for 1970, 1972, 1974 and 1976. I am glad to think that President Fry, were he still here, would rejoice in this highly promising phase of the ecumenical movement.

---

[1] On the preparation of the Revised Standard Version of the Bible, see Cavert, *Church Cooperation and Unity in America*, pp. 92-95.

[2] See the volume commemorating the founding of the National Council of Churches, *Christian Faith in Action*, New York, 1951. On pp. 25-29 S. M. Cavert gives an account of "The Decade of Preparation." Cf. Cavert, *American Churches in the Ecumenical Movement*, pp. 203-208.

75

J. Robert Nelson

Methodist

The former executive secretary of the Faith and Order Commission relates Dr. Fry's role in the genesis of the North American conference at Oberlin, Ohio, in 1957.

An Unexpected Boost for Faith and Order

The scene: the Gramercy Park hotel in New York, where many an ecumenical committee has met. The time: June 1954, just before the second assembly of the World Council of Churches in Evanston. The people: some of America's ecclesiastical establishment leaders plus Dr. Floyd Tomkins and the writer. The question: how to advance the interests of Faith and Order in America?

American Lutherans at that time were generally regarded to be very hesitant about becoming engaged in doctrinal studies and church union concerns. The National Council of Churches had been formed in 1950 (influenced in its constitution at many points by Dr. Fry) but with no provision for Faith and Order studies. Bishop Henry Knox Sherrill had agreed that it was premature for such activity in the council. It was to be presumed that Dr. Fry would share his caution. Nevertheless, during this committee meeting it was Dr. Fry himself who suggested that a North American conference on Faith and Order be held. Subsequently, when I visited him in Akron, it was he who first proposed the theme, which was destined to be most influential, "The Nature of the Unity We Seek." In all of his manifold ecumenical work, he was seldom involved in the work of the Faith and Order Commission. And yet, by initiating the idea and furthering the plans for the Oberlin conference of 1957,[1] he provided the possibility for the Faith and Order studies of the National Council of Churches.

[1] Official Report: *The Nature of the Unity We Seek*, ed. P. S. Minear, St. Louis, 1958.

(b. 1920) Dr. Nelson served in Geneva as executive secretary of the World Council of Churches' Commission on Faith and Order 1953-57. Since 1967 he has been chairman of its working committee. Before coming to Boston University in 1965 as professor of systematic theology he was dean of the Vanderbilt Divinity School (1957-60) and then professor at the Oberlin Graduate School of Theology.

76

George G. Beazley, Jr.

Christian Church (Disciples of Christ)

The current chairman of the Consultation on Church Union assesses Dr. Fry's personality and character, his leadership in relation to that of other ecumenical statesmen, and his position in regard to COCU.

Champion of Church

The sun shone down with all that clarity of light and intensity of heat to be found only in Greece. The buses wound around hairpin curves with the churchmen chattering as though they had never before discussed doctrine and order. All around plunged those red brown mountains, seeming to glory in that wild freedom which animated their native son, Nikos Kazantzakis, when he created Zorba the Greek. His Eminence, Eugenios Psalidakis, the archbishop of Crete, was entertaining his guests, the members of the Central Committee of the World Council of Churches.

Across the aisle from me sat my friends, Franklin Clark Fry and Mrs. Fry. Over his shoulder, Frank talked to me of what he was experiencing. It was August 1967, and he had last come down this way about forty-five years before when, as a young man just out of college, he and some friends had toured Crete. His father had given him a sizable sum, on his graduation, that he might fulfill the aspiration of a youth entranced by the archeology of the ancient world. Despite conflict on this island so marinated in war and history, he and his friends had worked their way across its surface with all the ingenuity which later was to enable Frank to handle a meeting of strong individuals from diverse traditions and from countries with conflicting interests. I could feel him recapture his youth as he talked. Evidently the strong will, the sharp intelligence, the pride verging on hubris, and the zest for life had been just as present in his early twenties as they were now in his late sixties.

(b. 1914) Since 1960 Dr. Beazley has been president of the Council on Christian Unity, the ecumenical office of the Christian Church (Disciples of Christ). He has been active in the National Council of Churches—a member of its General Board since 1961; in the World Council of Churches, as delegate to the assemblies of 1961 and 1968, a member of the Faith and Order Commission, and since 1968 a member of the central committee; and in the interdenominational merger project, the Consultation on Church Union, as member of its executive committee since 1962, secretary (1966), vice-chairman (1968), and chairman since 1970.

This self-directed tour (when would Franklin Clark Fry want someone else to plan for him!) had an interesting schedule. In rotation, each member of the group was expected to lecture to his friends on some archeological site. Phaestos, second most important site in Crete, toward which we were now traveling, was Frank's assignment. (When was he ever caught unprepared!) Now he relived that experience in his memory and looked forward to seeing again these twenty-five-hundred-year-old ruins through which he had guided his friends.

When we reached this "planned city" of Minoan culture, you could have fried eggs on the stones of its beautifully paved courtyard. A professional guide took us around. With characteristic courtesy, the chairman of the central committee listened, but I knew Frank was hearing other voices, living other days. Indeed, after a cool drink at the pavilion, as my wife and I were making our way back to the buses for the return trip, I found him and Mrs. Fry standing at the fence looking back at the ruins, and asked them to pose before the ruins for a slide as a memento of the occasion. When we stopped at a church with orphanage and old people's home attached on our way back to Heraklion. I was watching closely over my wife, Charlotte, who was already beginning to suffer from an infection which was to keep her in her hotel room until near the close of the meeting. I could hardly believe my ears when I heard that Dr. Fry had fainted in the church and Ernest Payne had had to make the remarks. The next morning Frank was back in his chair, presiding with his usual aplomb, but I never saw him alive again after the close of that meeting. With many others I attended the memorial service in New York and deeply mourned a kindly mentor and a generous friend.

Franklin Clark Fry was a rare combination of Graeco-Roman culture and Christian faith, those two strands that were woven together to produce Western culture, now in such a parlous state since it has decided that it can rely on the science and technology produced by this wedding and forget the parents that produced this modern child. No man whom I have ever known has combined constitutional awareness and deep churchly biblical commitment as did Franklin Clark Fry. A number of men have had one or the other. Few have had the combination. It was this blending, plus one of the two finest intelligences in the ecumenical movement of the recent past, which made me cleave to Frank as a person from whom to learn and one who was worthy of trust. Because his old friend and my predecessor, George Walker Buckner, introduced me to him at my first triennial assembly of the National Council of Churches in December of 1960, right after I became the chief executive of the Council on Christian Unity of the Christian Church (Disciples of Christ), I came to know Frank with a greater intimacy than I did that second scintillating mind, W. A. Visser 't Hooft. Though the relation was always that of the younger leader and the experienced warhorse, I came to know Frank very well. His brilliance everyone knew. Very early I sensed a warm pastoral heart, ready to guide the less experienced and willing even to sacrifice that monumental pride of his for a friend in such a way that most people did not know it had happened. He could flay an ideological enemy with an eloquence that sometimes outdid itself and frustrated his natural moderation as he became intoxicated with his marvelous facility with words, but he made a sharp distinction between issues and people and could turn in kindness to the victim soon after, if that person did not infuriate him with some further idea whose absurdity seemed easily apparent to Frank. To my mind, usually Frank was right, but when he made a mistake it had that more than life-size quality which characterized everything he did. There were giants in the ecumenical movement in those days, and they had all the Homeric exaggerations of the tragic heroes of Greek drama.

The floor of the General Board of the National Council of Churches was where I first learned to walk ecumenically. It was a great training ground. Among the many outstanding leaders, three stood out with great prominence, Henry Pitney Van Dusen, Eugene Carson Blake, and Franklin Clark Fry. Each had his peculiar weaknesses, but all were men towering far above the average. Much to my sorrow, the first disappeared from the floor shortly after I joined the crowd. The conflicts, agreements, and compromises of the other two dramatized the major issue which still dominates the ecumenical movement and remains even yet to be settled, if indeed it ever can.

Franklin Clark Fry was the champion of constitutional clarity and of the concept of councils as the creatures of the churches, confined to the roles the churches would let them play. Nothing was more guaranteed to launch him into a speech than doctrinal sloppiness which compromised the trinitarian faith rooted in the scriptures or a suggestion that groups other than true Christian churches should help make the decisions of the councils. I do not believe he was an opponent of church union, though he opposed many schemes, and I think he recognized a kind of churchly quality in the councils, but Frank believed in doing things "decently and in order" and respected the limitations which constitutional agreements placed on the present, by their existence.

Eugene Carson Blake was also dedicated to the traditional Christian faith, but he was more willing to strain doctrine or imply powers from the constitution than Frank, if he felt the present moment required some action that could not be justified by the letter of the present agreements.

Both men had a pride threatening to turn to arrogance when it was opposed. Some found this hard to take and resented their continual battles. Being a Kentuckian, with that background where style has always been more important than humility, and of a school of thought where pietism is always regarded as the harbinger of self-righteous selfishness, I found it both informing and refreshing to see two first-rate minds debate each other on important issues with all the verve of a Hector and an Achilles in mortal combat. Indeed, I should say that the departure of Franklin Clark Fry from the floor of the National Council's General Board several years before his death and his enforced absence from the World Council by human mortality has produced some of the confused situation which we have today. These two and their followers formed a kind of polarization which spun the dynamo of the ecumenical movement with great power. The death of Frank, and the departure of Gene in 1966 to be the general secretary of the World Council of Churches, created a vacuum in the National Council of Churches which has not been filled to this day. Many fine leaders have continued to fight these issues, but no dominant figures comparable to these two have arisen.

One wonders what would have happened in the National Council of Churches if Frank had still been on the floor when James Forman made his demands[1] or when the president insisted on giving every non-member pressure group its say at Detroit (1969). Possibly, even Samson would have gone down before the fusillade of raw emotionalism, but that Frank would have fought to the last for reason and for a true council of churches, I have no doubt.

One can almost hear him attack the idea of mission as inarticulate presence, in phrases of contempt worthy of a Christian Voltaire. His opinion of a Christian faith which let secular culture rewrite the gospel would have been even more fluent and eloquent than his magnificent impromptu introduction of Prime Minister Nehru at New Delhi (1961), and as full of vitriol as that introduction was of measured courtesy.

Frank and I did not always agree, but unlike many others, I never quarreled with him. I am sure our greatest difference would have been over the Consultation on Church Union.[2] I knew it was a rather forlorn hope, but I never ceased to urge that the Lutheran Church in America should become a participating church. Although I believe *A Plan of Union, 1970*, is a truly remarkable document and offers a remarkable opportunity for a group of American churches to find union, I know it would be a better document if the Lutherans had participated fully in the shaping of it, even though the task would have been far different. Frank could not see that participation.

We did not discuss his attitude in detail. I feel sure it had one subconscious cause, and two conscious ones. These we did not put into formal statements to one another, but I think I knew Frank's way of thinking well enough to correctly divine them from what he did say. Frank would have found it very hard to become a part of a movement which had been brought into being by a sermon preached by Gene. They were so used to opposing each other that it became almost a conditioned response. In a similar way Gene, realizing the deep problems involved, did not include the Lutheran Church in America as one of the specifically mentioned churches in his sermon. That they could really rise above this attitude toward each other when circumstances put them in a position where a great common cause was at stake is shown by the creative way they handled the situation when the Central Committee of the World Council in 1966 elected Eugene Carson Blake as general secretary and refused the resignation of Franklin Clark Fry as chairman of the central committee, which he had offered because he felt two such crucial offices should not both be held by citizens of the United States.[3] I can still remember His Eminence, Metropolitan John (Wendland) of the Russian Orthodox Catholic Church saying, "To us, these men are Christians first and Americans second."

Unfortunately, circumstances did not bring the Lutheran Church in America into the Consultation on Church Union,[4] so we never had a chance to see what creative work Gene and Frank could have done together there.

The two conscious reasons for staying out of COCU were Frank's conviction that Lutherans in the United States should unite before they attempted a larger union and his devotion to doctrinal agreement as an essential basis for union. I think he was wrong on both of these points.

I am convinced that confessional unions or the union of similar types, like those churches holding to believers' baptism, can stand in the way of the full reunion of the church by concentrating attention on the confessional or dogmatic peculiarities of a group too early in the process, before a church has had the needed exposure to a more diverse view, which I feel can come with fullness only in encounters as serious as those created by a union effort.

The second conscious reason for not becoming a participant in the Consultation on Church Union would probably have been Frank's assumption that union could rest only on a common dogmatic agreement. This is a presupposition of most systems growing out of the Reformation which, in my opinion, was, like my own tradition which was rooted in the Enlightenment, too exclusively intellectual in its treatment of man's relation to God. Of all the Reformation leaders, Luther was the most full-blooded and the most deeply rooted in an acceptance of life with its ambiguities. He had very little of the puritan about him, in contrast both to Calvin and to the Anabaptist leaders. It is this full-blooded character and its relation to creation that makes me fonder of Tillich and Sittler than of Barth and Bonhoeffer. It is one of the ironies of historical existence that at this moment in history many followers of Luther in the American scene should be so set on intellectual agreement about theological propositions, while many of the followers of Calvin should have accepted more fully the ambiguities of man's theological formulations and the need of rooting agreement in "the event of Jesus Christ" itself rather than in some proposition about it.

Frank was so full-blooded himself and had such a zest for all of life that I have never been able to understand how he could carry his insistence on intellectual clarity to the point where, to my eyes at least, it began to compromise full incarnation in favor of merely rational incarnation.

Often I find myself wishing that time and place had favored our thorough discussion of this, for we have needed and still need Lutheran participation in the Consultation on Church Union. Of course, the consultation has opted for full incarnational theology and has written the chapter on "The Living Faith" in *A Plan of Union* on these assumptions.

I shall always be glad that I began my ecumenical career early enough to know that creative era of Franklin Clark Fry and Eugene Carson Blake. Frank, like another student at Wittenberg, has been "sung to his rest." Gene still remains a creative force. The issues they fought will continue beyond both, and beyond most of us. It was good to call them both friends, and it is the measure of the comprehension of both men that I never had to choose between them.

---

[1] The "Black Manifesto" demanded "reparations" of half a billion dollars (later raised to three billion) from the churches for injustices suffered by black people. It was presented at the National Black Economic Development Conference in Detroit, April 1969, and at the National Council's General Board meeting the following month. The text is found in A. Schuchter, *Reparations: The Black Manifesto and Its Challenge to White America*, Philadelphia, 1970, pp. 196-202.

[2] COCU, a project of ten denominations to form one united church, resulted from a sermon by Eugene Carson Blake in 1960. See S. M. Cavert, *Church Cooperation and Unity in America*, New York: Association Press, 1970, pp. 337-342, 391. See also the memos of Harkins (No. 36) and Marshall (38).

[3] Other writers on this subject are listed with the memo of Lilje (No. 58).

[4] Dr. Fry never put into print a statement of his views on COCU.

77

John J. Cardinal Wright

Roman Catholic

Cardinal Wright shares a few episodes of intimate personal contact with Dr. Fry.

Permit me to recall three special memories of Dr. Franklin Fry, memories which intensified our friendship and sense of fraternity, despite our inevitable and conscientious differences.

The first concerns a television show on which we appeared, together with other theologians and a group of scientists, in order to discuss the ethics or morality of surgical "transplants," which were just beginning to be publicized.[1]

The discussion ranged far and wide, but it soon became clear that perhaps one of the scientists but certainly Dr. Fry and I were of one mind concerning the danger of men "playing God," while agreeing that men could and should be the instruments of God in using their talents, including those in surgical transplants, in accordance with God's will.

Before the hour was over the area of agreement between Dr. Fry and myself was clear not merely on the ethical and moral question at issue, but on so many other questions relating to God's providence, God's dominion and man's stewardship over creation, not to mention the primacy of life and its rights, that Dr. Fry passed me a note which I now wish I had kept. However, it is easy to remember and I will always cherish its message.

This is what the note said: "Why is it that we, who agree on so many and such fundamental things, disagree on *anything* that pertains to God and man?" It was a difficult question to answer. I took refuge in a returned note which, while it made him smile with affection and understanding, did not answer the question, at least not as of 1968. I suggested that we blame it all on the fifteenth and sixteenth centuries and content ourselves with hard work in the present and sincere commitments for the future, aimed at the ideal which his brief but beautiful note held forth.

(b. 1909) John Wright, professor at St. John's Seminary, Brighton, Massachusetts, was consecrated auxiliary bishop of Boston in 1947. He was installed as bishop of Worcester, Massachusetts in 1950, and transferred to the see of Pittsburgh in 1959. He helped to prepare the agenda on dogma and morality for the Second Vatican Council. In 1969 he was created a cardinal and appointed prefect of the Congregation for the Clergy in the Roman Curia, Vatican City.

My second memory of him is associated with the Lutheran Church in America convention held in Pittsburgh in 1964 while I was Catholic bishop there. I was invited to give one of the opening addresses of greeting.[2] I chose to speak of the debt of all Christendom, indeed of all civilization, to Lutheran piety, particularly as expressed in certain musical traditions, above all, that of Bach.

I am afraid that my love for music and particularly sacred music "ran away with me." Dr. Fry had been described to me by some of his own confreres as a relatively "cold fish," more given to efficiency and to presiding over meetings than to "feeling" in matters esthetical. However, at the interval following the greetings, he took me to one side for a wonderful quarter-hour conversation on the specific pieces of music that each of us liked—and why. Once again we found ourselves in complete unanimity, particularly with regard to works of Bach like "Jesus, Joy of Man's Desiring."

My third cherished recollection of Dr. Franklin Fry concerns the moment that I learned of his death. For years I had been at work with a clergyman of his denomination seeking to promote not the dreadful thing that is called "dialog," but the beautiful thing that is called "conversation" among Christians. I told my friend that I had just heard over the radio the news that we had lost a great churchman. He answered, and I agreed, that our loss was considerably greater: that we had lost a man of total integrity and of warm friendship which, once given, was never withdrawn.

I think I should like to end on that note, now that we are thinking of Dr. Fry in terms of his entrance into eternal life.

---

[1] CBS News Special, with Eric Sevareid as moderator: "Science and Religion: Who Will Play God?" on January 21, 1968. Participants were Dr. C. Walton Lillehei, surgeon; Dr. James Bonner, biologist; Walter Sullivan, NEW YORK TIMES science editor; and Bishop Wright, Dr. Harvey Cox, and Dr. Fry.

[2] The greeting was printed in *Ministers Information Service,* October 1964.

78

Bishop Henry K. Sherrill

Episcopal

An eminent Episcopal churchman recalls his visit to Germany in 1945 just after the end of the war, the formation of the National Council of Churches, and experiences in the Central Committee of the World Council.

My first meeting with Franklin Clark Fry was in December of 1945. He, Bishop Bromley Oxnam and I had been appointed by the Federal Council of Churches as a delegation to visit Germany and to hold out the hand of friendship to the leaders of the German churches. The Rev. Stewart Herman was our guide and interpreter. Oxnam and I flew to Germany together and met Fry and Herman in Frankfort. I do not know why but I had pictured to myself the president of the United Lutheran Church as an elderly gentleman with a full beard. I was astonished when Frank appeared, not much over forty, clean shaven, breezy, with great wit and enthusiasm. I told him of my expectation and said, "How did you make the grade?" Frank laughed and replied, "I will tell you. My father, grandfather, and I have been delegates to the general assembly of our church since the Civil War. As a result a third of the delegates thought that they were voting for my grandfather, two-thirds thought that they were choosing my father, and I was elected." This was the beginning of a friendship which meant a great deal to me in succeeding years.[1]

The assignment given us was not easy to carry out. It was so soon after the close of the war that great tensions of course existed. The balance between sympathy for the unhappy people of a defeated and largely destroyed nation and the necessity of justice in assessing Germany's responsibility for the war was difficult to achieve—a fact which at times created tension in our own group. Bishop Oxnam was inclined to be more critical of the Germans than were Fry and Herman. At one point the latter two decided that they could not keep on with the visitation, but

---

(b. 1890) Dr. Sherrill was Episcopal bishop of Massachusetts from 1930 to 1947, and presiding bishop of his church 1947-58. He was elected the first president of the National Council of Churches (1950-52) and a president of the World Council of Churches 1954-61. He has served on a number of civic bodies, a member of the USA president's Commission on Civil Rights (1947) and chairman of the Committee on the Maintenance of American Freedom.

after a long conference they agreed to continue. Frank, in later years with more experience, would not have reacted as strongly as he did. In the World Council of Churches he and Oxnam worked happily together. On our trip we visited the aged and greatly beloved Bishop Wurm. We attended a service with a great congregation addressed by Dr. Niemoeller and held a long talk with him in his home. We met with Bishop Meiser and with Cardinal Faulhaber in Munich as well as with Bishop Dibelius in Berlin. We attended a number of synods. In Berlin we had a long, frank, and cordial talk with General Clay. The Germans had many just grounds for complaint and these were frankly discussed with General Clay. At the time it was impossible to evaluate the significance of our visitation. A few years later I saw General Clay at a Yale commencement. I was gratified to have him state that our conferences with him had resulted in certain changes of policy and a greater understanding of the German church situation. We presented a report to the Federal Council after long discussion. In this report we did not minimize Germany's responsibility for the war but also described the quality of the German leaders and asked for understanding and for the relief of suffering.[2]

Frank and I were among a considerable number who worked in preparation for the formation of the National Council of Churches. I was impressed with Frank's attention to every detail. He was cautious in protecting the point of view of his own church. I kept thinking what an able lawyer he would have been. But always in the end he was conciliatory and helpful. In 1950 he was the presiding officer on the day when the Council was formally established, and what a superb presiding officer he always was.[3]

In March of 1956 Frank and I were members of a delegation from the National Council of Churches to visit the Russian Orthodox Church. We spent a number of days in Moscow, made trips to Leningrad and Zagorsk. We held long conferences with the primate of the Russian church and many others. I will not attempt to describe the many details of this visitation of which Eugene Blake was the chairman. Again Frank demonstrated his acute intelligence and wise yet firm understanding in many complex situations.[4]

My further contact with Frank was in connection with the World Council of Churches. Frank at the Evanston assembly became chairman of the central committee. As I have written, he was a wonderful presiding officer. He knew the names and the position of every member, which was not easy in such a varied assembly of people. He presided firmly but with unusual tact and sympathetic understanding. No details ever seemed to escape him. As the chairman he represented the committee at public gatherings in each nation in which the central committee met, in Switzerland, the United States, Hungary, Denmark, Scotland, Greece, and India during the years I was a president of the Council. A particularly difficult occasion was a state luncheon in Budapest when he had to be unusually careful in what he said due to the strained relations between church and state.[5] But at all times he handled perplexing situations with an unusual combination of common sense, humor and courtesy. During many years of his chairmanship he was in constant touch with the office in Geneva and many statements of policy were issued by Frank and the general secretary. At a Buck Hills Falls meeting before the 1961 assembly in New Delhi I urged Frank to decline a further term as chairman for I saw breakers ahead, which came after I was out of office, so I was not in immediate touch with the later situation which developed. But he was so committed to the World Council that he could not bring himself to a resignation—a step which would have saved him from some unhappy events in the selection of a new general secretary.[6]

---

[1] Bishop Sherrill also contributed a chapter to *Mr. Protestant,* pp. 31-37.

[2] "Report of Deputation to Germany," FEDERAL COUNCIL BULLETIN, January, 1946, pp. 6-7. See also memo 43 by Stewart Herman.

[3] See also memos by Cavert (73) and Weigle (74).

[4] See FCF's report of the visit in the *Pastor's Desk Book,* April 1956.

[5] See memos of Lilje (58) and Niles (86).

[6] Other writers on this topic are listed with Lilje's memo (58).

79

Henry Pitney Van Dusen

Presbyterian

An influential pioneer in the ecumenical movement, reminiscing on his first contacts with Dr. Fry in 1948, focuses upon their sharp differences over ecumenical principles, but also upon Fry's spirituality.

My earliest remembrance of Franklin Clark Fry is sharp and clear. The date was near mid-summer, 1948. Within a fortnight, the World Council of Churches was to meet in its constituting assembly at Amsterdam. A large number of the United States representatives had arranged to cross the Atlantic on the same sailing of the Queen Elizabeth. A select few—Negro bishops, some YWCA leaders, Southern Baptists (not, to be sure, official members of the World Council, but en route to the World Baptist Alliance in London with a brief stopover in Amsterdam)—were enjoying the lonely luxury of first class. Three or four, from financial stringency or proletarian sympathies, were in the bowels of the ship as third-class (steerage) passengers. But the great bulk, perhaps sixty to eighty, occupied appropriately "middle-class" accommodations in tourist or second class. These included most of those who had had major parts in the dozen years' preparations for the launching of the World Council. I recall sharing a stuffy, meagerly ventilated four-berth inside cabin with my colleagues, Reinhold Niebuhr, John Bennett, and another. By day, we lolled in deck chairs, the "preparatory volumes" piled high beside us, or strolled the decks as the top-heavy Elizabeth, rolling with the slightest ripple on the ocean's surface, plunged uncertainly through the humid fog-enshrouded Gulf Stream.

Everyone noted a solitary passenger, tall, heavy, even then slightly stooped, an old-fashioned schoolboy's cap pulled over his eyes, striding determinedly up and down the lurching decks. "Who is that?" we asked. "Franklin Clark Fry, president of the United Lutheran Church in America," someone replied. Doubtless, he may have sat at table in the dining saloon

---

(b. 1887) From 1926 a faculty member of the Union Theological Seminary, New York, Dr. Van Dusen was its president from 1945 to 1963. He was long an energetic leader in overseas missions and in the ecumenical movement. Among his many responsibilities he was chairman of the Faith and Order study committee (1939-54), member of the provisional committee of the World Council, and chairman of the joint committee which arranged the merger of the International Missionary Council and the WCC (1954-61).

with some fellow delegates to Amsterdam. Probably, he spoke with one or another from time to time. Certainly, I did not meet him. I do not believe Mrs. Fry was with him. In later years, Hilda Fry accompanied her husband to the annual summer ecumenical gatherings—as relaxed, friendly, and delightful as he was austere and aloof; I always found Hilda Fry one of the most charming and congenial among the "wives." But, on this initial appearance of Franklin Fry as an "ecumenist," the main impression was one of distance and coolness, a "loner" who conveyed an impression of indifference if not annoyance at this interruption of his summer holiday, of "strangeness" in non-Lutheran church circles. He had had no major role in the unnumbered meetings which led up to the World Council and which had knit many of us in close ties of ecumenical comradeship dating from the mid-1930s. He had not represented American Lutherans in August, 1937, at the Edinburgh meeting of the Faith and Order movement, one of the direct parents of the World Council. Like Protestant Episcopalians, Lutherans had a partiality for *this* parent. He was not present at the Oxford conference on "Church, Community, and State" in July of that same summer of 1937, called by the other parent, the Life and Work movement. Despite the fact that Life and Work owed its origin to the foremost Lutheran of the twentieth century, Archbishop Nathan Söderblom of Sweden, American Lutherans by and large held aloof from it.[1] Nor did Frank Fry appear at the numerous meetings of the "Provisional Committee of the World Council of Churches" during the "formative decade" of World War II and following.

In all probability, Franklin Fry would have continued a "loner," something of an "outsider" to the ecumenical movement, but for a momentous decision taken in the aftermath of the Amsterdam assembly—his election as vice-chairman of the World Council's Central Committee. I do not know who was responsible for initiating that shrewd decision, one of the most pregnant for the World Council's future. It placed Franklin Fry in one of the most crucial roles in leadership of the Council. Doubtless, some of the veterans may have raised questions that a newcomer should have been chosen for this key post. It determined that his firm character, strong convictions, and gifts of leadership should wield unmatched influence upon the whole ecumenical development. Through the following two decades, all other officers of the World Council changed; he continued as vice-chairman and then chairman of the central committee until his death—a personal embodiment of continuity as well as a unique force in the forming of policy and program.

* * *

From Amsterdam, 1948, until I retired from all active participation in World Council affairs at the third assembly at New Delhi in 1961,

Frank Fry and I were thrown constantly together, through much of that period in the National Council of Churches as well as in the World Council.

The editor of this volume has inquired whether Fry and I may have locked horns from time to time. Such a suggestion is wholly mistaken. Frank Fry and I understood and respected each other thoroughly, partly no doubt because we were in some respects so alike—impatient of pretense, sentimentality, and the stuffy self-importance to which ecclesiastics are so often prone; somewhat inclined, doubtless, toward personal authoritarianism; above all, insistent upon decisions and actions. I recall his blurting out to me at one of the gatherings that he had "had his fill," and my response of concurrence.

In ecumenical principle, we differed at one vital point; and we both fully recognized that watershed, with immense practical consequences for ecumenical structure and procedure. The difference was sharply defined, although casually and entirely by accident, in the most intimate conversation we ever had. At one of the innumerable small committees, a chance remark of mine had so offended a senior officer of the World Council that he burst forth in outrage, which shocked all those present. Happily, a week's respite intervened; I sought refreshment at the Salzburg festival. On return, I solicited Frank's counsel on how to repair the rupture. I happened to mention the fact that every one of my youthful contacts with the organized church had left a deposit of distaste and disdain, that I would never have thought of active participation in the church let alone its ministry had it not been for the influence of the Student Christian Movement, and later, of the ecumenical community of Union Theological Seminary. Frank, who had had no experience within that movement, replied quietly that he could not recall a time when his loyalty had not been wholly enlisted for the institutional, i.e., Lutheran, church.

This contrast in background may have predetermined our differing attitudes toward the role of the organized churches within the ecumenical movement.[2] Franklin Fry was by deep conviction, if not by temperament or predilection, an "ecclesiastic." He never wearied in insisting that both World and National Councils were "councils of *churches*." It would have been his preference if all appointments to Council committees should have been made by the member churches, as all major decisions on policy and program rested with their official representatives. On the other hand, like many others among ecumenical leadership, I had come into the Councils, not directly from church affiliation—I had been charged with heresy by my own church which threatened to bar me from its ministry, and was never appointed by my church to any ecumenical gathering or office until comparatively late—but as a "co-opted" participant. My first mentor in ecumenical matters was William Adams Brown, who likewise was not sent, for example, to the Oxford conference by his church, despite the fact that he was the American president of the body which sponsored that conference! However, it is to J. H. Oldham that the ecumenical movement owes the participation of non-ecclesiastical persons through the "principle of co-option"—in my judgment, the most pregnant and creative factor in the ecumenical movement, safeguarding it against exclusive domination by official ecclesiastics and assuring it the prophetic vision, wisdom, and drive of "non-ecclesiastics," which are largely responsible for its coming to birth, its advance, and its most significant achievements. *Pari passu*, the same is true of the National Council of Churches in the USA. Oldham introduced the "principle of co-option" through the Life and Work parent of the World Council at Oxford in 1937. Faith and Order, to which Franklin Fry's allegiance was initially given, has always looked askance at co-option. This principle, vindicated by the determinative influence of co-opted delegates at Oxford—incomparably the ablest, most distinguished, and most notable in the long sequence of modern ecumenical gatherings—was carried on into the World Council, not through the composition of its assemblies and their committees which, by its constitution, are reserved for official appointees of its member churches, but in the membership of its program committees through which most of the Council's pioneering and creative work is projected and carried out, for example, its Study Committee, of which J. H. Oldham himself was the first chairman, a post in which, at his insistence, I succeeded him in 1939 and continued for the first fifteen years of the Council's life. Thus, when Franklin Fry first assumed ecumenical leadership at Amsterdam in 1948, the "principle of co-option" was already firmly established. Somewhat unwillingly, he acquiesced in it, though never without some misgiving. Let me add, however, that his personal attitude toward me, a child by "co-option," was never other than the most cordial confidence.

Franklin Fry and I differed, therefore, on what is, for me, the central issue within ecumenical Christianity—the role of non-ecclesiastical individuals and groups. The issue has its most crucial illustration today in the place of Christian councils—what is sometimes labeled "conciliar ecumenicity"—within councils of churches at every level. In my view, all such councils should provide for two types of membership—churches, i.e., historical denominations, *and* Christian councils including councils of churches themselves.[3] On this proposal, Frank Fry continued to look askance. On the right resolution of this difference, more than on any other consideration, depends, I believe, the prophetic and creative future of ecumenical Christianity.

* * *

In my recollections of Franklin Fry, however, three moments of a quite different character stand forth as unforgettable.

At a meeting of the World Council's Central Committee at New Haven, as its presiding officer, he himself led the brief opening worship, the only occasion within my memory when he did so. It was magnificent, a model of profound and moving Christian devotion; I recall scribbling him a brief note of grateful appreciation.

During a Lenten season, zealous but ill-advised Union Seminary students invited him to speak at a weekday service. I had not been consulted; I would have vetoed the proposal, for I anticipated a minuscule congregation, altogether unworthy of the guest preacher. He faced a scattered handful in the James chapel. But he spoke movingly of "Brother Martin," and afterward accepted with characteristic grace my embarrassed apologies for the attendance.

My last meeting with him, I think, was at a meeting of the board of trustees of the Interchurch Center in New York. He was asked to offer the opening prayer. Again, it was matchless in dignity and depth. Again, I was moved to a message of thanks.

Among the unnumbered scores, hundreds, of occasions when we shared in ecumenical gatherings, on only these three did the "ecclesiastic," usually so formal and official in bearing and speech, give place to the man of God, steeped in profound and authentic Christian "piety." What a deprivation to the movements which so desperately needed what he, in these three brief moments, showed himself so superbly equipped to supply!

---

[1] On the Life and Work movement see R. Rouse and S. Neill, eds., *History of the Ecumenical Movement*, 1517-1948, 2nd edition, London, 1967, chapters 11-12.

[2] For other views on this subject see especially the memos of Reed (No. 2), Wentz (25), Cavert (73), and Niles (86).

[3] For the broad context, see Fey, ed., *The Ecumenical Advance,* especially chapters 1, 4 and 5, and Cavert, *Church Cooperation and Unity in America, 1900-1970, passim.*

80

Eugene L. Smith

Methodist

Dr. Smith assesses two incidents revealing Dr. Fry's place in the ecumenical movement: his exchange with Prime Minister Nehru at the New Delhi Assembly, and his role in the process of selecting a new general secretary of the World Council.

Two pinnacles tower over my other memories of the historic contribution which Franklin Clark Fry has made to the ecumenical movement.

The first occurred at the third assembly of the World Council of Churches at New Delhi, 1961. Prime Minister Nehru came to address the assembly. The announced time for his visit was short. The brilliance of Dr. Fry's welcoming statement obviously moved the prime minister. Nehru responded by speaking to the assembly in much greater length than was planned. Obviously, Dr. Fry had no opportunity to know in advance the content of the prime minister's address. Nevertheless, Dr. Fry's response to the prime minister was classic in perception and power. In felicity of phrase, precision of speech, clarity of statement, and in the whole matter of platform presence, Dr. Fry that morning showed himself clearly to be the equal or superior of one of the foremost statesmen and charismatic personalities of the twentieth century—Jawaharlal Nehru. This statement was made in a situation of high visibility before the world.[1]

The other pinnacle stands even higher, though its setting made it far less visible to the world's view. It was placed at the meeting of the Central Committee of the World Council of Churches at Enugu in 1965. At that meeting occurred the severest test to the inner unity of the Council that has yet developed. The central committee did not accept the nomination by the executive committee for a successor to Dr. Visser 't Hooft as general secretary. Dr. Fry was chairman of both committees. The exceeding danger of the tensions which developed is indicated by a statement of one prominent member of the executive committee that if its

---

(b. 1912) Since 1964 Dr. Smith has been executive secretary of the New York office of the World Council of Churches and general secretary of the WCC Division of World Missions. From 1949 to 1964 he was general secretary of the Methodist Division of World Missions. He has been a member of the National Council of Churches' General Board since 1950, and for a time vice-president of the Council. He has been active in the International Missionary Council and the WCC Commission of the Churches on International Affairs.

recommendations to the central committee were not adopted, the entire executive committee would have no choice but mass resignation. Dr. Fry's situation was incredibly difficult. Irreparable damage could have been done to the continuing unity of the Council. To Dr. Fry, more than anybody else, we owe the fact that the Council came through that crisis with its unity unimpaired and in many points strengthened. I happen to have some awareness of the personal anguish that he suffered, and the sleepless nights that he knew. In both committees he handled the explosive procedural and substantive issues with consummate skill. In the process, he performed what I believe to have been his most remarkable single ecumenical service. The achievement which that service represented was far less conspicuous than the shining moment of his response to Prime Minister Nehru. It was, however, far more deeply revealing of characteristics even more important than his platform brilliance—his competence as a churchman, and his commitment as a Christian.[2]

---

[1] Fry's welcome and Nehru's address have been preserved on tape. Reigner Recording Library, Richmond, Virginia, W 927 H 14 (December 4, 1961), reels 1 and 2.

[2] Other writers on the selection of the new general secretary are listed with the memo of Lilje (No. 58).

Part Five

Memos from *Overseas Christians* of sister churches

Christian leaders from three continents express themselves in Memos 81 to 92. The first three writers comment generally on Dr. Fry's ecumenical role. Thereafter the memos are arranged in approximately chronological sequence according to their major focus.

81

Archbishop Geoffrey F. Fisher

ENGLAND (Anglican)

The former primate of the Church of England offers a brief sketch of Dr. Fry, and in passing, draws a distinction between "oecumenism" and "oecumenicity."

Dr Franklin Clark Fry was a most attractive and entertaining companion; but I have no skill to re-create an impression of his personal graces. I watched him as chairman of the Central Committee of the World Council of Churches at work and in a quiet way I worked with him very happily. He was a wonderful chairman, patient, observant, fairminded, eirenic with occasional flashes of penetrating humour, almost but not quite always right. His chief care was (as it is of every good chairman) to get the business through to reasonable conclusions and to stop the gathering from doing anything unwise or extravagant. He was pretty good at that in my time as archbishop. It is my own personal belief that since then the World Council of Churches has been too much carried away by

---

(b. 1887) Emeritus archbishop of Canterbury since 1961, Geoffrey Fisher was consecrated bishop of Chester in 1932, bishop of London in 1935, and then primate of the Church of England 1945-61. He was elected a president of the World Council of Churches at its inception (1948-54). Upon his retirement in 1961 he was created a life peer, with the title Baron Fisher of Lambeth.

idealists who forget that the WCC exists only to *advise* its member churches, and not to tell them what they *ought* to do. There are dangers in oecumen*ism*[1] of which they are not sufficiently aware. It is not the same as oecumenic*ity*. The latter is of the Spirit; the former is professional and deals in schemes, programmes and organisations.

---

[1] For a different interpretation of the term *ecumenism,* see the memo of Archbishop Iakovos (No. 71).

82

Charles H. Malik

LEBANON (Greek Orthodox)

A distinguished Near Eastern layman assesses Dr. Fry's character as a Christian.

Dr. Fry was at once a man of God and a leader of men. I never felt that he pursued the cause of ecumenism by asking anybody to dilute or alter his most distinctive faith in Jesus Christ. He was the staunchest Lutheran and yet he was the most compassionate fellow Christian. He typified to me the great mystery of transcendent unity amidst profound difference—no encroachment whatever upon the privacy of what is dearest to one and yet the most certain spiritual unity in Jesus Christ. We are all the deeper and the richer in Christ because Dr. Fry had lived and because we have been privileged to know and associate with him.

(b. 1906) Lebanese philosopher, educator, and statesman, Dr. Mâlik has been a professor or an administrator at the University of Beirut since 1927, and a visiting professor at several universities in the USA. He has served his country as a diplomat in several important posts—minister and subsequently ambassador to the USA (1945-55), chairman of the Lebanese delegation to the United Nations (1945-54), president of the United Nations General Assembly (1958-59), a president of the UN Security Council in 1953 and 1954, minister of foreign affairs in Lebanon (1956-58). He has been prominent in World Council circles, particularly in discussions of international justice, and a member of the central committee 1954-61.

83

Sir Kenneth G. Grubb

ENGLAND (Anglican)

An English lay leader in the ecumenical concern for international affairs reflects on Dr. Fry's style as a churchman, and asks whether real communication with him was a problem for many people.

I first met Dr. Fry at the World Council of Churches, since I was chairman of the Commission of the Churches on International Affairs from 1946 to 1968. All my relations with him were within that setting.

I admired him from the start, partly because he was a very able chairman, and I have, for many years, had to chair large ecclesiastical bodies, although a layman. I found that, like myself, he was technically *interested* in the task of chairmanship, and he studied his papers (as I always did—I am now retired from most of my work) from the angle of a man who knew he had to guide a body of people, large or small, in debate. We used to discuss this a lot privately.

I consider him and Dr. Mott to be the ablest chairmen I have ever sat under in ecclesiastical affairs.

But his style in the chair was not mine at all. Indeed, in my experience at least in church work (and also in "secular" affairs), the American style is generally different from the English. An English chairman is expected to give positive and leading directions or advice to the meeting. An American chairman hesitates to do this and is more disposed to handle all questions as "open" questions until the meeting has clearly indicated its views.

I should have thought that an appraisal of Dr. Fry ought not to be too difficult. Not everyone liked his sense of humour, but in such a matter, tastes notoriously differ. It appealed to me strongly, and not least because it was obvious that when necessary he could take a very firm and decisive line. I was never engaged in a serious controversy with him: I think, indeed, that he had an exaggerated respect for my judgment. At World Council

---

(b. 1900) Sir Kenneth Grubb has had a distinguished career in church and state. A missionary in South America 1923-28, and president of the (Anglican) Church Missionary Society from 1944 to 1969, he has also occupied several positions in the British civil service. For more than two decades he was chairman of the World Council's Commission of the Churches on International Affairs (CCIA, 1946-68), and he was a member of the central committee from 1948 to 1954.

meetings he frequently consulted me privately about matters which were not strictly my concern, not only when I was a full member of the Central and Executive Committees of the World Council of Churches, but subsequently. I think he did this, not because my advice was of great value, but because he knew I guarded such confidences very closely.

On the lighter side of things, I can recollect one or two occasions when even a man so skilful as Dr. Fry in his use of words *inadvertently* made some very amusing statements. I remember him dismissing the executive committee before the New Delhi assembly with these words which I noted down in my private journal, on the same day, "When the new Executive meets we shall find ourselves with fresh faces." This struck me as a remarkable anatomical or physiological (perhaps physiognomical) operation.

On another occasion immediately after announcing the result of the election of a new board of presidents of the WCC, he said, "Let us rise and sing the Doxology—Praise God from whom all blessings flow." I did rise, but still cannot believe that *all* the blessings which God gives to men, or even to the church, can be subsumed in and under the persons of six presidents of the WCC. Perhaps I knew them all too well personally.

The unsolved problem in my mind about Dr. Fry is this. Did people feel that they really communicated with him, or did they feel that the brilliance of his address and wit, and the very quickness of his grasp and understanding, made real communication a problem? I did not feel this myself, but I knew some did.

84

M. M. Thomas

INDIA (Mar Thoma)

Recalling incidents covering nearly two decades, chiefly in the context of the ecumenical discussion of social issues, Dr. Fry's successor as chairman of the World Council Central and Executive Committees offers some observations on Fry's style of leadership and his spiritual depth.

I was never a member of the Central or Executive Committee of the World Council of Churches till Uppsala, 1968. Therefore I never knew Dr. Fry or the way of his working in the WCC in any intimate manner. But there have been some occasions when I participated in the meetings of the central committee either as substitute for the metropolitan or another member of the Mar Thoma church or as chairman of the working committee of the WCC Department on Church and Society. And looking back I have memories and impressions of Dr. Fry which I have never thought it necessary to recollect in any orderly manner. Since Dr. Fischer thinks that as his successor in the chairmanship of the Central Committee of the WCC, it would be appropriate if I make some contribution to the volume on Dr. Fry, I am putting down these stray and disconnected thoughts.

From 1947 to 1952 I was on the staff of the World Student Christian Federation. During this period, the metropolitan of my church asked me to attend the Chichester meeting of the central committee as his substitute. At that time Bishop Bell was chairman. But I recollect that on the train traveling from Chichester to London, I was with Dr. Fry and Dr. Visser 't Hooft in the same railway compartment, and this is my first recollection of him. I noticed that he was doing his crossword puzzle, throughout the trip. Dr. Visser 't Hooft and I were talking about the radical

---

(b. 1906) A veteran Indian leader in ecumenical social studies, M. M. Thomas was one of the group which in the 1940s popularized the expression, "the responsible society." Entering ecumenical work on the staff of the World Student Christian Federation (1947-52), he became influential throughout India and beyond as associate director (1957) and since 1962 director of the Christian Institute for the Study of Religion and Society, Bangalore. He has served the World Council in several posts, including staff consultant for Asia in the Department of Church and Society, and as chairman of the planning committee for the World Conference on Church and Society, Geneva 1966. In 1968 he was elected to the WCC Central Committee, and promptly chosen its chairman.

change coming in the status of the aristocracy of Britain. I expressed happiness about these changes and Dr. Visser 't Hooft criticised me for lacking a sense of pathos and historical tragedy in my happiness. When I commented that I was more concerned with the pathos of the lives which the common people had to live, I remember Dr. Fry looking at me without any comment, but with his usual smile. I am sure he must have thought of me then as a WSCF secretary from Asia who was a leftist in his ideology; and I had the impression of a conservative American, not particularly sympathetic with the tears shed over the fate of European aristocracy or with the happiness of an Asian at the political and social revolutions taking place. Later I learned that Dr. Fry checked with some of the American leaders of the WSCF, to know whether I had any deep Christian commitment along with my leftist views.

Later I saw Dr. Fry at closer quarters at the central committee meeting in Lucknow, India, 1952. I was there as convener of the first WCC Asian Consultation on Responsible Society in World Perspective.[1] The consultation formulated some very revolutionary findings about the transformation of the structures of traditional Asian societies and about Asian Christian stance in relation to the Big Power politics. I was also a consultant at the central committee, where I reported the findings of the consultation. I also participated in a small group drafting the message of the central committee to the member churches highlighting the issue of poverty and society as well as the unity of the churches.[2] I remember Dr. Fry was in that group for a period. And he raised the question whether the consultation on society at Lucknow was organized by the WCC, and when I said yes, he was quite willing to have its findings used in the message. I do not know how unsympathetic he was with the radical findings. Many of the WCC leaders were new to Asian realities and probably Dr. Fry was, too; and probably they were prepared to let the Asians have their say about their own societies. But what impressed me was the fact that as vice-chairman of the central committee he was quite prepared to be formally correct in permitting the use of the findings of a consultation by the committee even when he could not personally identify himself with them, because the consultation was sponsored by the WCC. Perhaps in later years he may have been prepared to be more than formally correct regarding social change in Africa, Asia, and Latin America. He could not have remained uninfluenced by the WCC study on Rapid Social Change.[3] On the enthusiasm for church unity which the draft message for Lucknow expressed, he was more critical.[4] I remember his comment that there is such a thing as syncretism to be guarded against, not only in the relation between religions, but also in that between churches. I thought it was a wise comment and it had come to my mind often, though my position always has been that whether in the relation between religions or between churches, truth and its relation to unity should not be discussed purely at the level of doctrine; they must be sought at a deeper dimension of the spirit, at the level of *faith,* of which *doctrine* is only a symbol though a necessary one.

Later at the New Delhi assembly in 1961 we were on opposite sides regarding the relation of Christ the Truth to the work of Christ in renascent religions and movements of secular humanism.[5] This was another aspect of the relation between truth and unity which we discussed at Lucknow, but more controversial. But I did respect the concern which he and many other Lutheran theologians deeply felt, namely, that we should guard the integrity of the core of the Christian faith—that there is no way to God other than Jesus Christ and there is nothing more inclusive than he. I shared this concern myself. But I held then and still hold that the discussion about the presence and activity of Christ in religious and secular movements outside the church is not irrelevant within this common commitment to Jesus Christ as the Truth.

Between the New Delhi and Uppsala assemblies I was chairman of the working committee of the WCC Department on Church and Society. And later when the department took up the organisation of the (1966) World Conference on Church and Society, I was made the chairman of its planning committee. In these capacities I had occasion to attend central committee meetings as adviser. I do not remember any occasion when I did not receive the courtesy of the chairman as I presented my reports, though I must confess that I was always nervous about his humor which seemed to me, perhaps wrongly, sometimes to have a touch of cynicism about it. At one time, besides being adviser, I was also alternate to a member. And as such I had rights of voice which I used while discussing Vietnam. At that time he almost put me out by asking whether I had the rights of a member of the central committee. And it took me a minute to find my bearings to clarify my double capacity. He took it with humour but I felt differently. Apart from this I did not have any occasion to feel bad about the way he as chairman dealt with me. Of course I had always felt that he was a little too rigid and formal in the chair, and that it did put out a good many members not well acquainted with the parliamentary procedure and afraid to make procedural mistakes; and naturally I have felt that a little more informality in procedures would be useful for an international body to make participation of members easier. I do not know whether it is correct. It remains to be tested.

I said that at Lucknow I felt he was prepared to let the findings of the WCC consultation influence the central committee. I had, however, a different feeling about the way he dealt with the report of the World Conference on Church and Society held in Geneva 1966.[6] Though it was very much more of an official WCC study conference, speaking *to* the churches though not *for* them, he was rather reluctant to let the central committee give its findings any recognition. Its findings were too radically revolutionary and too critical of America in world affairs, especially in South East Asia, for him to let them influence the policies of the World Council of Churches. Of course he was formally correct, but it was the one time when I felt that he was using a formality as an instrument of his own opinion. I felt it was but natural for him, but I felt disconcerted. Nevertheless, I was also quite sure that in matters of church and society, the ecumenical movement would have to take Geneva 1966 very seriously for the sake of the dynamism of its own Christian witness in the world as a world body.

Only once did I see him as preacher. That was at Strasbourg when the WSCF had its teaching conference, 1960. He preached on Jesus Christ who will come again.[7] And I said to myself, here was a dimension of the man which one seldom saw. The message and the man behind it impressed me deeply.

More is not expected of any man than to be faithful to his own vision. And he was so faithful in making his contribution to the ecumenical movement in a crucial period of its life. I am happy to have been able to join many others in giving my tribute to the memory of one of the fathers of the ecumenical movement.

---

[1] See the minutes and papers of the Lucknow conference: *Christ—the Hope of Asia,* Madras, 1953. For the context, see H. E. Fey, ed., *The Ecumenical Advance,* especially chapters 9 and 3.

[2] The WCC Central Committee's "Letter to the Churches in the WCC," in ECUMENICAL REVIEW, vol. 5, 1952-53, pp. 283-285, and in *The First Six Years,* Geneva, 1954, pp. 131-133. Section 1 deals with "The Imperative of Social Justice," Section 3 with "The Call to Missionary Obedience and Unity."

[3] A massive study launched in 1955. See E. de Vries, *Man in Rapid Social Change,* New York, 1961, and P. Abrecht, *The Churches and Rapid Social Change,* New York, 1961. Cf. Fey, *op. cit.,* chapter 9.

[4] "The Church's Call to Mission and Unity," a statement prepared by one section of the above-mentioned East Asia Study Conference at Lucknow, in ECUMENICAL REVIEW, 1952-53, pp. 287-291. On this issue see also the memo of Cavert (No. 73).

[5] See *The New Delhi Report,* London, 1962.

[6] See *Christians in the Technical and Social Revolutions of our Time,* Geneva, 1967: Report of the Geneva conference. Cf. Fey, *op. cit.,* chapter 9.

[7] Copy of sermon in LSTC Library. See *Source Register,* Section 8. See also the memo of Niles (No. 86).

85

Ernest A. Payne

ENGLAND (Baptist)

Vice-chairman of the central committee during the years when Dr. Fry was chairman, Dr. Payne writes from intimate association regarding Fry's ecumenical leadership, his keenness as a moderator and his witness as a Christian, the problem of the election of a new general secretary, and Fry's spirituality and humor.

My first clear recollection of meeting Dr. Franklin Clark Fry was at the WCC Central Committee in Lucknow in the closing days of 1952 and the first week of 1953. He was then vice-chairman of the central committee and proved throughout the proceedings a great help to Dr. Bell, the bishop of Chichester, who was chairman and not very well. On New Year's Day Dr. Fry had to preside in Dr. Bell's place over a meeting at which the governor of the United Provinces, Sri Rajyapal, welcomed the company. The governor praised the person of Christ and the humanitarian work of missionaries, but alleged that Christianity had come to his country linked with imperialism and that the day of proselytism—as he called it—was now over. Dr. Fry had to reply spontaneously and did so with great ability, courtesy, and firmness.[1]

During the Lucknow meetings I remember hearing for the first time one of his many stories, of which perhaps the most famous and oft-repeated was the one about his election as president of the United Lutheran Church being due to those who thought they were voting for either his grandfather or his father! He was a gifted raconteur, who enjoyed relaying jokes and witticisms. Not long before Lucknow, Dr. Fry had been in Yugoslavia and had been received by Marshal Tito. Tito's room, he said, was filled with pictures of himself. Tito was supposed to have soliloquised once before one of the portraits: "I wonder what they will do with you?" To which the answer came: "Oh, they're going to take me down and hang you up here instead!" Dr. Fry's laugh and the way he would slap his knee, if sitting down, were well-known and well-loved

---

(b. 1902) Dr. Payne was vice-chairman of the World Council Central and Executive Committees from 1954 to 1968. Since 1968 he has been a president of the World Council. He has served as general secretary of the Baptist Union of Great Britain and Ireland (1951-67), moderator of the Free Church Federal Council (1958-59), vice-president of the Baptist World Alliance (1965-70), and chairman of the executive of the British Council of Churches (1962-70).

characteristics. He was more sensitive than many realised and more dependent on appreciation and support.

It is true he could seem somewhat forbidding with his height and his keenness of mind. Sitting next to him at the chairman's table, I soon realised how tight a rein he had to keep on himself and how often he found the proceedings trying. But I was amazed at the way he carried the administrative burdens of his own church and was at the same time so responsibly involved in the WCC for twenty years, for six of which he was also president of the Lutheran World Federation. His judgments of men and movements were shrewd, based on wide knowledge and experience and on a strong faith. No one showed greater wisdom and patience than he in the protracted discussions regarding the integration of the International Missionary Council and the WCC, and in the initial contacts of the WCC with Russian churchmen and with the Roman Catholic church.

Between 1954 and 1968 when we served together as chairman and vice-chairman of the central committee and its Executive, it became his custom to take the opening devotions himself. They were always simple. He often culled prayers from Lutheran service books. A number of his brief addresses, I remember. Sometimes I thought they were synopses of sermons he had recently delivered, but from time to time they had a very direct relevance. I recall an address on Abraham, at a meeting in Geneva; his use of the Te Deum in a closing act of worship when the central committee met in Rhodes in 1959 (he had gone down with laryngitis on arrival there); another Geneva address, delivered in 1961, a few days after the death of his mother and based on Doddridge's hymn "Awake, my soul, stretch every nerve, And press with vigour on"; an address on Jeremiah in 1966 when he was under great strain and about to present his resignation to the Executive, following Dr. Blake's nomination as successor to Dr. Visser 't Hooft (he felt that the two chief officers of the WCC ought not both to be Americans); and the last devotional address of all at the Geneva Executive in February, 1968, based on Ephesians 3:14-15. These addresses helped one to understand the fortitude with which he carried on his work to the last and the calmness with which he faced death.

He was adept at welcomes and words of thanks on behalf of the WCC—when Pandit Nehru came to the New Delhi assembly in 1961, for example; on a rather difficult occasion in Rochester in 1962 after Mr. Averell Harriman had spoken; at a luncheon given by Archbishop Nikodim in Moscow in 1964.[2]

The last years were not easy ones for him. As early as February 1964 I noted: "There is some evidence that Fry is getting tired." A year later he seemed somewhat better, but during a visit to a monastery in Crete in August 1967 he fainted, and I think it was clear to all those of us close to him that he was somewhat seriously unwell. A letter he wrote to me three days before Christmas 1967 ended with the words: "1968, with a shiver, is upon us. God shield us in it!"

The discussions and the differences which emerged over the finding of a new general secretary for the WCC tried him greatly. The decision on procedure at Colgate-Rochester in August 1963 was not in accordance with his original suggestion, but he followed what was decided with meticulous care and spent himself in the negotiations and interviews which lasted from then until February 1966. That at times personal relationships were strained, distressed him greatly. During this period we met frequently and had many intimate and confidential talks.[3]

I remember how concerned he was to hear in July 1964, while in Germany, about the serious race riots in Rochester. He had assured us a few days earlier, that Barry Goldwater stood no chance of election as president unless there were so many disturbances that moderate opinion throughout America was swept aside. He told me he had heard the news of U. S. President Kennedy's assassination while in a plane over the Atlantic. In August 1967 when the executive and central committees met in Crete, the WCC officers had one or two preliminary engagements in Athens. Dr. Fry had Mrs. Fry with him and one evening they invited me to go with them to the "Sound and Light" spectacle on the Acropolis. A few months earlier, he had shown great personal kindness in coming to the annual Baptist assembly in London at which I had retired from the general secretaryship of the Baptist Union, giving on that occasion an address that was deeply appreciated by the delegates, as well as by myself.

In completing the report of the central committee to the Uppsala assembly, which Dr. Fry had to leave unfinished, I tried to express something of what he had meant to the WCC since its formation. What I wrote will be found in the Official Report, pages 284-285.[4] Personally I count association with him as colleague and friend, one of the great privileges of my life. At Yale in 1957 he spoke of there being in the WCC "a hierarchy of service, rather than authority." It was his unstinted and able service, and the selfless spirit in which it was undertaken, that gave him the commanding position he had come to occupy in the affairs of the WCC.

---

[1] See the memos of Manikam (No. 62) and Chandran (92).

[2] Other writers commenting on this talent are listed with Lilje's memo (58).

[3] Other writers on the selection of a new general secretary are listed with the memo of Lilje (58).

[4] *Uppsala Report,* Geneva, 1968. Dr. Fry's report on pp. 277-281, completed by Dr. Payne, pp. 281-285.

86

Daniel T. Niles

CEYLON (Methodist)

Shortly before his death Dr. Niles, the distinguished Asian ecumenist, submitted this ambivalent judgment of Dr. Fry, expressing respect for his genuine Christian faith, but disagreement over the role of confessionalism in the ecumenical movement. Included were some incisive observations about Fry's manner and personality.

At the inaugural assembly of the World Council of Churches in Amsterdam, 1948, one of the minor problems which arose in one of the committees was concerning the committee structure of the Youth Department. I was at that time co-chairman with Madeleine Barot of the Youth Department. The person appointed to help to solve the problem was Dr. Fry and I was asked to go and consult him. That was my first meeting with him. He left on me an impression of a quick and wise mind.

I next met him at the WCC assembly at Evanston in 1954, and since then I had maintained a relationship of personal friendship with him and his gracious wife. My wife was also present at Evanston and she too shared in this friendship. My wife and I have dined in the home of the Frys on two occasions and both times the memory is one of courteous hospitality and stimulating conversation. The conversation of Dr. Fry had an astringent quality. He could even be cynical. But while I have heard him in his most cynical vein about people, there was absolutely no sense of cynicism when he spoke of the church and its mission. He was gripped by the splendour of the enterprise and was sustained by his faith in its outcome.

In the assembly of the WCC at New Delhi, 1961, one of the issues which came up for debate was concerning the presence of the Christ incognito. Paul Devanandan, M. M. Thomas, and myself were on one side of the debate. So were most of the Asians. The Lutherans as a bloc showed themselves in strong opposition to what we were trying to say and Dr. Fry, from his place on the platform, indicated his position without

---

(1908-1970) Well known around the world as an ecumenical spokesman, D. T. Niles at the time of his death was a president of the World Council of Churches (1968-70). Among his many ecumenical posts he was secretary of the World Alliance of YMCAs (1939-40), general secretary of the National Christian Council of Ceylon (1940-42), and executive director of the WCC Department of Evangelism (1963-69). He was chairman of the World Student Christian Federation 1953-60, principal of Jaffna Central College 1954-60, and president of the Methodist Church of Ceylon 1968-70.

compromise. He felt that what was at stake was the church's faith in the historical person, Jesus Christ.[1]

I have with me one of the very last addresses of Dr. Fry. There, too, the same over-mastering concern is evident. In that address, he is seeking to interpret the place of the cosmic Christ in Christian faith. Dr. Fry preached the closing sermon at the Strasbourg conference of the World Student Christian Federation in 1960. His text was, "This same Jesus will return."[2]

The heart of Dr. Fry's theology was commitment to and conviction about Jesus of Nazareth. This Jesus was known through the scriptures, through the sacraments of water and of bread and wine, and through the mission—all of which were what constituted the Christian community. Any denigration of the church, Dr. Fry would characterise as "noxious and obnoxious."

One subject on which Dr. Fry and I disagreed, rather strongly, was on the place and purpose of confessional organisations.[3] His loyalty to the church led him into a confessional loyalty which made him see the ecumenical movement largely in these terms. There are those in the leadership of the World Council who see it as the coming together primarily of communions. I, on the other hand, belong to a group who would like to take each church in the World Council as a church in its own right and as representing the geographical and cultural realities of the place where it is set, and not only its denominational affiliation. I think that over the years, Dr. Fry and I came to understand each other's concerns with greater sympathy.

Dr. Fry could be very abrupt with people. I felt that in the conduct of meetings, he showed understanding patience with slow minds, but critical impatience with personalities that grated on him. It is unquestionably a Christ-like quality to like people as people and to enjoy them in all their variety. This quality Dr. Fry had to learn.

Dr. Fry was under great stress at Enugu, 1965, when the successor to Dr. Visser 't Hooft was to be appointed.[4] The question had become muddied and no one was sure what the right thing was to do. Dr. Fry had strong convictions on the subject. However, he did not allow his convictions to interfere with his role as chairman. His skill as a chairman was one way in which he maintained the openness of an assembly to the guidance of the Holy Spirit. I do not remember that he used his skill just to guide an assembly to some predetermined goal.

The last thing I want to say is the impression he left on my mind by the way he spoke at public functions. Both at the Lucknow meeting of the central committee, 1953, and at the meeting in Galyatetö, Hungary, 1956, in the presence of Hindu and Communist leaders, he spoke on behalf of the World Council of Churches with courtesy and understanding, but at the same time bearing unambiguous testimony to the Lord whom he served and the Saviour in whom he believed. He never compromised "the crown rights of the Redeemer."[5]

[1] See *The New Delhi Report,* London, 1962. See M. M. Thomas's memo (No. 84).
[2] Copy in LSTC Library. See *Source Register,* Section 8. See also Thomas (84).
[3] See also other memos in this volume, listed with the memo of Cavert (73).
[4] Other writers on this subject are listed with the memo of Lilje (58).
[5] See also the memos of Lilje (58) and Manikam (62).

87

Bishop Oliver S. Tomkins

ENGLAND (Anglican)

An experienced leader of Faith and Order comments on Dr. Fry's style of leadership.

When I first attended meetings of the Central Committee of the World Council of Churches as a member of its staff before and after the Amsterdam assembly, I witnessed the chairmanship of my own father-in-God, George Bell. As all who remember it still testify, it contained something of the ingratiating but infuriating characteristics which have more recently characterized Dr. Michael Ramsey's chairmanship of the tenth Lambeth conference. It would not be for me, an English Anglican, to say whether it is a characteristic of English Anglicans to believe leadership of this kind is best exercised with a high degree of informality if it is to retain a spirit of Christian freedom and not be in bondage to law—even the laws of democratic procedure.

So it was with some alarm that I anticipated the chairmanship of central committee by an American churchman who seemed at first glance to have all the characteristics of the American ecclesiastical tycoon. Again I hesitate to generalise as to whether there was foundation for my fears, but at least Franklin Fry proved them groundless. Although he certainly had the minutiae of democratic procedure as developed in the United States completely at his finger tips, there was always the saving grace of humour and informality which enabled those over whom he presided to feel that they were being shepherded and not bullied.

However, for the greater part of Frank Fry's chairmanship I was too preoccupied with the chairmanship of the Faith and Order commission to have time to attend the meetings of the central committee, though it was part of Frank's genius that those who had once been admitted to his friendship found the passage of years no barrier to the immediate resumption of intimacy. My last contact with him was a brief personal note written

---

(b. 1908) Bishop of Bristol since 1959, Oliver Tomkins was elected to the World Council Central and Executive Committees in 1968. He gained ecumenical prominence as assistant general secretary of the Student Christian Movement 1933-36 and associate general secretary of the World Council and secretary of the Commission on Faith and Order 1945-52. He was warden of the theological college at Lincoln from 1953 to 1959. He served as chairman of the working committee of Faith and Order 1952-67.

after the Enugu (1965) debates and decisions, for he was aware of the concern with which I had been following all that touched my friend Pat Rodger.[1] Suffice it to say that the letter showed very clearly how much he had been hurt, and he wrote that those days "have brought me one of the disheartening experiences of my life." But even now it must be too soon to see that episode in perspective.

It was a shock to learn he would not be at Uppsala, but there must be many of us there who, watching Ernest Payne's extremely competent taking of his place, remembered Frank Fry with frequent twinges of sorrow and gratitude.

[1] Other writers on the selection of a new general secretary of the WCC are listed with the memo of Lilje (No. 58).

88

Norman Goodall

ENGLAND (Congregational)

From intimate observation Dr. Goodall, veteran executive of the International Missionary Council and the World Council of Churches, presents a discerning appreciation of Franklin Fry the person and the ecumenical churchman.

Although I am proud to have counted Franklin Clark Fry as one of my dearest friends and closest confidants, I find it curiously difficult to recall and marshal the kind of information about him which might explain to others the enormous influence he had upon me. My first contact with him began unpromisingly. This was in 1945 or 1946, a few years before the launching of the World Council of Churches. As secretary of the International Missionary Council I had occasion to consult Dr Fry in New York about some details of what was then known as the "orphaned missions" service of the IMC.[1] This was the great war-time and post-war undertaking through which the work of great missionary societies cut off from their home base or fields of service by the exigencies of war was sustained through international and ecumenical cooperation. Between the International Missionary Council and the Lutheran World Convention (the forerunner of the Lutheran World Federation) agreements had been reached by which main responsibility in Lutheran areas was assumed by the LWC, while the IMC directed its relief energies elsewhere. In a few instances, however, there were inevitable overlappings of concern and responsibility and at the time of which I am writing some fresh adjustments needed to be made in Palestine. A luncheon party in New York had been arranged at which I was to meet Fry and discuss this particular situation. At that time, as to some extent subsequently, I think Fry looked upon the IMC with a touch of disdain, regarding it as belonging to a past that had not passed rapidly enough. I think he was also sensitive about possible encroachments by the IMC into Lutheran preserves. Anyhow, he arrived

---

(b. 1896) Dr. Goodall was foreign secretary of the London Missionary Society 1936-44, secretary of the International Missionary Council 1944-54, secretary of the joint committee to integrate the IMC and the World Council of Churches 1954-61, and assistant general secretary of the World Council 1961-63. He has served as chairman of the Congregational Union of England and Wales (1954-55), moderator of the International Congregational Council (1962-66), and moderator of the Free Church Federal Council (1966-67).

at the luncheon party, confronting me with his most majestic and official presence, and began the conversation with severity and with that most ferocious glare of which he was capable. My immediate reaction was to feel about as large as one of the pease on my luncheon plate. But long before the engagement ended I was treated to his disarming smile and a number of those anecdotes in which he so naively led the laughing applause; and what was more, I was assured of his confidence and cooperation in our further common tasks. I left him knowing that I had met a formidable character, but hoping that there might some day be a reunion with the chance to know him better.

After this episode I saw nothing of Fry until he was installed as chairman of the World Council of Churches' Central Committee and Executive Committee. I was still one of the secretaries of the International Missionary Council and for a year or two had only occasional close dealings with him. These always enhanced my impression of his worth, and from the moment of his assumption of these chairmanship responsibilities I recognized in him one of the world's ablest masters of assembly. Needless to say, this impression deepened with the years and although I have had the opportunity of working with and under a number of uniquely gifted chairmen I still put Frank Fry at the top of the list. In the technicalities of chairmanship, knowledge of procedure, and its apt and timely application, he was in my experience unrivalled. To these he brought not only swiftness of intellect and apprehension but a richly informed mind and theological equipment. All this helped to account for the depth of wisdom and perception which lay behind his handling of an assembly's affairs. Not the least addition to this was his characteristic humour. This could be very caustic sometimes—too much so for tender spirits. His irony could be devastating. Yet he was also able to sense the moment when a difficult corner could only be turned through a more gentle art and grace. In this same connection, I was to the end constantly surprised afresh by the patience which he could bring to his chairmanship. Most of all I think of the dignity with which he graced great occasions and the manner in which his conduct of worship, even the brief opening "devotions" at a small meeting, set a tone worthy of "the king's business."

Following the few years in which I saw him more distantly at work in the WCC, he became a member of the Joint Committee of the WCC and IMC, of which I was secretary.[2] I am no doubt a little prejudiced in thinking that this committee comprised one of the most interesting groups of people with whom I have ever had the privilege of working. Needless to say, everyone knew when Fry was present. Sometimes his looks and the changing expressions of that very expressive face made an almost decisive contribution to the matter under discussion. More often his contribution would be in the form of a challenging question and if it proved to be a difficult question, penetrating into a delicate area, it would be voiced with an air of great innocence. During the many years of this committee's life I think Fry's estimate of all that the IMC had stood for deepened in knowledge and appreciation. Although I think he came with some reluctance to the conviction that the integration of the IMC and the WCC was essential, he ultimately made one of his best personal contributions to its effective achievement. It was through this joint committee that some of my best friendships in the ecumenical movement were deepened and nurtured, and this became particularly true of my relationship with Frank Fry. I was normally due for retirement at the time of the New Delhi assembly, but when Visser 't Hooft generously urged me to stay on for another period as assistant general secretary of the WCC, it was Fry who greatly encouraged me to take on this further service and whose friendship became still more intimate during this remaining period. I had finally left the Council's secretariat by the time the main discussions on the future of the general secretaryship were embarked upon, but I had been entrusted with the chairmanship of the Council's Structure Committee, and events so turned out that I was closely involved in the delicate processes of finding the right successor to the inimitable Visser 't Hooft.[8] I do not think it would be right to say more about this period than to acknowledge that the brunt of the problem fell of necessity upon Fry as chairman of the central committee and of the executive committee which, against Fry's will but by action of the central committee, had been charged with the nominating responsibility. I will only add that as I recall this difficult process, two dominant impressions remain with me. The first is Fry's inner vulnerability to pain: he not only suffered much hurt, but had to cope with it with an inner tenderness of spirit constantly obscured, if not belied, by his confident exterior. The second impression is that of his unswerving loyalty to, and concern for the World Council of Churches and its own best interests. To this he was prepared to subordinate everything else, including his own private opinions and inward peace. In all this my estimate of his fundamental greatness was enhanced.

It was my loss that in spite of frequent official and semi-private opportunities of developing our friendship, life gave me too little chance of learning more of the full range of Fry's interests and convictions. I learned something of his churchmanship, its strong Lutheran anchorage and the reasons for it, together with his growing—dare I say it?—mellowing understanding of the full meaning of catholicity. I learned something of his love of literature and the breadth of his reading; of his interest in music, opera, and drama; and amongst my most cherished memories are relaxed evenings in his own home when I think I came nearest to the source of his strength and poise. But although I knew all too little of the deeper background to his official relationships, I believe that their breadth and depth had much to do with the quality of judgement and the kind of influence he could exercise through public assemblies. He was a theologian, but more than a theologian; a churchman, but more than a churchman. He was in some ways a man of the world, but more than a man of the world. A citizen of the kingdom and a humble—yes, sometimes strangely and wonderfully humble—disciple of his Lord.

---

[1] On aid to orphaned missions, see K. S. Latourette and W. R. Hogg, *World Christian Community in Action*, New York, 1949, and F. K. Wentz, *Lutherans in Concert*, Minneapolis, 1968. On the International Missionary Council, see Fey, ed., *The Ecumenical Advance*, especially chapter 7.

[2] Integration of the IMC and the WCC was accomplished in 1961. See Fey, *op. cit.*, especially chapter 2.

[3] Other writers on this subject are listed with the memo of Lilje (No. 58).

89

Bishop J. E. Lesslie Newbigin

INDIA (Church of South India)

Bishop Newbigin describes the change in his attitude toward Dr. Fry as he came to know him.

I first met Dr. Fry—so as to be really conscious of him—at the meeting of the Central Committee of the World Council of Churches somewhere about 1951. I did not like him. He stood for the things I distrusted—big American money linked with denominational power. He seemed to be scornful of the things I was most enthusiastic about—especially church union.

This antipathy deepened when I found myself pitched against him in battles over the integration of the International Missionary Council and the World Council of Churches at the meeting of the joint committee at Nyborg Strand, 1958.[1] However, at that time I became aware of his extraordinary power and ability. That did not make me like him any more, but it made me respect him! I still detected in him a deep antipathy to the sort of things that seemed to me important in the Indian background—a Gandhian feel for simplicity and distrust of power and money.

When I became a staff member, first of the IMC and then of the WCC, I saw much more of him. On the one hand, like (I suspect) most of the staff, I was nervous about having to make presentations of policies or projects in his presence. His scorn could be withering. He was described to me by a colleague as the only living man who could strut while sitting in a chair! At the same time, I grew increasingly to admire his extraordinary capacity to handle very difficult situations in the chairing of a meeting. In my heart I could never cease comparing him with George Bell, whose *métier* was so totally different. Yet I could not fail to admire Frank's remarkable gifts in that direction.

Slowly, also, I began to see that behind all this facade, there was a

---

(b. 1909) Beginning an eminent ecumenical career as a secretary of the Student Christian Movement in Glasgow (1931-33) and then as a Church of Scotland missionary in India (1936-46), Dr. Newbigin was influential in the formation of the Church of South India in 1947 and served as bishop of Madura 1947-59. He was general secretary of the International Missionary Council 1959-61, and associate general secretary of the WCC and director of the Division of World Mission and Evangelism 1961-65. Since that time he has been bishop of Madras.

humble man who was a devout believer and wanted friendship. I only really began to see this one evening when my wife and I asked him round for an evening at our Geneva flat. Things were going fairly tough for him by then. I came to recognise someone whom I had not been able to see before. I am sorry that this came so late. I saw him as a man of God in the simplest sense. I shall always be thankful that I was allowed to see that, and to cherish it thereafter.

---

[1] The two organizations were integrated in 1961. See Fey, *The Ecumenical Advance,* chapter 2.

90

Jan Cardinal Willebrands

THE NETHERLANDS (Roman Catholic)

Recalling two contacts with Dr. Fry, the head of the Roman Catholic ecumenical office comments on the pastoral character of true ecumenical leadership.

When the sad news came of Franklin Clark Fry's death, we were all conscious that a great Christian leader had left us. He had gone to the Lord, whom he had served during his life with all his talents—with his whole self. He had served the Lord in His church—both in a particular local congregation as the pastor of the flock entrusted to him, and on the worldwide scene, wherever he followed the Lord's call in the service of the gospel of unity. For he believed firmly that in work for unity he followed the path of the Lord—in the obscurity of faith yet in the light of the Holy Spirit.

It was my blessing to meet him on several occasions when he was chairman of the Central Committee of the World Council of Churches, and also during a meeting of church leaders in New York, where Cardinal Bea was the guest.

All who knew him admired his leadership, his ability, his decision towards persons. What struck me more about him was that as a leader he remained a pastor. Of course, I was not in daily contact with him, but I saw enough of him to be impressed with this specific quality. A church leader, even if he is in charge of an office which removes him from direct care of a parish, can never become a mere organiser, a mere bureaucrat, even a mere promoter of ideas. "Feed my lambs, feed my sheep"—this has been said to him, and thus he is responsible to the Lord of hosts in the service of His church. He has to be a witness and he has to serve. When he preaches or teaches the people of God, he speaks not for himself but brings to their remembrance what Christ has said. Whether giving

---

(b. 1909) As professor and then rector of the Catholic seminary at Warmond, Holland, Jan Willebrands became an energetic advocate of ecumenism, and in 1952 founded the Catholic Conference on Ecumenical Questions. He was made secretary of the newly created Secretariat for Promoting Christian Unity (1960-69). Consecrated titular bishop in 1964, he was appointed president of the secretariat in 1969 upon the death of Augustin Cardinal Bea, and elevated to the rank of cardinal. He is co-chairman of the joint working group between the Roman Catholic church and the World Council.

guidance to a single soul, or to a meeting or council, he chooses not his own way but follows "the way, the truth, and the life."

This mind, this resolve we call pastoral, in the sense in which Christ called himself the Good Shepherd.

Christian leadership has a special, intimate relationship to unity. "There shall be one flock, one shepherd." The leadership of Franklin Clark Fry was a service to unity. In his work for Christian unity he saw his specific vocation and his supreme charge. Yet he never ceased to be a pastor. Therefore it was that his leadership was selfless, wise, and strong, and earned the confidence of other Christian leaders with high responsibilities.

In my relatively few personal contacts with him, I had twice the chance to appreciate directly his profound Christian judgement and outlook. The first time was during the Central Committee meeting of the WCC at Rhodes in 1959. The Roman Catholic observers got into difficulties which involved me personally. After a meeting on the island of Patmos, on our way back from Rhodes to Athens, a short conversation with him about the matter quickly reassured me about his understanding and independence of mind, which led him to withhold judgement until the picture was sufficiently clear.

The second time was when representatives of the World Council of Churches living in the United States as well as representatives of the National Council of Churches received Cardinal Bea in New York, on March 31 and April 1, 1963, at the Lutheran Center and the Interchurch Center, respectively. These receptions took the form of meetings, and both were chaired by Franklin Clark Fry.

In the first of these meetings the conversation dealt mainly with possibilities of practical collaboration, with particular reference to social discrimination problems and those of Christian schools in countries which had recently obtained their independence.

In the second meeting the subject of mixed marriages was discussed. Cardinal Bea had always been personally interested in this subject, and had a keen insight into its ecumenical importance and urgency. I admired the way Franklin Clark Fry chaired this meeting, during which very divergent views were expressed on the theology of marriage by leaders of the different churches. Fry was able to appreciate every step forward which would benefit Christian conscience, without demanding that at once every wish would be understood and fulfilled. He was at the same time perfectly honest and frank in recognising that the theology of marriage was for many Protestants an underdeveloped area. The Vatican Council was engaged in the subject and it was not possible to foresee what the council would decide, since it was supreme and free both in its discussions and its decisions.

The meeting of the two men, Augustin Bea and Franklin Clark Fry, was in truth the manifestation of a common concern, alive in both of them yet towering above them: the concern of the Lord that all may be one.[1]

---

[1] On the ecumenical movement and the Roman Catholic church, see Fey, ed., *The Ecumenical Advance,* chapter 12.

91

Francis Akanu Ibiam

NIGERIA (Presbyterian)

A distinguished African layman shares his observations of Dr. Fry in the 1960s.

I first knew Dr. Franklin Clark Fry during the meeting of the third assembly of the World Council of Churches in New Delhi, India, 1961. The one and only honorary president and the six members of the praesidium had been elected by secret ballot followed by a careful and meticulous selection of the one hundred members of its Central Committee. There is no doubt, whatever, that the Central Committee of the World Council of Churches is not only all-powerful, but it is also the very soul of this famous world church organisation.

As one of the elected six presidents on that occasion, I attended the first meeting of the newly appointed central committee a couple of days later. The presidents are automatically members of both the Central and the Executive Committee of the WCC. There was an atmosphere of hush and expectation as we settled down in our seats. Then someone—I cannot now remember who—expressed the need for a chairman and a vice-chairman of the committee, and announced forthwith the names of Dr. Franklin Fry and Dr. Ernest Payne. Both Dr. Fry and Dr. Payne then came forward from a corridor nearby and presented themselves to the central committee which received and welcomed them with warm applause and congratulations.

A heavily and well built man, Dr. Fry was in full ministerial garb and looked every inch like a great preacher of the gospel of Christ. When he spoke he commanded rapt attention and his voice was pleasing to the ears. From the word go, I knew at once that he was thoroughly conversant with the work and trials of the chairman of the Central Committee of the WCC.

On at least two occasions I had the pleasure of observing the adroitness and masterfulness with which Dr. Fry conducted the affairs of both

---

(b. 1906) Dr. Ibiam, missionary and statesman, was a president of the World Council of Churches 1961-68. He was a medical missionary in Nigeria 1936 to 1957. He entered government service in 1947, rising to the position of governor of Eastern Nigeria 1960-66. He served meanwhile as president of the Christian Council of Nigeria (1955-58), and chairman of the provisional committee to form an All-Africa Council of Churches (1958-62).

the executive and the central committees. At this time, 1964, the World Council of Churches was in search for the man who would take on the mantle of office of Dr. W. A. Visser 't Hooft who was then preparing to retire and relinquish the highly responsible post of the general secretary of the WCC, a position he held with distinction and dedication and success for some twenty-five years from the inception of the organisation.

The search for a successor to Dr. Visser 't Hooft started in earnest during the meeting of the executive committee at Odessa in the Soviet Union in the fierce winter month of February, 1964. Several names were suggested, but only two names engaged the close attention of the committee for quite a long time. In the course of the discussion one of the persons concerned withdrew his nomination for personal reasons. It was the common sense (not so common as the name indicates) and sagacity of Dr. Fry and his profound knowledge of the mind and thinking of the World Council of Churches which guided him so unerringly to bring the committee to a welcome and accepted resolution—not to make the final recommendation, pending the next meeting of the central committee.

At Enugu, Nigeria, in January, 1965, where the next meeting of the central committee took place, the main and urgent consideration centred on the appointment of a new general secretary of the WCC. The debates were heated, and obviously there was a split within the ranks of the committee. One section, rather aggressive, attacked the executive committee for its presentation of a certain candidate for the office. The other section, although placatory in the assertion of its own views, was nevertheless forceful and unyielding. Dr. Fry took it all in with admirable self-composure and every now and again chipped in with a wise crack that brought laughter and a moment's relaxation to the assembly, reminding all that we were humble and imperfect Christians and servants of our Lord and Master, Jesus Christ first, and politicians thereafter.[1]

It is true that God the Father never lacks the tools which he uses to bring his blessed purposes to pass, but in the departure of Dr. Franklin Clark Fry to his Lord's nearer presence, the Christian church round the world has lost an outstanding Christian gentleman who was dignified in his person and who devoted his life in immeasurable capacity to the service of the kingdom of God. For me, he was a fine and admirable churchman and leader, and he inspired me enormously.

---

[1] Other writers on the selection of a new general secretary are listed with the memo of Lilje (No. 58).

92

J. Russell Chandran

INDIA (Church of South India)

Dr. Chandran, a veteran Asian ecumenist, offers a penetrating, judicious analysis of Dr. Fry's personality and leadership.

A Critical Appreciation

My acquaintance with Dr. Fry was through my association with the World Council of Churches, of which he was an officer from the time of its inauguration in 1948, first as vice-chairman and from 1954 as chairman of the central committee. Even though I first met him in 1948, I came to know him more closely only after I became a member of the Executive Committee of the WCC following the third assembly at New Delhi in 1961. From the beginning he impressed me as a rare type of person with a remarkable combination of physical, intellectual, and spiritual vitality, administrative competence, ecclesiastical statesmanship, and simple piety and devotion to Jesus Christ.

He was a disciplined and hard-working person, which was one of the secrets of his effectiveness. Even odd bits of time such as he had in an airport waiting for a flight, were well used by him either for reading or writing or for solving crossword puzzles. On the few occasions I had of flying with him, I noticed that he took some of his files with him and did a lot of work while on flight. I was not surprised to learn that even while in hospital during his last days he was working on the report of the central committee which he hoped to present at Uppsala. He also loved fun and jokes. He had a pleasant sense of humour, and even while discussing very serious matters he would often draw attention to the lighter side of things, without distracting from the main issue. Only

---

(b. 1918) Having joined the staff of the United Theological College, Bangalore, in 1950, Dr. Chandran has served as its principal since 1954. He has been president of the senate of Serampore College since 1968, and chairman of the Church of South India Synod Theological Commission since 1962. He was chairman of the East Asia Christian Council's Commission on Worship 1955-63, and is currently president of the Christian Union of India. He has been a member of the WCC Faith and Order Commission since 1952 (vice-chairman for a time), member of the WCC Central Committee since 1959 (vice-chairman 1965-68), and member of the executive committee 1961-68.

occasionally he yielded to the temptation of making jokes at the expense of others. Like many eminent men he could never "suffer fools gladly."

He was a warmhearted person and I have very pleasant memories of the warmth of friendship I received from him and the hospitality I enjoyed in his home in New York. He was also known for his great affection to his wife and other members of his family. It was while at Heraklion, in Crete, at the meeting of the WCC Central Committee in 1967, that he received the news of a major surgery one of his daughters-in-law had to undergo. Mrs. Fry was also with him. He openly expressed his concern for the daughter-in-law, his son, and the family. At the same time one could see the marks of the confidence and trust in God he had as a man of prayer. When he presided over the meetings there was no sign of the anxiety which he quietly bore. Perhaps as an after-effect of this strain or due to the ailment which finally took his life, he fainted during an excursion to a monastery in western Crete. When I visited him in the sick room on this occasion his words were, "I am all right." He attributed the fainting to climbing some steps, and went on to talk about other things and other people.

He also possessed a certain childlike simplicity. He often delighted in narrating his family history, particularly the story of how he got his names. He spoke of his sons with pride and was looking forward to have one of his sons as a member of the Uppsala assembly. He always carried an autograph book with him and collected the autographs of eminent people. At Crete he took the opportunity of the visit of the king and queen of Greece to get their autographs, and later told us of his meetings with several royal families and heads of states, including the scandals about some of them.

Dr. Fry had a remarkable gift of words. Whatever the occasion, whether the speech had to be extempore or prepared, he spoke with such choice of appropriate words and ideas that hardly anyone could think of saying anything more appropriate. I remember his reply to Dr. Radhakrishnan's talk on the occasion of the central committee meeting at Lucknow in January, 1953. As usual the great Indian philosopher, who at that time was the vice-president of India, had emphasised the equality of all religions, suggesting the irrelevance of the Christian concern in evangelism. In his reply, Dr. Fry remarkably combined courtesy to the guest and clarity and firmness of conviction about the church's commitment to proclaim the good news of Jesus Christ.[1]

His theology was consistently Christocentric. This came out in his opening devotions at the central committee and executive committee meetings and in his prayers. It was amazingly appropriate that for the last executive committee he chaired, namely, the one at Geneva in February 1968, he chose as the text of the devotional talk the great prayer of St. Paul in the Epistle to the Ephesians, "that Christ may dwell in your hearts in love—that you may be strong to grasp, with all God's people, what is the breadth and length and height and depth of the love of Christ."

He took the responsibilities of the chairman of the WCC Central Committee very seriously. He always chaired the meetings with great competence and dignity. The guidance he gave to the work of the World Council was marked by a thorough grasp of the facts and the issues involved. He would seldom let a decision be made without making the committee aware of all the implications. While he was flawless as a chairman, it was a serious weakness of his leadership that he never thought of sharing the responsibility of chairing meetings with the vice-chairman in the way his predecessor Bishop Bell had done.

He was genuinely committed to the World Council of Churches and to the ecumenical movement. He was deeply concerned about the financial support of the World Council and the strengthening of the cooperation from member churches. He was keen that his own church, the Lutheran Church in America, should fully participate in the work of the WCC. However, it may be mentioned that his ecumenical vision and dynamism were to some extent restrained by a certain conservatism which characterised his approach to several issues.

He was very much interested in the growth of the churches in Asia and Africa and was keen to encourage them. With a view to encouraging the representatives from the "younger churches" he often openly expressed his appreciation of the contribution made by them in discussions. Sometimes, however, his remarks about the "younger churches" and their representatives gave the impression of having a patronising attitude.

One was not always quite sure how evenly he divided the loyalties between Lutheranism and the ecumenical movement. There was no doubt that he was committed to ecumenism. But he was proud of his Lutheran heritage and was keen that in the ecumenical movement everything of value in the Lutheran tradition should be fully preserved. Therefore, he believed that the world confessional movements had a legitimate place. He was somewhat critical of the radical views expressed by the East Asia Christian Conference against world confessional movements.[2] But it must be acknowledged that the leadership he gave to the Lutheran churches and to the Lutheran World Federation resulted in the Lutheran churches becoming increasingly committed to ecumenical cooperation with other churches.

His conservatism also made him somewhat wary of any suggestion for radical changes in the structure of the WCC. During the period of negotiation for the merger of the International Missionary Council with the WCC (completed in 1961) he firmly opposed the suggestion for membership status to national Christian councils in the WCC, and pressed for the continuance of the original basis of membership. Even though in that context the decision taken was right, the basis of membership needs to be reviewed in the light of whatever theological answers we are able to agree upon about the ecclesiological significance of councils of churches.

Dr. Fry's reaction to the manner in which the central committee dealt with the election of the new general secretary should also, I think, be understood as due to his conservative approach and his image of the office of the general secretary.[3] That he resented the central committee's rejection of the proposal made by the executive committee was no secret. When I brought to his notice the widespread discontent about the choice made by the executive committee, he arranged for me to have an informal conversation, and during the talk his main point was the correctness and fairness of the procedures adopted.

Dr. Fry was certainly extremely competent to be correct and fair in the leadership of the WCC. This became specially evident in the manner in which he led the central committee at Enugu, Nigeria, in 1965, where a new nomination committee was appointed, and in Geneva, 1966, where the new general secretary was elected. But more than correctness and fairness, it was also necessary to recognise more fully the complexity of what the WCC is doing when it elects a general secretary, and the transformation that is taking place in the image of the office of general secretary. The choice of a person who should be acceptable to so many churches with such variety of ecclesiastical and cultural backgrounds is an unprecedented act, and it was not at all surprising that some of us had to be subjected to some unpleasantness and misunderstanding in the process. It is also important to remember that, whether we openly acknowledge it or not, the ecclesiological character of the WCC will demand that the general secretary, who is the executive officer, should be a person of proved and acknowledged leadership in a member church and not just a junior person with competence.

---

[1] See the footnote to Manikam's memo (No. 62), and the memo of Payne (85).

[2] See H. E. Fey, ed., *The Ecumenical Advance,* especially chapter 5. Other writers dealing with this subject are listed with the memo of Cavert (No. 73).

[3] Other writers on this subject are listed with the memo of Lilje (No. 58).

Source Register

The following register offers an inventory of Dr. Fry's writings and addresses, as far as I have been able to locate them, and sources of information about his career.

This catalog identifies most of the materials referred to by the contributors to this volume, and in many instances a wealth of parallel expressions. It brings into focus the range and profile and character of his public statements. It indicates developments in Dr. Fry's thought over a period of time, for example, on church polity, on strategies for promoting Lutheran unity, and on relations with Roman Catholicism.

The register is representative, but of course by no means exhaustive. Dr. Fry wrote comparatively little for publication. On the other hand, he maintained an overcrowded, jet-powered schedule of speaking engagements and of meetings, at many of which he delivered reports and addresses. He was often reluctant to have his speeches printed, but many of them were recorded on tape. Manuscripts of some addresses are at hand, but frequently he spoke from notes. Tapes or transcripts of some of his radio and television programs are extant, but many cannot be located.

Dr. Fry's public statements, therefore, have had to be gathered from widely scattered sources. Bibliographical indexes, magazines, and organization reports have been inspected. A dragnet of correspondence has gathered items from church offices, agencies, and institutions. Published appeals for information and materials have brought a gratifying response from individuals.

No doubt many more Fry materials will continue to turn up. A *Franklin Clark Fry Collection* of papers and audio-visual materials has been established at the Library of the Lutheran School of Theology at Chicago (which also has care of the ULCA and LCA Archives). Additions to this collection will be welcomed—both information on the location of items, and especially copies of items themselves. If subsequent acquisitions warrant it, a supplement to this Source Register will be published in due time.

—EDITOR

1. ARCHIVES AND FILES

Materials by Dr. Fry and about Dr. Fry

HOLY TRINITY LUTHERAN CHURCH, AKRON, OHIO

Dr. Fry was pastor here 1929-1944. Among the materials relating to FCF in the congregation's archives, as reported by Miss Ruth I. Simon, archivist, are the following items:

Call to FCF, and his letter of acceptance, 1929.

Bound copies of parish papers: *The Luther Leaguer,* 1929-33, *The Trinity Churchman,* 1941-44.

Reports to the church council and to the annual congregational meetings.

Sermon, "Through Architecture to God," 25th anniversary of dedication of the church, 1939. (Copy also in LSTC Library.)

Personal letters to FCF by young parishioners in the armed forces during World War II.

Letter of FCF to his former congregation, 11-6-1961, just before the New Delhi assembly of the World Council of Churches.

Clippings and pictures.

LUTHERAN CHURCH IN AMERICA (and the former UNITED LUTHERAN CHURCH IN AMERICA)

Archives of the LCA and the former ULCA are located at the Lutheran School of Theology at Chicago, 1100 E. 55th Street, Chicago. Access through permission of the president of the LCA. Archives contain:

Published Minutes of LCA/ULCA biennial conventions (also found in many libraries and church offices). Also recordings of conventions: Wire recording of 1948 convention, tapes from 1950 on.

Minutes of LCA Executive Council/ULCA Executive Board.

Minutes and Files of several boards and other agencies. E.g., the Men's Brotherhood (later United Lutheran Church Men); 14 volumes of correspondence, reports, minutes, and studies relating to the *Service Book and Hymnal* (published 1958), collected by Luther D. Reed (see especially Volume 1). Minutes and Files of the LCA Lutheran Church Women are at LSTC; those of the ULCA Women's Missionary Society (later United Lutheran Church Women) are in the library of the Lutheran Theological Seminary, Germantown Avenue at Allens Lane, Philadelphia.

File of the monthly mailing to pastors: (LCA) *Ministers Information Service,* 1963–/ (ULCA) *Pastor's Desk Book,* 1947-62 (see Section 5, below).

Minutes and Files of the Joint Commission on Lutheran Unity, 1955-62 (the commission which prepared the merger forming the LCA).

File of the LCA/ULCA President's Correspondence: Frederick H. Knubel (especially 1942-44), Franklin Clark Fry, 1945-68. A rich source, well filed. It includes FCF's correspondence on the Lutheran Council in the USA/National Lutheran Council, Lutheran World Federation/Lutheran World Convention, National Council of Churches/Federal Council of Churches, World Council of Churches, JCLU, etc.

At LCA headquarters, 231 Madison Avenue, New York, N. Y., the office of the Commission on Press, Radio & Television has a file of news releases of the News Bureau of the ULCA/LCA, issued since 1954 (also on file in several libraries), published features and photographs, and other materials on FCF, including a small quantity of films and tapes (see Section 9, *Audio-Visuals*).

Most widely distributed medium of communication in the church is THE LUTHERAN weekly magazine of the ULCA, since 1963 a biweekly of the LCA. Office of THE LUTHERAN, at 2900 Queen Lane, Philadelphia, has files of materials on FCF, correspondence between him and the editors, 1944-68, and an unpublished comprehensive index of the magazine. (See Section 6, below.)

LUTHERAN COUNCIL IN THE UNITED STATES OF AMERICA (and the former NATIONAL LUTHERAN COUNCIL)

Headquarters at 315 Park Avenue South, New York, N. Y. Its Archives of Cooperative Lutheranism include:

Minutes and Files of the LCUSA/NLC and of their agencies, e.g., file of Lutheran World Action bulletins since 1942; file of films in the LWA promotion office (see 9. *Audio-Visuals*); Lutheran World Relief, Inc.; and other cooperative Lutheran materials.

File of news releases of the NLC/LCUSA News Bureau and its predecessor, the Lutheran Bureau. These are the best single source on current events relating to Lutheranism, with a global scope. (File also found in several libraries.)

The NATIONAL LUTHERAN, journal of the NLC: quarterly 1931-38, bi-monthly 1948-59, monthly 1960-66. (The LUTHERAN FORUM, 1967–, is independent of the LCUSA.)

Minutes and Files of the USA National Committee of the LWF. Minutes of the LWF Executive Committee.

Papers of individual leaders with whom FCF had contact, such as Frederick H. Knubel, Abdel Ross Wentz, Paul C. Empie, et al. Dr. Wentz's papers are particularly important on beginnings of the World Council and Lutheran participation in its planning.

LUTHERAN WORLD FEDERATION (and the former LUTHERAN WORLD CONVENTION)

Headquarters at 150 Route de Ferney, Geneva, Switzerland, with Archives and Information Bureau. The USA National Committee of the LWF, formerly affiliated with the NLC, but since 1967 a separate agency, maintains offices at 315 Park Avenue South, New York, N. Y.

Proceedings of LWF assemblies (FCF participated in those of 1947, 1952, 1957, 1963) are published. Information Bureau has tapes of LWF assemblies from 1952 on, tapes of some other meetings, and a photograph file. Archives contain correspondence of the General Secretariat. Otherwise, the Geneva office has relatively little material by and about FCF which is not found elsewhere. His correspondence on LWF affairs is in the ULCA/LCA Archives at LSTC.

Executive Committee Minutes (also in LCUSA Archives, and archives of member churches).

LWF News Service, Geneva, produces occasional releases entitled *LWF Information*. (File also in the LCUSA Archives and in several libraries.)

LUTHERAN WORLD, published quarterly since 1954 (German edition: LUTHERISCHE RUNDSCHAU), contains articles, reports, notices, documentation, and a "Geneva Diary."

NATIONAL COUNCIL OF THE CHURCHES OF CHRIST IN THE USA (and the former FEDERAL COUNCIL OF THE CHURCHES OF CHRIST IN AMERICA)

Headquarters at 475 Riverside Drive, New York, N. Y., include Archives, Research Library, Office of Information, Broadcasting and Film Commission.

Reports of General Assembly meetings are published. Tapes are on file of all NCCC General Assembly meetings (see also Reigner Recording Library, below) and of almost all General Board meetings. See also minutes of various committees: FCF was chairman of the Policy and Strategy Committee 1955-61, the Constituent Membership Committee 1958-61, the Constitution and Bylaws Committee 1961-63.

File of periodicals: The FEDERAL COUNCIL BULLETIN, to 1950, the NATIONAL COUNCIL OUTLOOK, 1951-59. (Also in many libraries.)

Correspondence of the General Secretariat. (FCF's correspondence on affairs of the FCC and the NCCC is found in his ULCA/LCA presidential files.)

WORLD COUNCIL OF CHURCHES

Headquarters at 150 Route de Ferney, Geneva, Switzerland, include Archives and Library, Department of Information, Department of Television and Broadcasting, etc. See also the New York Office of the WCC, 475 Riverside Drive, New York.

Reports of Assemblies (1948, 1954, 1961, 1968) are published. Tapes of assemblies are on file in Geneva (see also Reigner Recording Library, below). Minutes of annual Central Committee meetings are published; tapes have been made of these meetings since 1967.

File of news releases entitled *Ecumenical Press Service,* issued since 1934. Best single source for ecumenical current events.

These and other printed records and related ecumenical literature are found in many libraries. (See William Adams Brown Ecumenical Library, below.)

Quarterly journal, CHRISTENDOM, and from 1948 the ECUMENICAL REVIEW. Correspondence of the General Secretariat is in Geneva. (FCF's correspondence on WCC affairs is found in his ULCA/LCA presidential files.)

RELIGIOUS NEWS SERVICE

43 West 57th Street, New York, N. Y. Has three large files of materials on FCF, probably the most complete record anywhere of his activities from 1945 on.

REIGNER RECORDING LIBRARY

At Union Theological Seminary, 3401 Brook Road, Richmond, Virginia. Has tapes of WCC and NCCCUSA assemblies, films, kinescopes and tapes of many radio and television broadcasts, tapes of addresses, and other materials. The Library publishes a catalog of its holdings. Tapes featuring FCF are listed under 9. *Audio-Visuals.*

WILLIAM ADAMS BROWN ECUMENICAL LIBRARY

At Union Theological Seminary, 120 Broadway, New York, N. Y. The chief center of ecumenical literature in the USA. In addition to its great collection of printed materials, it houses the papers of important ecumenists such as Henry P. Van Dusen.

2. BIOGRAPHICAL SKETCHES AND FEATURE ARTICLES ON DR. FRY

The most elaborate tribute to FCF is the little book honoring him on his 60th birthday anniversary: *Mr. Protestant. An Informal Biography of Franklin Clark Fry.* Board of Publications of the ULCA, Philadelphia, 1960. (Edited by Albert P. Stauderman.) Foreword by H. Torrey Walker. Essays by Franklin Drewes Fry, Harry J. Kreider, Thomas B. Kline, Henry Endress, Henry Knox Sherrill, Johannes Lilje, W. A. Visser 't Hooft, James F. Henninger. The 1958 TIME article is reprinted, and a biographical sketch given.

EARLY BIOGRAPHICAL SKETCHES

Current Biography, June 1946, pp. 199-200.

Who's Who in America: sketch first appeared in the 1946-47 edition.

FEATURE ARTICLES

"Big Fry," NEWSWEEK, 2-19-1951, p. 76.

Brief sketch of FCF appeared in "Toward Mutual Understanding. Two-Way Visit of American and Russian Churchmen," NATIONAL COUNCIL OUTLOOK, February 1956, pp. 6-10.

"Number One Protestant Statesman," LUTHERAN, 8-28-1957, pp. 12-15.

"World's Leading Protestant," LIFE, 9-2-1957, p. 100.

"Protestantism's Busy Lutheran," NEWSWEEK, 9-2-1957, p. 51.

"Lutherans and Mr. Protestant," TIME, 9-2-1957, p. 36.

"Dr. Franklin Clark Fry—New President of the LWF," NATIONAL LUTHERAN, November-December 1957, pp. 9-10.

"The New Lutheran," TIME, 4-7-1958, pp. 58-60+.

"Daughter Tells About Father," LUTHERAN, 4-16-1958, pp. 15, 17-18.

Article by George F. Harkins in ULCA *Pastor's Desk Book,* May 1958, commenting on publicity given to FCF in TIME and LIFE.

"Mr. Lutheran," CORONET, June 1958, pp. 144-148.

"Around the World with Franklin Clark Fry," LUTHERAN, 1-1-1964, pp. 6-9. Interview with Mrs. Fry.

Proceedings of the 4th Assembly [Helsinki, 1963] of the LWF, Berlin, 1965: Statement by the Resolutions Committee, p. 411; Dr. Schiotz's response to FCF's welcome, pp. 431-432; Bishop Giertz's tribute, pp. 432-433. Tributes at end of FCF's term as president of LWF.

"Franklin Clark Fry Resigns because of Illness," LUTHERAN, 6-19-1968, p. 23.

"Editor's Opinion," LUTHERAN, 6-19-1968, p. 50. Albert Stauderman on FCF's illness.

"TV's Fabulous Fry," LUTHERAN, 7-3-1968, pp. 47-48, by Richard T. Sutcliffe.

3. OBITUARY NOTICES AND TRIBUTES

The fullest obituary is the one printed in this volume as Memo 1, by Erik W. Modean, a release from the LCUSA News Bureau, 1968-53, June 7: "Dr. Franklin Clark Fry One of Towering Figures of the Christian World."

AMERICA, 6-22-1968, pp. 784-785. (Roman Catholic)

CHRISTIAN CENTURY, 6-26-1968, p. 834.

CHRISTIANITY TODAY, 6-21-1968, p. 43.

ECUMENICAL PRESS SERVICE, 6-13-1968, pp. 2-3: "Memorial Service for Dr. Fry Held at Ecumenical Centre [Geneva]." (WCC, Geneva)

ECUMENICAL REVIEW, July 1968, p. 301. (WCC)

LONDON TIMES, 6-8-1968. Copy in LSTC Library, per J. Stephen Bremer and Edgar S. Brown, Jr.

LUTHERAN, 7-3-1968, pp. 5-9: "Loss of a Leader," pp. 24-25: account of the funeral.

Minutes, Lutheran Church in America, 1968, p. 50 (cf. 407): Tribute by H. Ober Hess for the Executive Council. pp. 50-51: Prayer by Malvin H. Lundeen. pp. 51-52: Lundeen's tribute in awarding the "Servus Dei" medal posthumously, and Mrs. Fry's response.

LUTHERAN STANDARD, 6-25-1968, p. 15: "Mr. LCA." pp. 17, 30: "A Giant in the Land": Modean's article, abridged. (American Lutheran Church)

LUTHERAN WOMEN, September 1968, p. 32, by Dorothy J. Marple. (LCA Lutheran Church Women)

LUTHERAN WORLD, vol. 15, no. 4, 1968, pp. 318-319: Statements by other presidents of the LWF: Anders Nygren, Hanns Lilje, Fredrik A. Schiotz. (Lutheran World Federation)

LWF INFORMATION (23/68), 6-10-1968, pp. 1-6. Four articles, including tributes from leaders of LWF, World Council of Churches, Vatican, World Alliance (Reformed), and account of memorial service at Ecumenical Center, Geneva. (25/68), 6-12-1968, pp. 1-2: Tribute by LWF President Schiotz.

NEW YORK TIMES, 6-7-1968: Modean's article, abridged; 6-12-1968, p. 44.

NEWSWEEK, 6-17-1968, p. 88.

RADIUS, 6-18-1968, no. 59, by E. Theodore Bachmann: Includes quotations from addresses by Samuel M. Cavert and Archbishop Iakovos at the memorial service held at the Interchurch Center, New York. (Bulletin of the LCA Board of Theological Education)

SUOMI KONFERENSSIN KIRKOLLINEN KALENTERI, 1969, Hancock, Michigan, pp. 29-37, by Raymond W. Wargelin. (Annual of the LCA Finnish Interest Conference)

TIME, 6-14-1968, pp. 64+.

UPPSALA REPORT, Geneva, 1968, pp. 284-285: Tribute by Ernest A. Payne. (Proceedings of the 4th Assembly of WCC)

L. Sanjek, *The One Hundredth Anniversary of the First Vatican Council, with Memoir of the Octogenarian Author*. n.p., 1970. Chapter 5 is a memoir on FCF, pp. 59-66.

John Body and Rudolph Shintay, *History of the Slovak Zion Synod,* Pittsburgh, 1972, records a memorial tribute to FCF and an account of FCF's convening of the LCA Slovak Zion Synod in 1962.

Sermon at Dr. Fry's funeral, by Robert W. Stackel, 6-11-1968, is printed in the LCA *Ministers Information Service,* September 1968.

4. PRESIDENTIAL REPORTS TO BIENNIAL CONVENTIONS OF THE ULCA AND THE LCA, 1946-1968

These are among the most carefully prepared longer statements of Dr. Fry. Until 1966, a presidential report was always focused on a single theme; these documents, therefore, furnish an important index to FCF's ecclesiastical thought. The 1966 and 1968 reports consisted of FCF's personal commentary on issues coming before the convention, designed to offer guidance to the delegates (see report to 1966 LCA convention, *Minutes*, p. 33).

	ULCA Convention	*Minutes*	*Theme*
1946	Cleveland	pp. 21-25	Postwar responsibility.
1948	Philadelphia	22-27	Spiritual life.
1950	Des Moines	26-37	Interchurch relationships.
1952	Seattle	24-32	How the ULCA serves its congregations.
1954	Toronto	27-40	Organizational structure.
1956	Harrisburg	29-38	Christian unity.
1958	Dayton	29-72	Prospects of merger (JCLU report).
1960	Atlantic City	29-66	Details of the merger.
(1962	Detroit—adjourned meeting	659-665	President's valedictory.)
	LCA Convention		
1964	Pittsburgh	34-42	LCA as a channel for the Spirit of God (a call to church renewal).
1966	Kansas City	33-51	Personal commentary on issues coming before the convention.
1968	Atlanta	37-49	Comment on eight facets of church life.

5. (ULCA) PASTOR'S DESK BOOK (1947-1962) AND (LCA) MINISTERS INFORMATION SERVICE (1963-1968)

Beginning in November 1947, ULCA pastors received a monthly mailing of promotional materials and communications on various interests of the church. Dr. Fry reserved for himself one regular section, entitled "The State of the Church." (See his prospectus, November 1947, and his expression, "my column," January 1959.) Addressed to his "Dear Partners," these communications proved a remarkably effective device for helping pastors to feel well informed on a broad spectrum of current issues, both Lutheran and ecumenical, and therefore responsible for a ministry of national and international horizons. It gave them a sense of being taken behind the scenes in important current events.

These communications, therefore, being intimate in tone, more occasional and lively than the formal presidential reports, offer important insights into the range and depth and intensity of Dr. Fry's interests, his moods and opinions, and his style of work.

Beginning in 1950 he regularly published the full text of his biennial presidential reports in the summer months preceding a convention, so that all pastors would have them in advance. Since these are readily accessible in the ULCA/LCA *Minutes*, they are not listed below.

Frequent among the *Desk Book* releases are his world travel diaries. These often appeared also in the LUTHERAN, but usually in briefer form there.

A number of important addresses by Dr. Fry are found in the *Desk Book*, usually in abridged form.

Occasionally reports on ULCA/LCA matters would be drafted by another pen, but they usually passed his inspection before appearing in his "State of the Church" section. Often the article would consist of Dr. Fry's analysis of the particular topic and his comments on it.

Frequently—increasingly so in his later years—he would fill his column with other formal and informal materials which had impressed him. Here, too, Dr. Fry's mind is revealed in the range of his selections and the introductions which he wrote for them.

Because of the semi-confidential character of these "State of the Church" communications, they were not produced for general circulation. Some pastors have kept them on file. Complete sets are to be found in the LCA Archives at the Lutheran School of Theology at Chicago, and at the office of the LCA Board of Publication, 2900 Queen Lane, Philadelphia.

(ULCA) PASTOR'S DESK BOOK

The "State of the Church" section in the *Pastor's Desk Book* bears the code letters *NE,* with pages numbered consecutively from 1947 to 1962.

November 1947, NE-1 to NE-3. FCF's comment: Introduction to "State of the Church" section. Bishop Otto Dibelius to visit USA. CROP—Church World Service cooperating with Lutheran World Relief. Spiritual care and immigration of displaced persons. The LUTHERAN. Myron Taylor, President Truman's "personal representative" to the Vatican. Lutheran World Action.

December 1947, NE-5 to NE-8. Comment: Ministerial pensions. Myron Taylor. LWA. Hans Asmussen to visit USA. American Overseas Aid. Edwin Moll in Palestine.

January 1948, pp. 9-13. Comment: Lutheran progress around the world. Miracle at Lund (viz., that the LWF was founded)—"confidential." LWA goal reached.

February 1948, pp. 15-17. Comment: National Lutheran Council meeting at Richmond, where Ralph Long urged union of member bodies. The LUTHERAN.

March 1948, pp. 19-21. Comment: Funeral of Ralph Long. Coup in Czechoslovakia. CROP. (Asmussen's address to ULCA Executive Board.) ULCA apportionment.

April 1948, pp. 23-28. Comment: ULCA Committee on Faith and Life. Youth Work. (Letter from Moll: Israelis seize Syrian Orphanage in Jerusalem.) Pastors in Hungary. "The King's Business": training program for church councilmen. Article by Theodore Tappert countering Jonathan Perkins' republication of *The Jews and Their Lies* by Luther. Igor Bella returns to Czechoslovakia. Railway clergy fare.

May 1948, pp. 29-32. Comment: Myron Taylor. ULCA apportionment. Edwin Moll leaves Palestine. Preview of Philadelphia ULCA convention. Relations with Augustana Synod: An editorial by E. E. Ryden urging Lutheran union (3-24) and FCF's reply (LUTHERAN COMPANION, 4-21-1948, p. 2).

June 1948, pp. 33-37. Comment: The new Lutheran liturgy. Closer relations between UELC and ULCA? Income from church films. ULCA statistics. (Rome's view of tolerance: Fr. Cavalli on Spain's policy toward Protestants.)

July 1948, pp. 39-43. Comment: Lutheran DPs. Lag in Lutheran World Action drive. Asmussen's article on German confessionalism rejected by CHRISTIAN CENTURY. Lutheran unity: Danish Evangelical Lutheran Church interested. The LUTHERAN.

August 1948, pp. 45-47. Comment: Preview of Amsterdam WCC assembly (and excerpt from CHRISTIANITY AND CRISIS on the issue of confessionalism).

September 1948, pp. 49-53. Comment: Preview of Philadelphia ULCA convention, with excerpts of president's report.

October 1948, pp. 55-60. Comment: Echoes of the Amsterdam WCC assembly.

November 1948, pp. 61-64. Comment: What the WCC is not. Philadelphia ULCA convention. ALC on the offer of unity. FCF's letter to pastors on lag in the double apportionment drive.

December 1948, pp. 65-70. Comment: F. E. Reinartz's recovery. Lutheran unity: American Lutheran Conference meeting. Protestant DPs in USA.

January 1949, pp. 71-76. Comment: Lutheran self-analysis. (LUTHERAN WITNESS—Missouri Synod—on "Lutheran Power Politics.")

February 1949, pp. 77-82. Comment: Augustana President Bersell convenes NLC representatives to discuss union. Success of LWA drive. (Text: Pastoral letter of ELC District President Lawrence Field. FCF's schedule, January-February.)

March 1949, pp. 83-89. Comment: Mindszenty and Ordass, Communist oppression. Survey of local interchurch relationships.

April 1949, pp. 91-94. FCF's report of comments on the ULCA by President Prakasam (Andhra Lutheran Church). Comments: Dampened prospects of Lutheran unity.

May 1949, pp. 95-100. (Endress on church films.) Comment: A CHRISTIAN CENTURY article on Lutherans: "Would They Link Hands Today?"

July 1949, pp. 107-111. Comment: Pentagon invitation to orientation session for civilian leaders, with FCF's reply. ULCA statistics. Protestant DPs. Fundamentalist CHRISTIAN BEACON (American Council of Churches) article on a Rochester Lutheran church's secession because of opposition to affiliation with the Federal Council.

August 1949, pp. 113-118. Account of visit to Czechoslovakia by FCF and Bersell.

September 1949, pp. 119-124. Comment: FCF at WCC Central Committee meeting at Chichester. (Text: Message of LWF Executive Committee.)

October 1949, pp. 125-130. Comment: LWF Exec. Committee at Oxford. Lutheran World Relief.

November 1949, pp. 131-136. Comment: Lutheran unity: The "Committee of 34."

January 1950, pp. 143-147. Comment: Christian Higher Education Year appeal.

February 1950, pp. 149-153. Comment: LWA, failure of ULCA to reach goal.

March 1950, pp. 155-160. Text: Address for CHEY.

April 1950, pp. 161-167. Texts: Letter to synod presidents and letter to Secretary of State Acheson on Myron Taylor. (Quotations on Lutheran unity from ALC, ELC, and Augustana.)

July 1950, pp. 179-182. Text: Sermon delivered over Canadian Broadcasting Corporation: "Life Breaking In on You."

November 1950, pp. 205-210. Comment: ULCA's LWA drive lagging. CHEY. Lutheran World Relief. (Lutheran unity: ALC action at Columbus.)

December 1950, pp. 211-216. Comment: The Assumption of Mary dogma, and German Lutheran bishops' refutation. Invitation to the Communist peace conference, with FCF's reply. ULCA Pension Board's "Family Protection Plan." (Lutheran unity: Augustana action, American Lutheran Conference items.) LWA.

January 1951, pp. 217-222. Comment: Constituting convention of the National Council of Churches, Cleveland, December 1950.

February 1951, pp. 223-227. Text: FCF's statement to the 1950 ULCA convention on USA diplomat to the Vatican.

March 1951, pp. 229-234. Text: FCF's report of his world tour surveying the refugee situation, over National Radio Vespers ("One Great Time of Sharing": FCF interviewed by J. S. Bonnell. See also 6. *LUTHERAN*, 7. *Articles & Addresses*, 9. *Audio-Visuals*).

April 1951, pp. 235-240. Comment: USA Social Security and ministers. Texts: Correspondence to and from S. M. Cavert regarding a letter soliciting contributions to NCCC from ULCA congregations.

May 1951, pp. 241-247. Text: Address on church and state, at NLC seminar. (Augustana editorial on Lutheran unity.)

June 1951, pp. 249-255. (A woman's statement on Roman Catholic aggression and the problem of truth and tolerance, with FCF's comment.)

July 1951, pp. 257-267. Text: Address on the ULCA approach to interchurch relationships, at meeting of the Association of Council Secretaries, Williams Bay, Wis. Comments on NCCCUSA. (Text: LWF Theology Commission's study document for the Hannover assembly.)

November 1951, pp. 287-298. Comment: Appointment of Mark Clark as US ambassador to the Vatican, with a Roman Catholic reply to FCF.

December 1951, pp. 299-305. Text: Essay on ecclesiastical ethics. Comment: Vatican embassy.

January 1952, pp. 307-316. Text: Address on the state of the church, to ULCA executive secretaries, Buck Hill Falls, Pa. Comment: Vatican embassy.

February 1952, pp. 317-327. Report on ULCA's Part II budget plan (in the form of a "court trial," with leading churchmen as witnesses). (Re Vatican embassy: excerpt from Leo XIII's *Immortale Dei* (1885) on American democracy.)

March 1952, pp. 329-336. Text: Address on evangelism (Phil. 2:9-10), at Lutheran Evangelism Conference, Minneapolis Armory. (NLC statement on Vatican embassy. Report on LWA from an ALC representative in Germany.)

May & June 1952, pp. 345-354, 355-370. Japan and Korea diary.

August 1952, pp. 371-378. Comment: ULCA statistics. (Letter of Cavert on "National Council Day.")

November 1952, pp. 391-396. Text: Seattle ULCA convention sermon (II Tim. 1:7).

January 1953, pp. 403-408. Draft of report to ULCA Exec. Board on the Denver NCCCUSA assembly.

February & March 1953, pp. 409-416, 417-424. India diary.

April 1953, pp. 425-432. FCF's "observations and notes" for the new ULCA Commission on Organizational Structure.

May 1953, pp. 433-439. Comment on ministerial status, accompanying report of ULCA Commission on the Doctrine of the Ministry.

June 1953, pp. 441-445. Comment: Care of military service personnel.

October 1953, pp. 461-468. (W. P. Peery's report on flood in India, with introduction by FCF.)

November 1953, pp. 469-473. Text: Thanksgiving message (for Associated Church Press). . . .

January 1954, pp. 485-490. Text: Address, "The Church in an Industrial Society," at Board of Social Missions conference on the Church and Industrial Life, Muhlenberg College, June 1953.

February 1954, pp. 491-500. Comment: Missouri Synod–Wisconsin Synod controversy, with documents.

March 1954, pp. 501-510. Comment: Preview of the Evanston WCC assembly.

April 1954, (misnumbered 501-507, should be 511-517). Comment: Appearance of LUTHERAN WORLD (LWF journal); the journal's editor, Hans Bolewski.

May 1954, pp. 519-525. Comment: Lutheran Laymen's Movement offer of aid for congregational fund-raising.

March & April 1955, pp. 591-597, 599-607. Geneva and Vienna diary.

May 1955, pp. 609-618. FCF's report on ULCA's approach to Augustana, with documents (=genesis of the JCLU).

June 1955, pp. 619-624. . . . (Lutheran unity: A UELC opinion.) Comment: The ULCA Common Investing Fund.

November & December 1955, pp. 645-651, 653-660. Africa diary (Marangu Lutheran conference; visit to Liberia).

January 1956, pp. 661-670. Comment: Heresy trials in Wisconsin.

March 1956, pp. 681-690. Malaya diary.

April 1956, pp. 691-699. Russia diary.

January 1957, pp. 757-767. Comment: Lutheran unity: ALC-ULCA relations; Joint Commission on Lutheran Unity under way.

March 1957, pp. 777-784. Report of his evangelism mission in Hampstead, Maryland.

April & May 1957, pp. 785-792, 793-801. (FCF records reactions to the Midboe report (NLC) on service to military personnel.)

July 1957, pp. 809-815. (JCLU's first year report.) Comment: ALC-ULCA relations, on pulpit and altar fellowship.

October 1957, pp. 827-836. Report to the ULCA Exec. Board on the Minneapolis LWF assembly.

November 1957, pp. 837-848. Comment: Synodical budget priorities ("double budget").

December 1957, pp. 849-858. Comment: The Long Range Program of Parish Education.

February 1958, pp. 871-878. Ghana diary.

May 1958, pp. 901-909. (Harkins' comment on publicity given to FCF by TIME and LIFE.)

December 1958, pp. 985-996. Text: Address, "My Dream for the Future of Our Church," at Lutheran Laymen's Movement dinner, Dayton. . . .

January 1959, pp. 997-1004. Comment: Significance of four ULCA theological statements for the forthcoming merger. . . .

February 1959, pp. 1005-1013. Comment: Analysis of ULCA 1958 financial returns. . . .

March 1959, pp. 1015-1024. Comment: Pope's announcement of an "ecumenical council," with text of WCC Exec. Committee communiqué (drafted by FCF). Comment on statement in LOOK that he supported the candidacy of J. F. Kennedy.

December 1959, pp. 1071-1074. Notes on visit to the Holy Land. . . .

February 1960, pp. 1079-1085. Comment: How the new church came to be named.

March 1960, pp. 1087-1093. . . . (FCF's schedule, January-April.)

April 1960, pp. 1095-1101. British Guiana diary.

May 1960, pp. 1103-1117. (FCF's introduction, and 39 newspaper editorials censuring the US Air Force Manual which had incorporated slanders against the NCCCUSA and several churchmen.)

February 1961, pp. 1193-1202. Text: Communion sermon at Atlantic City ULCA convention (Matt. 23:8-9). . . .

April 1961, pp. 1213-1218. Comment: Confidential report on the Kennedy news conference at which FCF's name was mentioned. . . .

May 1961, pp. 1219-1224. . . . Comment: Pamphlet, "What Is Troubling the Lutherans?" circulated by Edgar Bundy's "Church League of America."

July 1961, pp. 1229-1237. Announcement of the application by the Russian Orthodox Church for membership in WCC, with FCF's comments.

November 1961, pp. 1251-1258. (FCF's schedule for trip around the world, October to January, with comment.)

December 1961, pp. 1259-1267. Report of chairman of the WCC Central Committee to the New Delhi assembly.

May 1962, pp. 1297-1300. Text: Sermon in the Helsinki cathedral (Luke 1:37).

September 1962, pp. 1313-1323. Valedictory to the ULCA convention.

(LCA) MINISTERS INFORMATION SERVICE (September 1963-)

The "State of the Church" section bears the code letters SC, with page numbering beginning afresh with each year from 1965 on.

September 1963, SC-1 to SC-3. Text: Second half of FCF's presidential address to Helsinki LWF assembly.

March 1964, SC-13 to SC-16. Text: Address to Conference of Synodical Presidents on "confirmed membership in good standing," benevolence, "ministers awaiting a call," pulpit and altar fellowship with ALC and Missouri Synod.

December 1964, pp. 51-73. (Harkins' manual of NCCCUSA relations, compiled for LCA Exec. Council; and editorial from Minneapolis TRIBUNE criticizing J. A. Stormer's *None Dare Call It Treason,* with FCF's comment on the "dementia americana" characterizing the latter work.)

April 1966, pp. 19-22. (WCC Central Committee minutes on FCF's attempted resignation in view of the election of E. C. Blake.) . . .

June to December 1967. Comments on the significance of the "Manifesto" ("God's Call to the Church in Each Place"), a statement adopted at the 1966 LCA convention:
June pp. 33-42 "Social Ministry and the Manifesto."
July-August pp. 51-52 "Ministries in Concert with the Manifesto" (American Missions).
September pp. 57-59 "Manifesto Emphases of the Commission on Stewardship."
October pp. 69-75 "The Manifesto and Lutheran Church Women."
November pp. 85-87 "Manifesto Emphases of the Commission on Evangelism."
December pp. 97-99 "The Manifesto and Parish Education."

January 1968, pp. 1-4. Comment: US crisis in race relations (six paragraphs from FCF's address to Pacific Southwest Synod pastors' conference, Asilomar, Cal., September 1967). . . .

February 1968, pp. 5-10. (Working paper of the joint working group of the WCC and the Roman Catholic church, on "Ecumenical Dialogue," with FCF's introduction on the current "dialogue.")

(September 1968. Robert W. Stackel's sermon, "Overwhelming Victory Is Ours," at FCF's funeral June 11, 1968, is printed in the *Miscellaneous* section, MS 31-34.)

6. DR. FRY IN "THE LUTHERAN"

THE LUTHERAN was the organ of the ULCA, and from 1963 on has been the organ of the LCA. Texts of FCF's addresses and travel diaries are often abridged in THE LUTHERAN; fuller texts are sometimes recorded elsewhere, such as the ULCA *Pastor's Desk Book* and the LCA *Ministers Information Service.* The same is true of FCF's presidential reports to the ULCA/LCA: abridged here, published in full in the *PDB/MIS* and subsequently in the convention *Minutes.* THE LUTHERAN frequently quoted brief remarks by FCF on various subjects; these are not listed below, nor are some interviews of FCF.

3-21-1935. "ULCA Committee on Evangelism: February Meeting Reported by Secretary Franklin C. Fry, Akron, Ohio." p. 7.

12-5-1935. "As a Consuming Fire" (Luke 12:49). One of a group of sermon synopses on "What Advent Means to Me." p. 11.

8-8-1936. "Stopped Half Way" (Gen. 11:32). Sermon synopsis. p. 10.

12-8-1937. Review of F. G. Beardsley, *Life of Charles G. Finney,* p. 18.

2-16-1938. "In Behalf of the Church" (I Cor. 11:12, I Tim. 3:15). Excerpts of a sermon of 1-18-1938 at Reading, Pa., on the 20th anniversary of the ULCA. pp. 12-13.

12-23-1942. Review of H. H. Farmer, *The Servant of the Word.* p. 22.

3-1-1944. Review of James Moffatt, *The Thrill of Tradition.* p. 20.

2-14-1945. "For the Love of Christ Constraineth Us." Lenten message to pastors. p. 8.

4-25-1945. "Church and Members Mourn." Statement on the death of Franklin D. Roosevelt. pp. 2, 23.

5-16-1945. "With One Accord." Statement to the churches on V-E Day ("Victory in Europe"). p. 3.

10-31-1945. "The Gospel's Present Opponents." Reformation Day message. p. 11.

2-27-1946. "It's the Plus That Counts: A Message to the Church in a Time of Testing." NBC radio address, 2-11-1946, on the postwar situation in Europe. pp. 16-20. (See also 10. *Sermons in Books.*)

6-5-1946. Letter to Lutherans on Lutheran World Action as an Eastertide task. p. 2.

10-9-1946. "Unless We Move Now." President's report to the ULCA Cleveland convention. pp. 13-17. (See 4. *Presidential Reports.*)

4-9-1947. "Nations in Trouble: Finland and Poland. pp. 12-16.

8-13-1947. "My Opinion of the Lund Assembly" (LWF). pp. 13-14.

3-17-1948. Remarks at the funeral of Ralph Long, 2-21-1948. p. 9.

8-3-1949. "The Future Comes Fast." Summary of addresses at synod conventions. pp. 18-21.

10-11-1950. "Why Lutherans Don't Unite." p. 13.

10-18-1950. Excerpts from acceptance speech on re-election as ULCA president, Des Moines convention. p. 6.

10-25-1950. Excerpts: address at ULCA convention.

3-7-1951. "It's Time to Share." Radio script: report on world refugee situation for "One Great Hour of Sharing." pp. 13+. (See also 5. *Pastor's Desk Book.*)

3-14-1951. "What Can Be Done?" Refugee report, continued. pp. 22+.

10-31-1951. Comment on appointment of US ambassador to the Vatican. p. 5.

12-12-1951. "We Must Speak Out Now." Protest against embassy to the Vatican. p. 13.

4-1-1953. "Indian Diary." Trip to India for World Council Central Committee meeting. pp. 15+.

4-8-1953. "Education Needs Religion." India trip, continued. pp. 17+.

4-29-1953. "Roads Are Rough in India." India trip, continued. pp. 15+.

11-25-1953. "Thank God." Thanksgiving message. pp. 12+. (Written for Associated Church Press, published in many journals.)

3-3-1954. Reply to accusations from the head of the Polish Lutheran Church. p. 8.

10-6-1954. "Miracle at Evanston." Report on WCC assembly. pp. 18+.

10-3-1956. "ULC President Goes to Moscow." pp. 12-15.

10-10-1956. "Can Church Survive?" Russia trip, continued. pp. 18-21.

10-17-1956. "It's Now or Never in Malaya." pp. 21-24.

10-24-1956. "Rough Road Ahead in Malaya." Malaya trip, continued. pp. 18-21.

11-7-1956. "Exploring Africa." pp. 16-19.

11-14-1956. "Africans Don't Become Christians Overnight." Africa trip, continued. pp. 17-20.

7-10-1957. "Running Down the Church Doesn't Make Sense." pp. 12-13.

7-31-1957. FCF's opinion of the Minneapolis LWF assembly. p. 5.

8-14-1957. "My Hope for Minneapolis." Interview on LWF assembly. p. 12.

9-17-1958, 9-24, 10-1, 10-8, 10-15. President's report to ULCA convention at Dayton.

12-23-1959. "Meaning of a Birthday." Christmas meditation. p. 20. (Written for Associated Press Newsfeatures, released under title: "Tyrants Still Fear the Infant Jesus." (See 8. *Miscellaneous.*)

5-18-1960. "Lutherans Do Well in Venezuela." pp. 20-22.

5-25-1960. "South American Journey." Continued: on Colombia. pp. 15-17.

7-11-1962. "We Strike Our Tents." Quotations: valedictory of the ULCA, 6-26. pp. 9-10+. (See 4. *Presidential Reports* and 5. *Pastor's Desk Book.*)

7-3-1963. Statement on US Supreme Court's decision invalidating compulsory Bible reading or prayer in public schools. p. 26.

7-31-1963. "The Christian Attitude toward Our Neighbors." Letter to LCA pastors and congregations on the race question. pp. 4-5. (See 5. *Ministers Information Service.*)

11-18-1964. "There Isn't Much Time Left." Guest editorial, on LCA benevolence. p. 50.

1-5-1966. Comments on Vatican II. p. 29.

7-6-1966. "This Is An Emergency." President's report to LCA Kansas City convention. pp. 6-9.

12-21-1966. "A Word for the New Year from the President of the Church." p. 50.

8-30-1967. "Today Is God's Day." Address to Lutheran Church—Missouri Synod New York convention. pp. 10-11. (See 8. *Miscellaneous.*)

10-11-1967. "Why I Am Thankful for the Reformation." Open letter. p. 50.

12-20-1967. "Christmas Begins at Home," as told to Will Oursler. pp. 9+. (Reprint from PARADE, the Sunday Newspaper Magazine, New York, 1966. Picture of FCF telling the Christmas story to children at Holy Trinity church, New Rochelle, N. Y.)

4-24-1968. Statement on the assassination of Martin Luther King, Jr. pp. 24-25.

6-19-1968. "Being Christian in a Violent Society." Dialogue between FCF and William S. Ellis, on "Protestant Hour" radio program 5-19-1968. pp. 14-17. (See also 8. *Miscellaneous,* and 9. *Audio-Visuals.*)

7. ARTICLES AND ADDRESSES BY DR. FRY IN JOURNALS, BULLETINS, MINUTES

Many of the addresses are abridged in their printed form. Various church offices, libraries, and individuals have kindly contributed copies of some of the items below to the LSTC Library.

"A Few Afterthoughts," HAMILTON LITERARY MAGAZINE, April-May 1920, pp. 226-227. Report by FCF on the Hamilton College debating season. (Copy in LSTC Library, per George Thompson.)

Essay in symposium on the ULCA and the Federal Council of Churches, in LUTHERAN CHURCH QUARTERLY, October 1942, pp. 417-419.

"Stones in Their Hands," LUTHERAN MEN (organ of the ULCA Men's Brotherhood, later called United Lutheran Church Men), March 1943, pp. 8-9. Lenten sermon, on John 8:59.

"To the Brotherhoods," LUTHERAN MEN, January 1945, p. 3. Message by the recently elected ULCA president.

("Report of Deputation to Germany," FEDERAL COUNCIL BULLETIN, January 1946, pp. 6-7. Report of Oxnam, Sherrill, and Fry on their visit in December 1945.)

"If Thine Enemy Hunger," LUTHERAN WOMAN'S WORK (organ of the ULCA Women's Missionary Society, later called United Lutheran Church Women), June 1946, pp. 7-8. For Lutheran World Action.

"World Council Representation by Families of Churches," CHRISTENDOM, Summer 1946, pp. 359-363. Appeal for confessional representation.

"The Work of the United Lutheran Church and the Lutheran Church Throughout the World, "*Minutes,* Women's Missionary Society triennial convention, Johnstown, Pa., October 1946, p. 112.

"A Crisis in Lutheranism," LUTHERAN OUTLOOK (organ of the American Lutheran Conference), January 1947, pp. 7-8. Appeal for the confessional principle at Uppsala, where plans were prepared for the formation of the LWF.

"Echoes from Amsterdam," LUTHERAN WOMAN'S WORK, January 1949, pp. 4-6+. Report on the formation of the World Council of Churches.

Essay for "The ULCA" in symposium, "Reaching Closer Relationships between American Lutherans," LUTHERAN CHURCH QUARTERLY, May 1949, pp. 165-168.

"What the Churches Expect from the World Council," *Minutes and Reports of the 2nd Meeting of the Central Committee* [of WCC] 1949, pp. 75-77. Address to the Central Committee.

"Meet the Women's Missionary Society," *Minutes*, WMS triennial convention, Grand Rapids, Mich., October 1949, pp. 114-115.

"Religion in Education," EDUCATIONAL NEWS (bulletin of the National Lutheran Educational Conference), January-February 1952. Address to the Association of American Colleges, 1-8-1952. (Copy in LSTC Library, per Donald R. Heiges.)

"Partners in a Common Task," LUTHERAN MEN, February 1952, pp. 10-11+. Address to a convocation of Boy Scout executives, East Lansing, Michigan.

"That Thy Way May Be Known," *Minutes*, WMS triennial convention, Philadelphia, September 1952, pp. 104-105.

"The Lutheran Church—A Series of Paradoxes," LUTHERAN MEN, November 1952, pp. 10-11. Address to Brotherhood convention.

"A Church for the Ages," *ULCA 1953 Yearbook*, pp. 4-5+.

"Thank God!" LUTHERAN WOMAN'S WORK, November 1953, pp. 12-14. Thanksgiving message, distributed through Associated Church Press.

"We Are Stewards of His Bounty," NATIONAL LUTHERAN (organ of NLC), November-December 1953, pp. 7-10. Thanksgiving message (="Thank God!").

Brief interview in "The Case against 'Easy' Religion," by William Peters, REDBOOK, September 1955, pp. 22-23+. (Copy in LSTC Library, per Linda Plants.)

Untitled address to WMS triennial convention, Cleveland, October 1955, *Minutes*, pp. 118-119.

"Lift Up Now Thine Eyes," LUTHERAN MEN, November 1956, pp. 7-9. Brotherhood convention banquet, Kitchener, Ontario.

"God Shows His Face," in *Marangu: Report of the All-Africa Lutheran Conference* [1955], Geneva 1956. Sermon, pp. 177-179. *Ibid.*, "Comments" on E. H. Flothmeier's address on evangelism and stewardship, pp. 71-73.

"The Unity of the Church," LUTHERAN WORLD (organ of LWF), March 1957, pp. 322-334. (=1956 ULCA presidential report, slightly revised. See 4.)

Sermon at concluding festival service, Minneapolis LWF assembly, August 1957, in *Proceedings of the 3rd Assembly of LWF*, Minneapolis, 1958, pp. 19-20.

"Lutheran World Federation Serves the Church in the World Today," *Minutes*, United Lutheran Church Women triennial convention, Toronto, September 1958, pp. 101-103.

"Dr. Fry Stresses Balance between Truth and Unity," *LWF Report to the Member Churches 1958*, p. 4. Address to LWF Executive Committee at Strasbourg. Reprinted in LUTHERAN MEN, December 1958, pp. 16-17. See also NLC News Bureau release #58-126, 11-5-1958.

LWF President's Report at Warsaw, Poland, June 1961, in LWF Executive Committee *Minutes*, 1961. (Copy in LSTC Library per Alice M. Kendrick.)

"It Is a Good Thing to Give Thanks unto the Lord," *Minutes*, ULCW triennial convention, Chicago, September 1961, pp. 106-109.

"To Be More Christian," NATIONAL LUTHERAN, October 1961, pp. 1, 6-7. Lutheran World Relief report.

"Today We Must Think," LUTHERAN WOMEN (organ of LCA Lutheran Church Women), November 1961, pp. 31-32. Address to United Lutheran Church Women convention, Chicago.

"He Leads Us On," *ULCA 1962 Yearbook*, p. 3.

"Paradoxes of the Ministry Today," PRINCETON SEMINARY BULLETIN, October 1962, pp. 4-11. 150th anniversary of Princeton Seminary.

Two addresses to the LCA Western Pennsylvania-West Virginia Synod, June 1963, on the work of the LCA, *Proceedings*, 1963, pp. 142-144.

Interview at LWF Helsinki assembly, in SUOMALAINEN (LCA Finnish Interest Conference), September 1963, p. 3. (Copy per Raymond W. Wargelin.)

Sermon on Ephesians 3:20 at LCA Pittsburgh convention. LCA *Minutes*, 1964, pp. 7-13.

"Christ Today," *Proceedings of the 4th Assembly of LWF* [Helsinki 1963], Berlin 1965, pp. 31-37. LWF presidential address.

Address to National Lutheran Council, Los Angeles, 2-10-1965, on the role of confessional bodies in the ecumenical movement, NLC *Minutes*, 1965, pp. 49-50.

"Educational Integrity and Church Responsibility," *Papers and Proceedings of the 51st Annual Convention of the National Lutheran Educational Conference*, 1965, pp. 14-16. 125th anniversary of Concordia Seminary, St. Louis.

"Ecumenical Perspective," *Minutes*, LCA Lutheran Church Women triennial convention, Cleveland, August 1965, p. 101. (LCW *Minutes* in Archives LSTC.)

"President Fry Chooses from the LWA Cornucopia," *Lutheran World Action Bulletin*, 1968, No. 1, pp. 1-2. (Copy per Rollin G. Shaffer.)

"Dr. Fry Warns Violence to Continue as Whites Fail to Support Equality," TEXAS-LOUISIANA LUTHERAN (synodical monthly), May 1968, pp. 7-8. Report of question-and-answer session at Texas-Louisiana Synod convention. (Copy per Willis Erickson.)

8. MISCELLANEOUS PUBLISHED AND UNPUBLISHED SERMONS AND ADDRESSES

Copies in LSTC Library

"Through Architecture to God," sermon at 25th anniversary of the dedication of Holy Trinity Lutheran church, Akron, Ohio, 12-17-1939. Pamphlet, 9 pp., no imprint. (Copy per Martha Baker.)

Sermon at funeral of Frederick H. Knubel, 10-18-1945 (Psalm 127:2). Published in two different pamphlets. Copies in ULCA Archives, LSTC.

"A Call from Christ," address on postwar situation in Europe, delivered at Souderton, Pa., 3-12-1946. Pamphlet, 16 pp., no imprint. Copy per Henry M. Kistler and Charles F. Brobst.

"We Dare Not Fail," FCF's closing address to ULCA convention, 10-11-1946. LCA pamphlet. (Copy per Rollin G. Shaffer.)

Excerpts of address on the present status of the church, at Buck Hill Falls ULCA Stewardship conference, 3-5-1948. (Copy per William P. Cedfeldt.)

Address in "Lutheran World Action Addresses," by Paul C. Empie, Clarence E. Krumbholz, and FCF, from the ULCA 1948 convention. Pamphlet, 18 pp. (Copy per Rollin G. Shaffer.)

Reformation Day address at St. Louis, Missouri, 10-31-1949 (text in St. Louis GLOBE-DEMOCRAT). (Copy per August R. Suelflow.)

"Our Relationships with the Vatican," informal address to ULCA convention, 10-10-1950, opposing US diplomatic relations with the Vatican. Transcript from tape, in LCA Archives at LSTC. (See 5. *Pastor's Desk Book.*)

"State of the Church," address to ULCA Stewardship conference, Wittenberg College, Springfield, Ohio, 6-14-1951. (Copy per William P. Cedfeldt.)

"Tyrants Still Fear the Infant Jesus," Christmas message, 1951, distributed through Associated Press Newsfeatures. (Copy per F. Eppling Reinartz.)

"God Sees," sermon at the Chicago Sunday Evening Club, 3-29-1953 (Gen. 16:13). (Copy per Francis Gregory.)

"What Is Protestantism?" transcript of WCAU-TV address, 8-19-1953. (Copy per William P. Cedfeldt.)

Christmas message, 1954. Abstract of message on NBC-TV "Frontiers of Faith," 12-19-1954, printed in ULCA Press-Radio-Television "Clipsheet," n.d. (Copy per Charles F. Brobst.)

"Reflections on the Educational Tasks of the Church," address to conference of ULCA synodical directors of parish education, Cincinnati, Ohio, 1-4-1956. (Copy per James Barkenquast. See also 9. *Audio-Visuals.*)

"Come, Lord Jesus," sermon at World Student Christian Federation teaching conference, Strasbourg, France, December 1960. (Copy per Donald Hetzler.)

Address at dedication of RVOG [Radio Voice of the Gospel] and inauguration of broadcasts, Addis Ababa, Ethiopia, 2-26-1963. (Copy per Ferdy E. Baglo.)

Two addresses at inauguration of Donald R. Heiges as president of Philadelphia Seminary, 10-21-1964, in student publication, *The Seminarian,* 10-28-1964. (Copies per D. R. Heiges.)

Address at Roanoke College, Salem, Virginia, for the college's financial appeal, 10-22-1965. (Copy per Raymond Petrea.)

Sermon at funeral of Luther A. Gotwald, Sr., 5-8-1966. (Copy per Luther A. Gotwald, Jr.)

Synopsis by William R. Smeltz of a question-and-answer session on the state of the church, at Lutheran Laymen's Movement conference, Seabury House, Conn., 9-1-1966. (Copy per William P. Cedfeldt.)

Address on evangelism, to the American Lutheran Church convention, Minneapolis, 10-23-1966. Pamphlet, 8 pp., printed by order of the convention. (Copy per Albert Dillemuth. See also 9. *Audio-Visuals.*)

"Worldwide Evangelism," address to the missionary conference sponsored by the LCA Board of World Missions, Carthage College, Kenosha, Wis., 7-10-1967. (Copy per James A. Scherer and David L. Lindberg. See also *Audio-Visuals.*)

Address to the Lutheran Church—Missouri Synod convention, New York, 7-11-1967 (Psalm 118:24). (Copy per Herbert Mueller. See also 6. *LUTHERAN,* and 9. *Audio-Visuals.*)

"Science and Religion: Who Will Play God?" CBS News Special television program, moderated by Eric Sevareid, with FCF a member of the panel, 1-21-1968. (Transcript per Albert Dillemuth. See also *Audio-Visuals.*)

Statement in panel discussion of F. A. Schiotz, FCF, and R. P. Wiederaenders on the race problem, in *A Consultation of Black Lutheran Clergymen, Chicago, May 7-10, 1968,* Chicago, n.d., pp. 36-37.

"Being Christian in a Violent Society," Protestant Hour program on the race crisis in USA, dialog between William S. Ellis and FCF, 5-19-1968. (Transcript per William W. Horlock. See also 6. *LUTHERAN,* and 9. *Audio-Visuals.*)

9. AUDIO-VISUAL MATERIALS

Increasingly it is becoming the practice of churches, church councils, and other agencies to record their *proceedings* on tape. FCF's participation in a number of such meetings is catalogued below (see also 1. *Archives and Files*). Recordings of ULCA and LCA biennial conventions since 1948 (by wire recordings 1948, by tape from 1950 on) are in the ULCA/LCA Archives at LSTC. These include sermons, remarks, etc., as mentioned or summarized in the *Minutes:*

1948, p. 5 Sermon based on the invocation "In the Name of the Father, etc."

1948, p 686 Lutheran World Action address.

1950, p. 5 Sermon on I Corinthians 4:1.

1950, p. 920 Remarks on US Vatican embassy (see 8. *Miscellaneous*).

1952, p. 5 Sermon on II Timothy 1:7 (text in *Pastor's Desk Book,* see 5.).

1956, p. 7 Sermon on Hebrews 2:8.

1956, pp. 1105-1106 Prayer for unity.

1960, p. 7 Communion sermon on Matthew 23:8-9 (text in *Pastor's Desk Book,* see 5).

1964, pp. 7-13 Sermon on Ephesians 3:20 (text printed).

1964, p. 678 Comments on first biennium of LCA and the spirit of the 1964 convention: response to a speech commending his leadership. (Summary printed.)

The LCA Press, Radio & Television office in New York has several tapes of remarks by FCF at sessions of the conference of synod presidents and the LCA cabinet of executives, tapes of several radio and TV interviews, tapes and photos and slides of the FCF funeral, and a few other items.

The LUTHERAN gives ample but incomplete notice of FCF's appearances on *radio and television programs.* Though recordings of many of these programs have not survived, the list below gives several examples still extant in the form of kinescope, tape, or record. Occasionally the text of a program will be found transcribed (see 7. *Articles,* 8. *Miscellaneous*). Sometimes the broadcasting systems have turned over kinescopes of their programs to the National Council of Churches' Broadcasting and Film Commission for educational purposes; a number of these recordings have been collected in the Reigner Recording Library, Richmond, Va.

Churches and church agencies use films, filmstrips, tapes, and records for *promotional* purposes. Notable among those in which FCF appeared are the materials prepared by Lutheran World Action and by the Lutheran Laymen's Movement or the Commission on Stewardship of the ULCA/LCA.

Finally, tapes of a number of *miscellaneous addresses* have been kindly reported by several church offices and individuals.

Materials in the REIGNER RECORDING LIBRARY, Union Theological Seminary, 3401 Brook Road, Richmond, Virginia (Copies may be purchased):

KINESCOPES of NBC-TV panel discussions, "Frontiers of Faith":

"World Council of Churches," 9-5-1954.

"Christian Responsibility of Newspapers," 7-17-1955 (FCF moderator).

"Why Church Union?" 7-19-1955 (FCF moderator).

"What Is Happening to the Bill of Rights?" 9-18-1955.

"Religion in the News," 9-16-1956.

"The Gods We Live With in International Affairs," 7-26-1959.

"What Do the Emerging Nations Need from Us?" 7-17-1960.

"Is Christianity Standing Up to Communism?" 7-9-1961.

TAPES

"Diplomatic Relations," 11-6-1960, with W. Averell Harriman. ABC radio program, "Pilgrimage": award-winning series on "Christianity and Communism."

"What Is the Ecumenical Movement Trying to Accomplish?" 2-5-1961. ABC radio program, "Faith in Action."

"The Meaning of Christian Unity for Today," May 1966. Address to the American Baptist Convention, Kansas City, Mo.

World Council of Churches Evanston assembly, 1954: FCF appears 14 times, presiding, reporting, and participating in discussion.

World Council of Churches New Delhi assembly, 1961: 9 times, including Report of the Central Committee, and welcome to Prime Minister Nehru. (Copy of welcome in LSTC Library.)

National Council of Churches general assemblies: St. Louis, 1957, Philadelphia, 1963, Miami, 1966: a few items.

FILMS on file in the LUTHERAN WORLD ACTION promotion office, 315 Park Avenue South, New York, N. Y.:

"March of Faith": film of the LWF Lund assembly, 1947. FCF appears only briefly.

"Fruit of the Living Word": LWF Hannover assembly, 1952. Abridged version entitled "Report from Hannover" produced for use in USA and Canada. Film contains excerpt of address by FCF.

"Your Lutheran World Federation": LWF Minneapolis assembly, 1957. Version entitled "The Third Assembly" produced for use in Europe. Film contains a long conversation between Bishop Lilje and FCF.

"Viewpoint Helsinki": LWF Helsinki assembly, 1963. Includes address of FCF, especially about the Radio Voice of the Gospel, Addis Ababa.

The office also has a FILMSTRIP entitled "The Midnight and the Dawn," prepared from FCF's report to the 1946 ULCA convention on his summer 1946 visit to Finland, Poland, Germany, and Sweden. (For recording of the original address, see below. See also 6. *LUTHERAN*.)

LUTHERAN CHURCH SUPPLY STORES, 2900 Queen Lane, Philadelphia, Pa. (and other cities), can furnish two FILMS featuring FCF:

"A Living Church," produced by the ULCA Department of Stewardship in 1957. FCF appears as preacher.

"Dr. Franklin Clark Fry on the Ecumenical Movement," 1966, produced for the LCA Board of Parish Education.

MISCELLANEOUS TAPES, FILMS, AND RECORDS

"The Lutheran Church Faces the Midnight and the Dawn," LWA address to ULCA convention, 10-6-1946, on his visit to Finland, Poland, Germany, and Sweden. Four 78 rpm RECORDS, in ULCA Archives at LSTC. (See also LWA FILMSTRIP, above, and 6. *LUTHERAN*.)

"And Now I See," ULCA stewardship FILM produced in 1947. Copy in LSTC Library, per William P. Cedfeldt.

"Home Is Nowhere," FCF's report on the world refugee situation. FILM produced to promote the 1951 Protestant "One Great Hour of Sharing" appeal, on file at the NCCCUSA Broadcasting and Film Commission, New York, N. Y. (See also 5. *Pastor's Desk Book*, 6. *LUTHERAN*.)

"The Man of God," address on theological education, at the inauguration of Harry F. Baughman as president of Gettysburg Seminary, 10-4-1951. Two RECORDS in Gettysburg Seminary Library.

ULCA New York Synod convention, June 1952: Question-and-answer period on the work of ULCA; address to mass meeting on same theme; ordination sermon. Three TAPES held by Franklin D. Fry.

"Distinctive Characteristics of the Lutheran Church," address at sesquicentennial of ULCA North Carolina Synod, 5-6-1953. TAPE at synodical office, Salisbury, N. C.

"Reflections on the Educational Tasks of the Church," address to conference of ULCA synodical directors of parish education, Cincinnati, Ohio, 1-4-1956. TAPE at LCA Board of Parish Education office, Philadelphia, Pa. Transcript in LSTC Library. (See 8. *Miscellaneous*).

"American and Foreign Missions," 5-21-1958. TAPE in ULCA Archives at LSTC.

Four Bible Study periods at the United Lutheran Church Men convention, Wagner College, Staten Island, N. Y., August 1961. TAPES in LSTC Library, per Samuel Weicker.

Commencement address, Pacific Lutheran Seminary, 5-10-1962. TAPE in seminary business office, Berkeley, Cal.

Banquet address, ULCA Pacific Southwest Synod, Berkeley, Cal., 5-10-1962. TAPE held by David H. Romeis, Walnut Creek, Cal.

"One Lord, One Faith," FILM of the LCA merger convention in Detroit, June 1962, produced for the Commission on Stewardship. On file at New York and in LSTC Library.

Press conference at the Luther League of America convention, San Francisco, September 1962. TAPE held by David H. Romeis, Walnut Creek, Cal.

Interview on Easter and Protestantism, by Hugh Downs, on NBC "Today" program, Easter season, 1963. FILM at LCA/PRT office, New York, N. Y.

Address at LCA Nebraska Synod, Grand Island, Neb., 5-20-1963. TAPE held by Ernest W. Switzer, Diller, Neb.

Interview at radio station KMMJ, Grand Island, Neb., 5-20-1963. TAPE held by Ernest W. Switzer, Diller, Neb.

"The Christian Revolution," one-hour Telstar satellite program (one of the earliest), produced jointly by CBS-TV "Town Meeting of the World" and the British Broadcasting Corporation, 10-15-1963. Eric Sevareid was the moderator in New York. FCF spoke from the Princeton Seminary chapel, Bishop J. E. Lesslie Newbigin from London, and Cardinal Laurian Rugambwa (Tanganyika) and Professor Hans Küng from Rome. Due to technical difficulties, FCF carried the first half of the program almost single-handedly. TAPE at LCA/PRT office, New York, N. Y.

Address at inauguration of Stewart W. Herman as president of the Lutheran School of Theology at Chicago, 5-3-1964. TAPE in LSTC Library.

Banquet address, LCA Florida Synod, 5-13-1964. TAPE in LSTC Library, per Royall A. Yount.

Commencement address, California Lutheran College, 5-30-1965. TAPE at the college, Thousand Oaks, Cal.

"The Church's Ministry to Its Students," address at Catawba College, Salisbury, N. C., 1-23-1966, for LCA North Carolina Synod's financial campaign to support campus ministry. TAPE at synod office, Salisbury, N. C.

LCA Maryland Synod, June 1966: Report on work of LCA; address, "Religious Aspects of the World Situation"; question-and-answer period. Three TAPES at synod office, Baltimore, Md.

Tribute to Dwight F. Putman, retiring president of LCA Central Pennsylvania Synod, 6-7-1966. TAPE at synod office, Harrisburg, Pa.

Sermon at inauguration of John W. Rilling as president of LCA Ohio Synod, 10-9-1966. TAPE in LSTC Library, per Dr. Rilling.

Address on evangelism to the American Lutheran Church convention, Minneapolis, 10-23-1966. TAPE at ALC Department of Public Information, Minneapolis, Minn. (Printed text: see 8. *Miscellaneous.*)

"The Manifesto—Interpretation and Application in Terms of Evangelism," address to conference of synodical directors of evangelism, Dearborn, Mich., 1-10-1967. TAPE at LCA Commission on Evangelism, New York, N. Y.

Four-man interview: FCF; Carl E. Waisanen, dean of Suomi College; Jacob W. Heikkinen, professor at Gettysburg Seminary; Cyril Sheehy, president, Sheehy Construction Co., St. Paul, Minn., June 1967. A wide-ranging conversation on contemporary Christianity. FILM in Suomi Junior College Library, Hancock, Mich.

Address to LCA Board of World Missions missionary conference, Carthage College, Kenosha, Wis., 7-10-1967. TAPE at LCA/BWM office, New York, N. Y. (Transcript in LSTC Library, see 8. *Miscellaneous.*)

Address to the Lutheran Church—Missouri Synod convention, New York, 7-11-1967 (Psalm 118:24). TAPE at LC—MS Archives, St. Louis, Mo. (See 8. *Miscellaneous.*)

Pastoral conference, Asilomar, Cal., September 1967: Communion sermon; question-and-answer period. Two TAPES, held by Franklin D. Fry.

Brief addresses by Jerald C. Brauer, Stewart W. Herman, and FCF, to be played on the day of dedication of the LSTC, 10-22-1967, in supporting LCA congregations. RECORD in LSTC Library.

Address at dedication of Lutheran School of Theology at Chicago, 10-22-1967. TAPE in LSTC Library, per Wesley J. Smuzer.

Address to LCA Minnesota Synod, at Moorhead, Minn., 11-21-1967, for Gustavus Adolphus Leadership Appeal. TAPE in LSTC Library, per R. E. Anderson.

"Science and Religion: Who Will Play God?" CBS News Special television program, with Eric Sevareid as moderator. Panel: Dr. C. Walton Lillehei, surgeon; Dr. James Bonner, biologist; Walter Sullivan, NEW YORK TIMES science editor; Bishop John J. Wright; Dr. Harvey Cox, theologian; and FCF, 1-21-1968. On "space, transplants, genetics and the mind." TAPE held by Franklin D. Fry. (Transcript in LSTC Library, see 8. *Miscellaneous.*)

"Being Christian in a Violent Society," dialog between William S. Ellis and FCF on the race crisis in USA, on the "Protestant Hour," 5-19-1968. TAPE at LCA/PRT office, New York, N. Y. (See 6. *LUTHERAN*, 8. *Miscellaneous.*)

"American Mission and World Mission," address to LCA Michigan Synod, May 1968 (FCF's last public address). TAPE held by Dr. Fry's daughter, Mrs. Richard I. Preis.

10. SERMONS PUBLISHED IN BOOKS

"The Quest for Happiness: Whither It Leads," sermon on Matthew 5:6, in E. L. Keller, ed., *Great Sermons by Young Preachers,* New York, 1931, pp. 85-97.

"Washington's Spirit Must Live," sermon on Matthew 10:39, in *History of the George Washington Bicentennial Celebration,* Washington, 1932, Volume 2, pp. 484-486.

"Compulsions of the Cross," five Lenten sermons, in *From Throne to Cross,* Rock Island, Illinois, 1940, pp. 117-141.

"God and Bread," sermon in P. Z. Strodach, ed., *Calling All Christians,* Philadelphia, 1942, pp. 95-107.

"Lest They Be Defiled," sermon on John 18:28, in S. J. Sebelius, ed., *A Faith for These Times,* Rock Island, 1942, pp. 133-141 (with a "sermon biography," pp. 125-133).

"It's the Plus That Counts," sermon in C. P. Butler, ed., *Best Sermons,* New York, 1947, pp. 281-285.

"Living Communication," in *Share Christ Today* (Sermons and Addresses from the Lutheran Evangelism Conference, Minneapolis), Lutheran Evangelism Council, Minneapolis, 1952, pp. 106-110.

"Interruptions," in *In the Unity of the Faith,* Foreword by E. T. Dahlberg (a book of sermons and meditations), Philadelphia, 1960, pp. 44-50.

11. DR. FRY'S FOREWORDS AND GREETINGS, BRIEF REPORTS, AND TRIBUTES TO COLLEAGUES

Dr. Fry was a master of the brief statement. This section, therefore, which otherwise might be considered too trivial for inclusion, is given a place in the Source Register.

Only a few examples are listed of the many letters or speeches of tribute by FCF to his close colleagues.

A large file containing several hundred of FCF's greetings and congratulations on special occasions to congregations, institutions, and individuals (carbon copies from his correspondence) is in the *Franklin Clark Fry Collection* in the LSTC Library.

Foreword to V. J. Eylands, *Lutherans in Canada,* Winnipeg, 1945.

Tribute to Ralph H. Long (funeral of the executive secretary of the National Lutheran Council), in the LUTHERAN, 3-17-1948, p. 9.

Foreword to American edition of R. N. Flew and R. E. Davies, eds., *The Catholicity of Protestantism,* Philadelphia, n.d. (original English edition 1950).

Tribute to H. Reed Shepfer (retirement of president of ULCA Pittsburgh Synod), in LUTHERAN MONTHLY (of Pittsburgh Synod), May 1950, p. 4. (Copy in LSTC Library, per E. Jerome Alexis.)

"Ansprache" (German address at close of Hannover LWF assembly), in *Es soll durch meinen Geist geschehen,* München, 1952, p. 40. (Copy of LSTC Library, per Gottfried Klapper.)

("Greetings from the World Council of Churches" in *Marangu: Record of the [1955] All-Africa Lutheran Conference,* Geneva, 1956, p. 18.)

Greeting to the Second International Congress for Luther Research, Münster, Germany, 1960, in V. Vajta, ed., *Luther and Melanchthon,* Philadelphia, n.d., pp. 11-12.

Greetings from ULCA, in 1961 *Augustana Annual* (Yearbook of Augustana Lutheran Church), Rock Island, Illinois, p. 67.

(*Mission in South Africa, April-December, 1960,* Geneva, 1961, a pamphlet prepared by a six-man WCC delegation to the Consultation in December 1960 chaired by

FCF, contains two letters dated 5-12-1960, addressed to the churches and the church leaders in South Africa, signed by FCF, Ernest A. Payne, and W. A. Visser 't Hooft.)

Foreword in *Evanston to New Delhi* (Report of the Central Committee to the 3rd assembly of WCC), Geneva, 1961, pp. 2-4.

Foreword in *Proceedings of the 4th Assembly [Helsinki 1963] of LWF*, Berlin, 1965, pp. 9-10.

Presentation of new president, Fredrik A. Schiotz, to the Helsinki LWF assembly, in *Proceedings of the 4th Assembly of LWF*, Berlin, 1965, pp. 430-431.

Tribute to Dwight F. Putman (retirement of president of LCA Central Pennsylvania Synod, 6-7-1966). Tape in Central Pennsylvania Synod office, Harrisburg.

Foreword to Enok Mortensen, *The Danish Lutheran Church in America*, Philadelphia, 1967, pp. v-vi.

Foreword in F. C. Fry, hrsg., *Geschichtswirklichkeit und Glaubensbewährung*, Festschrift für Friedrich Müller (Lutheran bishop of Transylvania), Stuttgart, 1967, pp. 17-18 (German Vorwort, pp. 19-20).

Tribute to Ernest A. Payne (retirement of general secretary of the Baptist Union of Great Britain and Ireland), reported in BAPTIST TIMES, London, 5-4-1967, p. 8. (Copy in LSTC Library, per Dr. Payne.)

Foreword in *New Delhi to Uppsala* (Report of the Central Committee to the 4th Assembly of WCC), Geneva 1968, pp. 5-6.

Grusswort von Franklin Clark Fry, in *Christus Praesens*, Vorträge, Aufsätze, und Predigten von Landesbischof D. Hermann Dietzfelbinger (Lutheran bishop of Bavaria), München, 1968.

(Message from FCF and Eugene Carson Blake to the Beirut Conference on World Cooperation for Development, co-sponsored by WCC and the Pontifical Commission on Justice and Peace, in ECUMENICAL REVIEW, July 1968, p. 301.)

12. SOURCES IN THE FRY FAMILY'S POSSESSION

Mrs. Franklin Clark Fry informs me that she has several boxes of materials as yet unclassified:

A few hundred sermons and addresses, many merely in the form of notes.

A few tapes and records of addresses.

Dr. Fry's "travelogue" letters to his family.

Some clippings of press interviews.

Unsorted papers.

The Reverend Dr. Franklin Drewes Fry has in his possession

A number of sermons and addresses.

Six tapes of addresses (listed under 9. *Audio-Visuals*).

Some clippings.

Dr. and Mrs. Fry's daughter Constance, Mrs. Richard I. Preis, has one tape (listed under *Audio-Visuals*).

Index of Persons

A. Writers for This Volume

Boldface numbers indicate the writers' memos.

B. Other Persons Mentioned

Persons are identified chiefly according to their positions during their association with Dr. Fry, especially as mentioned in the memos.